CW01368010

A NEW WAY TO BAKE

For my family.

For every person that has dared to question the status quo.

For all the bakers, the sweet-toothed cakers and sweet-treat makers looking for a new way to bake.

May this book be a source of inspiration, joy and hope. Together, we can create a future that's kinder, more compassionate and more sustainable for all.

PHILIP KHOURY

A NEW WAY TO BAKE

Hardie Grant
BOOKS

PHOTOGRAPHY BY MATT RUSSELL

Introduction 7
A very brief history of cake 13
The plantry 17
Essential tools 41
The weigh to bake 43

SWEET RISEN 47

Vrioche 49
Pain aux Raisins 53
Sticky Date and Cardamom Buns 54
Cinnamon Slice 56
Vostocks 61
Pistachio (and Rose) Vostocks 62
Stollen 65
Chocolate Hazelnut Babka 67
Hot X Bun 71

BISCUITS AND COOKIES 75

Anzac Biscuits 77
Nut Shortbreads 78
Glazed Gingerbread 81
Banana Chip Cookies 82
Chocolate Chip Cookies 84
Chocolate Tahini Cookies 88
Sugar Cookies 91
Maamoul 93
Almond Amaretti 94

TARTS AND PIES 97

Red Berry Tart 99
Apple Pie 102
Pecan Pie 107
Chocolate Ganache Tart 108
Tarte Bordaloue 111
Banoffee Pie 113
Bakewell Tart 117
Lemon Tart 120
Sweet Potato Pie 122

About the author 243
Thanks go to 244
Index 246

CAKES 125

Financiers 128
Fluffy Scones 130
Madeleines 134
Carrot Cake 137
Maple Cake 138
Apple Cake 143
Victoria Sponge 144
Lamingtons 147
Extra Virgin Olive Oil Cake 150
Earl Grey Loaf Cake 154
Banana Bread 156
Lemon Drizzle Loaf 158
Pumpkin Spice Loaf Cake 161
Orange and Almond Cake 162
Banana Tatin Cake 164
Pear, Hazelnut and Almond Gâteau 166
Baked Cinnamon and Citrus Cheesecake 170
Fluffy Baked Silken Tofu Cheesecake 173
Two-tone Chocolate Cake 175
Triple Chocolate Fudge 177
Mille Crêpes Praline 181
Sacher Torte 185
Double Chocolate Brownies 188

DESSERTS 191

Molten Centre Chocolate Cakes 193
Tiramisu 194
Sticky Toffee Date Pudding 196
Crème Caramel 199
Crème Brûlée 200
Eton Mess 202
Rice Pudding 207
Nut Gelato 208
No-churn Ice Cream 210
No-churn Chocolate Ice Cream 211

CONFECTIONS 215

Nama Ganache 216
Chocolate Truffles 219
Gianduja 221
Turkish Delight / Lokum 224
Coconut Sea Salt Caramels 226

BASE RECIPES 229

Short Sweet Pastry 230
Flaky Pastry 231
Sweet Flaky Pastry 232
Shortening 232
Nut Butter 233
Oat Crumble 233
Chocolate Crème Pâtissière 235
Crème Pâtissière 235
Fresh Whipping Cream 236
Thick Whipped Cream 237
Fruit Jam with Pectin NH 238
Fruit Jam with Agar-agar 238
Exotic Clear Glaze 239
Baking Glaze 239

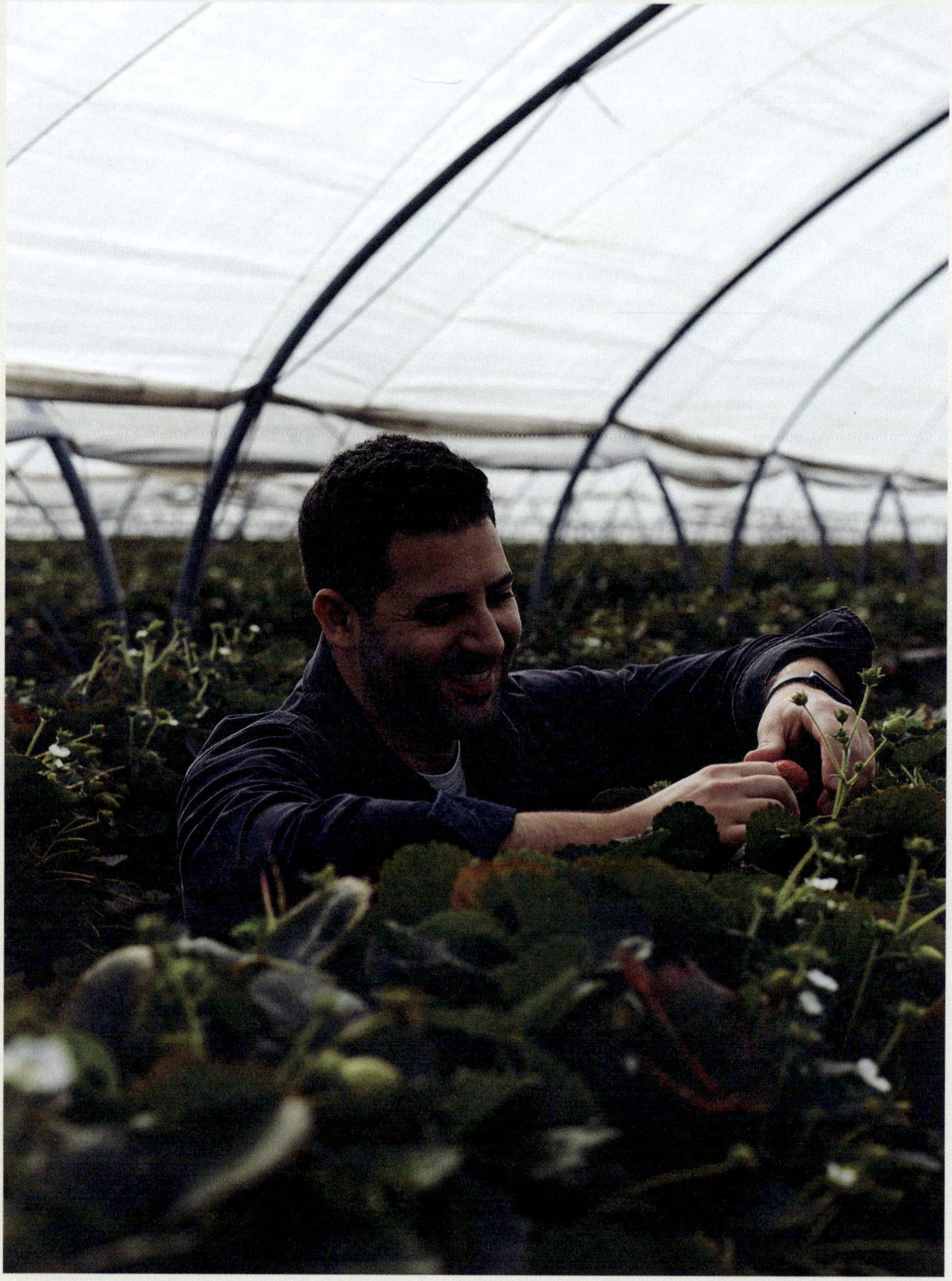

INTRODUCTION

Beneath the Saint-Sulpice Church in Paris, I found myself perched on a park bench, cradling a bag of pastries. I was making a pilgrimage to the boutique of one of my pâtissier heroes – Pierre Hermé. I took a bite into his divine mille-feuille and in that glorious moment, the clouds may have parted and celestial choirs may have sung. At the time, I was a baking-obsessed graphic design university student who would spend weekends whipping up confections to bring into my design internship on Mondays. My boss posed a question that would change my life: why not pursue baking professionally? This was the first time I had ever considered it.

My career as a pastry chef started fairly conventionally. As an apprentice I went to college once a week and worked for some brilliant chefs the other days. I have an inquisitive streak that probably frustrated my teachers, and I always asked 'WHY?' Why does an ingredient need to be blended at a specific temperature? Why does sugar need to be sprinkled into a meringue and not added at the beginning? I was very unhappy to accept that the books and people I worked with could know everything – granted they might have, but I wanted to know why! How did everything work and were there other ways of doing things.

At Quay, the first restaurant I worked in, I made 10 small batches of meringue every morning for the restaurant's signature dessert – the infamous Snow Egg – which was immensely popular off the back of its appearance on *MasterChef Australia*. Over the next year I was able to test the same meringue recipe over 2,000 times and found that the difference between adding the sugar upfront when you begin whisking, or sprinkling it in after a foam had formed, made no noticeable difference to the volume of the meringue or how it baked. I learnt that if egg whites were at room temperature of a minimum of 19°C (66°F) they did whisk up much faster, and the presence of some acid or cream of tartar did indeed increase stability. Similarly, making a batch of scones every working day for 3 years also taught me about doughs!

I went on to work for Australia's most acclaimed pâtissier, Adriano Zumbo, and after successfully competing in a couple of local Australian competitions I was plucked out of the production kitchen to help Adriano establish a new department, and eventually led research and development for all new products. It was like being taken behind the curtain into a magician's workshop to learn the method to the magic. I delved deeper into pâtissèrie, wanting to make desserts that were 'cleaner', using less fat and sugar and which presented finer flavours and textures.

My next major move was to London. I applied for the position of the Queen's pastry chef (a role I did not get!) – but another opportunity very quickly presented itself not far away at the terracotta palace in Knightsbridge. Harrods' legendary Food Halls are decked with the most exotic and luxurious foods available. As Head Pastry Chef, I help lead a brigade of pastry professionals – one of the largest brigades left in the world serving a single site – from underneath its famed Food Halls. Again, the eggs are free range and the dairy from the highest welfare cows fed on lush pastures, but this time I was acutely aware that this was the exception, not the rule and that cruel industries still feed commercial food production in the rest of the world.

With the opportunities and encouragement that Harrods provided, I challenged myself to begin experimenting with entirely plant-based desserts. There was barely any existing technical information to work from, and as a pastry chef with my background and training I couldn't compromise my values in provenance, taste and quality – nearly all the recipes I could find called for margarines made from refined oils or hydrogenated fats or substitute ingredients only accessible in certain markets, along with other chemicals and additives. However, sticking with my approach of staying true to the principles of using whole, high-quality ingredients, I developed and launched 20 (and counting) new plant-based products at Harrods, but without telling anyone before they tasted them that they were plant-based. I think the look of disbelief on people's faces after I revealed the secret said it all!

I have since learned through experience that there are countless ways to whisk a meringue or emulsify a ganache, and most of them are written for the success of the recipe at hand. Chefs have it fairly easy in that there's a lot of standardisation of equipment, industry-wide sharing of knowledge and technique, and most skilled chefs look at the ingredients in a recipe and know what to do with them.

How did eggs and dairy end up in just about everything? My single goal has been to try and look at things in a different way, asking a simple question: if I was trying to create some of the classic treats and some new ones from a new perspective, how would that look and can they be naturally plant-based?

Many have asked how I learned about vegan pastry, and the truth is there's no bible or handbook. There's the synthesis of some very old recipes crafted during times of religious fasting, and some completely new ones guided by a long history of learning about the functionalities of ingredients through trial and error, as well as being guided by a sense of intuition and rather hedonistically the pleasure I get from eating. I love good cake!

The recipes in this book have gone through hundreds of tests and iterations. In the process of starting out from scratch, guided only by taste and experience, the single requirement is that all the ingredients are natural and in their purest form, or have been in use for over 100 years and are widely available all around the world.

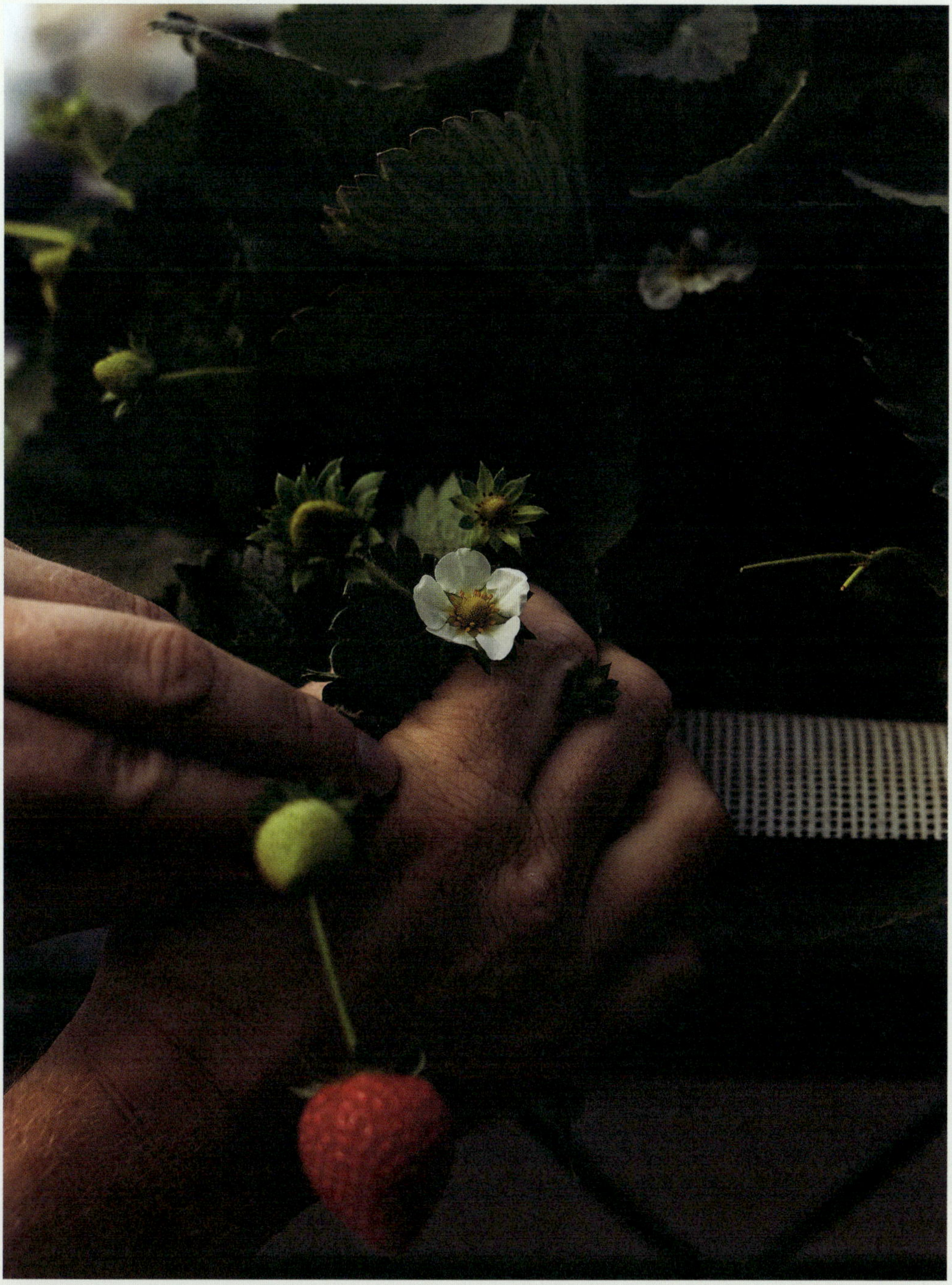

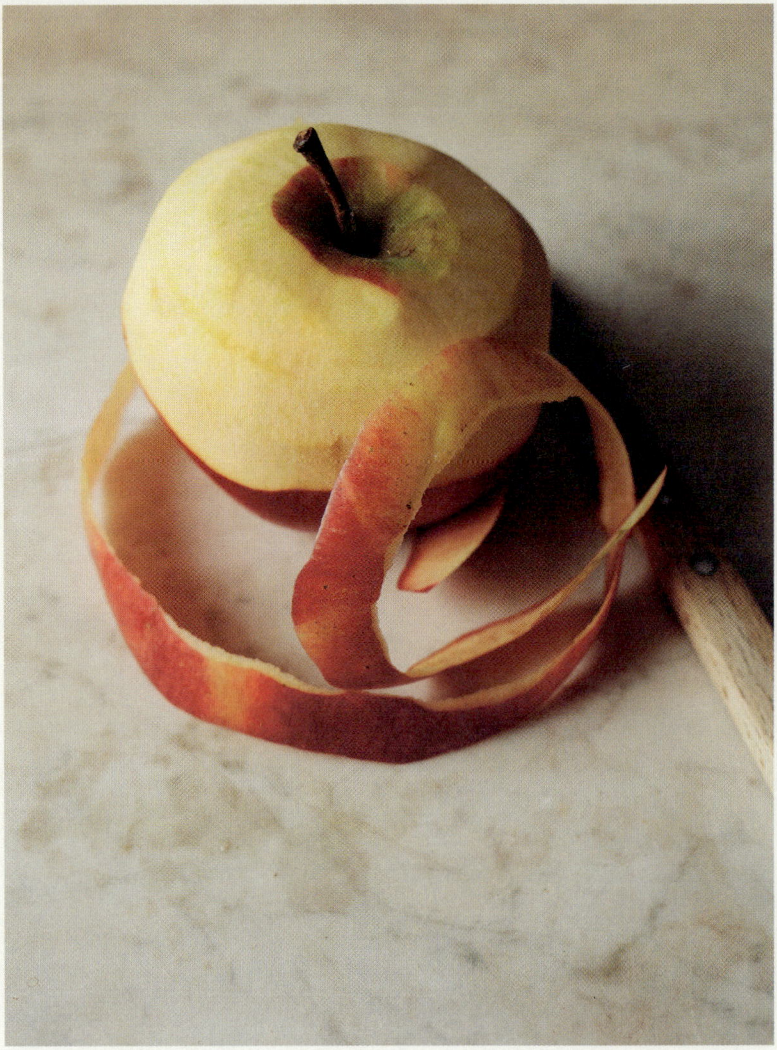

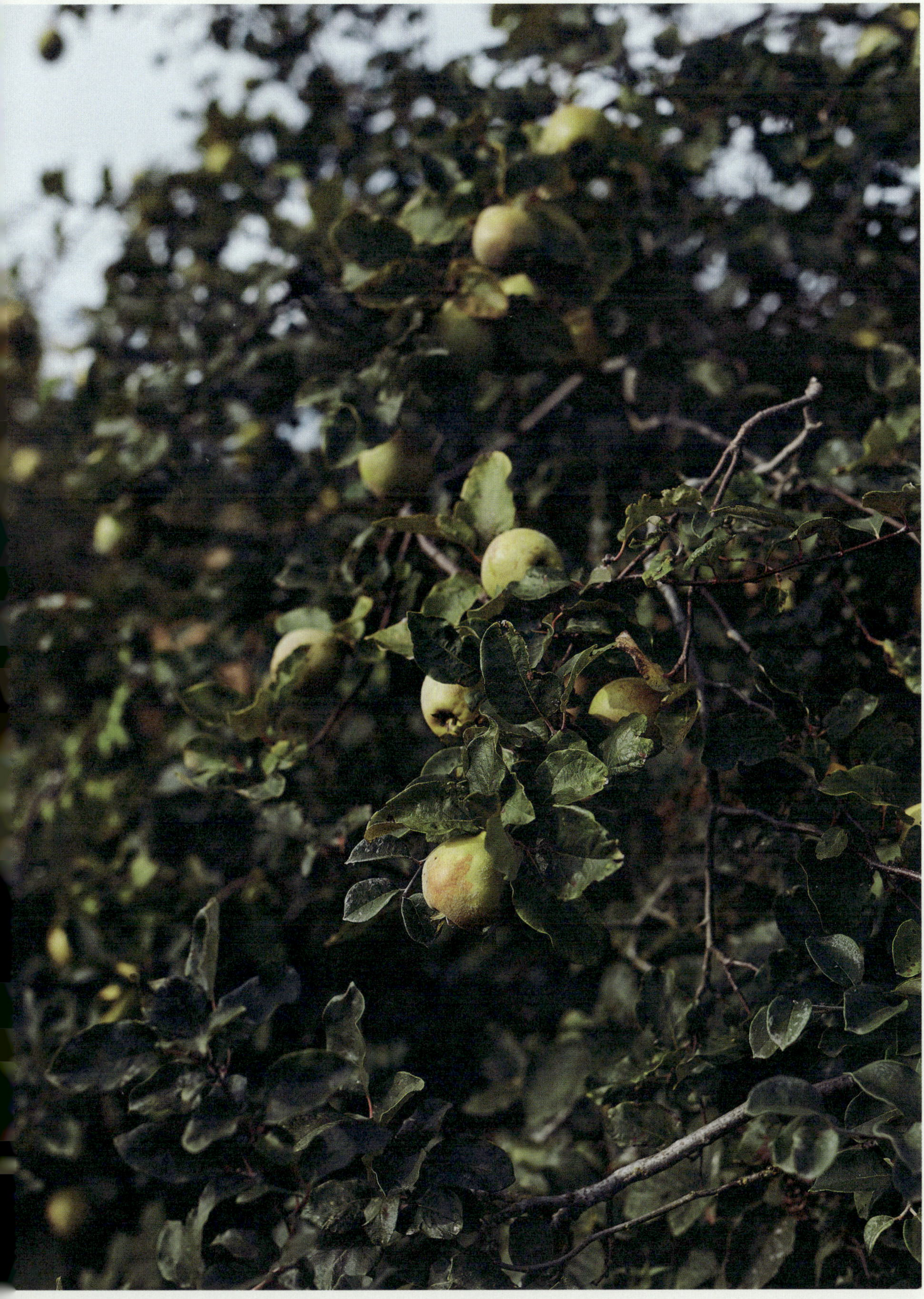

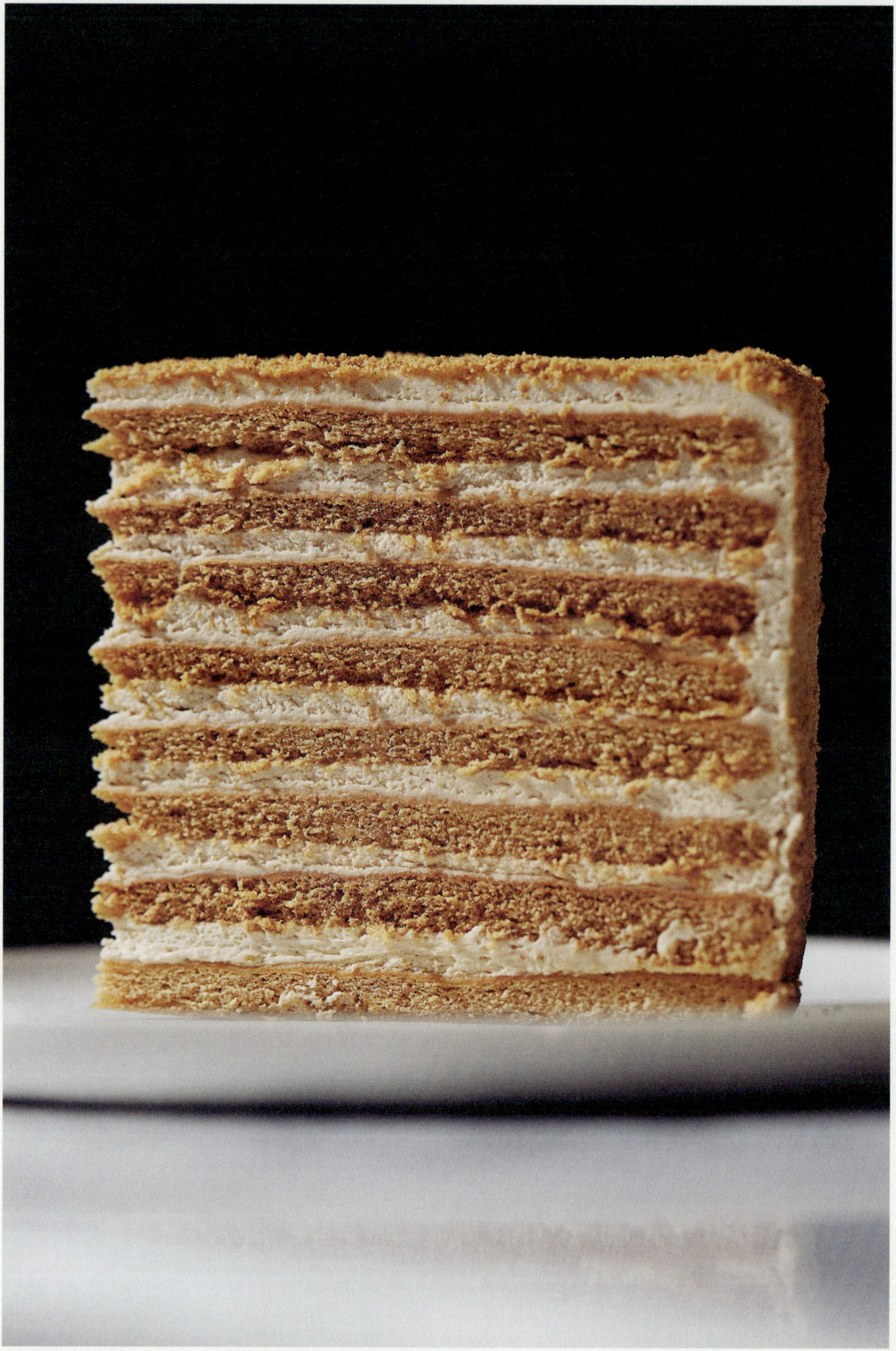

A VERY BRIEF HISTORY OF CAKE

Cake as we know it is a new innovation in the history of mankind, evolved from a number of transformations in farming and agriculture, chemistry and technology.

Most foods that we consider traditional are relatively new and are the products of industrialisation. Many of the recipes that we now consider traditional were hailed as new not so long ago. Moist sponges and cakes evolved from breads that were enriched with honey and milk, and later sugar, butter and eggs. Eventually cooks found that if you beat the eggs or butter you could incorporate air, which then led to the creation of something that resembles cakes as we know them.

Domesticated animals have long been tied to the history of agriculture. They've been needed to till fields and help sow crops, their waste has been used as fertilisers and they've been killed for their meat. In a time gone by, using dairy and eggs seemed like a natural thing to do. After all, butter is a healthy and delicious fat eaten in moderation. You get about 60–80 g (2–2.8 oz) butter from 1 litre (33.8 fl oz) milk. In the 1970s the average Holstein-Friesian cow produced 10 litres (338.14 fl oz) milk a day, while in 2012 the average was 21 litres (710.1 fl oz) a day. The standard 23 cm (9 in) round cake can contain up to 250 g (8.8 oz) of butter, which will have taken 3.5 litres (118 fl oz) of milk to make.

The ancestors of the egg-laying hens used to lay 20 eggs a year. Now the modern broiler chicken will lay almost one per day. The average 23 cm (9 in) cake might use 5–8 eggs, so this has spawned very cruel and intensive industries to keep up with our insatiable demand.

Two hundred years ago, if you had chickens, using their unfertilised eggs as food, as well as to enrich cakes, could have seemed like a natural evolution. Chickens have been selectively bred and put into manipulated environments that are arguably the worst conditions of any farmed animal. Living in extreme confinement and unable to perform any form of natural behaviour, they suffer day after day in conditions that no living creature should ever have to endure.

I don't want to be confronting or make you feel uncomfortable by sharing some of the facts about how intensively farmed animals are raised, but the reality is confronting and it is uncomfortable.

I think in a time when we have become so disconnected to where and how food is produced and we live to eat whatever we want, on demand, we need to have more options that are less impactful on the planet, and don't rely on animal exploitation. Sure, there are organic and high-welfare options that most can't afford, but I believe there is a better way to get our sugar fix.

This book is about arming you with a new outlook and tools to bake a better future.

THE RULES

1 Read (or watch) the recipe from start to finish

If you're doing something for the first time, the recipe is there to help you find your bearings! QR codes load videos of the recipe so I can show you exactly how and why to do things.

2 Use scales please!

Digital scales are affordable and easy to use. Grab the bowl or jug mentioned in the recipe and weigh directly into it for fuss-free and consistent baking.

3 Don't substitute

I have tried to build in plenty of flexibility into the recipes to cater for different allergens. As a general rule, don't substitute different ingredients because they work differently and this book was written so accessible ingredients could be used. Gluten-free options are also mentioned. By all means use the recipes as a new foundation and experiment, but do try them as they are written first.

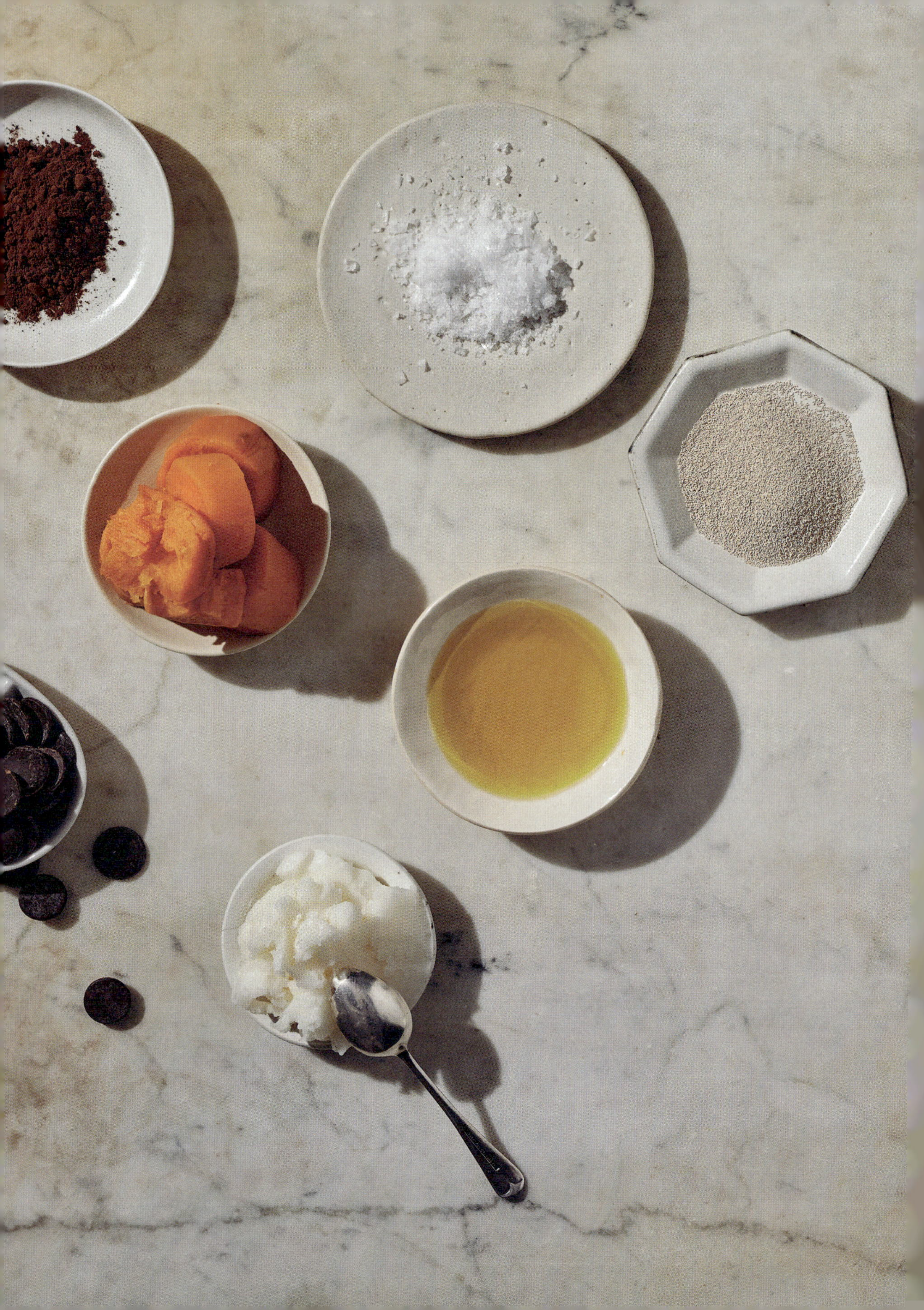

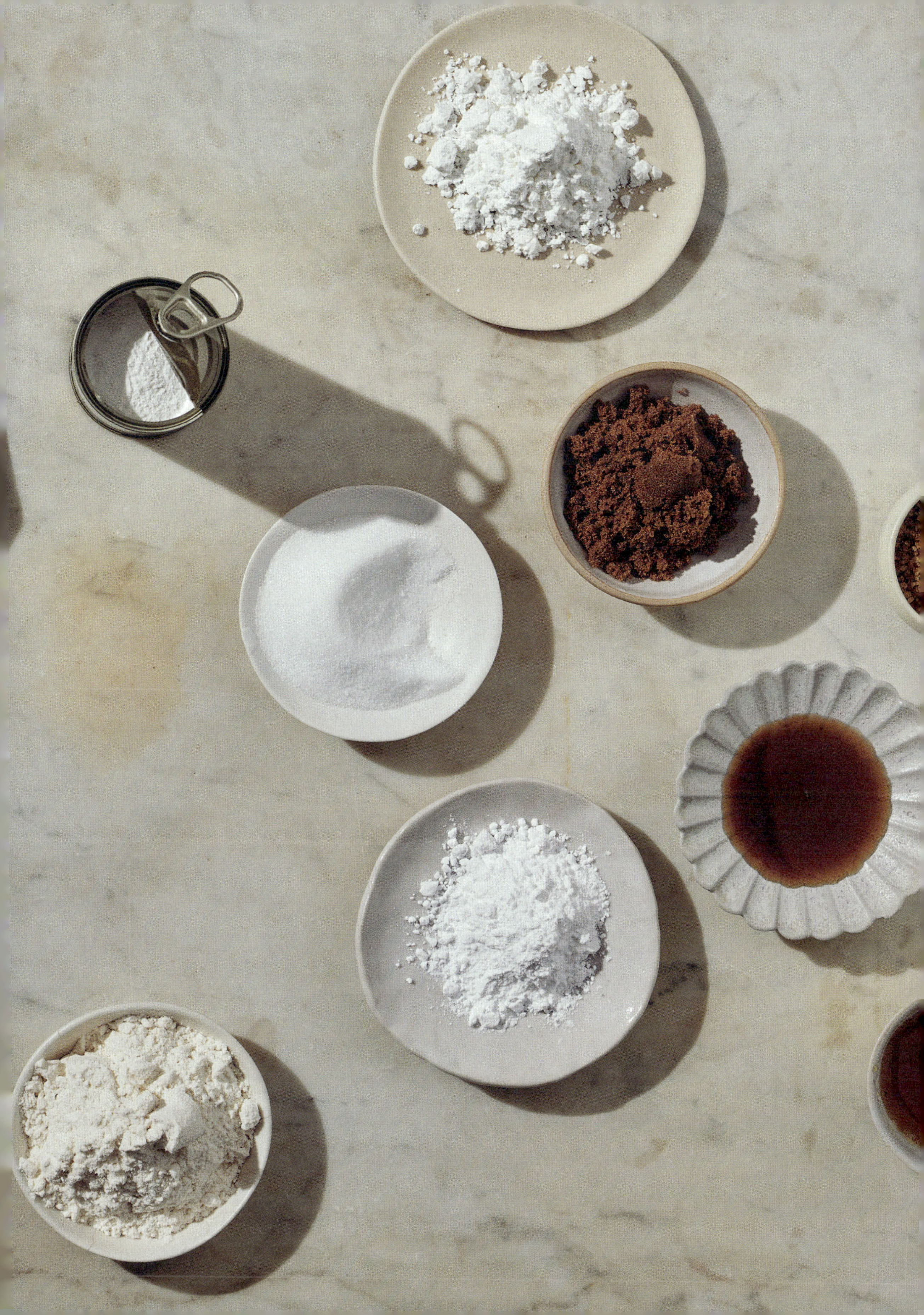

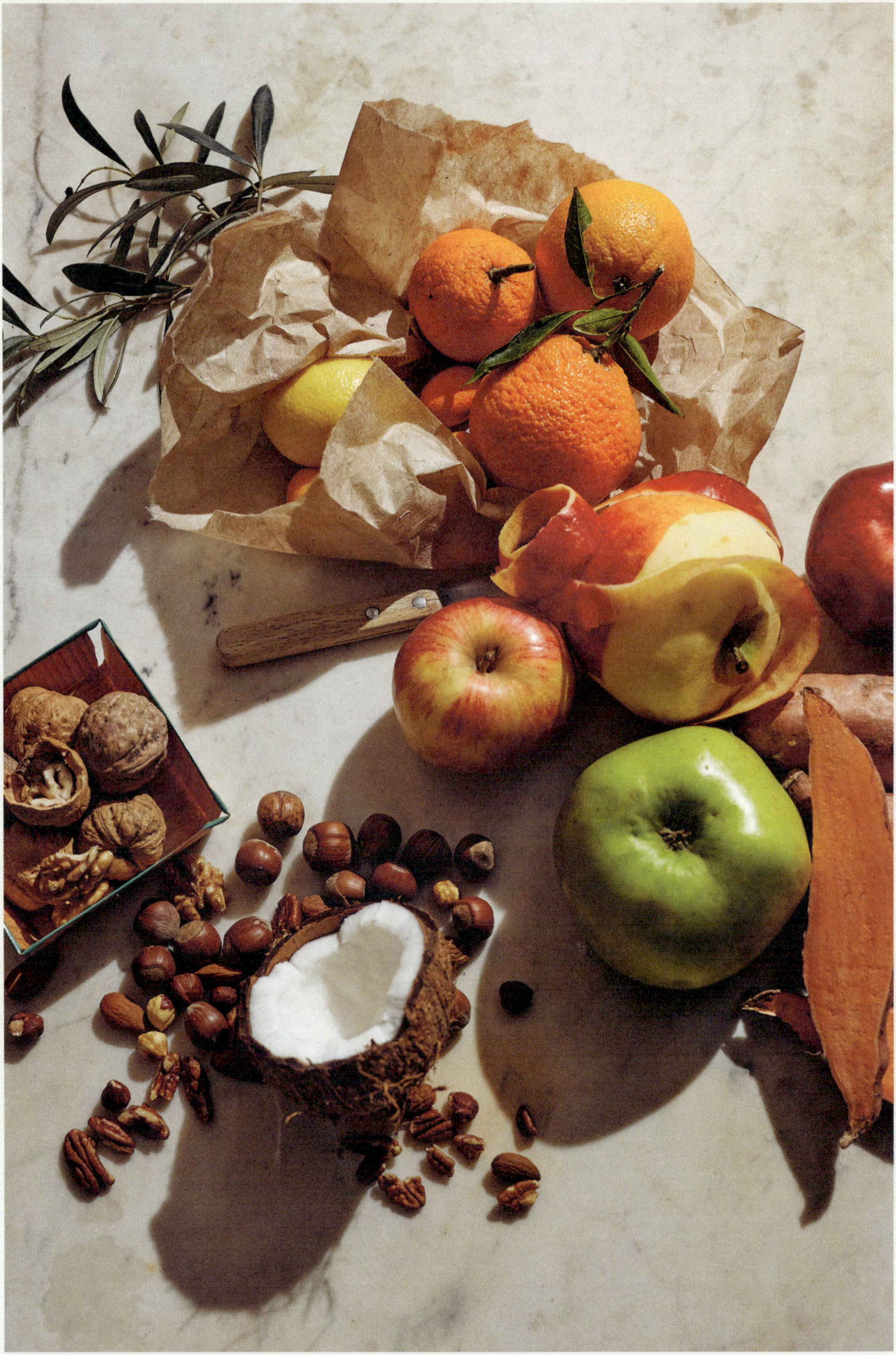

THE PLANTRY

**MAIN AND SPECIAL INGREDIENTS WITH
ALL THEIR FUNCTIONALITIES EXPLAINED**

The key to my approaching more natural, plant-based baking required a new way of looking at our existing pantry and allowing the functionalities of ingredients we already use shine in different and often new ways by revisiting formulas, tweaking ratios and oftentimes just starting completely from scratch. In this section is a short dive into the ingredients that make up the 'plantry' so you can get some insight into how they are produced and how they work in recipes, with my recommendations.

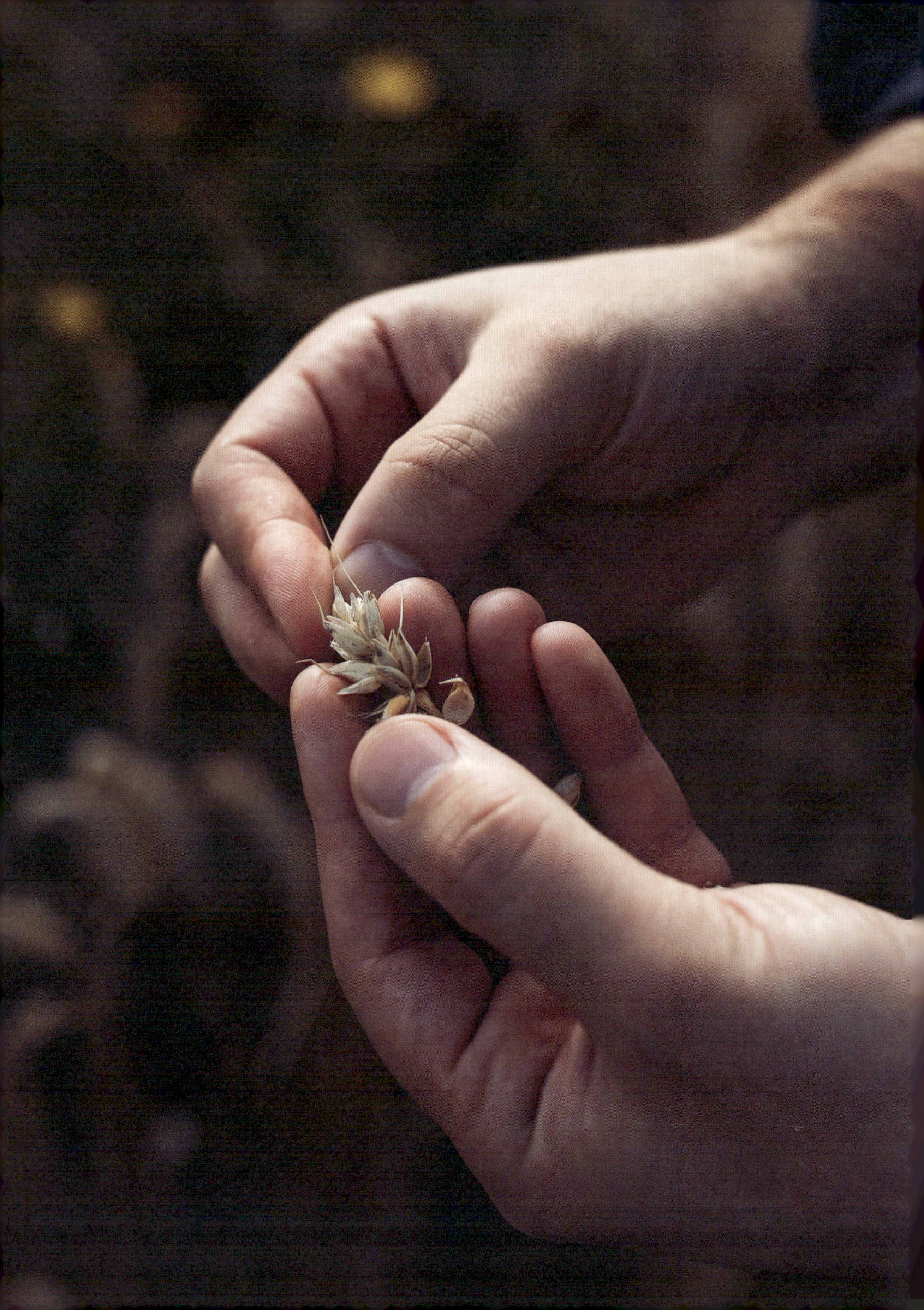

WHEAT FLOUR

Wheat flour is an incredible ingredient made from the milled berry of wheat grass. It forms a humble yet vital foundation that nearly all baked goods and many foods have evolved from. Humans have consumed it for thousands of years and records date back to the Egyptians.

Picture vast stretches of wheat fields, uniform and impressive, yet hiding a secret. These monoculture systems, though efficient, have unintended consequences. Much has changed in the farming of wheat in the last 200 years with the advent of industrial and intensive monoculture farming and the use of fertilisers. Modern farming uses pesticides to eliminate pests, herbicides to remove weeds and fertilisers to feed the wheat grass, resulting in soil that is lacking in any biodiversity or micronutrients – leaching carbon out of the ground when it is tilled. It leads to soil degradation and the depletion of natural resources, while the use of synthetic chemicals to maintain high yields can harm both the environment and human health. Some experts estimate that with traditional monoculture farming, we have a mere 60–100 years of crops left, primarily due to soil degradation.

But fear not, for there is hope on the horizon. It comes in the form of the wildfarmed method. This more sustainable, regenerative approach to wheat cultivation nurtures the land by incorporating a diverse mix of up to four plants alongside our precious wheat. The benefits are abundant: healthier soil through enhanced fertility and structure, a thriving ecosystem with increased biodiversity, CO2 capture and a reduced reliance on synthetic chemicals. This method ensures that the healthy, live soil will bear crops of nutritious, flavoursome wheat in perpetuum.

The art of milling is crucial in the transformation of wheat into the flours we know and love. The traditional milling process involves cleaning the wheat to remove impurities, followed by grinding the grains to separate the endosperm, bran and germ. Finally, the flour particles are sifted to obtain the desired granulation. Within this process lies a beautiful alternative: the stoneground milling method. By gently grinding the grains between two large stones, the bran and germ are preserved, resulting in a more nutritious and flavoursome flour. So, as you gather your ingredients and embark on your next culinary adventure, take a moment to consider the story behind a bag of flour. Seek out regeneratively farmed wheat and traditional stoneground milling, for it not only helps preserve our precious planet but also elevates the simple pleasures of our baking.

When flour is mixed with water to a batter or dough a network of protein called gluten develops which provides web like structure and strength. When the batters or doughs are baked, the proteins and starches create a gelling effect and the mixture becomes firm. Many people have developed sensitivity and intolerance to gluten – the protein in wheat which forms in the presence of water. For these people there are many brilliant blends of gluten-free flours consisting mainly of rice and tapioca flours and potato starch. They work well in a number of recipes, but some require total reformulation.

Flours are made from different types of wheat, grown under different conditions or seasons to achieve specific profiles and protein levels. While there's an incredible range of flours, the two main flours I use in the recipes are:

1. Plain (all-purpose) flour (10–13 per cent protein) for cakes

2. Bread (strong) flour (12–15 per cent protein) for yeasted/sweet risen doughs

LEAVENERS/ RAISING AGENTS

Before yeast was commercialised it was a crude preparation of flour and water and was prone to the weather, spoiling and off flavours. Baking was heavily skills based, time consuming and the domain of wives and daughters. Cooks in those days had very different ovens and inconsistent flour, which they even had to dry in the oven. Chemical leaveners, such as potash and pearl ash, first made an appearance in recipes as early as the 1780s when the ancestors of baking powder were mixed with an acidic ingredient, such as lemon juice, vinegar or buttermilk. The reaction created air (gases) that was trapped and this resulted in lightening the recipe as the batter or dough heated and firmed up during cooking.

CHEMICAL

Bicarbonate of soda | In recipes bicarbonate of soda (baking soda) provides the 'first rise' or leavening of a batter or dough. This is what happens when the dough is mixed and an acidic ingredient (like lemon juice or brown sugar) and the bicarbonate of soda combine in the presence of water. It also promotes browning and caramelisation in biscuits (cookies) and sponges when it is included without an acidic ingredients to neutralise it.

Baking powder | It was in the 1840s that baking powder as we know it came to exist. Alfred Bird, the British inventor and food scientist, created 'single-acting' baking powder for his wife who was allergic to yeast (he also created custard powder for his wife as she was also allergic to eggs) and mixed it with bicarbonate of soda (baking soda) and cream of tartar (an acidic powder leftover from wine production). When added to a recipe, this would create an instant reaction or leavening effect in recipes that did not require an acidic ingredient.

In the 1860s 'double-acting' baking powder was invented by Eben Norton Horsford. This type of baking powder becomes active when it comes into contact with a liquid, and as the mixture warms up to above 60°C (140°F) a second acidic compound dissolves and gives the mixture a second wind. Starches start to gel at this temperature too. Nearly all blends of baking powder have had formulations that have been the same for the last 200 years. 'Single-acting' baking powder is only available to industrial bakers for specific applications, so now all baking powder is 'double acting'.

BIOLOGICAL

Yeast | Yeast as we know it (in fresh or dried form) is a relatively modern invention, newer actually than baking powder. Prior to 1876 when it was introduced by the Fleischmann brothers at the Centennial Exposition, 'yeast' had to be prepared much like the sourdough starters most might be familiar with now. Their invention isolated *Saccharomyces cerevisiae* (also known as brewer's yeast), a single-celled fungus responsible for many fermentation processes and also one of the most widely studied organisms. These simple organisms consume starch and simple sugars and produce carbon dioxide as a result of dividing and multiplying. How they will be added to a recipe mainly depends on how they have been processed/dried. Fresh and instant types can be added directly to a recipe, whereas active yeast needs to be 'activated' or dissolved in liquid first.

In this book, the most commonly available yeast – instant dry yeast – is recommended for everyone's convenience. If you prefer to use fresh (also called cake) yeast you need to multiply the amount by three. Fresh yeast can be added directly to a recipe and mixed into a dough.

Most brands of yeast will work very well but may contain an emulsifier or an outer layer of deactivated yeast (from the drying processs), which makes it necessary to dissolve them in liquid first – make sure the liquid is lukewarm and does not exceed 59°C (138°F) as this will kill the yeast and make it useless.

If you can find it, I recommend seeking out an organic brand of instant dry yeast, as it will only contain the active yeast and the ingredients will list *Saccharomyces cerevisiae*. Unlike conventional yeast, organic yeast is produced using organic cereals without the use of chemical additives during fermentation. Selected strains of yeast and lactic acid bacteria cultures are bred in a wholly organic nutrient solution made from organic grain, pure spring water and enzymes. All microorganisms and raw materials used are guaranteed non-GMO, organic ingredients.

Instant dry yeast is a finer granule size and can usually be added directly to a recipe.

Active dry yeast has been dried at a slightly higher temperature so it has a coating of deactivated (dead) yeast cells that need to be dissolved or 'activated' in lukewarm water or liquid in a recipe before use. Times the instant amount by 1.3 times for the active dry.

Compressed fresh (cake) yeast contains 70 per cent water and can be added directly to a recipe. It is popular with bakers who can use it in its short use-by (expiration) date as it typically doesn't last more than a week or two. Three times more than the instant amount is needed for the fresh.

I recommend using instant dry yeast. It can be purchased in packs or in small cans and has a very long shelf life (2 years from date of manufacture) and doesn't need to be refrigerated like fresh.

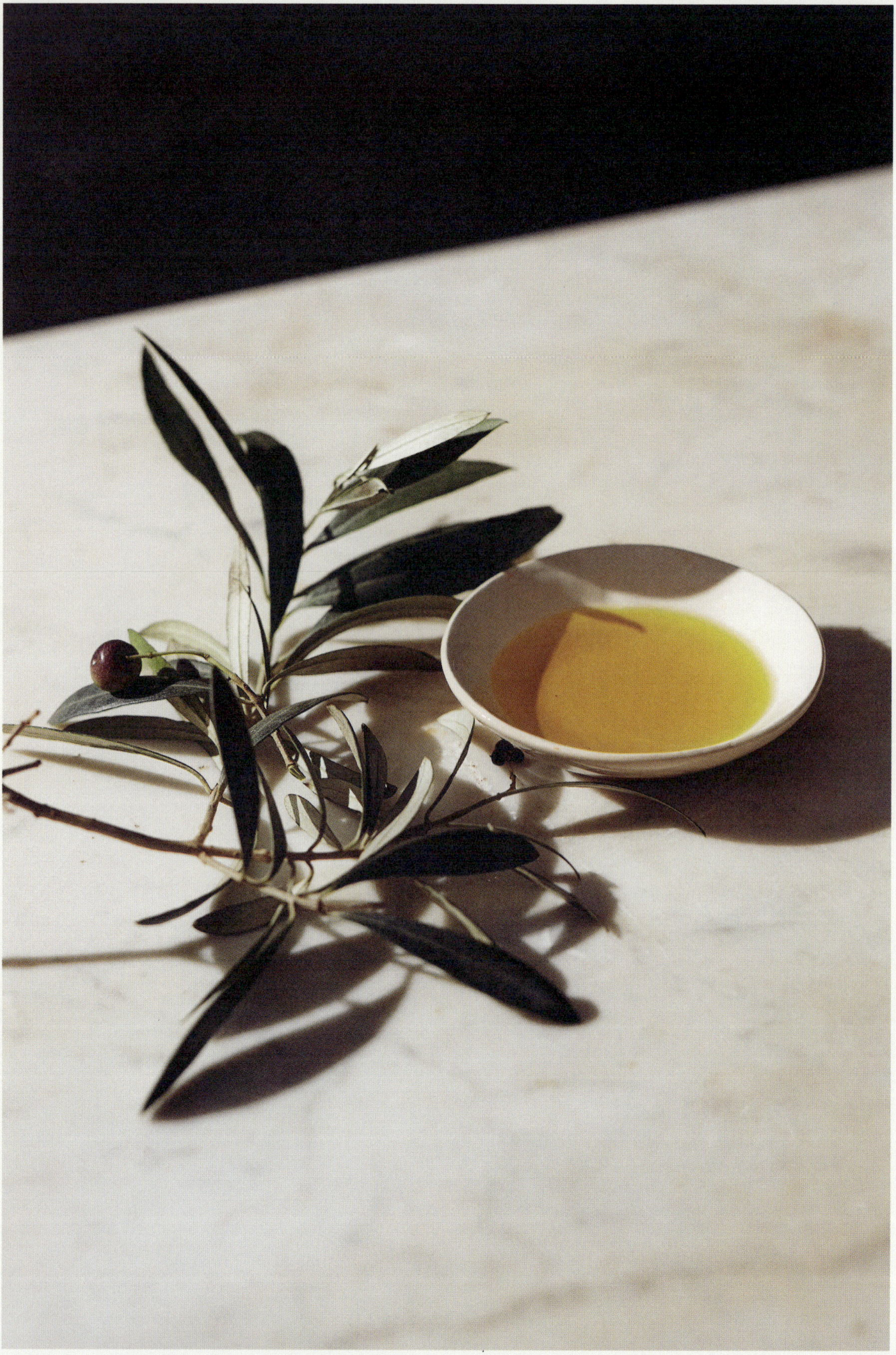

OILS

Oils are naturally plant based and I hope that people will discover the beautiful flavour and qualities of cold-pressed and organic oils that should be celebrated for their provenance and flavour in the way we celebrate wine and honey. My recipes have a significant reduction in fat compared to traditional bakes, and I use high-quality oils as the expense is comparative. Cheap highly refined oils should be avoided (see below).

Oils are fats that are liquid at room temperature. This is a critical characteristic that makes them so useful in many delicious foods. In a sponge they penetrate the batter so readily creating a tender, moist crumb. This is different to solid fats that need to be manipulated (beaten or melted to specific textures in order to be incorporate into a recipe). When the temperature drops below 20°C (68°F), cakes made with butter and other solid fats tend to become firm and eat with a 'dry mouthfeel', especially if they have been refrigerated – it takes a lot to warm bakes back up to the temperature where a solid fat might become soft on the palate again.

UNREFINED VS REFINED OILS

Unrefined oils are ones that have been pressed by mechanical means usually by some form of pressing. Oils that are certified organic will have been processed this way too. These oils usually contain higher amounts of vitamins and minerals, and residual compounds that flavour the oil. These same compounds increase the chance of the oil oxidising and spoiling faster as well as reducing their smoke point. The smoke point is the temperature an oil can be heated to before it starts to break down and release harmful chemicals and taste bitter. All unrefined/low-processed oils have a lower smoke point for frying, but this isn't relevant to baking as the batter or dough never exceeds 100°C (212°F), well below the smoking point for most oils. These oils should be used at the peak of freshness and stored in cool dark places or containers. Choose oils that have mild or complementary flavours. I use extra virgin olive oil and organic or virgin sunflower oil in nearly everything from pastry to many cakes. Some organic oils may be steam refined, which is a gentler method of deodorising the oil where boiling steam is pumped into a chamber under vacuum to help remove volatile aroma compounds. This is still a far cry from the solvents and processing used for many refined oils.

Refined oils have been extracted using chemical solvents and should be avoided. They are ultra-processed ingredients. It's this very reason I have purposefully formulated recipes without margarines which are made from refined oils (sometimes hydrogenated to make them solid at room temperature). Some oils are also very high in omega-6 fatty acids and can contribute to known health risks if not kept in check.

Extra virgin olive oil | Not all oils were created equal and extra virgin olive oil is the undisputed queen of all the oils. It has been produced by purely mechanical means – this is a strict control on its classification and how it is labelled. Extra virgin olive oil is a staple of the Mediterranean diet and has been used in food for thousands of years. It is high in polyphenols, antioxidants and monounsaturated fats, all of which have been studied extensively for their positive effects on health. Most people will associate a peppery and savoury flavour with olive oil, but there are many varieties and origins for olive oils.

Through extensive testing, I have found robust extra virgin olive oil to work brilliantly in nearly all of my recipes. In baked products the flavour I thought would be there just lends a delicious complexity, and in raw products like a ganache it gives a fresh fruity flavour. In fact, I am such a huge fan of baking with olive oil I should have called this book 'Baking with Olive Oil'.

Many have suggested that olive oil is too strong a flavour for general baking, but I think this is an untested theory and to my surprise it has worked brilliantly in almost every recipe I tested (although this is also because my recipes use a lot less fats/oils than is traditional). The oil can be tasted in cakes where there is no competing flavour, such as a plain vanilla sponge, but it was nearly the only application where I would have recommended using an alternative oil like cold-pressed sunflower oil, or any lightly flavoured oil of your choice. I initially worried that its use could be tasted or be overpowering, but this assumption quickly disappeared as quickly as the Nut Shortbreads (page 78) melts in the mouth. It was an assumption.

Extra virgin olive oil has a robust herbaceous flavour and should be used when this complements the dessert you're making. It pairs very well with items containing fruit. But, I have tested all my recipes with robust olive oil.

Sunflower oil | This is an oil produced from the pressing of sunflower seeds and has a mild, nutty flavour. Sunflower oil originates in cooler eastern Europe (Ukraine and Russia accounted for half of global production) where it is the most popular oil to cook with.

I recommend a cold-pressed or organic sunflower oil in items where chocolate, caramel or other 'brown' flavours are being highlighted.

GROUNDNUT / PEANUT OIL

Peanut oil, also referred to as groundnut oil or arachis oil, is a vegetable-derived oil made from the edible seeds of the peanut plant. Although the peanut plant flowers above ground, the seeds or peanuts actually develop underground. This is why peanuts are also known as groundnuts. Peanuts are often grouped with tree nuts like walnuts and almonds, but they are actually a type of legume that belongs to the pea and bean family.

Depending on processing, peanut oil can have a wide range of flavours that vary from mild and sweet to strong and nutty. Peanut oil is widely used around the world but is most common in Chinese, South Asian and Southeast Asian cooking. It became popular in the United States during World War II when other oils were scarce due to food shortages. It has a high smoke point of 225°C (437°F) and is commonly used to fry foods.

There are several types of peanut oil and each one is made using different techniques:

Refined peanut oil | This type is refined, bleached and deodorised, which removes the allergenic parts of the oil. It is typically safe for those with peanut allergies. It is commonly used by restaurants to fry foods like chicken and French fries.

Cold-pressed peanut oil | In this method, peanuts are crushed to force out the oil. This low-heat process retains much of the natural, mild peanut flavour and more nutrients than refining does.

Gourmet peanut oil | Considered a speciality oil, this type is unrefined and the peanuts are usually roasted, giving the oil a deeper, more intense flavour than refined oil.

Peanut oil blends | Peanut oil is often blended with a similar-tasting but less expensive oil like soybean or corn oil. This type is more affordable but has been highly refined.

I recommend cold-pressed, unroasted peanut oil for it's milder flavour when peanut allergies are not a concern, and sunflower when it is.

COCONUT OIL

The pressed oil from coconut flesh is a saturated fat that may raise the levels of good cholesterol.

Virgin | Fresh coconut flesh is scooped out of the shell and then cold pressed making coconut milk, which separates to leave the oil on top. Unrefined or virgin coconut oil has a very strong coconut flavour, a slightly lower smoking point and is prone to rancidity faster. It can be used in baking but only in recipes where the flavour would be complementary. I generally don't use it.

Refined | Made from dried organic coconut meat, or copra, it is gently steam-refined through a certified organic process to achieve a neutral scent and flavour. If it's organic, absolutely no chemicals will be used, but if not, it will likely go through additional refining steps to purify the oil.

I recommend seeking out a steam-deodorised, odourless coconut oil. I use coconut oil in recipes where I need some hardness or for a creamy texture when blended, such as in a custard or to make your own whipping cream.

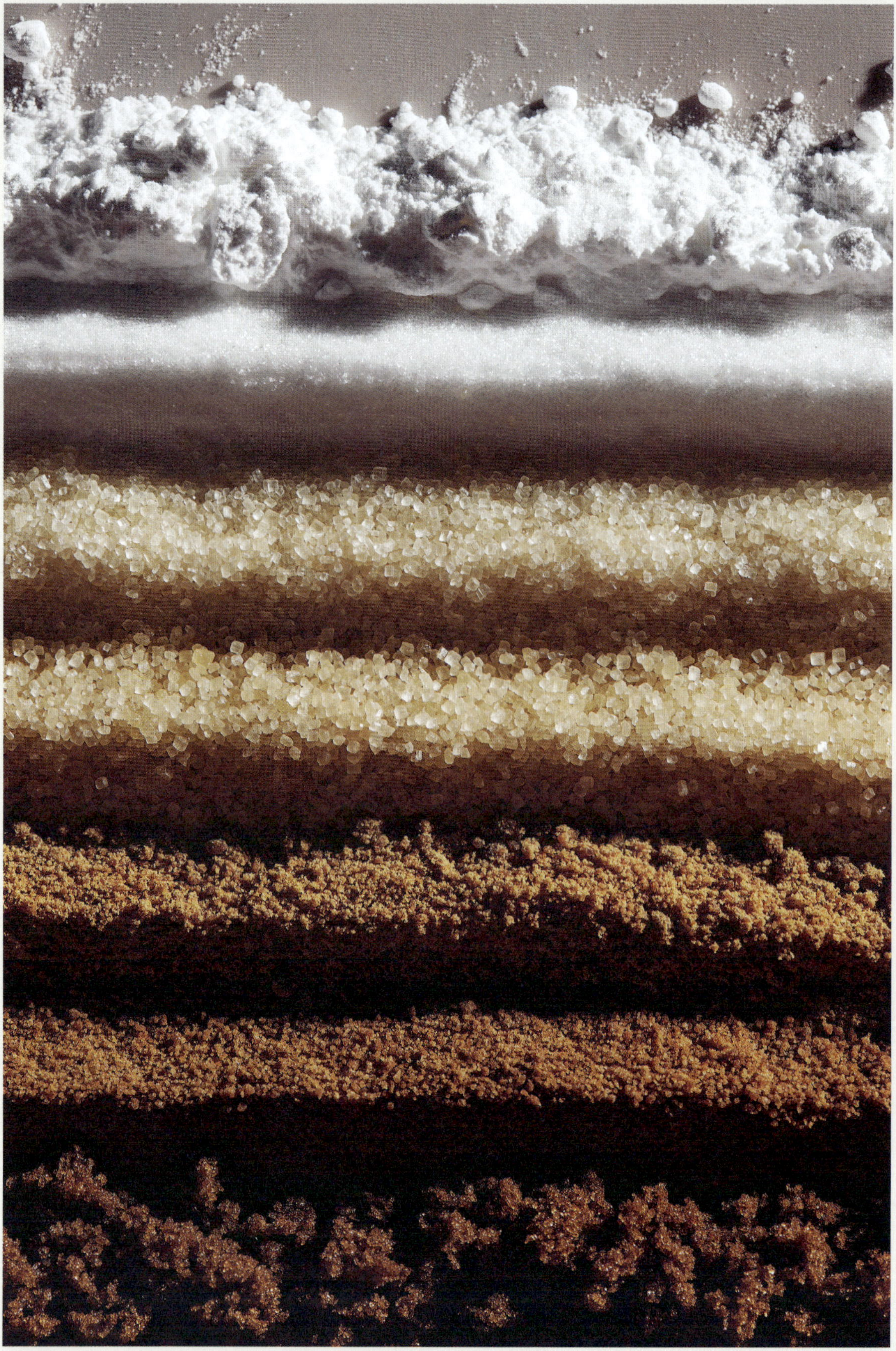

SUGAR BY ANY OTHER NAME WOULD TASTE AS SWEET

Who knew one base ingredient could have over 50 names and forms. Mostly, they vary by the amount of molasses and how 'purified' they are, but how they are named comes down to marketing, local laws and politics. Sugar comes in a variety of forms. The difference in processing between a number of classes of products can be small, but the finished sugar can appear very different. Take light and dark brown sugars: these are technically more processed than white sugar because white sugar is made and molasses is then added back into it to make brown sugars as opposed to muscovado sugars which have a similar but richer flavour and are less processed but similar in a number of ways.

UNREFINED VS REFINED OR CENTRIFUGED VS NON-CENTRIFUGED

Even 'unrefined sugars' go through a refining process – I will outline each process so you can understand the differences and make decisions about which sugar you are happy to use. With the exception of panela, other artisanal dark sugars and muscovado sugars (which are only made from sugar cane juice) nearly all sugars will need to be refined to remove the molasses. Non-centrifuged sugar has all the molasses content retained and has trace amounts of nutrients. Even sugars we consider raw or which are marketed as non-refined, often mean that they have been through less 'centrifuges' in the final stages of production.

Brown sugars are more often used to add beautiful toffee and caramel flavours to baking, due to their molasses content, but are rarely used alone as they may add too much of these lovely flavours (too much of anything can be a bad thing – a fitting sentiment to discuss in the sugar section of a baking book!) They also melt and behave differently because the higher molasses content can burn easily and leave a burned or overpowering flavour when used in caramels for example.

No matter what the marketing says, anything other than this is 'processed', which isn't necessarily always a bad thing and manufacturers have found cleaner ways of processing and refining sugar.

HOW SUGARS ARE PRODUCED AND REFINED

1 Crushing

Obtain sugar juice by crushing or milling sugar cane or beets.

2 Clarification

Remove impurities from the juice by heating and adding lime, followed by filtration.

3 Evaporation

Concentrate the clarified juice by evaporating water, resulting in a thick syrup.

4 Crystallisation

Encourage sugar crystallisation by boiling the syrup in vacuum pans.

5 Centrifugation

A centrifuge is used to separate sugar crystals from the syrup (molasses).

6 Washing

Increase the purity of sugar crystals by washing with hot water or steam.

7 Drying and cooling

Dry and cool the sugar crystals before packaging or further refining.

TYPES OF SUGARS

Common white (and golden) |
White sugar (sucrose) is what we are most commonly familiar with and measure sweetness by. It comes from two main crops: sugar cane (a grass) accounting for 70 per cent and grown in warmer climates, and sugar beets (related to beetroot) which is grown in temperate climates. In processing, beets will always be refined to produce white sugar products (and in turn can be made into 'brown' sugar) whereas cane sugar can produce various types of sugar. Their juice is extracted, which is boiled under vacuum to concentrate the sugars. It is then crystallised and washed to remove the dark molasses, then it is made into syrups through a number of stages that are progressively clarified.

White sugar has been refined to be 99.95 per cent sucrose. It is pure, white with no other flavour than sweetness.

Raw sugar is refined to about 99 per cent sucrose with traces of molasses, which give it a light golden colour and a light toffee flavour.

White sugar is available in various granule sizes. Granulated, the sugar you stir into coffee; finer ground sugar like caster (superfine) sugar, used in baking – the type that I recommend for the way it dissolves into recipes; and icing (confectioners') sugar, which is further pulverised to be very finely ground and is great for icings (frostings). In an emergency, you can make icing sugar yourself by blending either granulated or caster sugar in a high-powered blender and sifting the fine powder.

Raw sugar also called plantation white, turbinado, Demerara |
The crystals have just a hint of molasses flavour and a pale blond colour and trace amounts of the original cane molasses are retained around the crystals, which gives them colour and flavour. They contain less than 2 per cent molasses and their crystals are medium-size or slightly larger than table sugar.

Organic sugars with a blond colour are slightly less refined than table sugar but much less processed and contain about 99 per cent sucrose. To compare, table sugar is 99.95 per cent sucrose. Both of these sugars are purified by crystallisation and centrifugation. The difference is white sugar goes through more series of crystallisation and centrifugation cycles to achieve higher 'purity'.

Light or dark brown sugar |
Brown sugar is refined white sugar with molasses added back into it. Muscovado sugar is less refined, so it retains much of its molasses component. The amount of molasses determines whether it is 'light' or 'dark': the darker the sugar, the more molasses it contains. It is technically more processed than white sugar, as it has been through more centrifuges before molasses are added back in. Dark brown sugar is a suitable substitute for muscovado sugar with a similar flavour and texture.

Dark muscovado |
Muscovado sugar is made by extracting the sugar cane juice, then clarifying and cooking it until it crystallises and moisture evaporates. The brown syrupy molasses created during cooking remains in the final product, resulting in a moist, dark brown sugar that has the texture of wet sand. The high-molasses content also gives the sugar a complex flavour with hints of toffee and a slightly bitter aftertaste. Some companies that produce muscovado remove a small amount of the molasses to also create a light variety. Muscovado is often called an artisanal sugar, as the production methods are relatively low tech and labour intensive. In many cases it is a non-centrifuged sugar, depending on the manufacturing process and country of origin, but some processing can be partially refined.

Traditional artisan sugars

Artisan sugar is a non-centrifugal sugar that comes straight from freshly harvested cane. Traditional non-centrifugal sugars are produced close to cane fields using hundreds of years of knowledge. They are often made on a small scale for local markets with simple equipment and little capital. Put simply, their processing involves collecting the cane juice, clarifying it and boiling its water off through slow simmering in open kettles. Other dark artisan sugars of the world include muscovado from Mauritius Island and the Philippines, rapadura from Brazil, panela from Colombia, piloncillo from Mexico, kokuto from Japan and jaggery from India. Each of these have specific flavour profiles or *terroir* as in wines, coffee or chocolate.

In summary, I use the below main types of sugar:

1. Golden or white caster (superfine) sugar for the way that it can be incorporated into batters and doughs or dissolves quickly when making a syrup. Use white caster (superfine) sugar for making caramels as the molasses content is prone to burning.

2. Pure icing (confectioners') sugar (no added starches or anti-caking agents) for icings (frostings) that recrystallise beautifully. If you would like to use raw sugar, then blend raw sugar in a high-powered blender.

3. Dark muscovado or dark brown sugars for their toffee and butterscotch flavour and colour. in recipes where I specify muscovado, I am referring to dark muscovado.

Glucose (corn syrup)

Maize (corn) is commonly used as the source of the starch in the US, where the syrup is called 'light corn syrup', but glucose syrup is also made from potatoes, wheat and even cassava or rice. Glucose syrup is created by hydrolysing, or breaking apart, the strings of glucose molecules that make up starchy foods by cooking it with water and introducing an acid or enzyme. It is great at keeping things moist and helps give an elastic texture to caramels.

Golden syrup or light treacle

With the texture of honey, golden syrup is produced in a number of ways around the world. Generally it is a dense sugar syrup that has been cooked for a long time, some citric acid (or other acid) is added and the composition of the sugar changes to invert sugar – the resulting syrup doesn't crystallise. It is a popular topping syrup and a fantastic and easy-to-use inverted sugar with a unique light molasses flavour. Invert sugar helps to retain moisture in cakes and biscuits (cookies) and promotes nice caramelisation.

If you can not get golden syrup, agave syrup is a suitable direct substitute.

Sweet potato | I use sweet potatoes in sweet yeasted dough to soften the texture by adding extra moisture, as well as a golden sweet aromatic tinge to all baked goods. I wholeheartedly recommend preparing them in advance and freezing them so they're always ready to use.

To prepare sweet potatoes, peel them with a vegetable peeler, cut into 2 cm (¾ in) thick rounds and add to a saucepan of water over a medium heat. Set a timer for 15–20 minutes and cook until a knife inserted into a potato meets no resistance. Drain and cool at room temperature, then freeze in a freezer-proof container.

Aquafaba | An exciting discovery was made in 2014 when a musician called Joel Roussel found that the water from tinned beans and chickpeas (garbanzos) showed some foaming capabilities. This is due to the trace amounts of protein, starch and other soluble solids in the liquid. In my personal experience it is great for making meringues, foams and for emulsifying a mayonnaise. It does not gel or coagulate and set like an egg white so I would not call it an egg white or egg replacer, broadly speaking.

Making Concentrated Aquafaba

For sweet application, tinned white beans and chickpeas work well. When using aquafaba, it is best to reduce it by boiling half the liquid off on the stove to concentrate its foaming abilities. You should have about 300 ml (10½ fl oz) of aquafaba liquid from two 400 g (14.1 oz) tins. Just use beans that are in water and not brine. Strain the liquid over a measuring jug. Set the chickpeas or beans aside in a container, cover and keep in the refrigerator for up to three days to use in other recipes. Pour the aquafaba liquid into a large saucepan, bring to the boil, then reduce to a simmer over a low-medium heat. You want to reduce the volume to 150 ml (5 fl oz), which should take around 10 minutes. You can use it immediately, or keep in a container in the refrigerator for 3 days or frozen for up to 3 months.

Gluten-free flour | Great strides have been made in the area of gluten-free baking. Wheat flour contains a protein which some people are sensitive or downright allergic to (coeliac disease). Symptoms vary widely from mild discomfort for those who are sensitive/intolerant from eating a product containing gluten, down to intense agony and distressing physiological symptoms from consuming foods containing even a trace amount of gluten. More and more people are diagnosed with varying degrees of sensitivity each year. Coeliacs need to eliminate gluten from their diet completely.

There are many flours that don't contain gluten, such as buckwheat, teff, hemp, oat, rice, coconut, almond and potato flours, but I would never recommend swapping ANY flour directly for wheat flour as this will not work the same way.

Gluten-free replacements for plain (all-purpose) flour have become increasingly popular. These are commonly a combination of very finely milled rice, and either/or all of potato, tapioca or maize starch. A common formula for a versatile gluten-free flour contains two-parts finely milled rice flour, one-part potato starch and one part tapioca starch. Where moisture retention is important, 1 teaspoon of xanthan gum can be added per 120 g (4.2 oz) of the blend.

Some cake and cookie recipes will allow for simple substitution of a plain gluten-free flour. I have noted these where it works very well. I have also kept some recipes intentionally gluten free where possible.

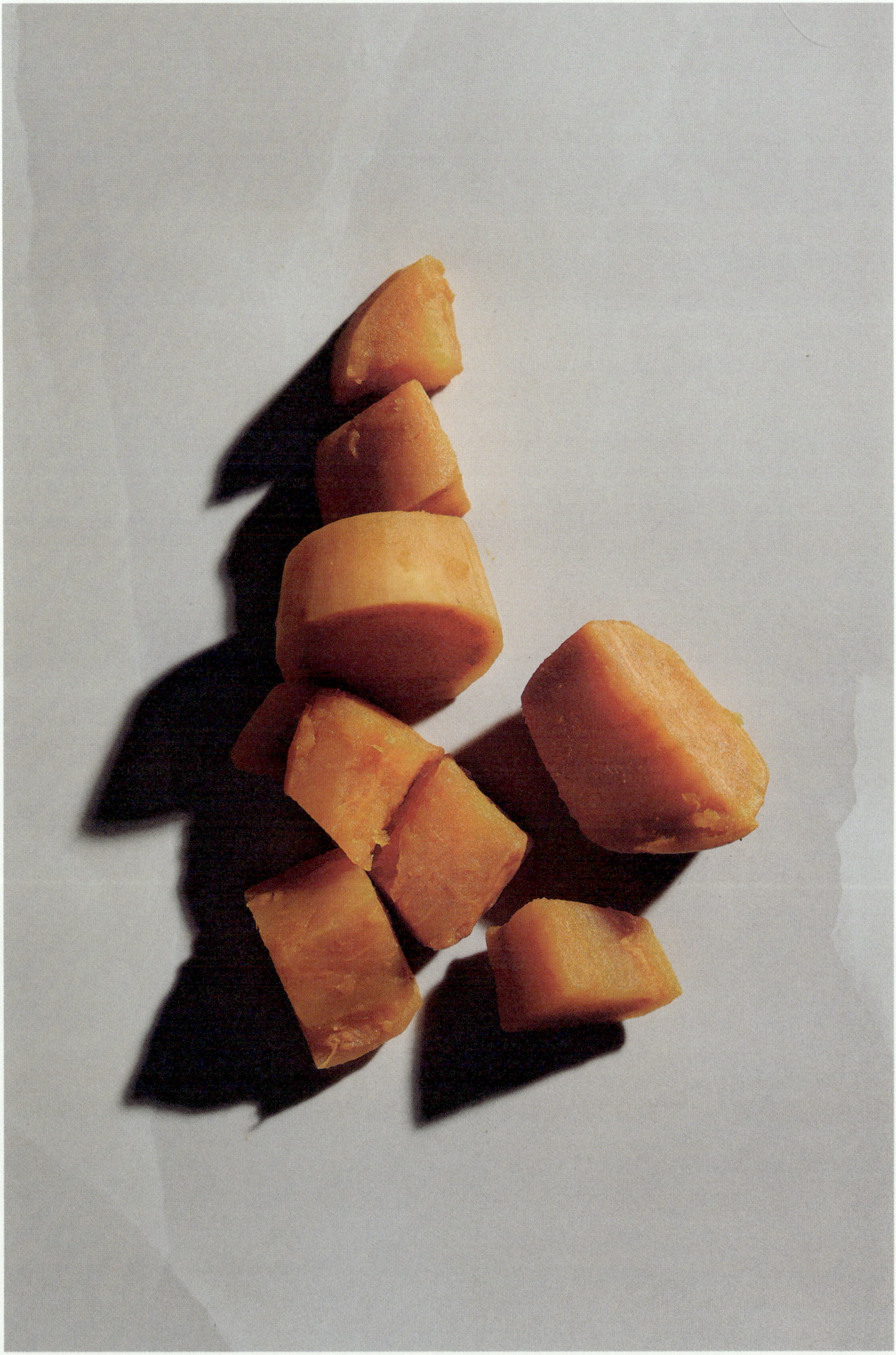

CACAO

Cacaofruit or *Theobroma cacao* is the pod of a cacao tree. From a pod, about 30 per cent is the beans and the rest is mucilage, a pulp surrounding them. This has a delightful, tropical sweet flavour that reminds me of mango, pineapple, passion fruit and lychee. The whole beans are fermented with the mucilage, which imparts lots of fruity flavours to the beans, then roasted to develop cocoa flavours. The outer shell husk is then removed to leave the cocoa nibs, which are about 50 per cent cocoa solids and 50 per cent cocoa butter. The nib is then conched (rolled between stone or steel rollers) with sugar for hours until glossy and smooth with a particle size that is imperceptible to the tongue and melts to nothing.

Chocolate can be used as an ingredient or tempered for coating and decoration. Buy from chocolate makers/brands that can guarantee they don't use child slave labour, pay their farmers fairly and guarantee traceability. Cocoa is hard to produce, so should be treated with care and respect. It should be expensive and traceable so you know exploitation (usually of children) hasn't taken place in its farming.

Dark chocolate | High-quality dark chocolate should only have two or three ingredients – cacao and sugar and maybe lecithin. The percentage on dark chocolate refers to the amount of cocoa content (cocoa solids and cocoa butter) – the rest is sugar. Some brands will add vanilla and/or extra cocoa butter to make it more fluid for professionals. Use a high-quality dark chocolate for chocolate recipes and try to find 'couverture', a grade that has more cocoa butter.

I use a 65–70 per cent dark choclate (couverture grade) in my recipes.

Cocoa powder | When cocoa nibs are pressed for cocoa butter, the cake of solids left over is the cocoa powder. It can be further processed to alter the fat content. Natural cocoa powder has a slightly fruitier and acidic flavour because cocoa is naturally slightly acidic. An alkali (potassium carbonate) can be added and results in a woodier flavour profile and darker colour (called Dutch process).

You can use any type of cocoa powder you like; the main difference will be the colour.

Cocoa butter | Cocoa butter is the fat pressed from the nib. It can be virgin and have a very strong flavour that can be rather overpowering when used, or it can be deodorised gently with steam processing.

I only use deodorised cocoa butter as an ingredient.

PLANT-BASED MILKS

Cows have been milked to make dairy milk that is highly nutritious and necessary to grow a 36 kg (79 lb) newborn calf into a 600 kg (1,323 lb) cow within two years. It is estimated almost 70 per cent of the world has a form of lactose (the sugar naturally present in milk) intolerance, due to not having the enzyme to break it down. A huge variety of milk alternatives now exist, anything from nuts like almonds, to soy, oats, seeds, rice and coconut! Plant-based milk lends a creamy flavour and body to baking. In many cases, water could be used without much fuss but there's something I can only describe as 'milky' to the flavour that I prefer.

I rank milk alternatives according to nutrition, flavour and functionality. 'Barista' and professional milks are also widely available – these have had a stabiliser like a gum added to them to keep the milk from separating when added to coffee, or foam when steamed for espresso-based beverages. Some have had oils blended into them to make them creamier. I recommend reading the labels of the brands before you buy them, and seek out plant-based milks that are unsweetened so you can control the flavour and also contain the fewest ingredients. Try to buy organic if possible.

Soy milk | Products made from dried soybeans have been prepared for thousands of years and are highly nutritious. Soy has come into question recently for contributing to deforestation in the Amazon. It turns out that 80 per cent of the soy is actually grown to feed livestock. Soy milk is made by soaking dried soybeans in water and then grinding them together. This milk has the most protein of all natural milk alternatives and has a creamy texture and mild flavour. The protein content has lots of functionalities too as it helps with emulsification.

Soy milk is my preferred plant-based milk.

Oat milk | Oat milk has a lovely cereal flavour to it. It is prepared by grinding oats with water, then adding an enzyme that breaks down the starches into sugars. This stops the starches from becoming slimy and gelling when heated. Oat milk may contain gluten due to processing or growing near wheat crops, but you can find oat products that are certified gluten free. Find an organic brand with as few ingredients as possible.

Almond milk | Almond milk is made by grinding almonds and water with a tiny bit of salt. Sweeteners and stabilisers may be added. A number of issues have arisen due to the industrialisation of almond farming. Almonds are a thirsty crop requiring a lot of water and need bees to pollinate the flowers. Specific species of bees are shipped around to pollinate these farms, but many die and spread diseases that kill off other native species of bees, which are crucial to pollination and biodiversity of the area. I don't use almond milk for this reason, as well as because some people may be allergic to it and it can make a recipe that might otherwise have been nut-free contain nuts.

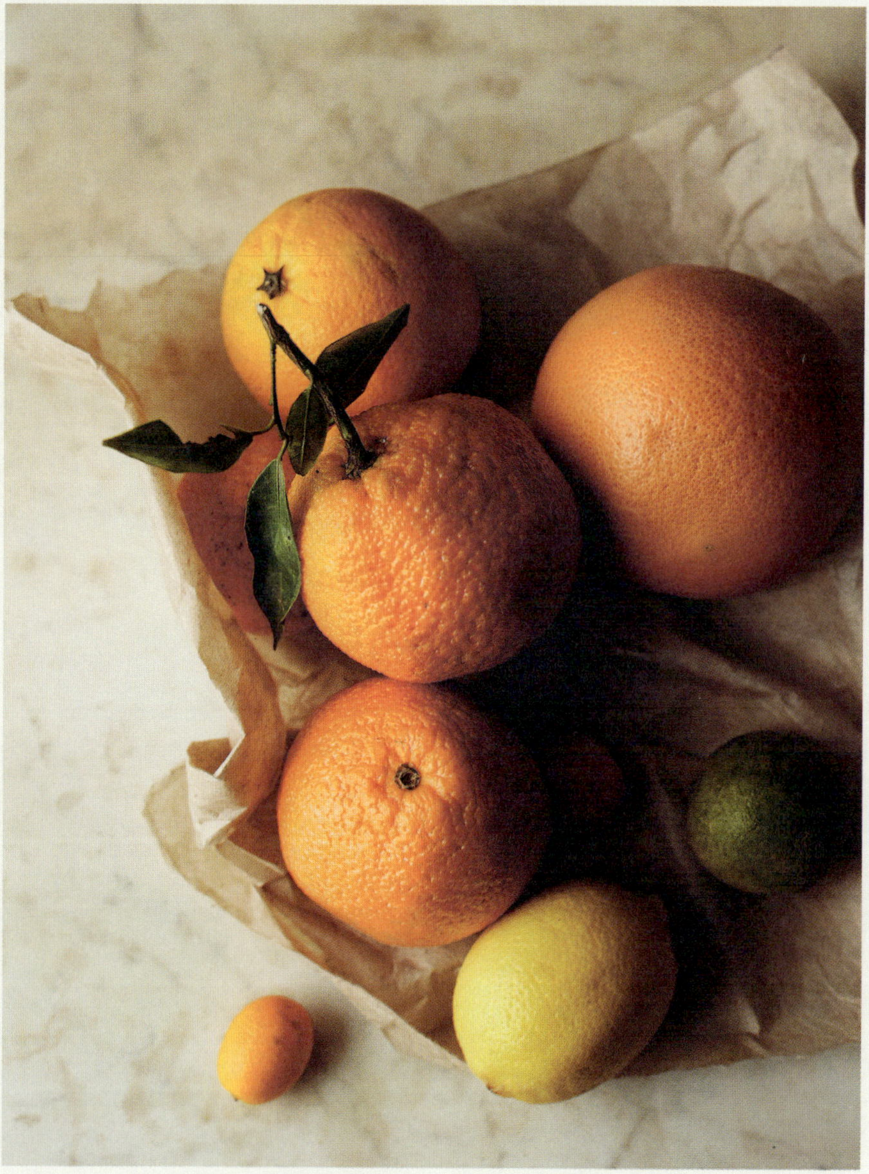

INGREDIENTS THAT FORM GELS

Cornflour and cornstarch | Cornflour in the UK is what North Americans call cornstarch. I think cornstarch is a more accurate name for the product and its qualities. The corn that's used for milling starch isn't much like the kind you eat from the cob. The breeds meant for eating fresh have lots of sugars for sweetness and they're harvested before they mature. The kind meant for milling is starchy rather than sweet and it's left on the cob until it's stone-hard. Corn in that form isn't easy to work with, so the first step in extracting the starch is to soak the corn kernels for a day or two in huge vats. This loosens the husks, moistens the rest of the grain and generally gets the corn ready for the rest of the process. From there the corn goes through a series of screens, designed to separate the grain into its various parts. The hulls and germ are removed to be processed into corn bran and corn oil. The endosperm, which has a lot of protein as well as starch, is separated out for a variety of other uses. What's left is a wet slurry that's made up of water and starch. The water is drained out and replaced with fresh water to wash the starches until they are really pure. Finally, the starch is dried and milled to a fine powder. That's the cornstarch you buy from the supermarket.

Pectins | Pectin is found in fibres that come from fruit. It is usually extracted from citrus fruits and comes in a powder. This powder is mixed with sugar (so it doesn't clump) before it's added to liquids. It is then simmered and a gel is formed when it's cooled. It is often used in jam (jelly) making.

There are a few types of pectin available, but the one I use in these recipes is pectin NH – a type of pectin that gels with low sugar and acidity meaning you can make jams or jellies that freeze and defrost very well. If you are not freezing your cake, feel free to use the recipe with agar-agar powder.

Pectin NH is available in nearly all countries, although you may need to find an online supplier – 20–30 g (0.9–1.1 oz) is required to set 1 kg (2 lb 4 oz) of gel or jam, so a little goes a long way. There are other types of pectin like Ball RealFruit Low or No-sugar Needed Pectin or Pomona's Universal Pectin and they should be used according to the packet instructions.

The most common type of pectin is often just called pectin or yellow pectin and requires a high amount of sugar, and acid to create a gel. This is desirable in a jam where you have a lot of sugar and acid from lemon juice. I have not used it in any of the recipes in this book but I have provided a recipe for jams that uses pectin NH so it can be frozen and defrosted.

Agar-agar powder | Agar-agar is extracted from red seaweed. It can be added in very small amounts to liquids and then boiled to make a gel at 38–40°C (100–104°F) as it cools. Use high-accuracy microscales scales when dealing with agar-agar, because only a small amount is needed to set a large amount of liquid. Recipes will usually specify small amounts. When using acidic liquids such as cranberry juice, lime juice or pineapple juice you may need to use more.

A soft jam or gel with very low sweetness can be made by blending a set agar gel and used in a fresh cake. They contain significantly less sugar than most commercial varieties which often have as much as 1:1 fruit and sugar. This low-sugar jam has a short shelf life but can be a delicious addition to fresh cakes that don't need to be stored at room temperature for extended periods.

Agar-agar mainly comes in two forms – a powder and strips. The powder is made from grinding down the strips and is the one I recommend using, as it's easier to weigh and use. It can be mixed with some sugar from a recipe and easily blended in liquids and them boiled out to activate.

NUTS

Technically speaking, nuts are a bit confusing, and what we know as culinary nuts include a range of seeds, legumes and drupes (a nut is a fruit encapsulated by a hard shell; true nuts include hazelnuts, chestnuts and acorns, but culinary nuts include pecans, walnuts, pistachios, almonds, macadamias, pine nuts, and so on.). Nuts are nutritionally dense and contain lots of protein and unsaturated fats which can be pressed for oil, ground to make nut butters, or ground to a coarse flour. Nuts can go rancid or oxidise if kept too long, so store them in airtight containers and taste them before using if they've been kept a long time. They should smell and taste nutty and not smell plasticky or taste bitter. Using rancid nuts is an easy way to ruin a bake.

Grind with flour | A great way to use nuts in cookie (Nut Shortbreads, page 78) and cake batters (Pear, Hazelnut and Almond Vanilla Cream Gateau, page 166) is to grind them with the flour to extract their oils and flavour, plus it also coats the gluten, making the cookie or sponge softer. Each nut has a beautiful characteristic flavour. Explore as many as you can!

Roasting nuts | I like to use nuts with their skin on, as the skin is often a rich source of fibre and antioxidants. To roast nuts, preheat the oven to 150°C fan (300°F/gas 2), then spread them on a large baking sheet in a single layer and roast for 15–20 minutes. This lower oven temperature allows the nuts to roast evenly and all the way through to the centre.

Nut butter | To make a nut butter, you will need to fill your food blender or food processor about three-quarters full to generate enough friction to blend them efficiently. Blend the toasted nuts until they start to clump as the oils are released. As they blend the mixture will start to look wet and generate some heat. Continue blending until the mixture is smooth! Store in an airtight jar away from direct sunlight and stir well before use as there will be some separation over time. I have also successfully used a small high-powered blender too. Just make sure to pulse it, then scrape the sides of the blender down regularly between pulses, and blend until smooth and liquid. See page 233.

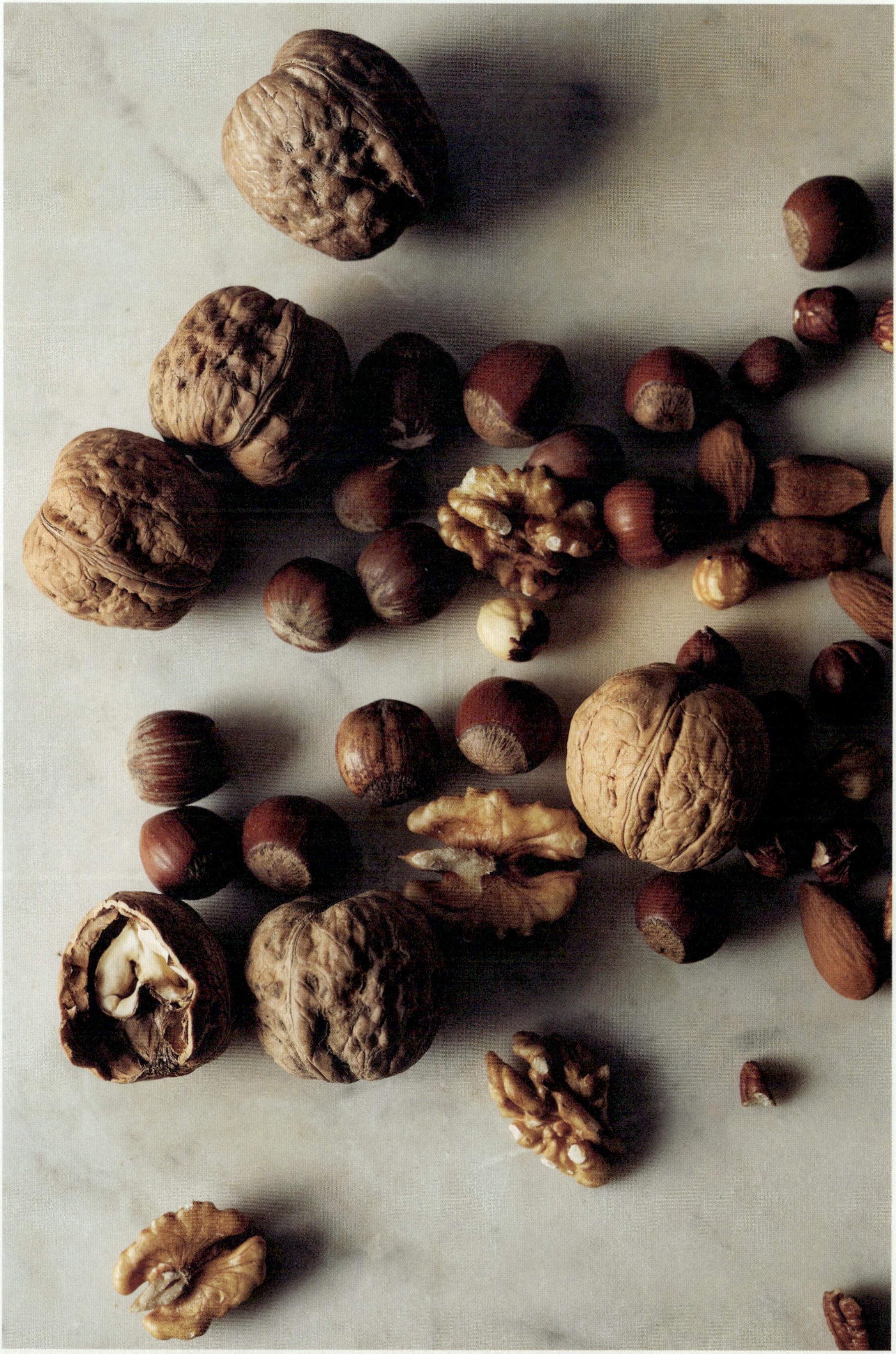

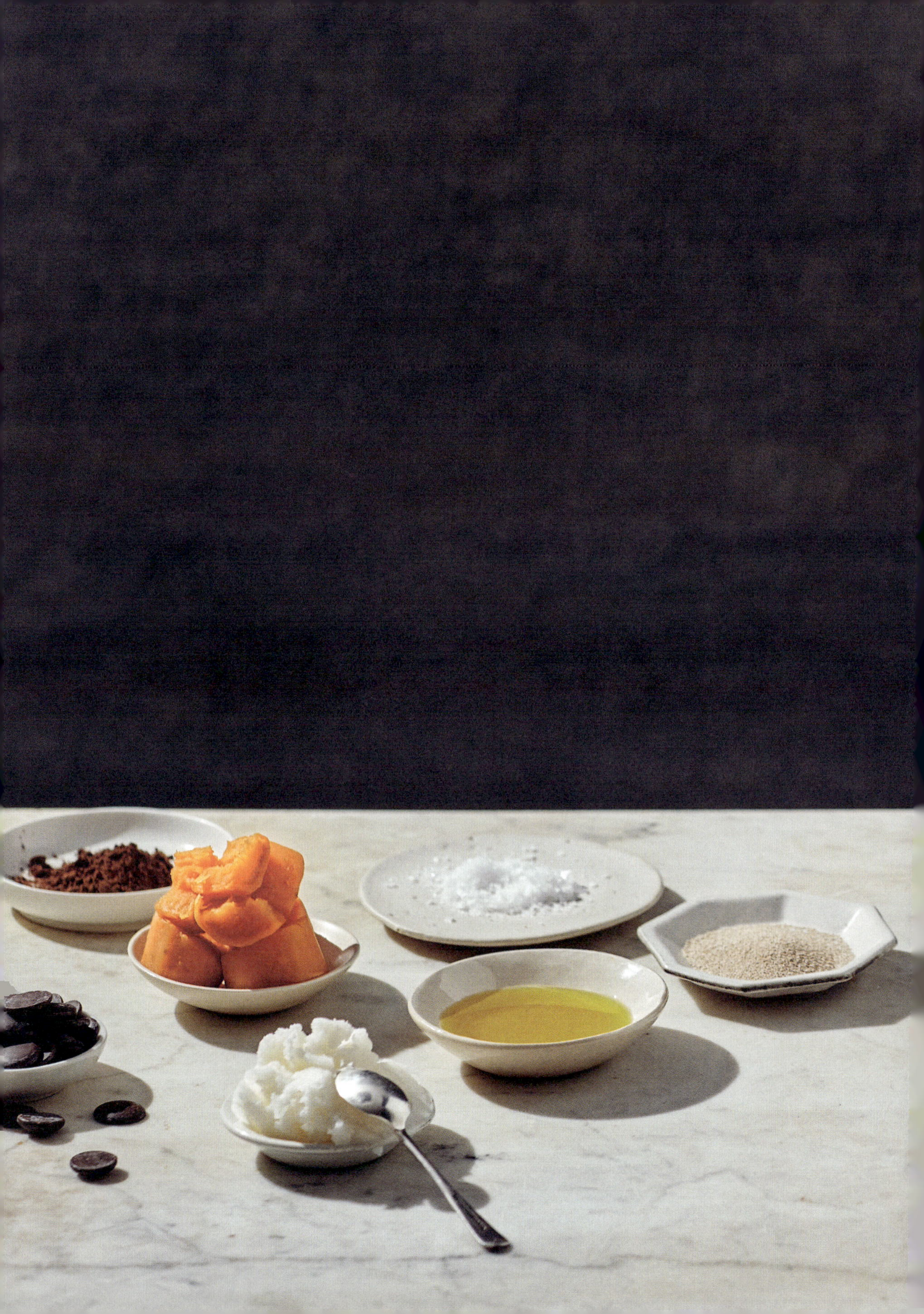

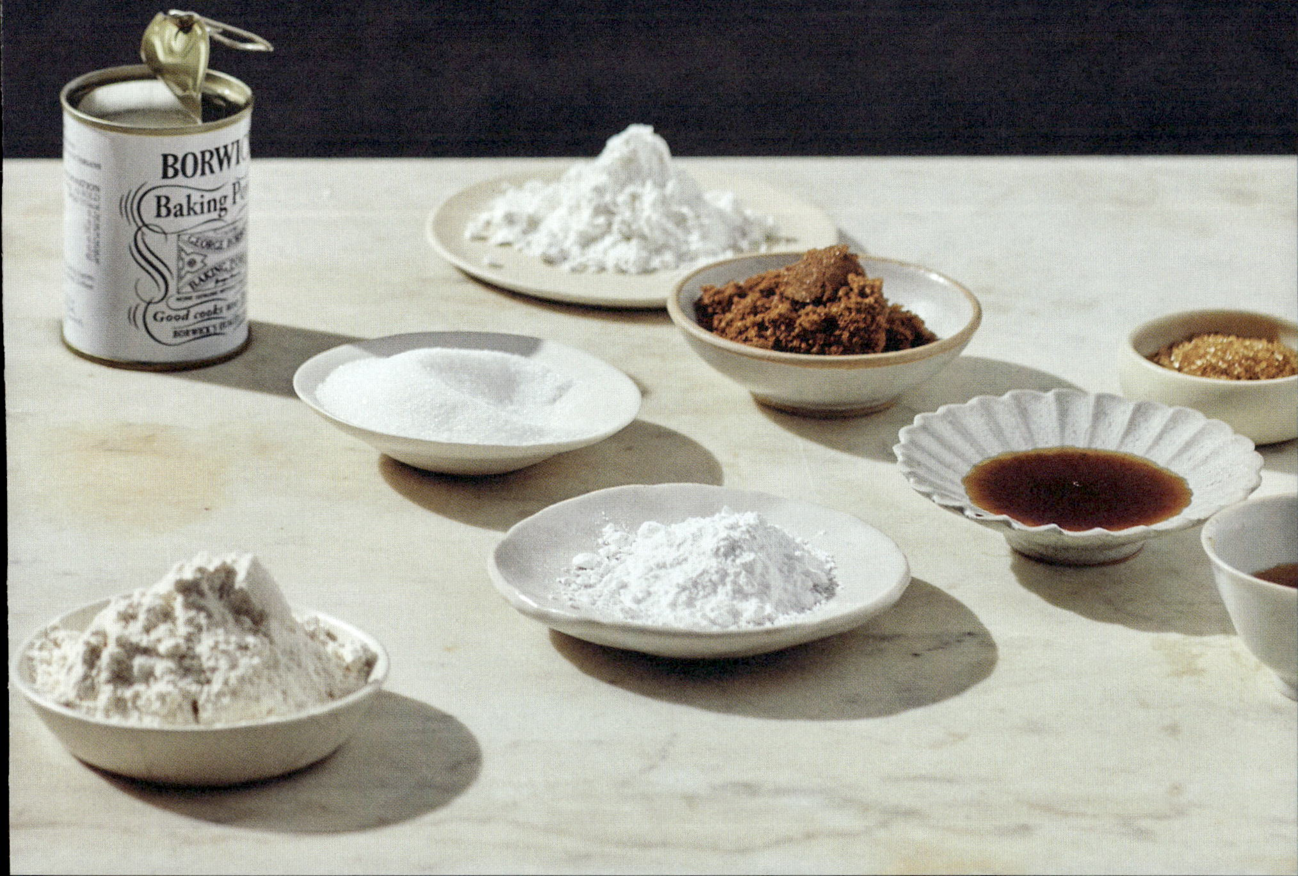
BORWIC
Baking

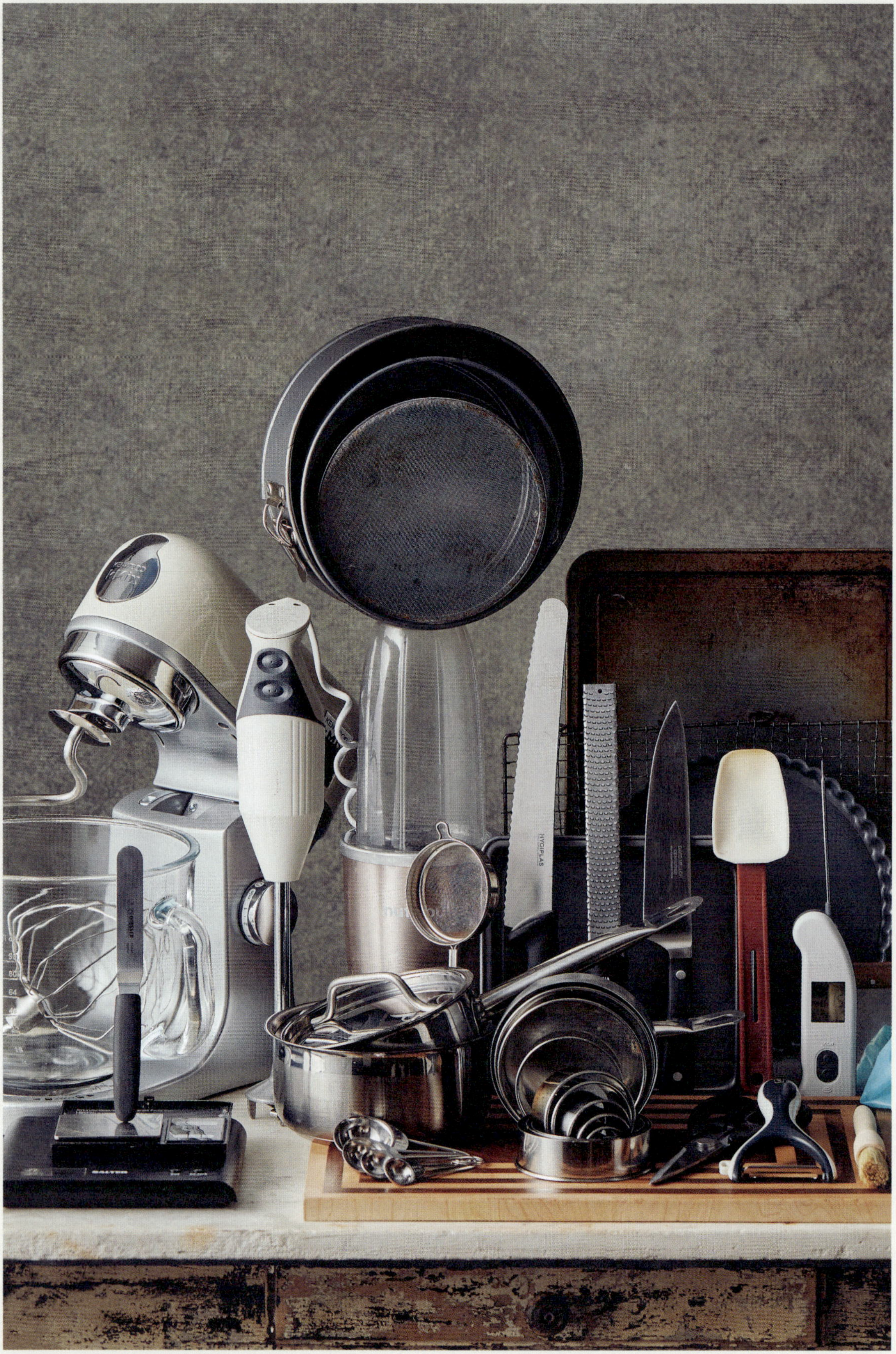

ESSENTIAL TOOLS

Tools and equipment for repeatable results.

Digital scales | More accessible and accurate than ever, these come in slim-line easy-to-stow away shapes and sizes.

Microscales | Available online, they are great for measuring micro amounts (for me that's anything less than 10 g (½ oz), where an extra gram greatly affects the finished product.

High-powered blenders | Very useful for grinding nuts and blending emulsions. Nutribullet, Vitamix or Thermomix are great machines.

Immersion stick blender | I love using a hand-held blender and they come with a number of food processor attachments. If you're in the market for one, find one that has a sturdy metal blender mechanism. Bamix, Waring and Braun have great machines that I use to 'emulsify' my homemade whipping cream (page 236), or ganaches where there is fat and water that needs to be combined well, as well as any liquids, gels, custards, and so on. Helps minimise washing-up too!

Silicone spatula | This is indispensable for mixing. Select a spatula that's firm with some flex that allows you to scrape against a bowl and combine ingredients.

Metal whisk | Great for combining ingredients swiftly. I don't sift dry ingredients, I just stir my flours and dry ingredients in a bowl gently to mix and 'lighten' them, or sift the ingredients and break up any clumps.

A range of bowl sizes

Saucepans and pots | When making caramels, use a pot or pan with high sides that will have plenty of space for liquid that expands as it boils. I prefer stainless-steel saucepans especially for caramel so I can see the colour as it cooks.

Sieves (strainers) | Large and fine

Large baking sheet or cookie sheet pan | 43 × 31 cm (17 × 12¼ in)

Wire rack | To cool things quicker and prevent moisture condensing on a baked good.

Cake tins | I like springform cake tins (pans) for baking round cakes, or cake rings, about 20 cm (8 in) and often use two of these for a two-layer cake as the portion is much taller than 23 cm (9 in).

23 cm (9 in) springform tin (pan) | The size I use for large single-layer cakes.

Small pudding tins (pans) | For Crème Caramel (page 199) and Molten Centre Chocolate Cakes (page 193).

Madeleine moulds made from silicone or tin

Silicone dome or mini muffin mould | 45 mm (1¾ in) in diameter for making soft centres for the Molten Centre Chocolate Cakes (page 193).

Non-stick silicone baking mat | This is a great alternative to baking parchment.

Rectangular cake tin (pan) | 23 × 33 × 5 cm (9 × 13 × 2 in)

Square cake tin (pan) | 20 × 20 × 5 cm (8 × 8 × 2 in)

Small loaf tin (pan) | 900 g (2 lb) / 22 × 12 × 7 cm (8½ × 4½ × 2¾ in)

Round cutters set

Pastry brush

Rolling pin

Large serrated knife | For trimming and halving sponge cakes.

Small paring knife | Serrated ones are versatile and great for cutting small fruits.

Piping tubes and silicone piping (pastry) bags | Buy a small and large one.

An electric stand mixer (with whisk, dough hook and paddle attachments) | This is recommended to knead doughs, whip creams/meringues, mix batters faster and more efficiently and with less mess! I personally mix all batters by hand because they're really easy, but use the mixer for whipping cream, meringues and kneading dough – although even doughs can be kneaded by hand. Kenwood or KitchenAid machines both work great and come with many attachments.

Oven | Most ovens nowadays are electric and will have a conventional setting (top and bottom element) and fan-forced/assisted setting. I recommend fan-force for most bakes but if you are cooking in a conventional, non-fan-assisted oven, you should increase the temperatures by 10–20°C (50–60°F/2 gas marks).

Microplane | I find this to be invaluable for extracting the precious and explosively flavoursome essential oils from citrus. Rotate and press the citrus as you move it along the microplane, directly over the bowl.

THE WEIGH TO BAKE

The metric behind the magic

I'd like you to cast your imagination back a hundred years... ingredients didn't come standardised in neat little packages, the home oven was fuelled by temperamental and dangerous fire and not electricity, cups and teaspoons came in different sizes, scales were cumbersome and difficult to use and even harder to transport.

Believe it or not, baking nowadays is easier and better than ever. Digital scales are compact, cheap and accurate. Using ingredients as prescribed and in the exact quantities will be one of the best ways to guarantee the consistency and the success of a recipe for the experienced and non-experienced baker alike.

The professional works in formulae and tables of ingredients that can be precisely calculated to produce the batches or volumes the day calls for. This translates here so that you can be afforded the same flexibility, precision and confidence that your recipe will turn out with consistency every time.

In the new way of baking, especially in small recipe amounts like one that bakes 10 cookies, precision is critical – a few grams of extra baking powder (the difference between a standard or non-standard US or UK or Australian spoon) can drastically alter a finished product. It's for this reason that you can even use microscales – I use these for weighing anything under 10 g (0.4 oz) with supreme confidence, especially for ingredients like baking powder, agar-agar powder or even salt in small recipe quantities.

As a pastry chef, I can vouch that the baking professional universally weighs their ingredients – so take it from the pros – it's our not-so-secret little secret to perfectly consistent bakes.

Weighing in grams produces the best results, but I wanted the book to be as accessible as possible and therefore have included imperial measurements as an alternative.

Adapting recipes for different-sized tins

Round tins (pans) | I have based round cakes on the 20 cm (8 in) tins, which serves 8 generous portions or 12 sensible portions.

My recipes for single-layer cakes are in 23 cm (9 in) round tins, and the ones that call for two baked layers and which are tall, use two 20 cm (8 in) tins.

Loaf tin (pans) | I have used the most widely available 900 g (2 lb) loaf tin measuring 18 cm (7 in) long, 11 cm (4¼ in) wide and 6 cm (2½ in) tall, which serves 8–10.

Fluted tart tin (pan) | 23 cm (9 in) which serves 10–12.

If you'd like to make any of the other common sizes, simply multiply each amount by the numbers in each chart.

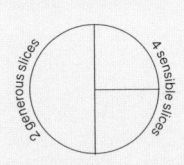

10 cm (4 in) x 0.18

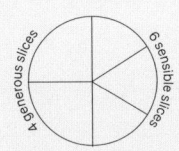

13 cm (5 in) x 0.31

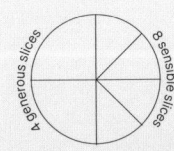

15 cm (6 in) x 0.42

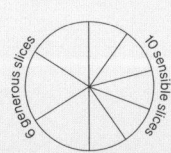

18 cm (7 in) x 0.61

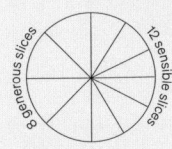

20 cm (8 in) x 0.75

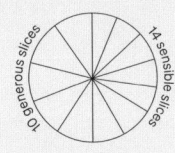

23 cm (9 in) x 1

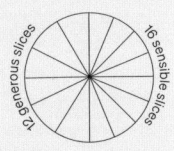

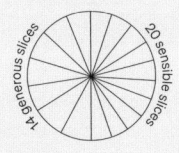

25 cm (10 in) x 1.18

28 cm (11 in) x 1.48

THE WEIGH TO BAKE

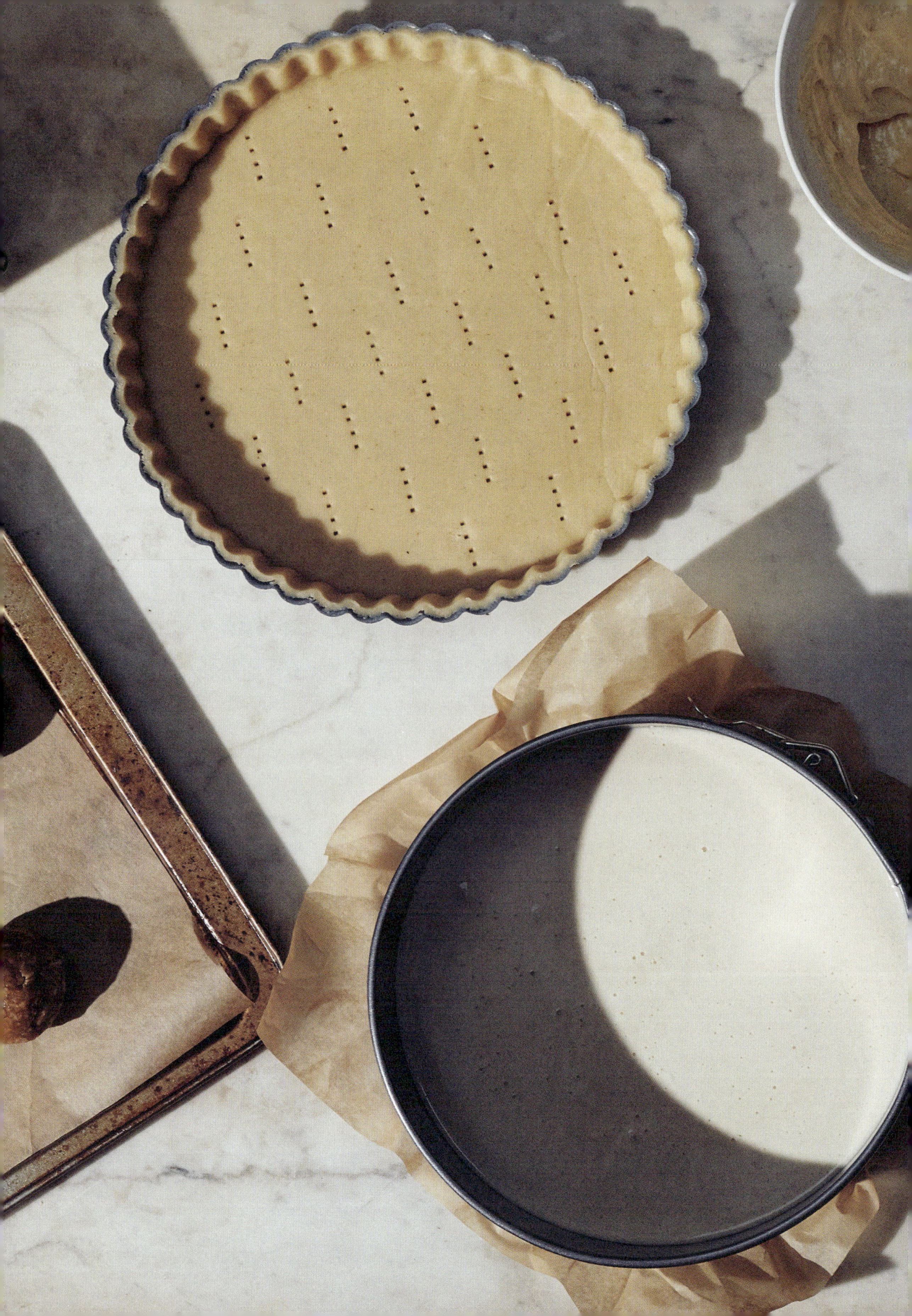

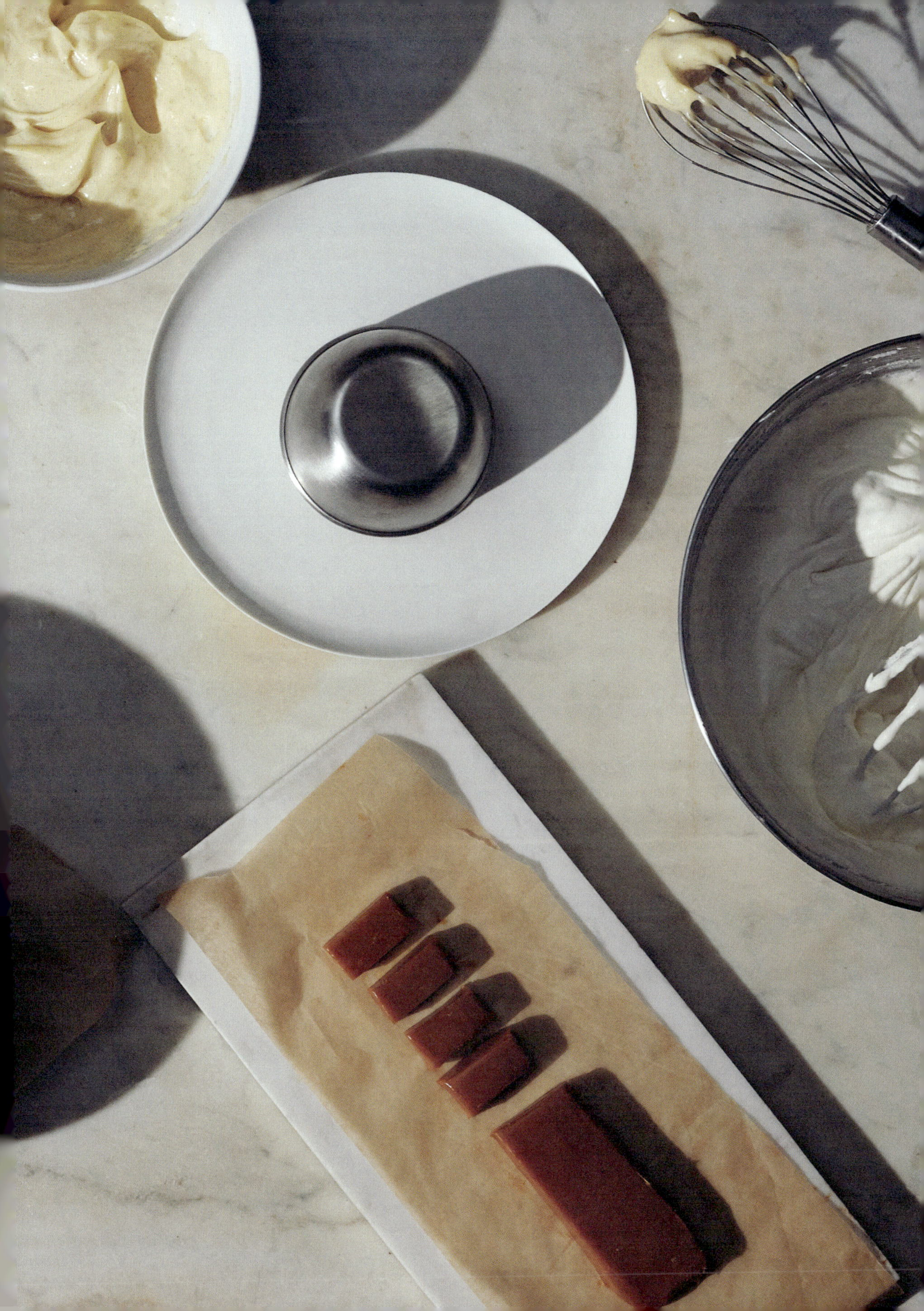

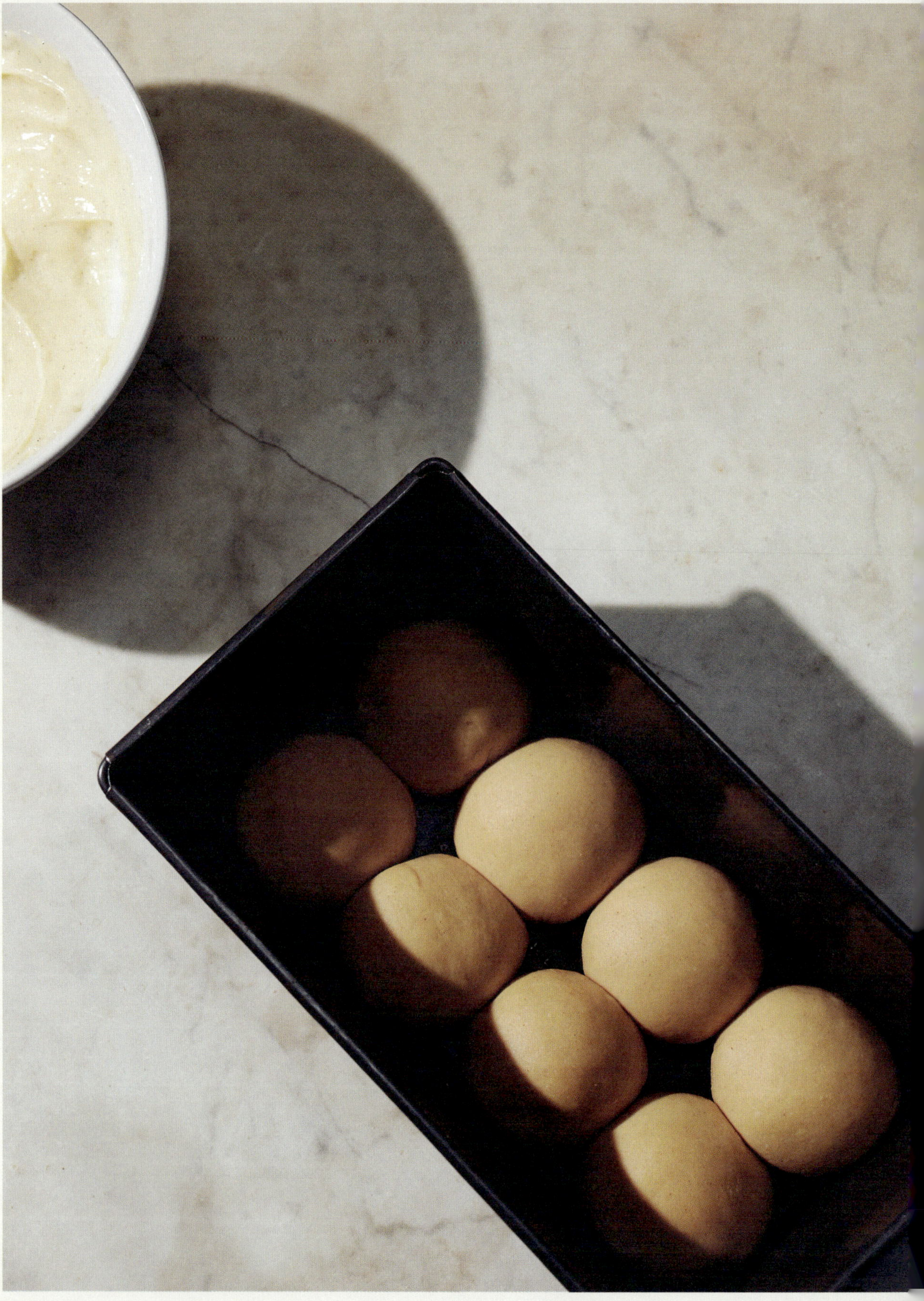

1 SWEET RISEN

This section revolves around the variation of one beautiful and very versatile, soft, sweet and yeasted dough – vrioche. In the countless trials and hundreds of hours (at least 4 hours every attempt!) developing this recipe, I wanted to create a dough that was super-soft, only lightly sweet, but with the richness and flavour we love of traditional brioche. There are two techniques that go into producing this dough – one can be done far ahead in time and stored in the freezer, the other can be done up to a day ahead and kept in the refrigerator. This allows us to produce a beautiful dough with extra virgin olive oil that keeps soft for days, and can be used as the base for any number of recipes.

Tangzhong | This 'cooked flour' or yudane method is from Asia (Yvonne Chen first wrote about it in the 1990s as being based on a Japanese technique). It gives extra softness to many Asian-bakery-style soft breads, perhaps most famously the Hokkaido milk bread.

To make the tangzhong, add the flour and water to a small saucepan and cook over a medium heat, stirring constantly, until it becomes a thick paste (it will thicken when the starch gelatinises at 65°C/149°F and the mixture is cooked through). This allows us to add more moisture to a recipe while still having a dough that is easy to handle. If you were to add too much water directly to a dough it would be too soft. Pour the cooked gel onto a rimmed baking sheet and leave to cool to at least room temperature, although I recommend chilling it in the refrigerator. This can be done when you start the recipe or up to 2 days in advance and stored wrapped in the refrigerator.

Sweet potato | Sweet potato is cut into pieces, cooked in boiling water until tender, then drained and cooled. These cooled pieces can be stored in a freezer-proof container or bag in the freezer for 3 months. Just defrost pieces as needed. I use sweet potatoes a lot for the buttery and sweet fragrance and flavour as well as the warm golden buttery hue. Using cooked potatoes in the dough also allows us to add more moisture to the dough without adding water directly, which would make the dough too soft to handle. I would recommend keeping a batch of these pre-prepared and frozen as they will certainly come in handy.

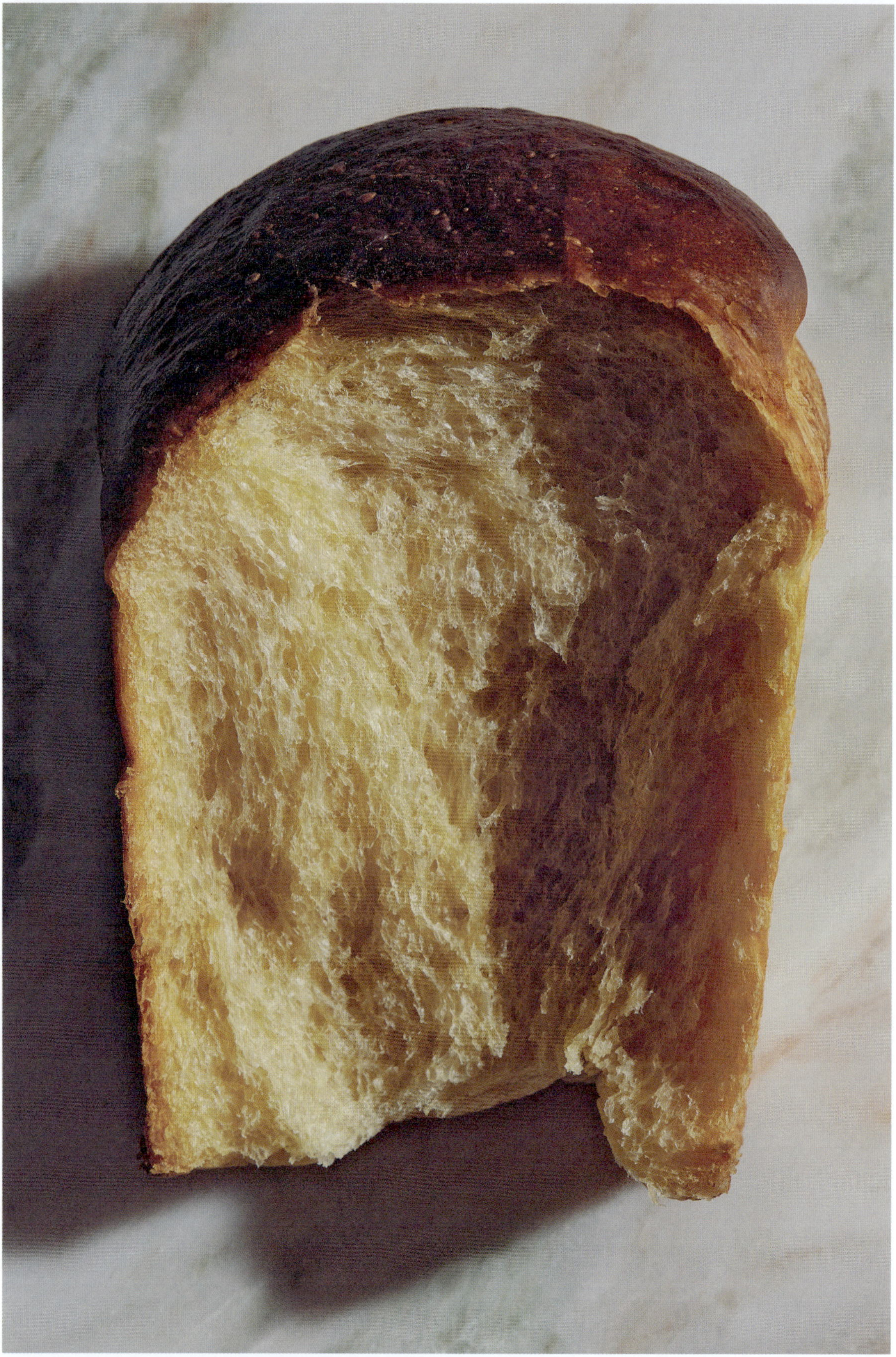

VRIOCHE

Traditional brioche gets its beautiful feathered texture, softness and flavour from a lot of butter and the shaping technique. Here, I have developed a recipe which in conjunction with the tangzhong technique and the inclusion of a healthy dose of olive oil, produces a beautiful and versatile dough. Prepare, then chill the tangzhong and proceed to mix the dough, then add the tangzhong last, once the dough has developed enough. This recipe can be prepared by hand, but a stand mixer will make *much* lighter work of it.

	500 G	1 lb 2 oz	650 G	1 lb 7 oz	750 G	1 lb 10 oz	1 KG	2 lb 4 oz
bread (strong) flour (1)	12 g	0.4 oz	15 g	0.5 oz	18 g	0.6 oz	24 g	0.9 oz
water	60 g	2 oz	75 g	2.7 oz	90 g	3.2 oz	120 g	4.2 oz
soy milk, at room temperature	96 g	3.4 oz	120 g	4.2 oz	144 g	5.1 oz	192 g	6.8 oz
instant yeast	4 g	1 tsp	5 g	1 tsp	6 g	1.5 tsp	8 g	2 tsp
bread (strong) flour (2)	240 g	8.5 oz	300 g	10.6 oz	360 g	12.7 oz	480 g	16.9 oz
caster (superfine) sugar	20 g	0.7 oz	25 g	0.9 oz	30 g	1.1 oz	32 g	1.1 oz
golden (or agave) syrup	20 g	0.7 oz	25 g	0.9 oz	30 g	1.1 oz	40 g	1.4 oz
salt	5 g	1 tsp	6 g	1.5 tsp	7 g	1.5 tsp	8 g	2 tsp
sweet potato, cooked and cooled	40 g	1.4 oz	50 g	1.8 oz	60 g	2 oz	80 g	2.8 oz
extra virgin olive oil	32 g	1.1 oz	40 g	1.4 oz	48 g	1.7 oz	64 g	2.3 oz
tangzhong (from above)	70 g	2.5 oz	90 g	3.2 oz	105 g	3.7 oz	140 g	4.9 oz

SIZE AND WEIGHT GUIDE FOR BUNS AND LOAVES

STANDARD BUN SIZES	WEIGHT		BAKING TEMPERATURE		BAKING TIME
burger bun (large)	130 g	4.6 oz	190°C	375°F/gas 5	13–14 minutes
burger bun / roll (standard)	100 g	3.5 oz	190°C	375°F/gas 5	13 minutes
small bun / dinner roll	60 g	2 oz	190°C	375°F/gas 5	11–12 minutes
slider buns	30 g	1.1 oz	190°C	375°F/gas 5	11–12 minutes
bostock	75 g	2.7 oz	190°C	375°F/gas 5	13 minutes
hot dog roll	90 g	3.2 oz	190°C	375°F/gas 5	13 minutes
Nanterre balls for loaves	50 g	1.7 oz	180°C	350°F/gas 4	20 minutes
small pullman loaf pan 11 × 19.5 × 11 cm (4.2 × 7.7 × 4.4 in)	450 g	15.9 oz			
standard pullman loaf pan 23 × 10 × 10 cm (9 × 4 × 4 in)	750–850 g	1 lb 10–1 lb 14 oz			

VRIOCHE DOUGH

1 Prepare the tangzhong by adding the bread flour (1) and water to a small saucepan and mixing it together to dissolve the flour. Heat over a medium heat and cook, stirring constantly with a silicone spatula so it doesn't catch, until it is thick all the way through (a temperature probe will read 65°C/149°F minimum). I have not had any ill effects from just bringing it to the boil while stirring well. Pour the tangzhong into a shallow dish or baking tray (pan), cover the surface with cling film (plastic wrap) and leave to chill in the refrigerator for 1 hour, or until cool to touch.

2 Pour the soy milk into a bowl, add the instant yeast and stir to dissolve. If using active dry yeast you may need to leave it to stand for 10 minutes to dissolve the coating.

SWEET RISEN

3   Add the bread flour (2), sugar, golden syrup, salt, sweet potato and olive oil to a stand mixer fitted with a dough hook attachment. Add the milk–yeast mixture and the sweet potato mixture and start mixing on low speed. A dough will start to form. Once all the flour is combined, increase the speed slightly and mix for about 5 minutes – the dough should be smooth and developed. Keep kneading until a windowpane test shows a well-developed dough.

4   Add the chilled tangzhong to the dough and mix until it is incorporated and smooth. The dough may look like it's beginning to become wet and separated, but keep mixing until the dough starts to climb up the hook and come away from the sides of the bowl. This stage of mixing should take about 3–5 minutes, taking about 10 minutes in total. You can tip the dough out onto a lightly oiled work surface to shape it into a ball, then place it back into the bowl, cover in cling film (plastic wrap) and leave it to rise in a warm place for 1½–2 hours until doubled in size.

TIP This initial rise – or what professionals call a 'bulk ferment' – allows the dough to develop flavour and to rest. Timings are always a guide, based on a room temperature of 20–22°C (68–72°F). If your room is warmer or colder your timings may need to shift. Yeast is a living organism and if it's warmer it works quicker and if colder it's much slower, so read your dough for its visual cues rather than rigidly sticking to timings.

5   When the dough is ready to use, knock it back by punching all the air out in the bowl. Try to avoid mixing it at this stage as you want to keep the dough flexible for rolling or shaping into your desired shape – although not a huge problem, as this can be remedied by a 15-minute rest on the work surface before shaping.

6   Use a scraper or knife to cut the dough into desired weights, then proceed to shape according to the recipe.

7   Once you have shaped the buns, arrange them on a sheet of baking parchment or directly onto a lightly greased and floured baking sheet. Make sure there is just over the width of one item distance between each one and just over half the distance from the edge of the baking sheet.

TIP Make sure there is plenty of space if baking individual shapes. A bun will expand twice its initial size during the proving stage. If lightly flouring the baking sheet (use a pencil if using baking parchment), mark this size as a guide so you know when it is proved and how far apart you need to place your buns.

8   When proving, I recommend just brushing a layer of water to keep your dough supple, then placing the baking sheet in a large clean storage container with a clip-on lid that fits the sheet (I have bought a couple of slim storage containers for just this purpose that can be stacked and stowed once done). Alternatively, place a piece of cling film (plastic wrap) loosely on top of the baking sheet. Try to keep them in a warm place (about 25°C/77°F), although at room temperature 20–22°C (68–72°F) it should take roughly 1 hour for them to *double* in size.

TIP Proving is the one stage most inexperienced bakers will rush but it is crucial to ensure light fluffy products that eat beautifully. Underproved doughs result in a dense, unenjoyable eat. You will know most doughs have fully proved once they have doubled in size or pass the jiggle test – where a gently wobbled baking sheet makes the buns jiggle. I also find it useful to mark the size of the buns before proving.

9   About 30 minutes into proving, preheat the oven to 190°C (375°F/gas 5), making sure the oven rack is in the middle.

10   Bake until golden all the way over the top, or in larger loaves (especially babkas) until a temperature probe reads 90°C (194°F).

11   Once baked, transfer to a wire rack to cool. Wrap or add the fully cooled vrioche to an airtight bag and store at room temperature for up to 4 days, or freeze for up to 3 months.

NOTE

Ovens do vary, so do take a visual check that they are nice and golden all over and they will be ready. Except babka and large loaves, which can brown on top before the centre is cooked fully – the internal temperature measured with a temperature probe should be 90°C (194°F).

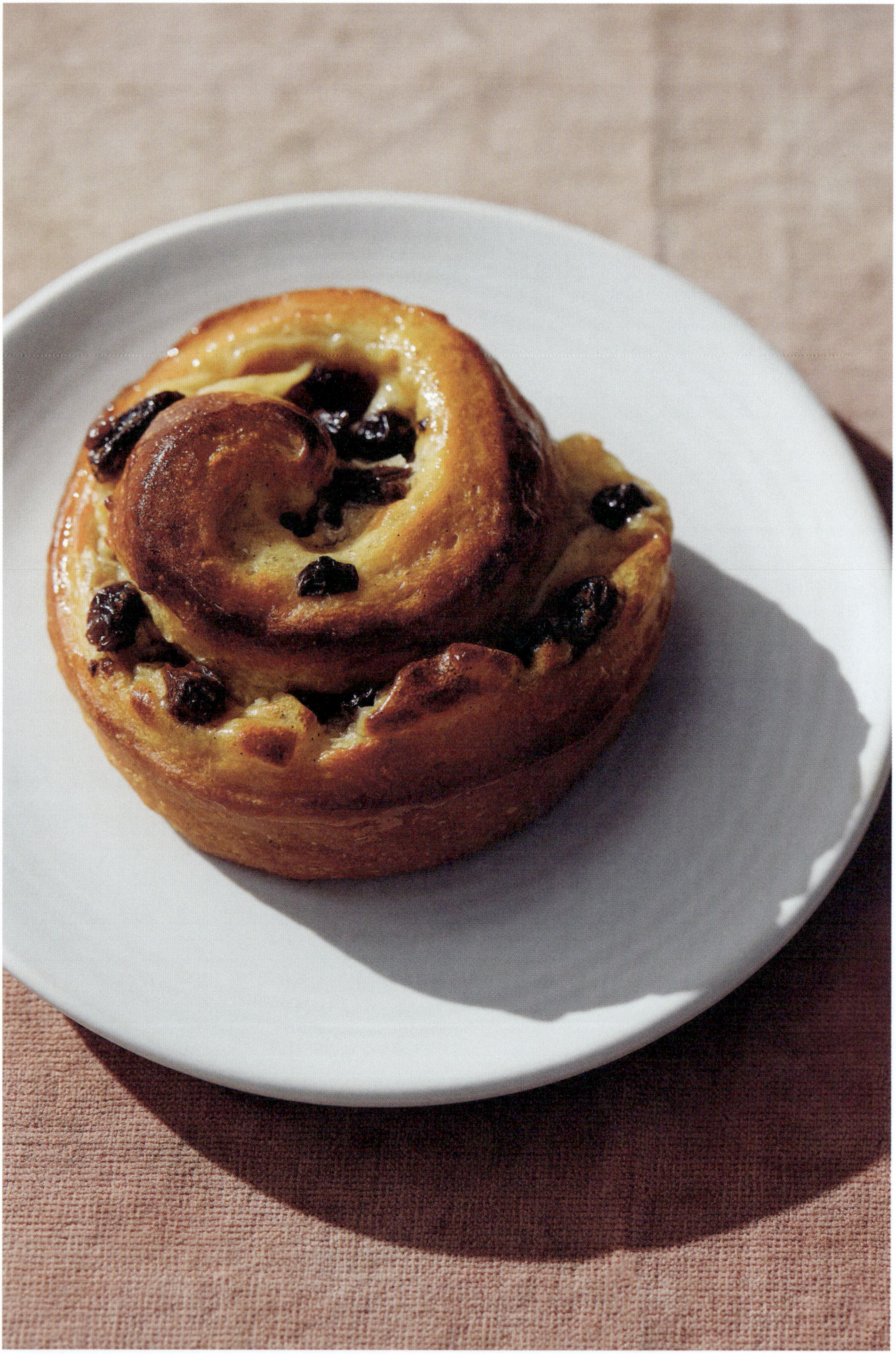

PAIN AUX RAISINS

Makes 12 scrolls

Closer to the northern European and North American version of a classic pastry, these pain aux raisins – literally 'bread of raisins' use the three types of dried grapes (raisins, sultanas/golden raisins and currants), though you're welcome to just use one or your favourite type! Dipping the base of the buns into some Demerara sugar adds a nice caramel crunch and brushing with some of the glaze adds an additional fresh perfume. Bake directly on a steel baking sheet lined with baking parchment.

SOAKED FRUIT

1. The night before, combine all the ingredients together in a bowl and leave to soak and rehydrate overnight. They will plump up to 2–3 times their dried size. You can store them in the refrigerator for up to 4 days. Drain well before use.

currants	50 g	1.8 oz
sultanas (golden raisins)	50 g	1.8 oz
raisins	50 g	1.8 oz
orange juice	150 g	5.3 oz
dark rum	30 g	1.1 oz

TO ASSEMBLE AND BAKE

2. Prepare the vrioche dough following the instructions on pages 51–52 and leave it to bulk ferment. Lightly flour the work surface, then turn out the dough and sprinkle lightly with flour to help you roll it out easily. Press the air out of the dough and roughly into shape, then roll the dough into a rectangle, about 30 × 40 cm (12 × 16 in) long.

3. If the crème pâtissière is set, use a whisk to just soften it slightly, then spread it over the dough, leaving a 2 cm (¾ in) border.

4. Pat the drained raisins dry with paper towels and sprinkle over the crème pâtissière custard.

5. Roll a tight scroll using a long side of the triangle. Taking a long edge of the rectangle, fold it over and start to roll a scroll until it reaches the other side.

6. Line two baking sheets with baking parchment, and have a small plate of Demerara sugar ready nearby.

7. Use a sharp serrated knife to gently saw through the log at 3 cm (1¼ in) intervals – this will make roughly 12 scrolls. Pull the outermost end of the scroll outwards to stretch the dough slightly, then tuck it to one side of the scroll which will be the bottom.

8. Dip the scrolls into the Demerara sugar, then arrange on the lined baking sheet. Fit six scrolls onto each sheet, with plenty of space in between. Lightly brush with water to keep them moist while they are proving, then cover with cling film (plastic wrap) to prevent the dough drying out.

9. Leave to prove for 30 minutes–1 hour until doubled in size and jiggly. About 15 minutes or 30 minutes into proving, preheat the oven to 190°C fan (375°F/gas 5).

10. Bake for 13–15 minutes until golden all over the top. Remove from the oven and leave to cool on the baking sheets for 15 minutes before transferring them to a wire rack to cool.

11. Brush some of the hot liquid glaze onto the cooled buns. Store in a sealed container at room temperature for up to 2 days.

ALSO NEEDED

Vrioche dough (pages 51–52)	500 g	1 lb 2 oz
plain (all-purpose) flour	for dusting	
Crème Pâtissière (page 235)	400 g	14.1 oz
Demerara sugar	100 g	3.5 oz
Exotic Clear Glaze (page 239)	100 g	3.5 oz

NOTE

When cutting scrolls, you might have two ends that are offcuts. Cut them into 12 even-sized pieces, press them into flat discs and tuck them under the middle of each scroll for added volume.

SWEET RISEN

STICKY DATE AND CARDAMOM BUNS

Makes 10 buns

Butterscotch glazed, sticky date-laced knots punctuated with the unmistakable, warm lingering aroma of cardamom. Roll the chilled dough quite thin, spread the date and cardamom seed paste, then load up the video tutorial to see a very cool knotting technique!

DATE FILLING

1. Pulse the dates and water in a high-powered blender until the dates are chopped and still somewhat chunky. Transfer them to a bowl and leave to stand for 30 minutes. The water will rehydrate the dates slightly and thicken them up.

dried dates	150 g	5.3 oz
water	100 g	3.5 oz

BUTTERSCOTCH SAUCE

2. Mix the plant-based milk, sea salt, cornflour and sugar together in a small saucepan, then bring to a rolling boil. Add the coconut oil and whisk until melted and well-mixed through. Leave to cool. Set aside to brush over the cooled buns.

plant-based milk	150 g	5.3 oz
sea salt	2 g	½ tsp
cornflour (cornstarch)	8 g	2 tsp
muscovado sugar	40 g	1.4 oz
coconut oil (deodorised)	10 g	0.4 oz

TO ASSEMBLE AND BAKE

3. Carefully peel the grassy pod away from the cardamoms, then put the seeds into a spice grinder, pestle and mortar or a high-powered blender, add the sugar in and grind to a powder. Mix them into the dough.

4. Prepare the vrioche dough following the instructions on pages 51–52 and leave it to bulk ferment, or double in size in the bowl.

5. Lightly flour the work surface, then turn out the dough and sprinkle lightly with flour to help you roll it out easily. Press the air out of the dough and roughly into shape, then roll the dough into a rectangle, about 20 × 50 cm (8 × 20 in) long.

6. Spread the date paste over half of the dough, then fold the dough in to shorten the rectangle. Transfer the dough to a baking sheet and chill in the freezer for 40 minutes.

7. Line two baking sheets with baking parchment and set aside. Lightly dust a work surface with flour, then place the dough on top. Cut the dough into 2.5 cm (1 in) strips, then clear the work surface and twist a dough strip from either side and tie into a knot.

8. Arrange six knots onto each lined baking sheet, leaving plenty of space in between them. Lightly brush with water to keep them moist and supple while they are proving, then cover with cling film (plastic wrap) to prevent the dough drying out. Leave to prove in a warm place for 30 minutes–1 hour until doubled in size and jiggly. After about 30 minutes, preheat the oven to 190°C fan (375°F/gas 5).

9. Bake for 13–15 minutes until golden all over the top. Remove from the oven and immediately brush with the butterscotch sauce. Leave to cool on the baking sheets for 15 minutes before transferring them to a wire rack to cool completely. Store in a sealed container at room temperature for up to 2 days.

ALSO NEEDED

cardamom	7 pods	
caster (superfine) sugar	30 g	1.1 oz
Vrioche dough (pages 51–52)	500 g	1 lb 2 oz
plain (all-purpose) flour	for dusting	

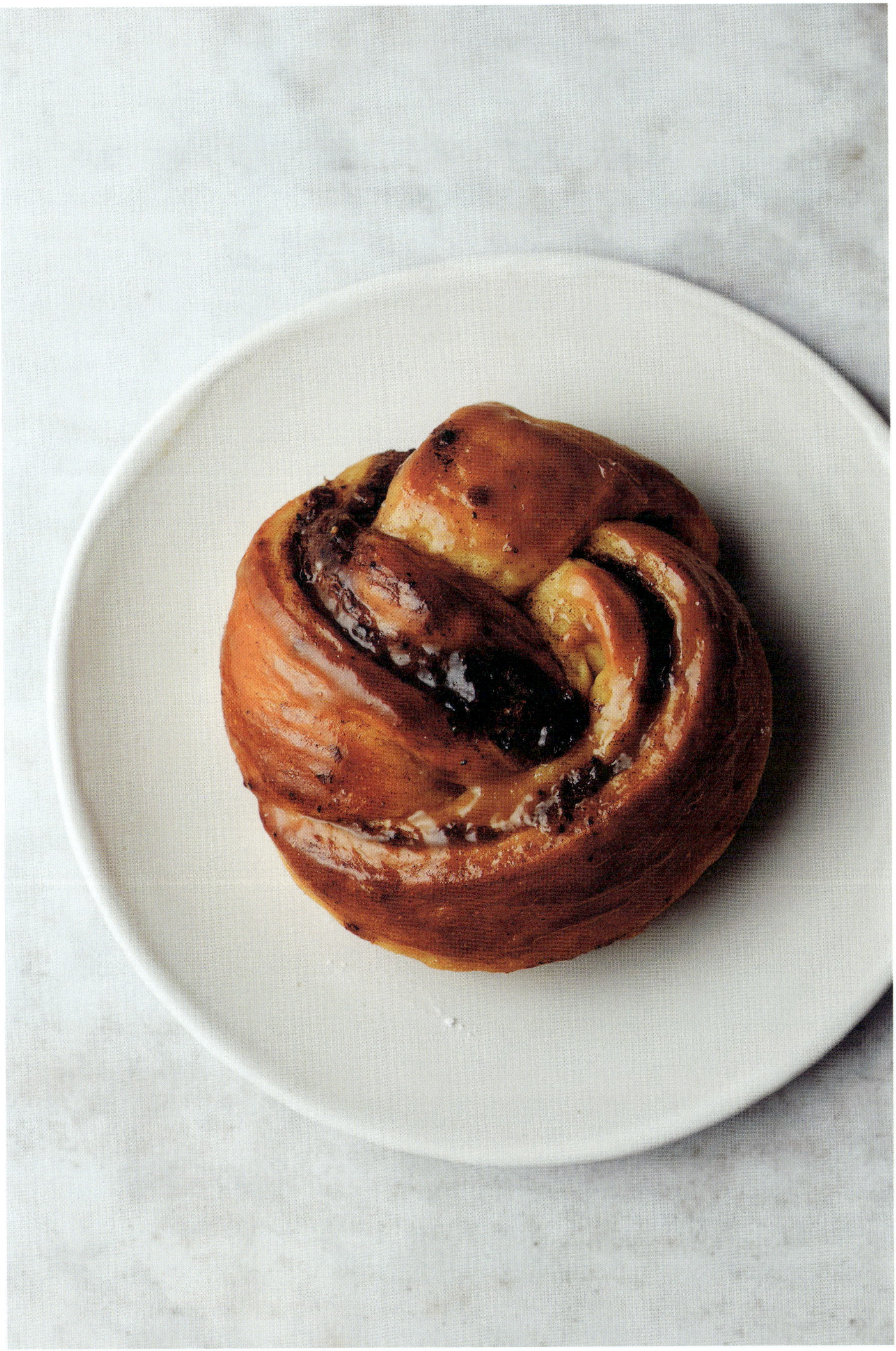

CINNAMON SLICE

Makes 6 large slices

When I moved to London, a friend ironically introduced me to a Danish chain bakery called Ole and Steen, an offshoot of the (much harder to pronounce) Lagkagehuset bakery of Copenhagen. This pastry comprises of a pretty plait (braid) of custard and cinnamon and got me through my first British winter. It also directly inspired this recipe.

CINNAMON FILLING

1. Place all the ingredients in a small high-powered blender and blend until smooth. You can make this filling ahead and keep it in the refrigerator for 2 weeks or freeze for 3 months.

TO ASSEMBLE AND BAKE

2. Prepare the vrioche dough following the instructions on pages 51–52 and leave it to bulk ferment or double in size in the bowl. Line a large baking sheet with baking parchment and set aside.

3. Lightly flour the work surface, then turn out the dough and sprinkle lightly with flour to help you roll it out easily. Press the air out of the dough and into a flat square shape, then roll the dough into a rectangle, about 25 × 40 cm (10 × 16 in) long.

4. If the crème pâtissière has set, whisk it in a large bowl just to soften it up slightly, then spread it along half of the dough. Spread the cinnamon filling on the other half.

5. Take a long edge of the rectangle, fold it over and start to roll a scroll until it reaches the other side.

6. Use a sharp pair of clean scissors to cut vertically almost down to the bottom of the scroll, at 2.5 cm (1 in) intervals, then push each cut section over to alternating sides of the scroll so it resembles a plait (braid).

7. Arrange the scrolls on the lined baking sheet, making sure there is plenty of space in between them. Lightly brush with water to keep them moist and supple while they are proving, then cover with cling film (plastic wrap) to prevent the dough drying out.

8. Leave to prove in a warm place for 30 minutes–1 hour until doubled in size and jiggly. When they are at around the halfway mark, preheat the oven to 190°C fan (375°F/gas 5).

9. Bake for 13–15 minutes until golden all over the top. Remove from the oven and leave to cool on the baking sheet for 15 minutes, then transfer to a wire rack to cool completely.

10. Spoon the icing (frosting) into a resealable bag and drizzle diagonally along the cooled scroll. Leave it to set, then slice into six pieces. Store in a sealed container at room temperature for up to 2 days.

muscovado sugar	50 g	1.8 oz
sweet potato, cooked and cooled	50 g	1.8 oz
ground cinnamon	6 g	2 tsp
coconut oil	40 g	1.4 oz

ALSO NEEDED

Vrioche dough (pages 51–52)	500 g	1 lb 2 oz
Crème Pâtissière (page 235)	200 g	7 oz
Vanilla Water Icing (page 81)	40 g	1.4 oz

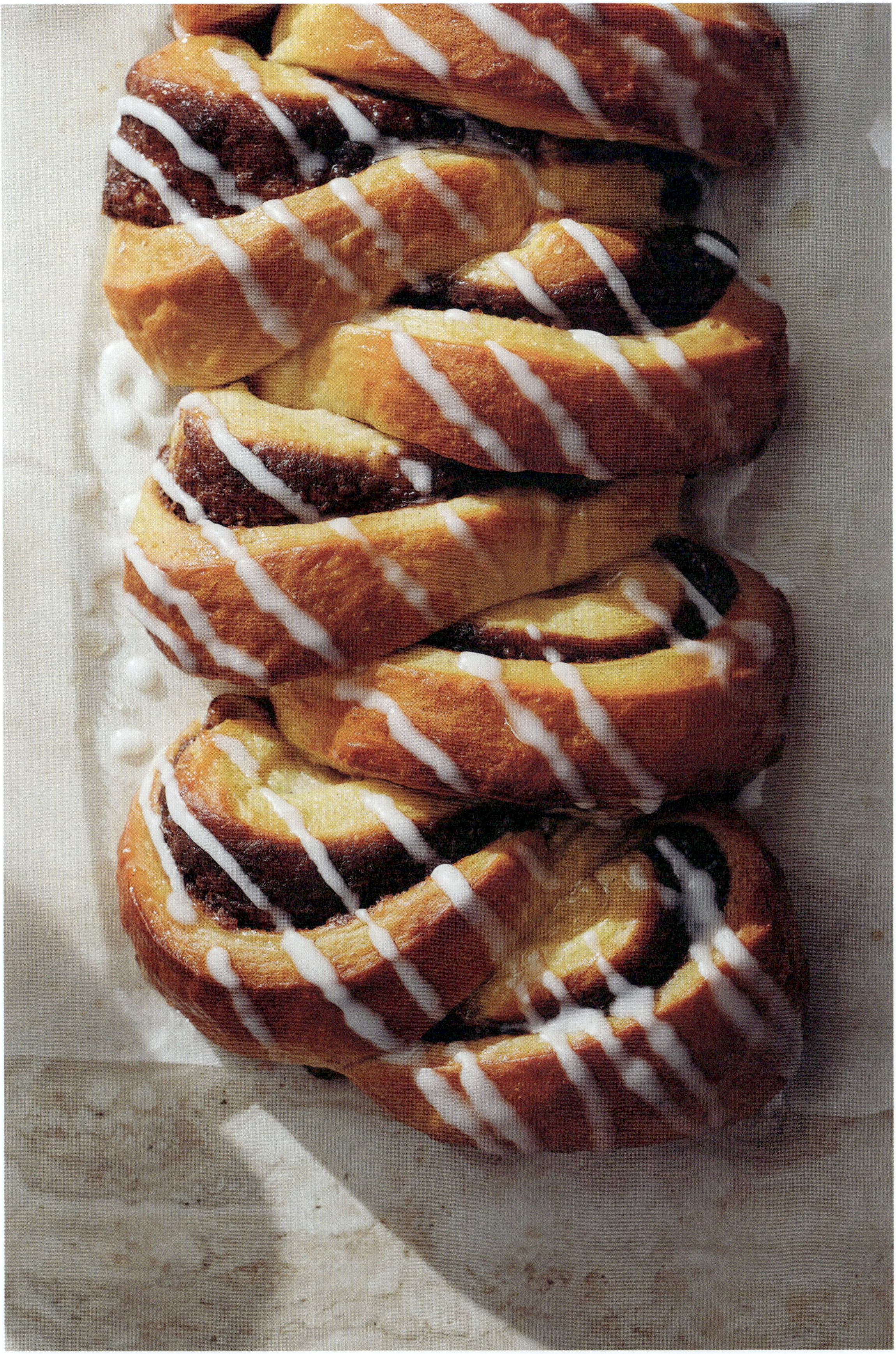

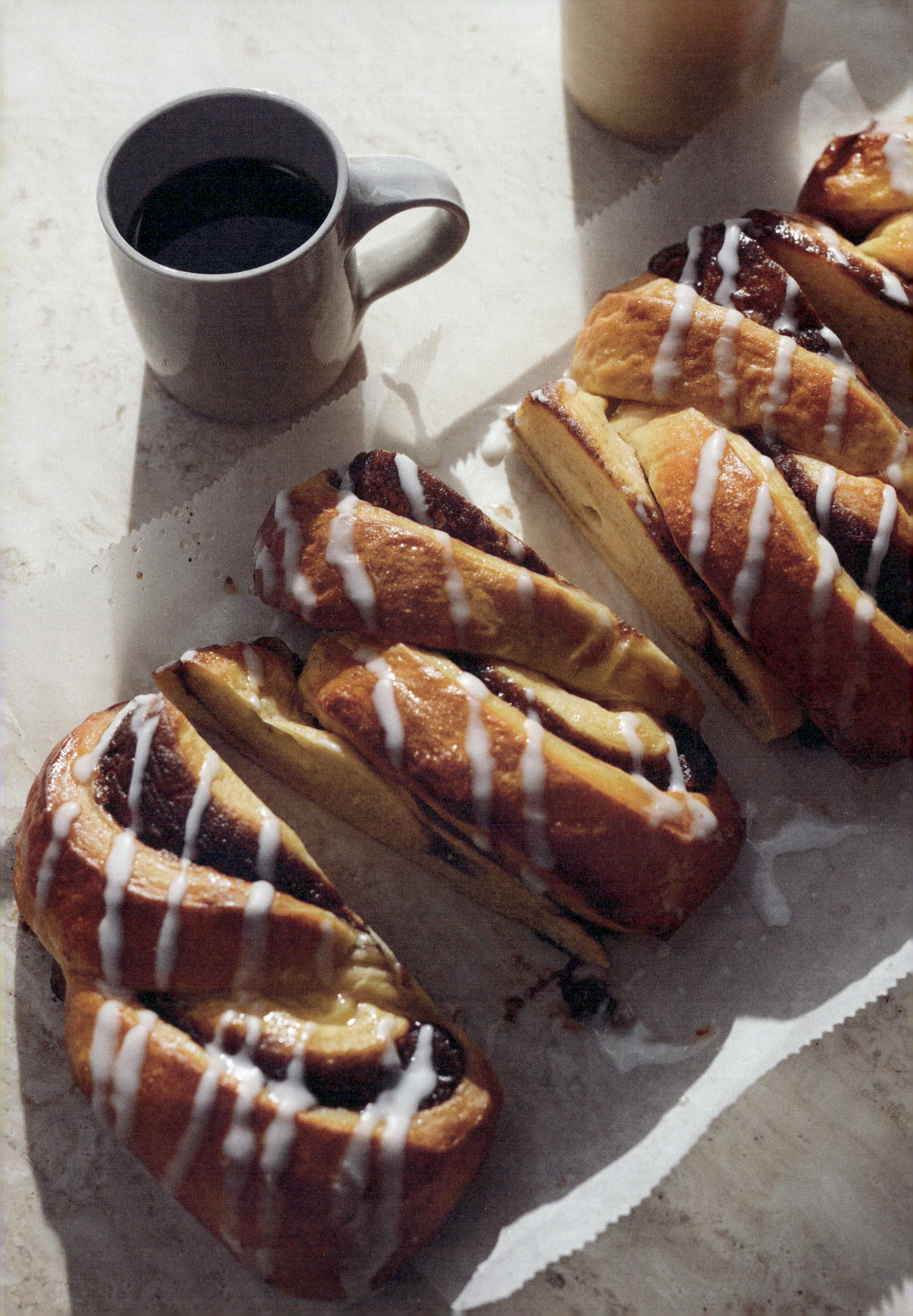

SWEET RISEN

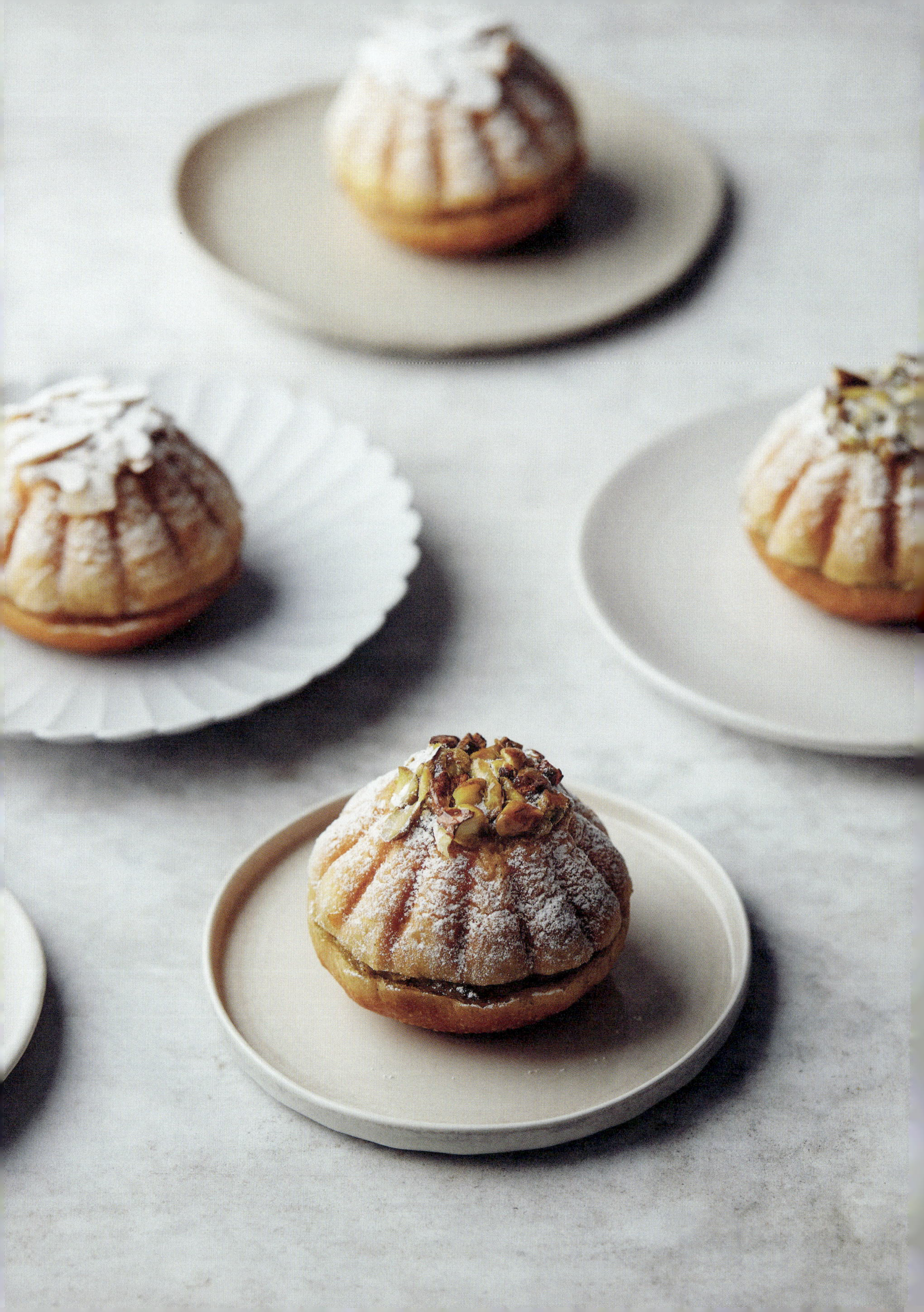

VOSTOCKS

Makes 10

The French bostock is a brioche slice (usually stale or leftover) revived with a dip in a syrup, then topped with almond frangipane and sliced almonds, and baked again. A vostock is a bun of vrioche dipped in syrup, sandwiched with frangipane, topped with more frangipane and nuts, then baked again. Think of it as a cross between a bostock and almond croissant!

ALMOND FRANGIPANE

1. Pulse the nuts, sugar and cornflour in a small high-powered blender to a fine powder, then add the milk, oil and almond extract (if using) pulse again until a creamy thick consistency is reached. Set aside.

raw almonds	200 g	7 oz
caster (superfine) sugar	130 g	4.6 oz
cornflour (cornstarch)	30 g	1 oz
plant-based milk	105 g	3.7 oz
extra virgin olive oil	13 g	0.5 oz
bitter almond oil extract (optional)		¼ tsp

BUNS

2. Prepare the vrioche dough following the instructions on pages 51–52 and leave it to bulk ferment or double in size in the bowl. Lightly flour the work surface, then turn out the dough and use a scraper to cut 75 g (2⅗ in) portions, making sure to use scales to weigh them.

3. Shape as buns, using 8 cm (3¼ in) broche moulds or tart cases, if you have them, to shape them for a cute bottom edge.

4. Place two buns per baking sheet (you will need two) and leave to prove for about 1 hour, or until doubled in size. After 30–40 minutes of proving, preheat the oven to 190°C fan (375°F/gas 5).

5. Bake the buns for 12–15 minutes until golden all over, then remove from the oven, transfer to a wire rack and leave to cool completely.

VANILLA AND RUM SYRUP

6. Combine all the ingredients in a small bowl that will fit a 9 cm (3½ in) bun when dipped and stir to dissolve the sugar. Set aside.

water, hot	200 g	7 oz
caster (superfine) sugar	100 g	3.5 oz
vanilla bean paste	5 g	1 tsp
dark rum (optional)	20 g	0.7 oz

ALSO NEEDED

Vrioche dough (pages 51–52) to make 10 × 75 g (2¾ oz) buns	750 g	1 lb 10 oz
plain (all-purpose) flour		for dusting
chopped pistachios or sliced almonds	100 g	3.5 oz
icing (confectioners') sugar		for dusting

TO FINISH

7. Cut each bun in half across the equator, then dip each cut side of the bun into the syrup.

8. Spread the nuts out on a plate. Pipe or spread with a palette knife a generous tablespoon of filling onto the bottom half of each bun and sandwich together, then pipe a thin layer of filling, about 3 cm (1¼ in) in diameter, on the top. Gently press into the nuts.

9. Preheat the oven again to 180°C fan (350°F/gas 4) and line a large baking sheet with baking parchment.

10. Return all ten buns to the lined baking sheet (they don't need to be spaced out) and bake for 6–8 minutes. You will know when they are done as the frangipane will have puffed up slightly and the nuts have taken on a golden hue.

11. Remove from the oven and leave to cool completely for 1 hour, then dust with icing sugar and enjoy. Store in a sealed container at room temperature for up to 2 days.

SWEET RISEN

PISTACHIO (AND ROSE) VOSTOCKS

Makes 10 buns

Pistachio is almost universally adored, whereas rose can be polarising (usually because the flavouring is poor, as not pure rose water has been used, or it has simply been overdosed). You can leave the rose water out if it's absolutely not your thing, but if you add even just a tiny bit (a couple of drops) it just elevates the pistachio ever so slightly. I very highly recommend it – otherwise I wouldn't have made a recipe for it! Think of it as the gateway to rose appreciation. Avoid rose flavourings at all costs and find an authentic rose water.

PISTACHIO FRANGIPANE

1. Pulse the nuts, sugar and cornflour in a small high-powered blender to a fine powder, then add the milk, oil and rose water (if using) and pulse again until it is a creamy, thick consistency. Set aside.

2. Follow the instructions for almond vostocks on page 61, using the pistachio frangipane and chopped pistachios, then dust with icing sugar. Store in a sealed container at room temperature for up to 2 days.

raw pistachios	150 g	5.3 oz
caster (superfine) sugar	100 g	3.5 oz
cornflour (cornstarch)	24 g	0.9 oz
plant-based milk	80 g	2.8 oz
extra virgin olive oil	10 g	0.4 oz
rose water (optional)	4 g	1 tsp
icing (confectioners') sugar	for dusting	

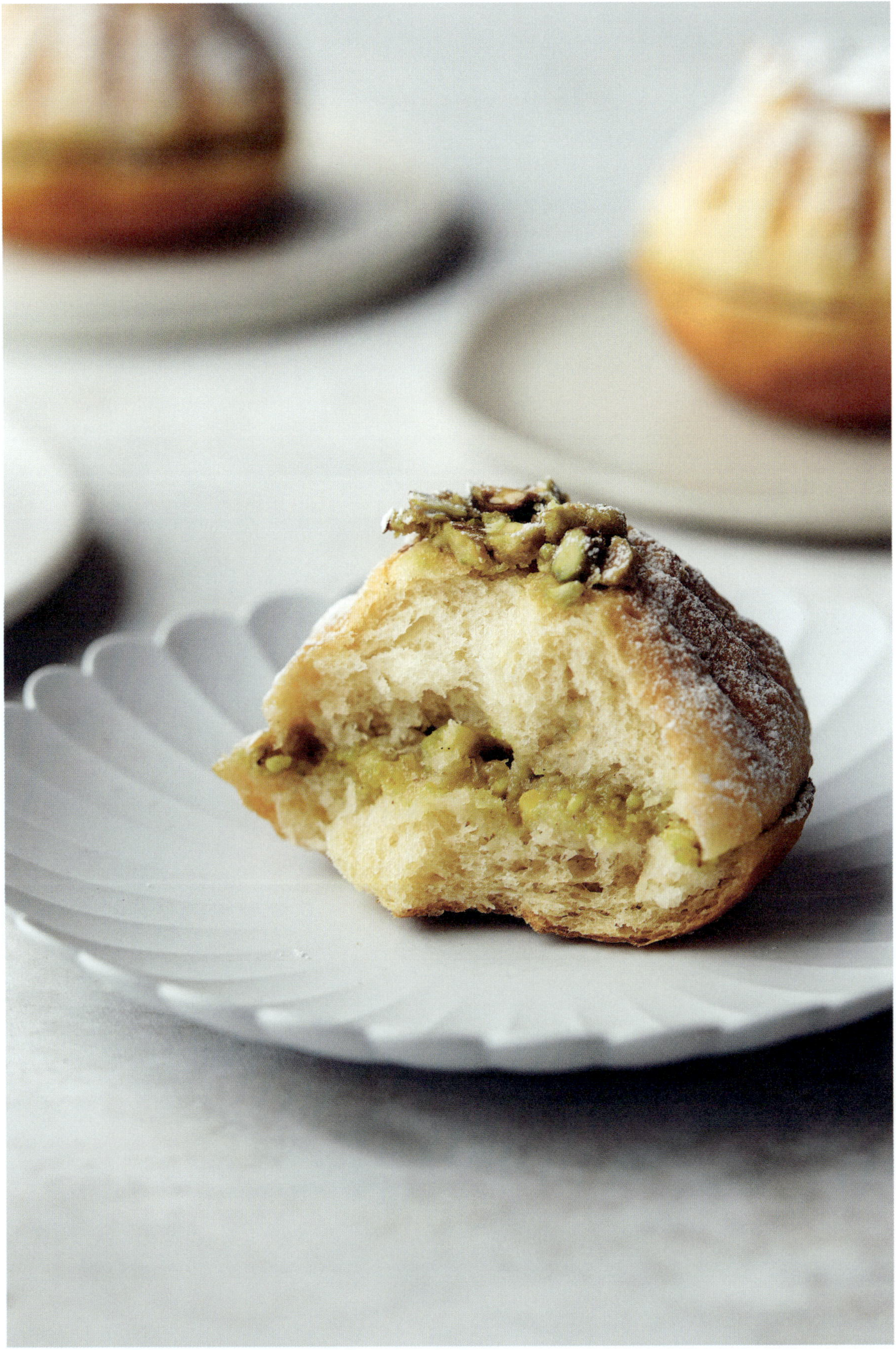

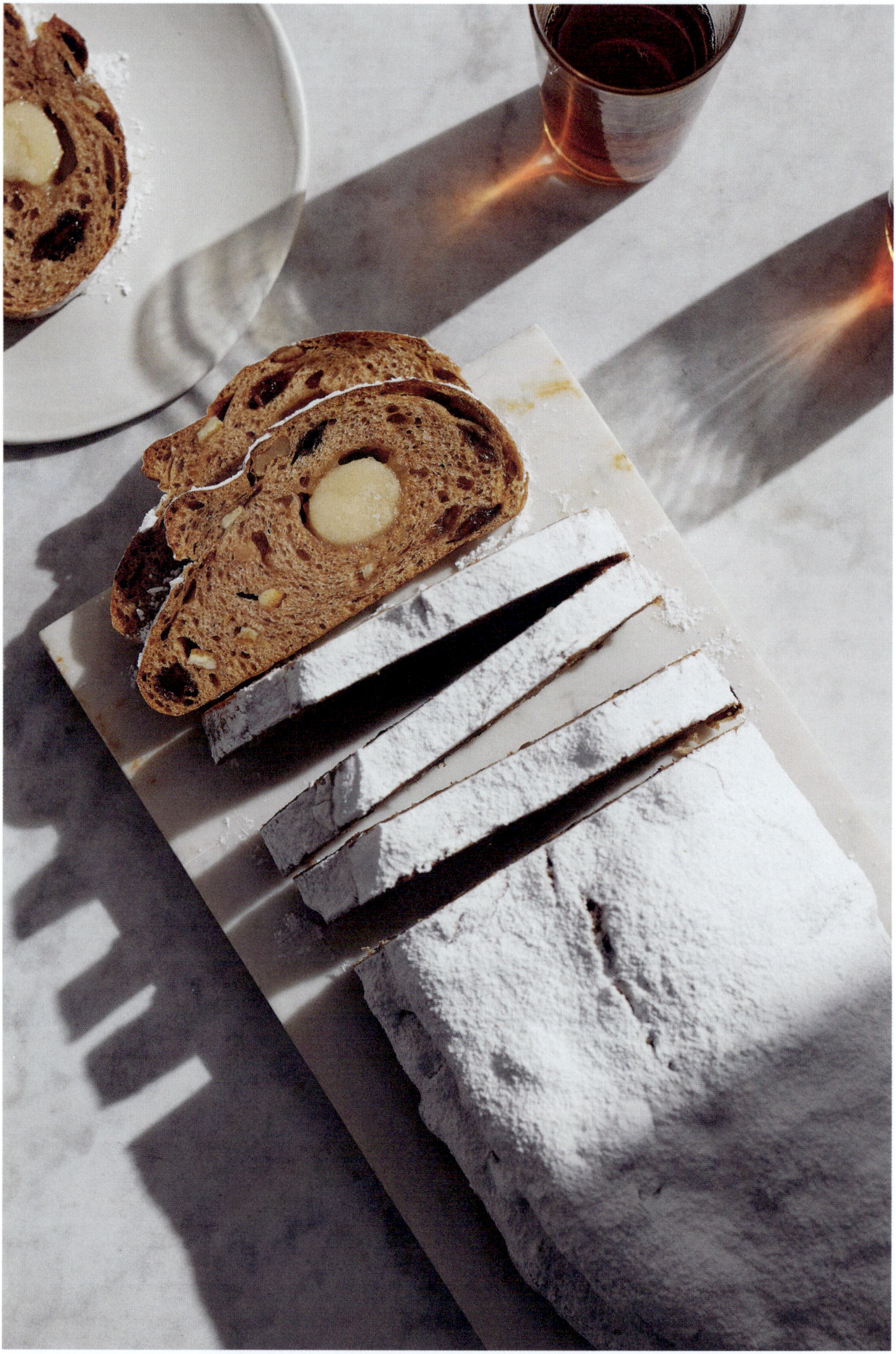

STOLLEN

Makes 2 loaves

Stollen come in many variations, and have evolved from the 700-year-old original recipe. The evolution continues and this one is a version of Christmas stollen (or Christstollen in Germany). This recipe is a 'direct dough' where you mix the dough all at once. There's no tangzhong, just a little sweet potato for richness, as this isn't a dough you necessarily want to be too soft or fluffy.

1. In a small bowl, soak the raisins in the rum a few days before making the stollen. However, if you are short on time then cover the bowl in cling film (plastic wrap) and microwave in 30 second bursts until piping hot. Toss to allow the rum to coat. Leave to cool completely.

2. Stir the yeast into the milk and leave to stand for 5–10 minutes to dissolve.

3. Add the milk and yeast mixture to a stand mixer fitted with a dough hook, followed by the flour, sweet potato, muscovado sugar, vanilla paste, cinnamon, nutmeg, lemon zest, salt and olive oil and mix on low speed until everything is combined.

4. Knead the dough on the second speed of the mixer for 6 minutes, or until the windowpane test shows a well-developed dough. Add the rum-soaked raisins, mixed peel and chopped walnuts to the dough and mix until they are combined. Alternatively, turn the dough out onto a work surface and roll out the dough, then sprinkle the fruits and nuts over the top and fold the dough until they are well incorporated. You can sprinkle some flour on the work surface or the dough to make it easier to handle.

5. Remove the dough from the bowl (if it's still in the bowl), lightly oil the bowl, then return the dough, cover loosely with cling film (plastic wrap) and leave it to rise in a warm place or lightly warmed oven (just barely warm) for 1–2 hours until nearly doubled in size. Line a large baking sheet with baking parchment and set aside.

6. Turn the risen dough out onto a floured work surface and cut it into two equal halves. Each should weigh 500 g (1 lb 2 oz). Press or roll each piece into an 18 × 12 cm (9 x 4½ in) rectangles, about 2.5 cm (1 in) thick.

ingredient	metric	imperial
raisins	140 g	4.9 oz
dark rum	30 g	1.1 oz
instant yeast	5 g	1 tsp
plant-based milk, chilled	200 g	7 oz
bread (strong) flour	350 g	12.4 oz
sweet potato, cooked and cooled	70 g	2.5 oz
muscovado sugar	30 g	1.1 oz
vanilla paste	4 g	1 tsp
ground cinnamon	2 g	½ tsp
ground nutmeg	2 g	½ tsp
lemon zest		½ lemon
fine salt	6 g	1.5 tsp
extra virgin olive oil, plus extra for greasing	35 g	1.2 oz
candied mixed peel	100 g	3.5 oz
walnuts, chopped	60 g	2 oz
marzipan/almond paste	200 g	7 oz
cocoa butter (deodorised) or coconut oil		for brushing
icing (confectioners') sugar		for dusting

7   Roll each piece of marzipan into a log the length of the rolled out dough (16–18 cm/6¼–7 in), then press the marzipan gently into the middle of the dough. Fold the left side of the dough over to cover the marzipan, then fold the right side over on top of the left side so that the edge of it sits just left of the middle of the stollen to cover the marzipan. Use the bottom edge of your hand or a slim rolling pin to press down along the length of the stollen towards the right of the centre to create a divot and characteristic hump.

8   Arrange the stollen on the lined baking sheet, cover loosely with cling film and leave to rest in a warm place for 40 minutes–1 hour until puffed up. This dough doesn't need to double in size like most doughs. At this point you can remove any raisins that are sticking out of the dough as they will burn during baking.

9   Towards the end of proving, preheat the oven to 180°C fan (350°F/gas 4) and bake the stollen for 25–30 minutes until golden. You can use a probe thermometer to aim for an internal temperature of 90°C (194°F).

10 Leave the stollen to cool completely, then brush the stollen with some deodorised cocoa butter or coconut oil and generously dust with icing sugar. You may want to dust with more icing sugar after leaving it for 30 minutes. This stollen will keep for a week if well wrapped. Enjoy in nice thin slices.

TIP

If using very firm marzipan, knead in orange juice or water to make it softer, by mixing in a few drops at a time as you knead it. It should have the texture of modelling clay.

CHOCOLATE HAZELNUT BABKA

Makes 2 × 450 g (15.9 oz) loaves or 1 × 900 g (2 lb) loaf

I was pretty good at school, although in my final year of high school I just gave up, much to my parents' dismay. They told me to get a job by the end of the week or live to regret it, so I put together a CV a week before my final exams and started handing it out at my local shopping centre. I ended up with a job in a shoe store, which I hated, but it led me to my first pastry-related job at a chocolate café called Max Brenner. It was a totally new and brilliant concept and the stuff of my 18-year-old dreams. I became obsessed with hospitality and wanted to learn how to make coffee and serve basic desserts. It's a long way off from where I am now, but that was a fun six-month introduction to a field I had no idea about. One of the things on their menu I loved was a chocolate babka, a sweet yeasted bread elaborately layered with a filling; in this case, chocolate and hazelnut.

CHOCOLATE HAZELNUT FILLING

1. Bring the milk, sugar and cinnamon to a simmer in a small saucepan over a medium heat. Add the cocoa powder and whisk until it is combined and lump-free.

2. Add the chocolate and hazelnut butter and whisk until smooth. Cover the surface with cling film (plastic wrap) and chill in the refrigerator for 30 minutes to cool to room temperature. You can also prepare the filling ahead of time and leave in the refrigerator for up to a week, heating gently in the microwave to soften.

TO ASSEMBLE AND BAKE

3. Prepare the vrioche dough following the instructions on pages 51–52 and leave it to bulk ferment or double in size in the bowl. Lightly flour the work surface, then turn out the dough and punch it down to deflate the air. Roll the dough out into a 22 × 30 cm (9 × 12 in) rectangle.

4. Spread the filling over the dough, leaving a 2 cm (¾ in) border at one short edge. Sprinkle with the chocolate chips, chopped hazelnuts then place on a baking sheet and leave to chill in the refrigerator to set the filling. Line the loaf tin (pan) with baking parchment.

5. Roll the chilled dough from the opposite short edge to where you have your 2 cm (¾ in) border, then brush with water and stretch and press it to seal the log.

6. Using a serrated knife, cut the log in half lengthways using a gentle sawing motion to cut all the way through.

   TIP To make the twisting easier and neater, chill the two halves of the rolled log for 15 minutes in the freezer.

7. Twist the two halves around each other so that the cut side showing the chocolate is on top, then tuck the ends in. Put it into the lined loaf tin, brush the top lightly with water to keep it supple, then wrap the tin loosely with cling film (plastic wrap) and leave to prove in a warm place for 1–1½ hours until the loaf doubles in size.

plant-based milk	75 g	2.7 oz
caster (superfine) sugar	70 g	2.5 oz
ground cinnamon	4 g	1 tsp
cocoa (unsweetened chocolate) powder	12 g	0.4 oz
dark chocolate with at least 66–72% cocoa solids, chopped	75 g	2.7 oz
hazelnut butter	75 g	2.7 oz

ALSO NEEDED

Vrioche dough (pages 51–52)	600 g	1 lb 5 oz
plain (all-purpose) flour	for dusting	
chocolate chips	80 g	2.8 oz
hazelnuts, chopped and toasted	50 g	1.7 oz
Exotic Clear Glaze (page 239)	50 g	1.7 oz

8 Preheat the oven to 180°C fan (350°F/gas 4) and bake the loaf for 25 minutes, or until a probe thermometer reads 90°C (194°F). Babka loaves can be deceptive because they will brown nicely on top before they are fully baked inside due to the size and shape of the loaf.

9 Remove from the oven and cool in the tin for 5 minutes then remove gently. Once cool, brush the top of the loaf with the exotic clear glaze.

10 Leave to cool in the tin. Many a warm babka breaks up when it's prised too early from the tin. You might need to run a sharp knife along the edge of the tin to help ease it out. Store well wrapped at room temperature for up to 4 days, or frozen for 3 months – slicing before wrapping always helps!

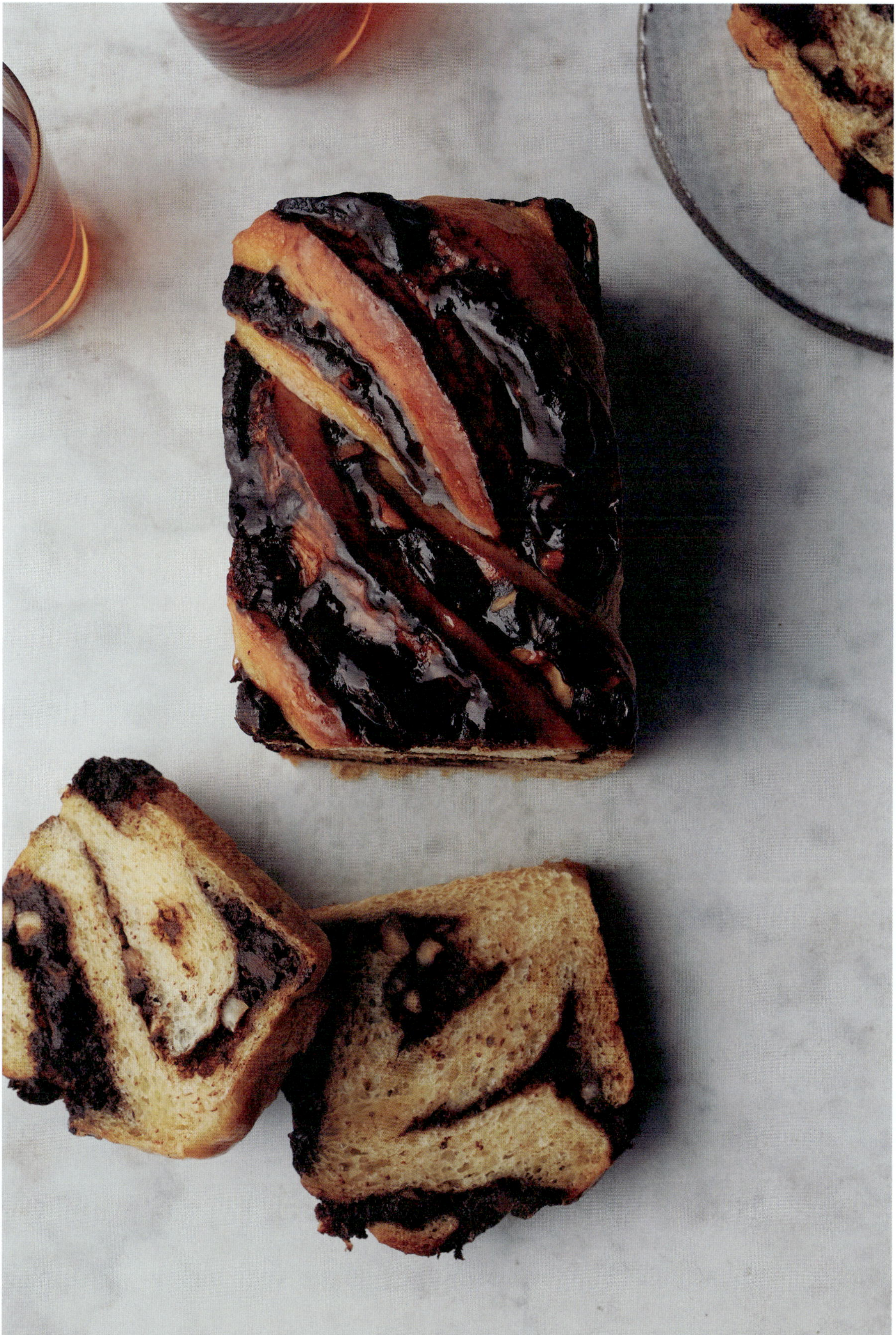

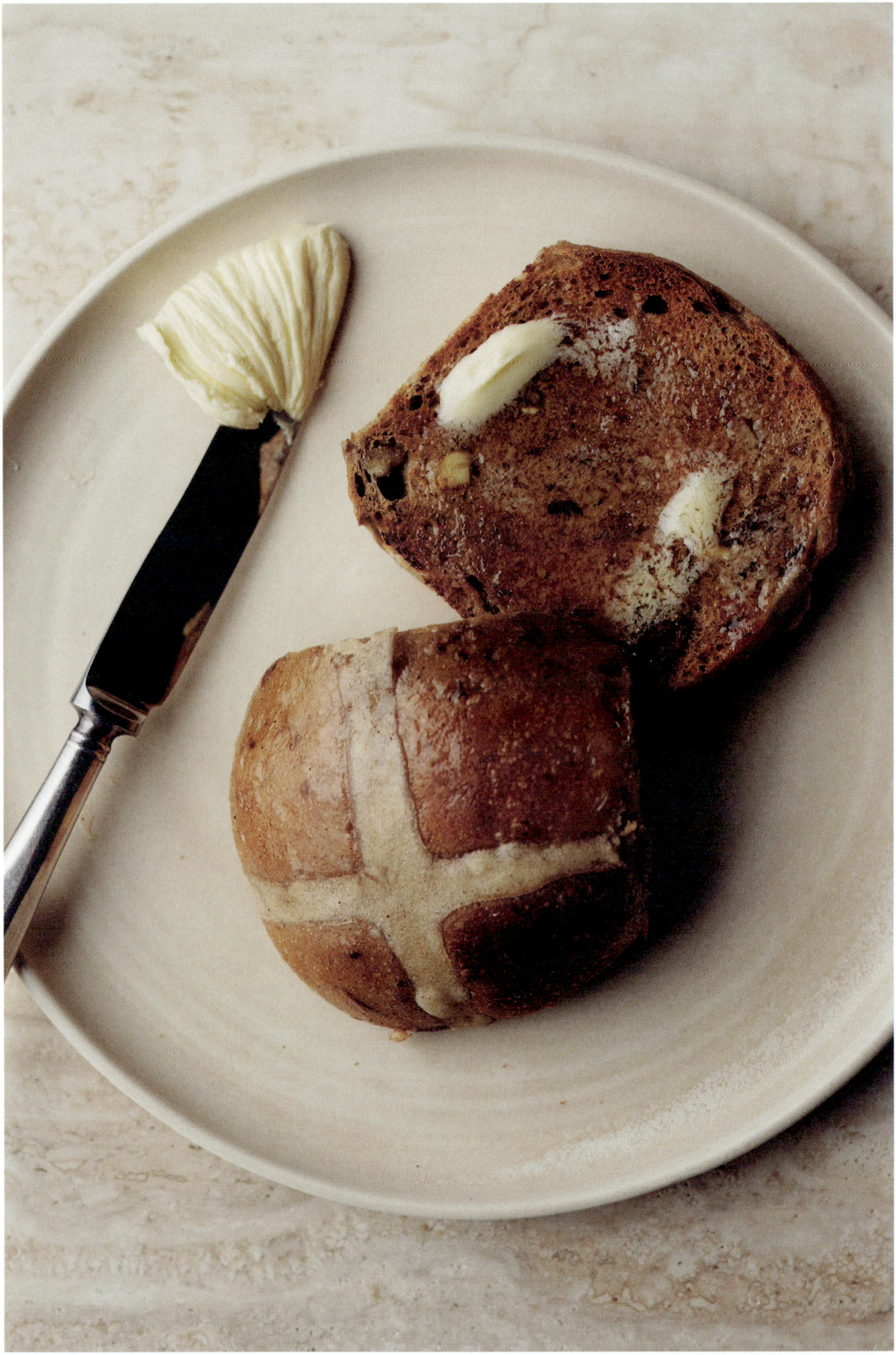

HOT X BUNS

Makes 12 buns

Hot cross buns have a tendency to be dense, but also dry out and become stale pretty quickly. Using the tangzhong technique ensures that these will be fluffier and stay moist for as long as possible. Fruit and spice are generously accounted for in this recipe. Be prepared to share!

bread (strong) flour (1)	25 g	0.9 oz
water	125 g	4.4 oz
plant-based milk or water, cooled	170 g	6 oz
instant yeast	5 g	1 tsp
bread (strong) flour (2)	350 g	12.4 oz
muscovado sugar	50 g	1.7 oz
fine salt	5 g	1 tsp
ground cinnamon	2 g	1 tsp
ground nutmeg	2 g	1 tsp
ground cloves	1 g	½ tsp
orange zest	¼ orange	
extra virgin olive oil, plus extra for greasing	30 g	1.1 oz
tangzhong (see above)	120 g	4.2 oz
sultanas (golden raisins)	160 g	5.6 oz
candied citrus peel	60 g	2 oz

TANGZHONG DOUGH

1. Prepare the tangzhong by adding the bread flour (1) and water in a small saucepan and mixing until the flour is completely dissolved. Heat over a medium heat, stirring constantly with a silicone spatula until the mixture thickens. Place cling film (plastic wrap) on top, then chill in the refrigerator until cool to touch.

2. Pour the plant-based milk into a bowl, add the instant yeast and stir to dissolve. If using active dry yeast you might need to leave it to stand for 10 minutes to dissolve the coating.

3. Add the bread flour (2), sugar, salt, spices, orange zest and olive oil to a stand mixer fitted with a dough hook attachment. Add the milk and yeast mixture and the chilled tangzhong and start mixing on low speed. A dough will start to form. Once all the flour is combined, increase the speed slightly and mix for about 5 minutes – the dough should be smooth and developed. Keep kneading until a windowpane test shows a well-developed dough.

    TIP If you don't like candied citrus peel, use the zest of a whole orange instead.

4. Tip the dough out onto a lightly oiled work surface and press it into a flat disc. Add the sultanas and candied citrus peel and keep folding and kneading the dough until everything is incorporated. Lightly oil the bowl with a little oil, then return the dough to the bowl. Cover with cling film and leave it to rise at room temperature for 1½–2 hours until doubled in size.

    TIP This initial rise – or what professionals call a bulk ferment – allows the dough to develop flavour and to rest. Timings are always a guide, based on a room temperature of 20–22°C (68–72°F). If your room is warmer or colder your timings may need to shift. Yeast is a living organism and if it's warmer it works quicker and if colder it's much slower, so read your dough for its visual cues rather than rigidly sticking to timings.

5. When ready to use, knock the dough back by punching all the air out in the bowl. Try to avoid mixing it at this stage as you want to keep the dough flexible for rolling or shaping into your desired shape – although not a huge problem, as this can be remedied by a 15-minute rest on the work surface before shaping.

6. Use a scraper or knife to cut the dough into 75 g (2.7 oz) portions, then shape them into balls by pressing the weighed portion into a disc, pinching the sides into the centre, then flipping them over so the smooth side is on top.

SWEET RISEN

TO ASSEMBLE AND BAKE

7. Once you have shaped the buns, arrange them on a sheet of baking parchment or directly onto a lightly greased and floured baking sheet. Make sure there is half the distance of a dough ball's worth of space (about 2–3 cm/1 in) in between if you would like them joined together as is traditional, or give them plenty of space if baking individual buns.

   TIP Make sure there is plenty of space if baking individual shapes. A bun will expand twice its initial size during the proving stage. If lightly flouring the baking sheet (use a pencil if using baking parchment), mark this size as a guide so you know when it is proved and how far apart you need to place your buns.

8. When proving, you can place the baking sheet in a switched-off oven with a roasting tray in the bottom, which is half-filled with water, to create a humid and warm environment. Leave for 40 minutes–1 hour, then remove and preheat the oven for baking immediately after. Alternatively, place a piece of cling film (plastic wrap) loosely on top and wrap the baking sheet. Try to keep them in a warm place (about 25°C/77°F); at room temperature (20–22°C/68–72°F), it should take roughly 1 hour for them to double in size.

   TIP Proving is the one stage most inexperienced bakers will rush but it is crucial to ensure light fluffy products that eat beautifully. Underproved doughs result in a dense, unenjoyable eat. You will know most doughs have fully proved once they have doubled in size or pass the jiggle test – where a gently wobbled baking sheet makes the buns jiggle. I also find it useful to mark the size of the buns on the tray before proving.

SPICED BUN WASH

9. Make the bun wash while your dough is proving, or any time before the buns come out of the oven, because you want to brush the buns as soon as they come out of the oven, otherwise they stay sticky on top. Bring all the ingredients to a simmer in small saucepan, then set aside.

ground cloves	1 g	¼ tsp
ground cinnamon	1 g	¼ tsp
caster (superfine) sugar	30 g	1.1 oz
muscovado sugar	30 g	1.1 oz
water	50 g	1.8 oz

PIPING MIX

10. Prepare the piping mix by mixing all the ingredients together in a medium bowl until combined, then spooning into a piping (pastry) bag. Use a 4 mm (⅛ in) plain piping tube or cut a hole 3–4 mm (⅛–⅙ in) across. This can be prepared up to 3 days in advance and stored in the refrigerator.

plain (all-purpose) flour	60 g	2 oz
water	70 g	2.5 oz

11. About 40 minutes into proving, preheat the oven to 180°C fan (350°F/gas 4), making sure the oven rack is in the middle.

12. Before putting your buns into the oven, use the piping mix to pipe the crosses on the top of the buns.

13. Bake the buns for 12–15 minutes until golden all the way over the top. As soon as the buns are ready, remove them from the oven and immediately glaze with the spiced wash.

14. Carefully transfer the buns to a wire rack to cool. Store well wrapped or in a sealed container at room temperature for up to 5 days. You can also wrap and freeze for up to 3 months. Defrost at room temperature before slicing in half along the bun's equator and toasting.

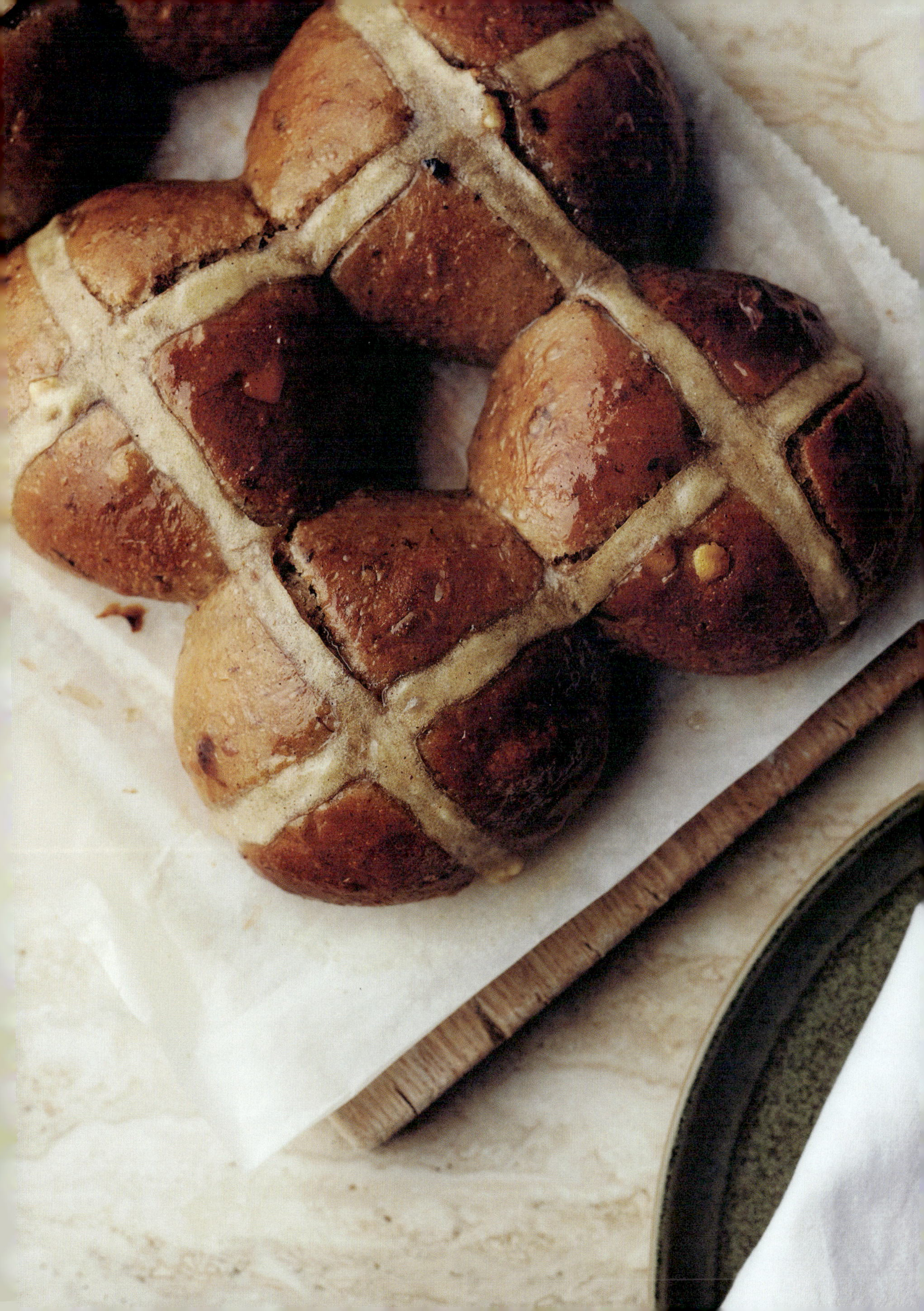

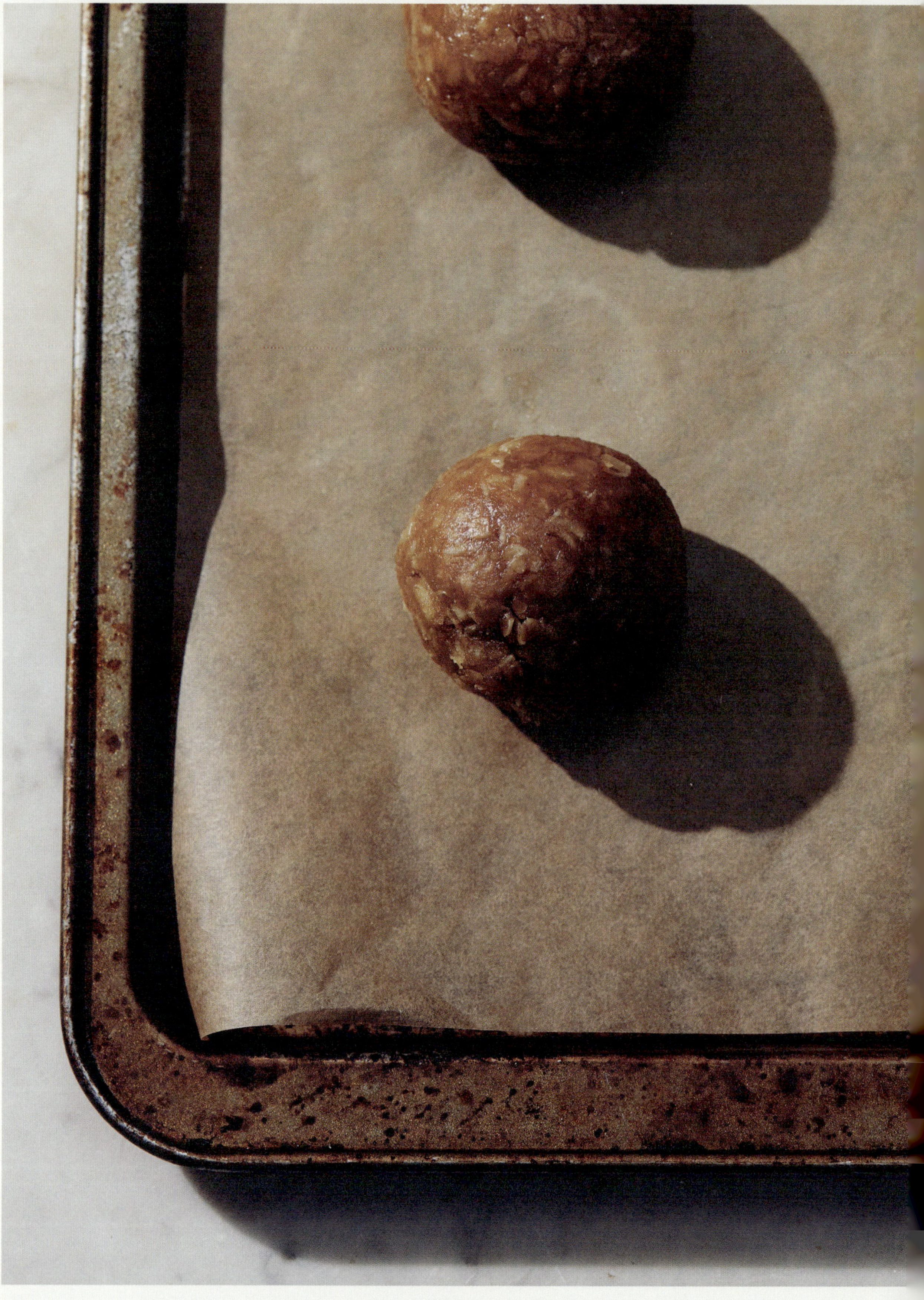

2 BISCUITS AND COOKIES

Some readers may remember the fancy tins that biscuits (if you're British) or cookies (if you're North American) used to come in. Whether they were Dutch butter cookies or English shortbreads, the tin signified indulgent discovery in my childish mind (before it got upcycled to a household sewing kit or miscellaneous cable box). Over the years, supermarket brands sold the staples in 'family packs' with something to please everyone. This is how you should view this chapter of the book!

There is one common technique used in these recipes. I whisk (or blend) oil, water and sugar together into a syrup, then mix them into the dry ingredients to form a dough. If you were to just add them separately, you would end up with a very crumbly dough that doesn't form, roll, scoop, bake or eat well! The sugar helps combine the oil and water in a stable emulsion which hydrates or wets the flour at an even rate. This dough can appear just slightly softer than dough made with solid fats, but this is remedied by a 30-minute rest in the refrigerator. The result contains less fat, has a superior shelf life and widely varying flavours. The following recipes are ones I'm most proud of. I hope that as you bake through these cookies it will be like opening a tin of fine treats, waiting to discover which one is your favourite.

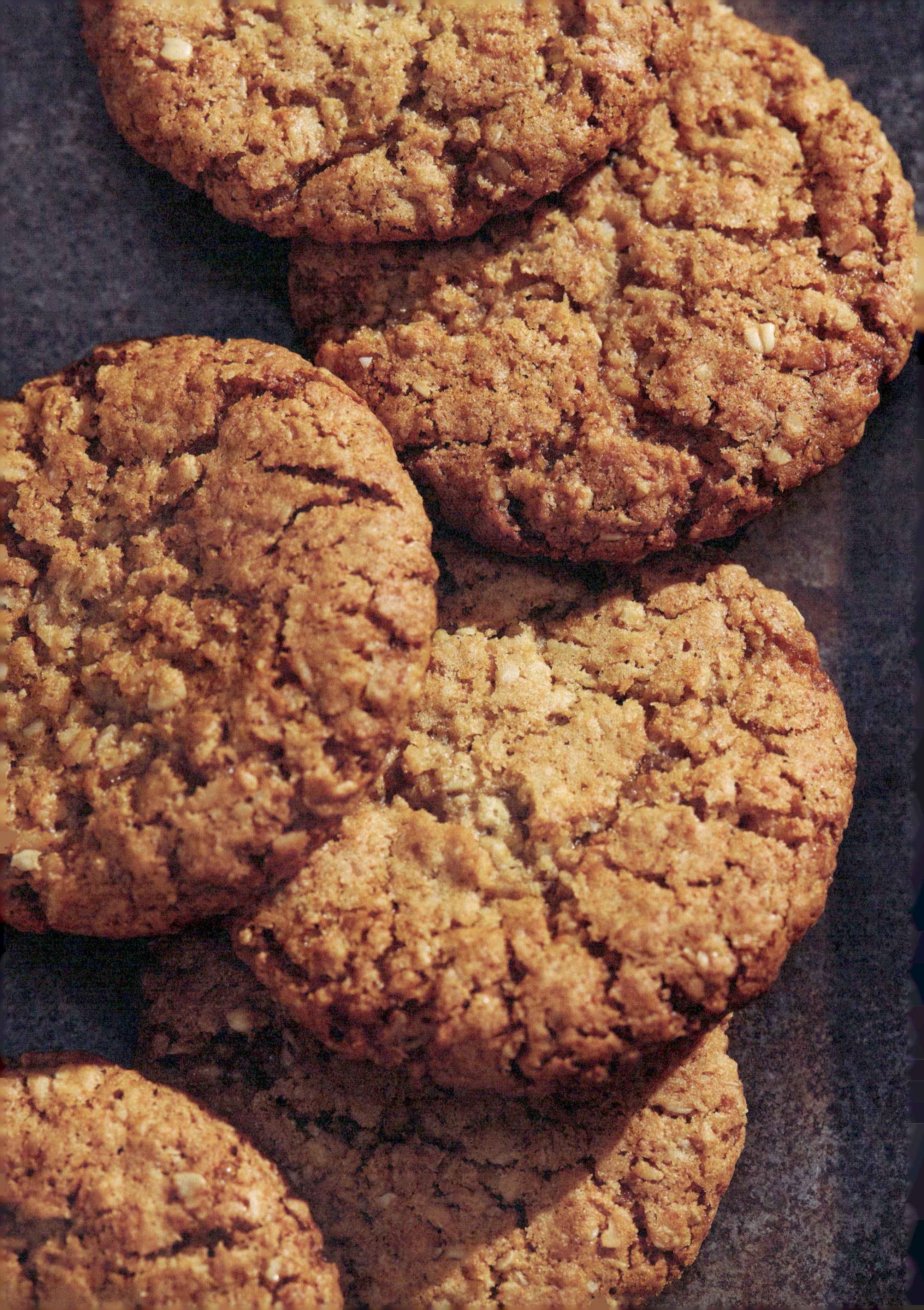

ANZAC BISCUITS

Makes 10 cookies

Legendary by name and by heritage, the Anzac cookie captures the spirit of the Australia–New Zealand bond. It is the only product allowed to be sold with 'Anzac' in the name (and only when it prefixes 'biscuit' – not 'cookie') because it would otherwise seem to be commercialising on the sacrifices of war – a sad reminder that there are no winners at war. Despite its origins, these biscuits (cookies) whenever I see them, whether in an Aussie- or Kiwi-founded café in London, or New York, signify a shared history and a warm bond. These biscuits are chewy and golden with a hint of salt, which I love – it tempers the sweet molasses of the muscovado or brown sugar.

1. Add both sugars, the golden syrup, water, olive oil and sea salt to a large bowl and whisk until fully combined and there are no oily streaks. This is the syrup.
2. In another large bowl, use a whisk to gently stir the flour, bicarbonate of soda, oats and coconut together.
3. Add the syrup to the dry ingredients and mix until a dough forms, then leave to rest for 30 minutes to allow the moisture in the recipe to hydrate the dry ingredients.
4. Preheat the oven to 180°C fan (350°F/gas 4). Use a 6 cm (2½ in) spring-loaded scoop or weigh 60 g (2.1 oz) and roll into balls. Arrange them on a large baking sheet, lined with parchment paper, 5 cm (2 in) apart.
5. Bake the cookies until evenly golden all over – 10 minutes for a more chewy cookie and 12 minutes for a crispy one. The cookies will look puffed up straight out of the oven but they will deflate slightly to crackly once they are completely cooled on the baking sheet or wire rack. Store in an airtight container for up to 5 days.

muscovado sugar	65 g	2.3 oz
caster (superfine) sugar	100 g	2.3 oz
golden (or agave) syrup	30 g	1.1 oz
water	60 g	2 oz
extra virgin olive oil	60 g	2 oz
sea salt	1 g	¼ tsp
plain (all-purpose) flour	150 g	5.3 oz
bicarbonate of soda (baking soda)	5 g	1 tsp
porridge oats	90 g	3.2 oz
desiccated (dried shredded) coconut	80 g	2.8 oz

BISCUITS AND COOKIES

NUT SHORTBREADS

Makes 12 shortbreads

These shortbreads have an intense nut flavour and superb shortness meaning there's no chew or bite – it just surrenders to and melts in the mouth. This type of recipe is a category of its own and the variations are endless! It is almost an all-in method in a food processor or blender. In making these I tried to minimise the use of any additional fats and the shortness relies on the abundance of natural oils in the nuts themselves. The portion sizes are small because they are indulgent, especially doused in icing (confectioners') sugar. The texture of these shortbreads is definitely inspired by qurabiya in the Middle East, kourabides in Greece and polvorones in many Spanish-speaking countries.

1. Preheat the oven to 160°C fan (325°F/gas 3) and line a large baking sheet with baking parchment.
2. Add the nuts, flour, baking powder and sea salt to a food processor, and pulse until the nuts are blending into the dough and it starts to clump together. Pour into a mixing bowl.
3. In a small bowl, use a whisk to combine the icing sugar, olive oil and water until glossy. Add this mixture to the bowl of ground nuts.
4. Using a silicone spatula or your hands, mix and knead the mixture until well combined and a dough forms. Press together onto a sheet of parchment paper, and place another piece of parchment paper on top. I roll to 1 cm thickness between these sheets of parchment paper, then remove the top layer and use a cutter to cut desired shapes and place onto a baking sheet.
5. Bake for 12–14 minutes until golden.
6. Leave to cool to room temperature, then generously dust with icing sugar. Store in a sealed container for up to a week.

nuts, any type, such as pistachio, hazelnut, peanut, almond, cashew, pecan or walnut	120 g	4.2 oz
plain (all-purpose) flour (gluten-free flour also works well)	50 g	1.8 oz
baking powder	2 g	½ tsp
sea salt, crushed	1 g	¼ tsp
icing (confectioners') sugar, plus extra for dusting	50 g	1.8 oz
extra virgin olive oil	30 g	1.1 oz
water	15 g	1 tbsp
chopped nuts (optional, for texture)	40 g	1.4 oz

TIP

Unfortunately a food processor or blender is necessary for this method. A version could be made with pure nut butters although this would be expensive and need adaptation.

BISCUITS AND COOKIES

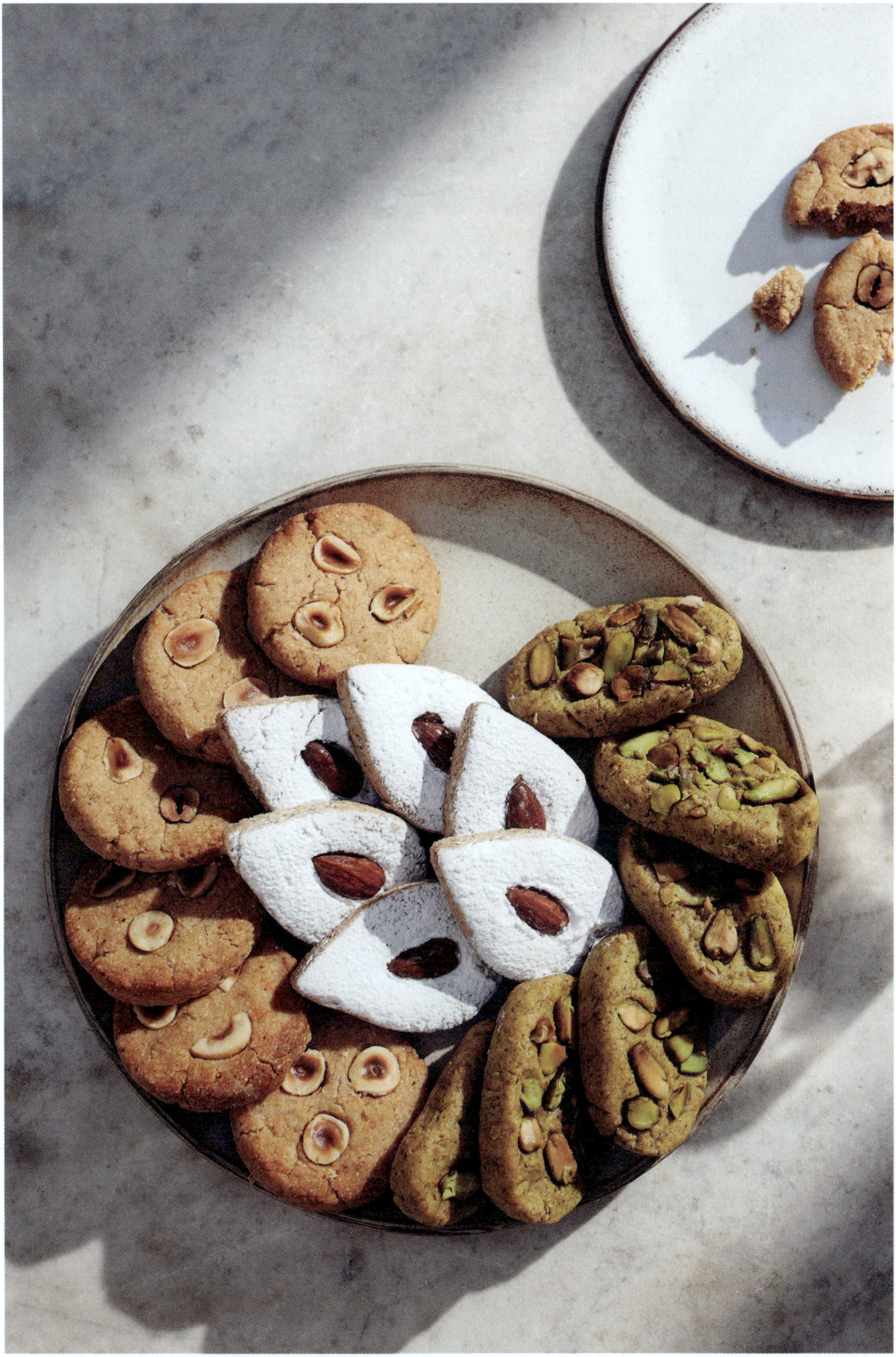

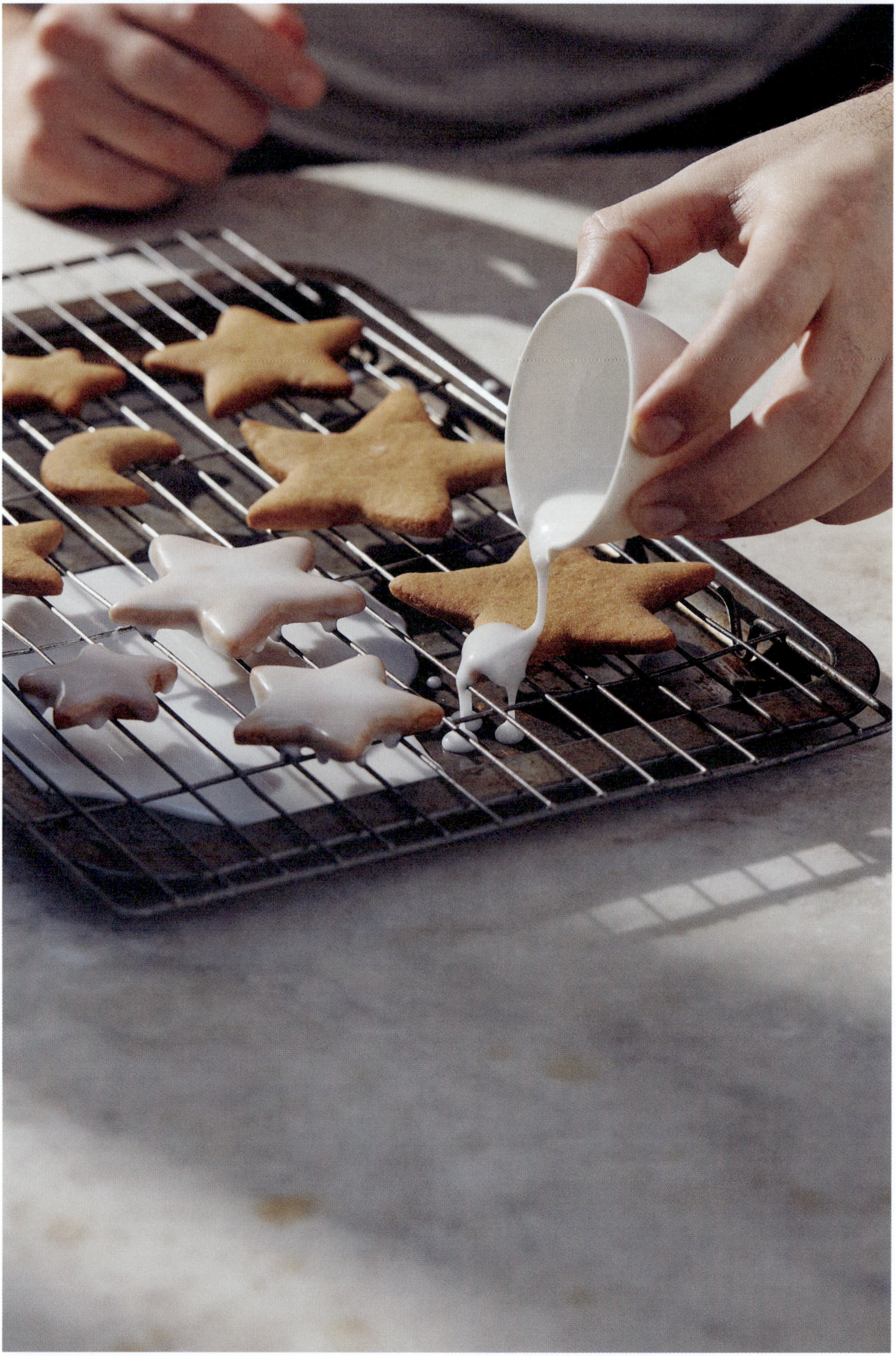

GLAZED GINGERBREAD

Makes 25–30 cookies

A soft gingerbread for people who might not like gingerbread is another way of saying that this is a 'safely' spiced dough that will appeal to most palates. The dough is soft when freshly mixed so be sure to give it a full 30-minute rest for much better handling. If a darker, spicier flavour is more your vibe then by all means feel free to ramp up the spices and replace the golden (or agave) syrup for molasses. This recipe gets fantastic depth from the natural molasses from the dark muscovado sugar, while the golden syrup is an invert sugar which attracts moisture and keeps the cookie soft. Adding an optional thin layer of a vanilla water icing crystallises around your cookie for a touch of extra festive sweetness, and patterned cookies come out beautifully with this finish. You can also roll little balls of the gingerbread dough for a treat akin to lebkuchen, or as soft, moreish cookies with piped icing (frosting).

GINGERBREAD

1. Mix the flour, baking powder, salt and spices together in a large bowl.

2. Combine the sugar, molasses, milk and oil in a measuring jug or cup and blend them until they are well mixed and there are no oily streaks. This is the syrup.

3. Add the syrup to the dry ingredients and mix until everything is combined, a dough forms and it is streak free.

4. Press the dough into a flattened disc in the bowl, cover in cling film (plastic wrap) and leave to rest in the refrigerator for at least 30 minutes, or overnight.

5. Preheat the oven to 180°C fan (350°F/gas 4) and line a large baking sheet with baking parchment.

6. Roll the rested dough between two sheets of baking parchment until it is 5 mm (¼ in) thick. Use a cutter to cut whatever shapes or sizes you like and arrange them on the lined baking sheet, 2 cm (¾ in) apart.

7. Bake for just 9–11 minutes. The dough will feel soft (maybe even puffy) but it will firm up once it cools. Leave to cool on the baking sheet for 10–15 minutes, then transfer to a wire rack to cool completely. Store in an airtight container for up to a week.

plain (all-purpose) flour	320 g	11.3 oz
baking powder	4 g	1 tsp
salt	1 g	¼ tsp
ground nutmeg	2 g	½ tsp
ground cinnamon	2.8 g	½ tsp
ground ginger	4 g	1 tsp
ground cloves	2 g	½ tsp
muscovado sugar	90 g	3.2 oz
molasses or dark treacle	28 g	1 oz
plant-based milk	70 g	2.5 oz
extra virgin olive oil	60 g	2 oz

VANILLA WATER ICING (OPTIONAL)

8. If you are using the icing (frosting), then mix all the ingredients together in a bowl. Dip the biscuit into the glaze, let the excess drip off and place onto a wire rack to set. Leave to set.

icing (confectioners') sugar	300 g	10.6 oz
water	65 g	2.3 oz
vanilla bean paste	4 g	1 tsp

TIP

These cookies need to 'age' overnight for all the spices to come alive in the finished gingerbread.

BISCUITS AND COOKIES

BANANA CHIP COOKIES

Makes 12 cookies

This cookie has a rich, sweet banana flavour. It's a perfect recipe for using up bananas that are too brown. These cookies evoke banana bread in a bite-sized morsel of soft, chewy, chocolate-studded goodness.

1. Pulse the banana and sugars with a hand-held blender in a blending jug to combine into a syrup.

2. Melt the coconut oil in the microwave in 30-second bursts or in a small saucepan over a low heat, then pour it into the banana mixture and pulse again to combine.

3. Weigh all the remaining ingredients into a large bowl, add the banana mixture and mix with a silicone spatula until a dough forms. Leave to rest in the refrigerator for at least 30 minutes. This is a wet dough, so I recommend chilling and resting it in the refrigerator to make it easier to handle.

4. Preheat the oven to 180°C fan (350°F/gas 4) and line two large baking sheets with baking parchment.

5. Use a 5–6 cm (1½–2½ in) or size #20 spring-loaded scoop to scoop balls of the dough (70 g/2½ oz each) and arrange six balls on each lined baking sheet, 5 cm (2 in) apart from each other and 3 cm (1¼ in) away from the edge.

6. Bake for 12–14 minutes until golden around the edges. Transfer to a wire rack to cool completely. Store in an airtight container for up to 5 days.

bananas, ripe and mashed	200 g	7 oz
brown or muscovado sugar	100 g	3.5 oz
caster (superfine) sugar	100 g	3.5 oz
coconut oil (deodorised)	40 g	1.4 oz
vanilla extract	5 g	1 tsp
plain (all-purpose) flour	300 g	10.6 oz
baking powder	8 g	2 tsp
bicarbonate of soda (baking soda)	3 g	1/2 tsp
fine salt	1 g	⅛ tsp
ground cinnamon	0.5 g	⅛ tsp
dark chocolate chips	180 g	6.3 oz

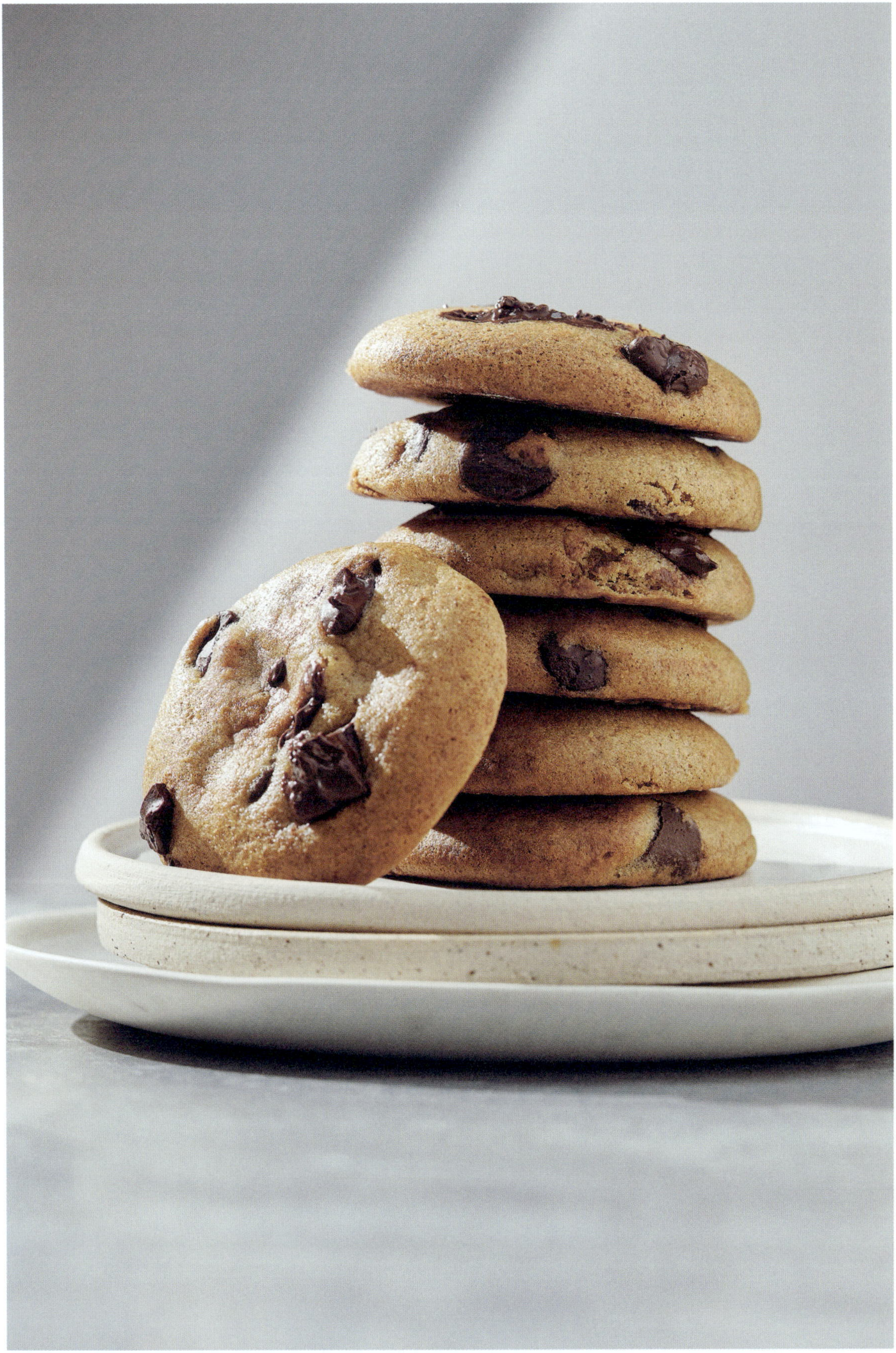

CHOCOLATE CHIP COOKIES

Makes 12 cookies

This chocolate chip cookie is crispy around the outside and soft and chewy within. With rivers of dark chocolate flowing through the middle, it is a straight-up dough that just needs a 1 hour rest to firm up and hydrate the flour. This is chocolate chip cookie stripped down to its most functional components, each one carefully allocated a role in the delicate balancing act that gives the cookie its specific and much-loved qualities and attributes. Having said that, measure the baking powder and bicarbonate of soda (baking soda) carefully as they have been calculated to give just the right amount of lift, spread and browning.

1. Whisk both sugars, the cinnamon, milk, olive oil and vanilla extract together in a large bowl until fully combined and there are no oily streaks. This is the syrup. You can also use a hand-held blender and measuring jug.

2. In another large bowl, mix the flour, baking powder, bicarbonate soda, fine salt and chocolate chips together.

3. Add the syrup to the dry ingredients and mix with a silicone spatula until a dough forms, then mix in the chopped chocolate or chips. Leave the dough to rest for 1 hour in the refrigerator.

4. Preheat the oven to 180°C fan (350°F/gas 4) and line two large baking sheets with baking parchment.

5. Divide and weigh the dough into 70 g (2.5 oz) portions, then roll into balls and arrange them on the lined baking sheet, spaced 5 cm (2 in) apart and away from the edge. Sprinkle a few flakes of sea salt onto the dough.

6. Bake for about 12 minutes for a soft, fudgey cookie and up to 15 minutes for cookies that are crispier around the edges. Straight out of the oven, you can make your cookies sexy and perfectly round – use a plain cutter that is 2 cm (¾ in) wider than the baked cookie, and rotate it around the cookie quickly to tuck in and 'round' the edges. These keep well for up to 7 days stored in an airtight container, although they are especially good on the first day before the chocolate has cooled down and reset into chunks.

caster (superfine) sugar	120 g	4.2 oz
brown or muscovado sugar	120 g	4.2 oz
ground cinnamon	0.5 g	⅛ tsp
plant-based milk	80 g	2.8 oz
extra virgin olive oil	100 g	3.5 oz
vanilla extract	5 g	1 tsp
plain (all-purpose) flour	260 g	9.2 oz
baking powder	4 g	1 tsp
bicarbonate of soda (baking soda)	3 g	½ tsp
fine salt	2 g	¼ tsp
dark chocolate chips or block dark chocolate, coarsely chopped	180 g	6.3 oz
sea salt flakes		to sprinkle

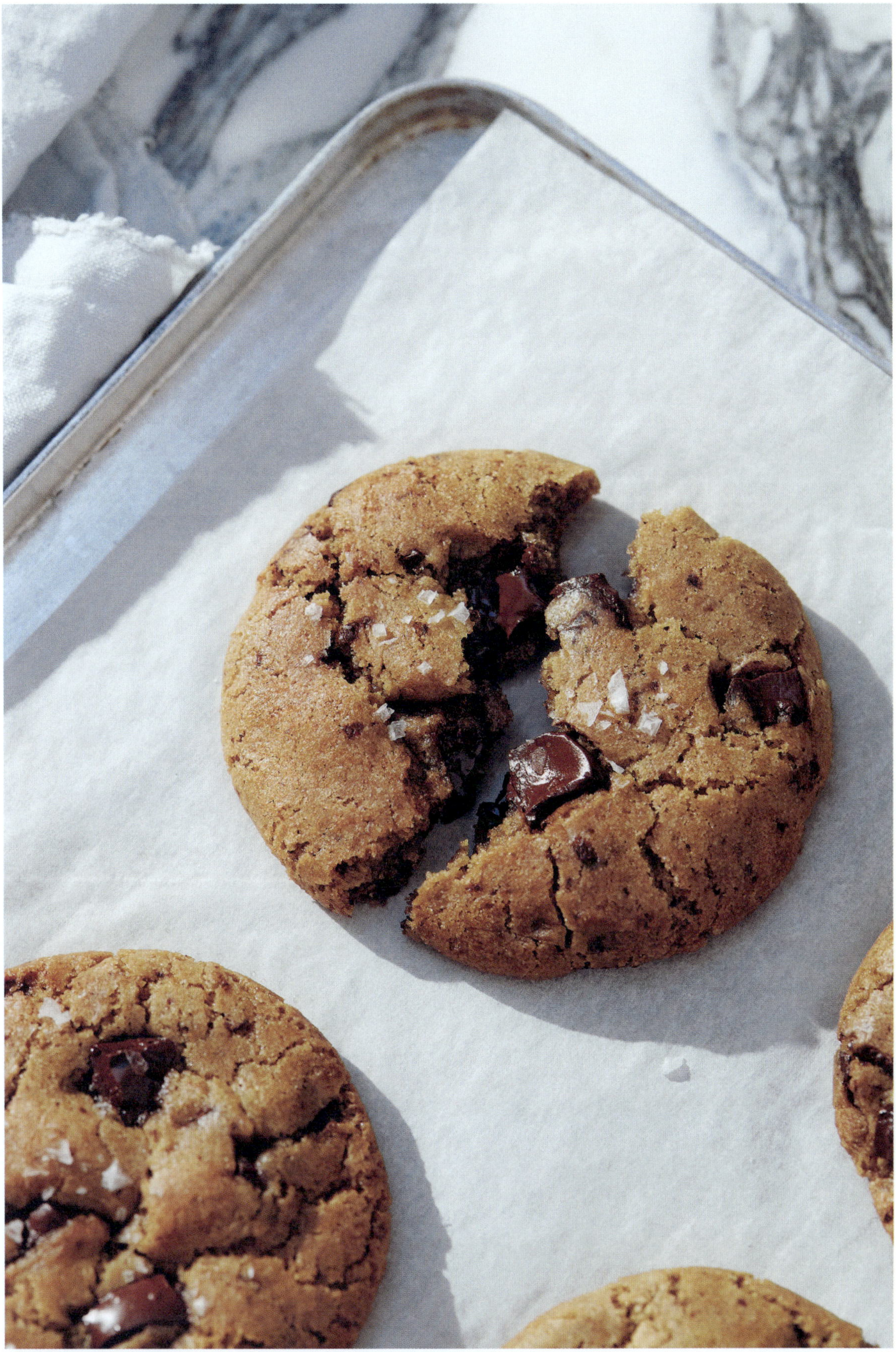

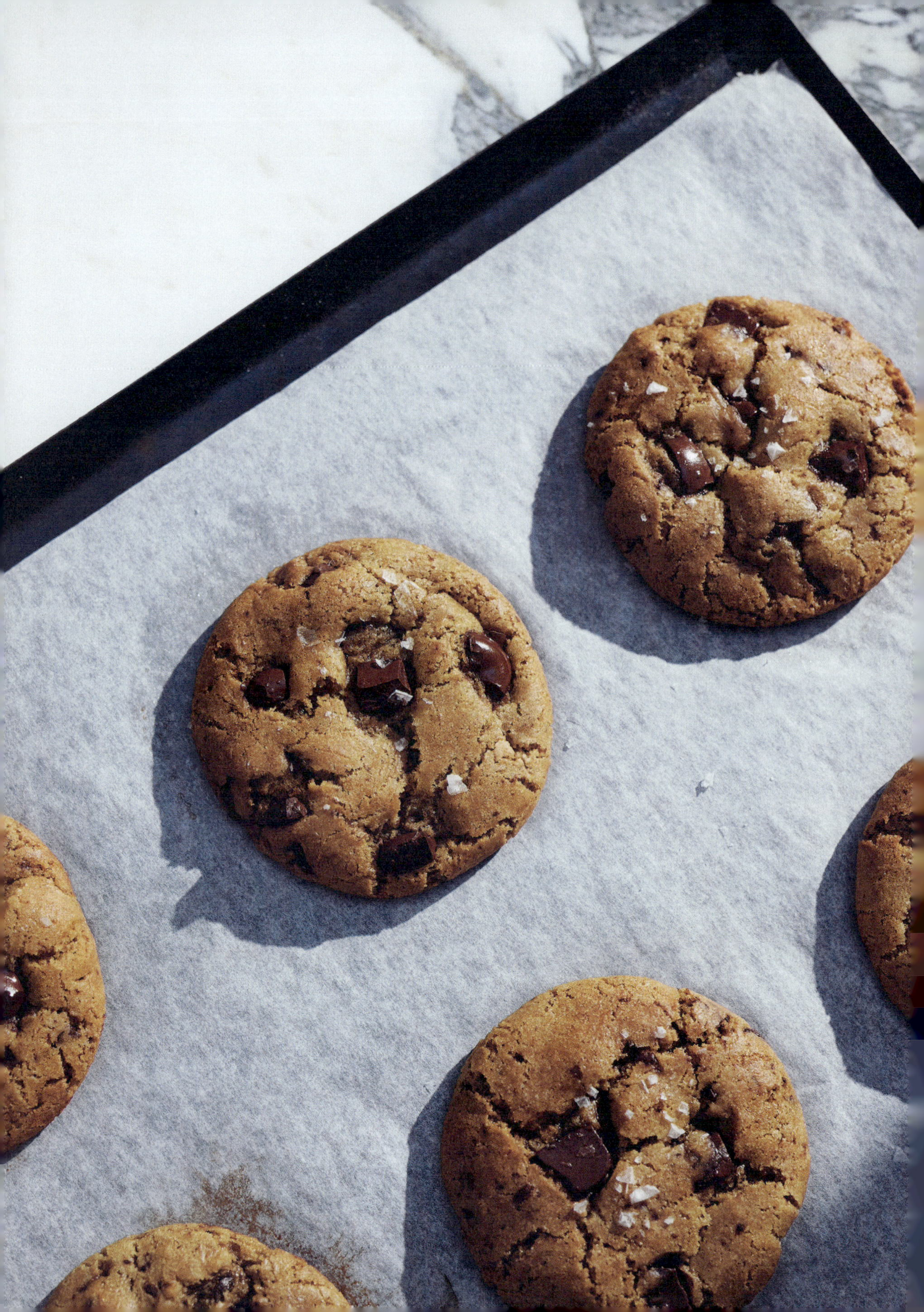

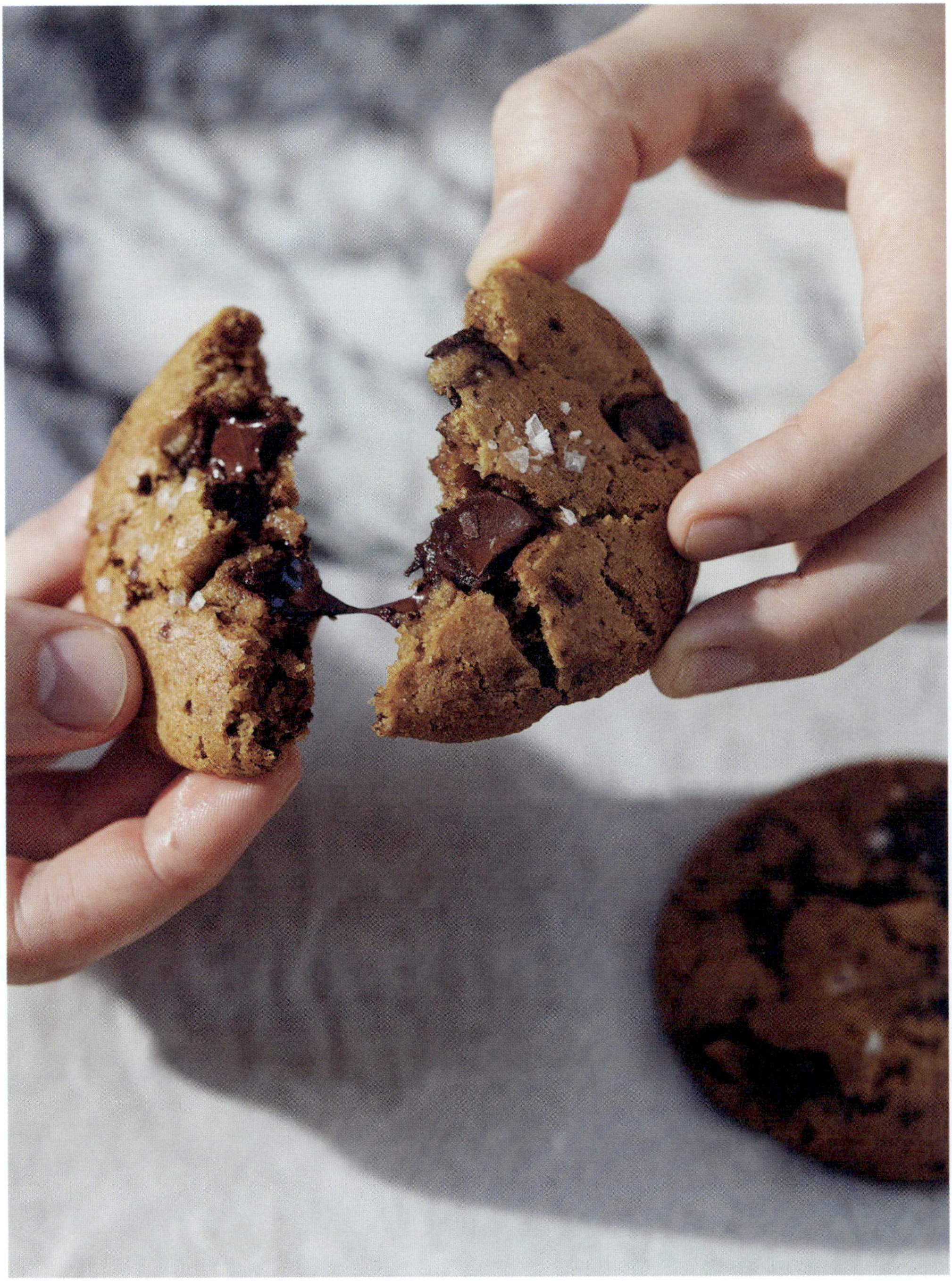

CHOCOLATE TAHINI COOKIES

Makes 12 cookies

These cookies are super cakey and chocolatey with a subtle smoky nutiness from the tahini. The beauty of this recipe is that tahini can be replaced with peanut or hazelnut butter for more variations.

1. Preheat the oven to 170°C fan (325°F/gas 3) and line a large baking sheet with baking parchment or a silicone mat.
2. Melt the chocolate in a microwave-safe bowl in the microwave in 30-second bursts, stirring in between, or in a stainless-steel bowl set over a pan filled with 1 cm (½ in) simmering water, stirring until melted, then remove from the heat.
3. Mix the tahini, muscovado sugar and cinnamon into the chocolate to combine, then add the milk and whisk until the mixture is smooth and glossy.
4. Add the flour, baking powder and bicarbonate of soda and mix with a silicone spatula until everything is well combined and streak free.
5. Weigh the batter into 50 g (2 oz) balls or use a small spring-release scoop to scoop the dough. It doesn't need to rest. Arrange the balls on the lined baking sheet.
6. Bake for 10 minutes for a soft and fudgey cookie. The chocolate content firms up when it cools so it is best to 'underbake' these. Store in an airtight container for up to 5 days.

dark chocolate with at least 70% cocoa solids, coarsely chopped	180 g	6.4 oz
tahini	100 g	3.5 oz
brown or muscovado sugar	180 g	6.4 oz
ground cinnamon	1.4 g	½ tsp
plant-based milk	100 g	3.5 oz
plain (all-purpose) flour	150 g	5.3 oz
baking powder	4 g	1 tsp
bicarbonate of soda (baking soda)	4 g	¾ tsp

TIP

To make a tidier looking cookie, straight out of the oven, use a round cutter that's slightly larger than the cookie, press it on the try, rotate it quickly around the cookie to tuck in the edges.

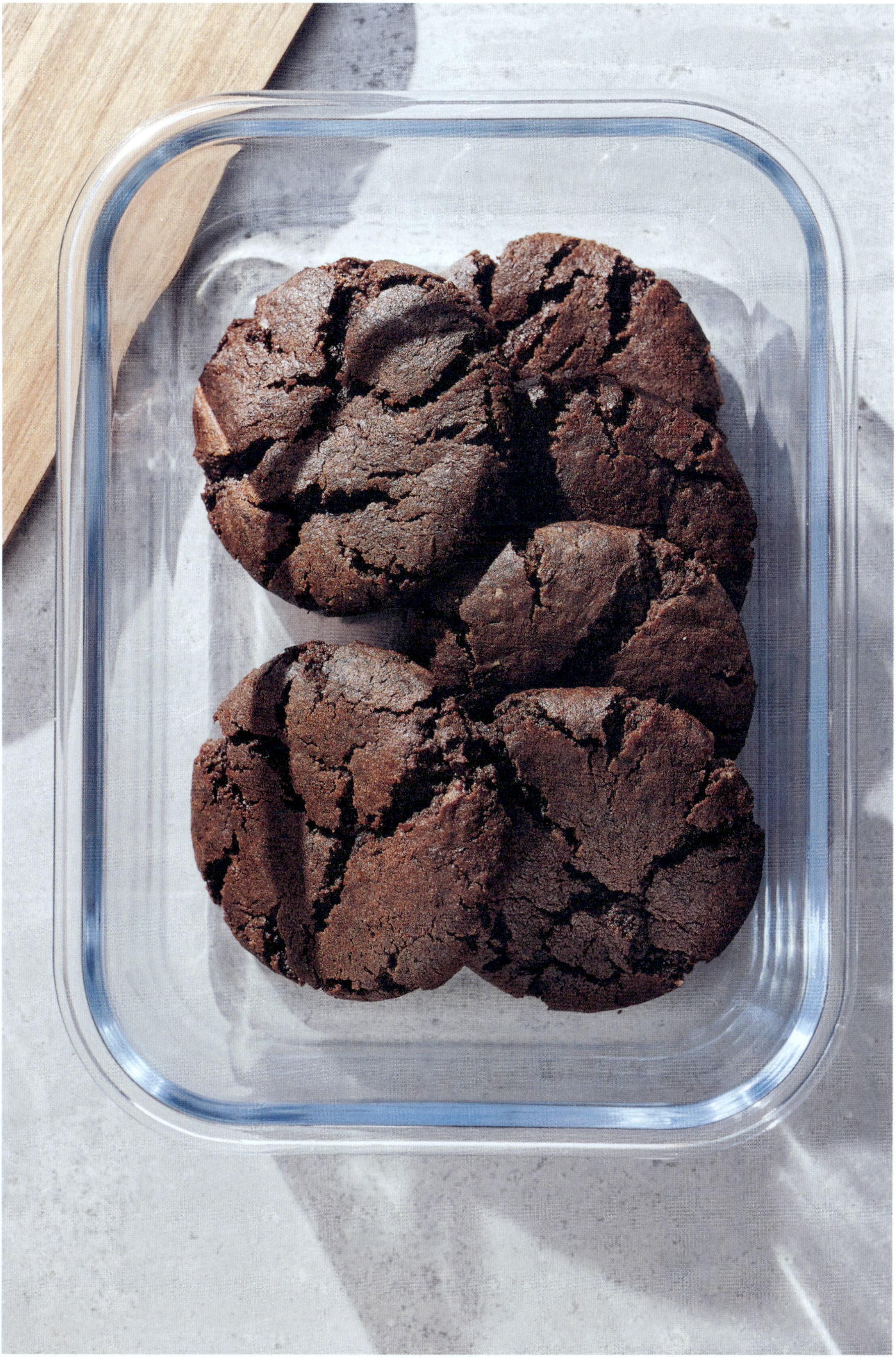

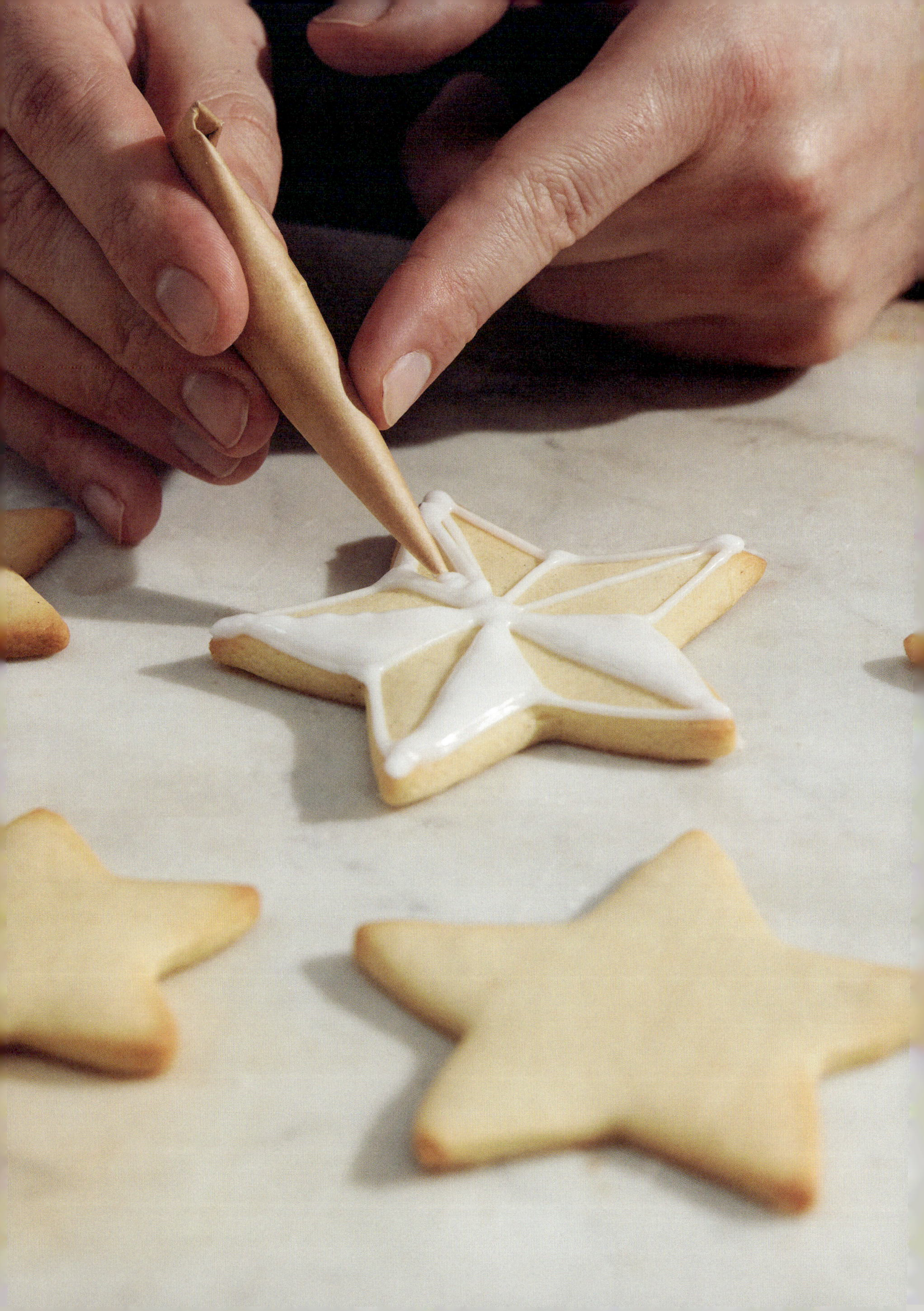

SUGAR COOKIES

Makes 20 cookies

A sugar cookie is a tender, sweet treat and the perfect base for iced (frosted) biscuits (cookies) which you can cut in any size and shape you desire. If cutting a small shape then bake for the shorter recommended time, and for larger shapes bake for the longer recommended time. These only need a quick bake to stay soft, puffy and pale.

SUGAR COOKIE DOUGH

1. Add the flour, baking powder and salt to a large bowl.
2. Add the melted coconut oil, milk, golden syrup, vanilla and sugar to a small blending jug and blend until creamy and pale. This is the syrup.
3. Pour the syrup into the dry ingredients and mix well with a silicone spatula until a dough forms. This can be done in a stand mixer fitted with a beater attachment for larger quantities.
4. Place the dough between two sheets of baking parchment and roll it out until it is 3–4 mm (⅛–⅙ in) thick or whatever thickness you desire, keeping in mind the dough does puff up very slightly. Transfer the sheet to a large baking sheet and leave to rest in the refrigerator for 15 minutes. Preheat the oven to 160°C fan (325°F/gas 3) when ready to bake. Line a large baking sheet with baking parchment or a silicone mat.
5. Using sharp cutters (I recommend steel ones for a sharp clean cut), cut out the cookies, then carefully pick up each cookie and arrange on the lined baking sheet. Bake for just 6–8 minutes – the paler the better as it produces a soft, melt-in-the-mouth texture. If this cookie is golden it will have a crunchy snap to it! Transfer to a wire rack to cool before icing (frosting).

plain (all-purpose) flour	270 g	9.5 oz
baking powder	5 g	1¼ tsp
salt	1 g	¼ tsp
coconut oil (deodorised), melted	60 g	2.1 oz
plant-based milk	60 g	2.1 oz
golden (or agave) syrup	50 g	1.8 oz
vanilla extract	4 g	1 tsp
caster (superfine) sugar	100 g	3.5 oz

ROYAL ICING

6. Mix all the ingredients in a stand mixer fitted with a whisk attachment on low speed until everything is combined. You can do this by hand to avoid a cloud of sugar dust.
7. Once the mixture resembles a paste, increase the speed to high and whisk until it is a thick pipeable consistency.
8. Spoon into a piping (pastry) bag fitted with a very small size piping nozzle or tip, and pipe desired patterns onto your cookies.
9. Leave the iced biscuits for 2 hours until the icing hardens. Store the iced and un-iced cookies in an airtight container for up to a week.

icing (confectioners') sugar	400 g	14.1 oz
aquafaba, reduced in half (page 30)	50 g	1.8 oz
vinegar, any type	5 g	1 tsp
cream of tartar	3 g	¾ tsp

TIP

Silicone mats are great for this type of cookie because they insulate from the heat of the steel baking sheet and keep the cookies pale and soft.

Make sure to keep your icing covered by a moist tea towel (dish towel) to avoid it drying out in contact with the air, otherwise it will start to create a crust.

BISCUITS AND COOKIES

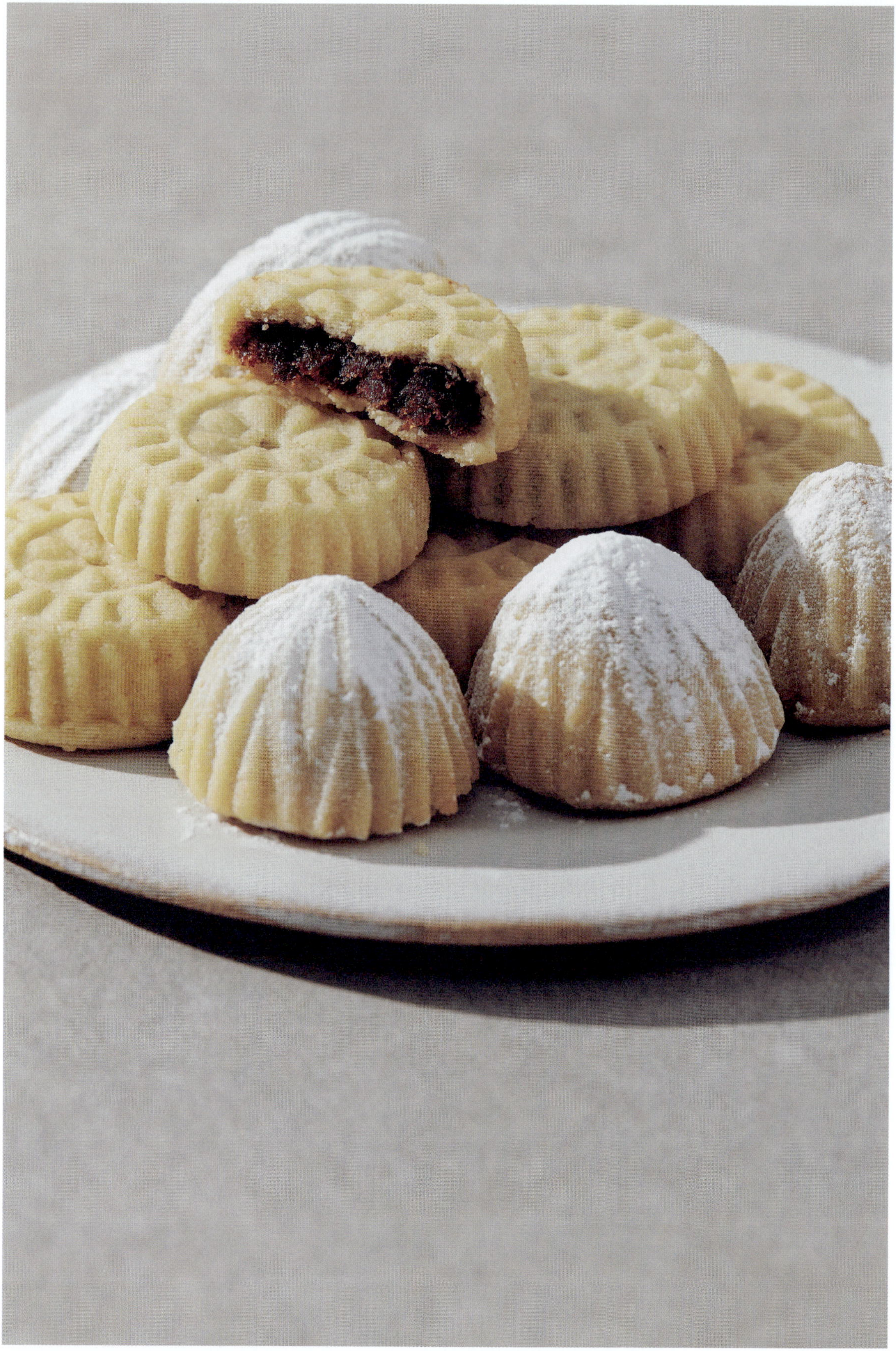

MAAMOUL

Makes 20 cookies

Maamoul is famous throughout the Middle East. It is a semolina cookie encasing a sweet date paste or crushed nuts, and they are often scented with orange blossom water or rose water but more traditionally with mahleb made from the seeds of the St Lucy cherry stone, akin to the flavour of bitter almond. I love that, though they are now commonly served all year around, they show the incredible way that food transcends religion – in a region where conflict has been a constant, this treat is enjoyed by the three major religions at Easter, Ramadan and Purim. If only we could celebrate more what we have in common rather than be divided by things that we don't. Seek out a specific maamoul mould which is similar to a mooncake mould. They were traditionally made by carving a medallion shape into a small wooden paddle, but nowadays many are just made from heavy plastic. The moulds are available online and at Middle Eastern grocery stores.

SEMOLINA BISCUIT DOUGH

1. Add the fine semolina, flour and baking powder in a bowl.

2. Add the caster sugar, melted coconut oil, extra virgin olive oil, orange blossom water, rose water and milk in another bowl and use a balloon whisk to whisk very well. Add the liquids to the flour mixture and mix with a silicone spoon until a dough forms. Wrap the dough in cling film (plastic wrap) and leave to chill in the refrigerator for 30 minutes.

3. Preheat the oven to 200°C fan (390°F/gas 6).

fine semolina	220 g	7.8 oz
plain (all-purpose) flour	45 g	1.6 oz
baking powder	1 g	¼ tsp
caster (superfine) sugar	65 g	2.3 oz
coconut oil (deodorised), melted	80 g	2.8 oz
extra virgin olive oil	20 g	0.7 oz
orange blossom water	15 g	0.5 oz
rose water	4 g	1 tsp
plant-based milk, room temperature	70 g	2½ oz

NUT FILLING

4. Pulse all the ingredients together in a food processor until it comes together, but retains nice chunks of nuts. I like to premould by filling it halfway and tapping it out before wrapping in dough.

pistachios or walnuts	150 g	5.3 oz
caster (superfine) sugar	60 g	2.1 oz
orange blossom water	30 g	1.1 oz
icing (confectioners') sugar	for dusting	

DATE FILLING

5. Pulse the dates and orange blossom water in a food processor to a paste. You can lightly oil your hands and then roll the filling into balls, about 15 g (¾ oz) and 1.5 cm (⅜ in) in diameter.

Medjool dates, pitted	200 g	7 oz
orange blossom water	20 g	0.7 oz
oil (optional)	for greasing	

TO ASSEMBLE AND BAKE

6. Cut the chilled dough into 25 g (1 oz) pieces and press into discs with your hands. Place each filling inside and wrap the dough around it to fully encase it.

7. Press the ball of dough into the mould, then tap it out with a swift movement against the work surface.

8. Arrange the cookies on a large baking sheet and bake for approximately 10–12 minutes until the bottom edges are golden. Be careful not to overbake the cookies as this can cause them to be tough and crack open.

9. Leave the date-filled cookies plain (they're sweet enough!) and dust the nut-filled maamoul with icing sugar.

NOTE
Mould sizes do vary. It's recommended that you test the fillings to test the quantities for size.

BISCUITS AND COOKIES

ALMOND AMARETTI

Makes 15–20 small amaretti

Raw almonds give these chewy, marzipany, Italian-inspired morsels a distinctive almond flavour. You are welcome to add a couple of drops of almond extract (especially if you choose to use ground almond meal and oat flour and forgo using a food processor). I like to use up scraped dried vanilla pods I have lying around in this recipe where all the dry ingredients are blitzed to a fine powder before the addition of some water forms a rich dough. I recommend rolling in an Amarena or glacé cherry for extra nostalgic decadence.

1. Preheat the oven to 200°C fan (392°F/gas 5) and line a baking sheet with parchment paper.

2. Place the almonds, caster sugar, rolled oats, baking powder and scraped vanilla pod in a food processor. Pulse to a fine powder, then add the water and pulse until it starts to clump or come together.

3. If making plain amaretti, weigh 25 g (0.9 oz) pieces and roll into balls, coating in icing sugar before placing on a tray 2.5 cm (1 in) apart.

4. If making a cherry-filled amaretti, weigh 20 g (0.7 oz) pieces. Roll the dough around each cherry by pressing it with your thumb, then pinch the dough together and roll until round. Then roll in icing sugar (make sure your fingers are dry) and place on the baking sheet 2.5 cm (1 in) apart.

TO FINISH

5. Bake the amaretti for about 8–10 minutes until they have become crackly and taken on a light golden hue – the plain amaretti will be flatter and the cherry-filled ones a bit rounder.

6. Remove from the oven and allow to cool completely. Store in a sealed container for up to a week.

raw almonds	200 g	7 oz
caster (superfine) sugar	125 g	4.4 oz
rolled oats	45 g	1.6 oz
baking powder	2 g	½ tsp
vanilla pod, leftover dried (optional)	1 pod	
water	40 g	1.4 oz

ALSO NEEDED

Amarena cherries in syrup, drained, or high-quality glacé cherries (optional)	approx. 20 cherries
icing (confectioners') sugar	for rolling

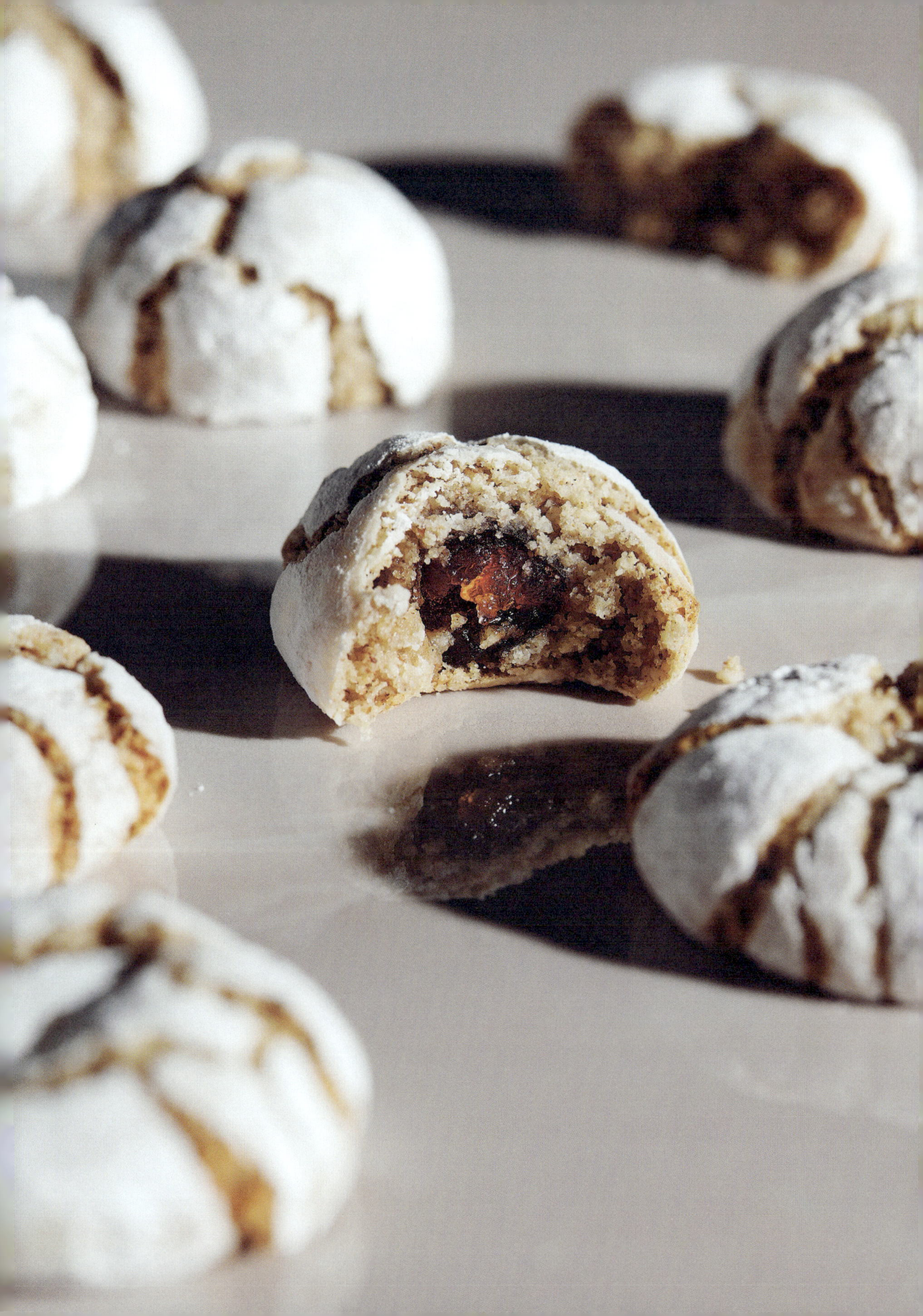

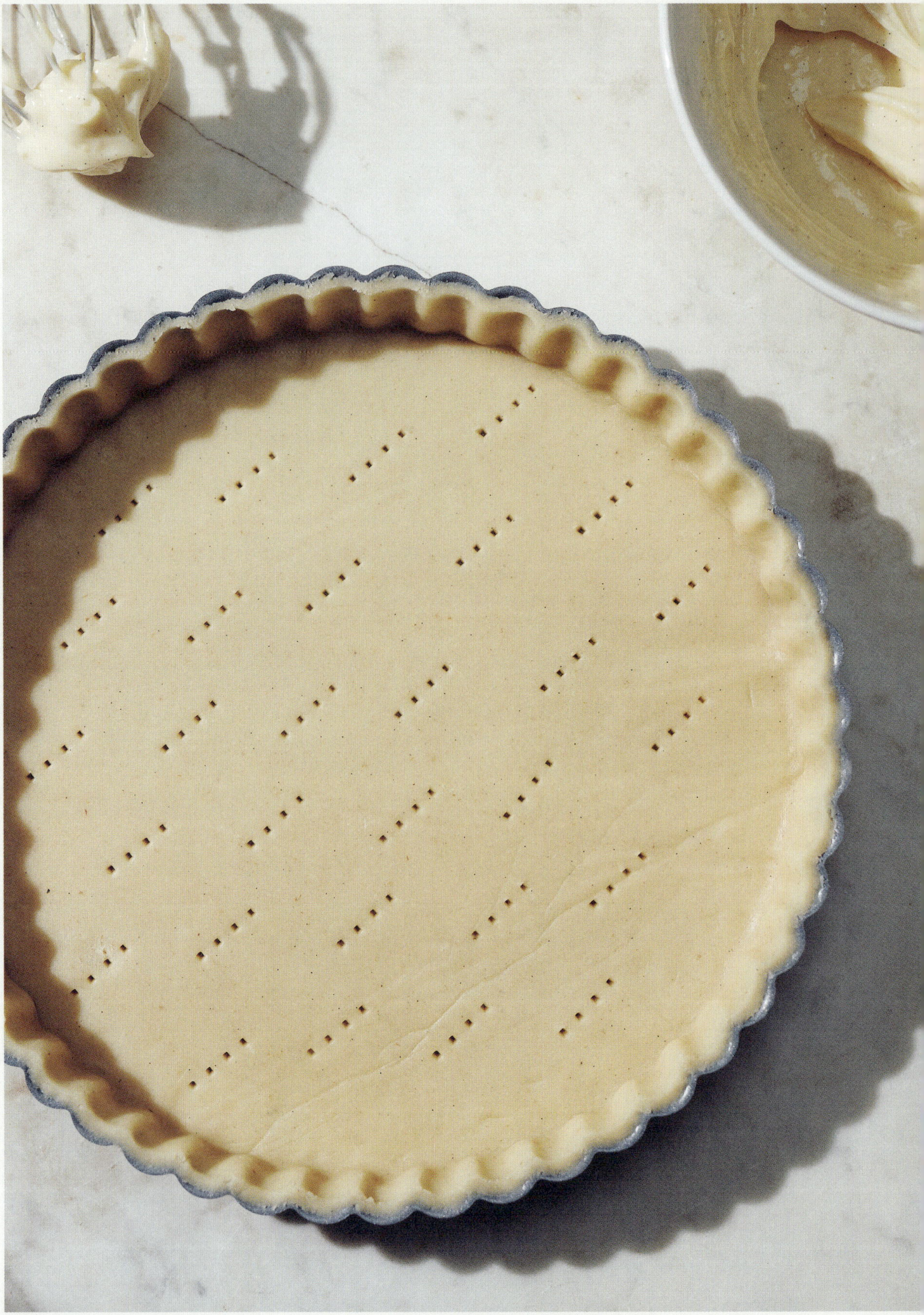

3 TARTS AND PIES

Trying to define the difference between tarts and pies will be impossible – depending on which country you're from will provide different answers. Some will say a tart is a pie if it can be removed from the dish it was baked in – others will put them all into the same if-it-has-a-base-it's-a-pie camp, while others will try to tell you that pies have a thinner crust than tarts.

I like to remove all my tarts or pies from the dish they were baked in so they can be neatly sliced and served, but that is probably the pâtissier in me coming out. Whatever you think it should be called, I promise I won't mind so long as you love to make and eat it! Ranging from rustic to fine, these tarts provide a range of culinary experiences most will know and love.

In the basics section, you'll find recipes for three pastries. These mostly form the basis for the tarts and pies. They're made with virgin or cold pressed oils, and they made me question how I thought butter worked in traditional shortcrust. You'll be surprised how easily they come together. They will be softer but I will share a tip for how to handle them easily.

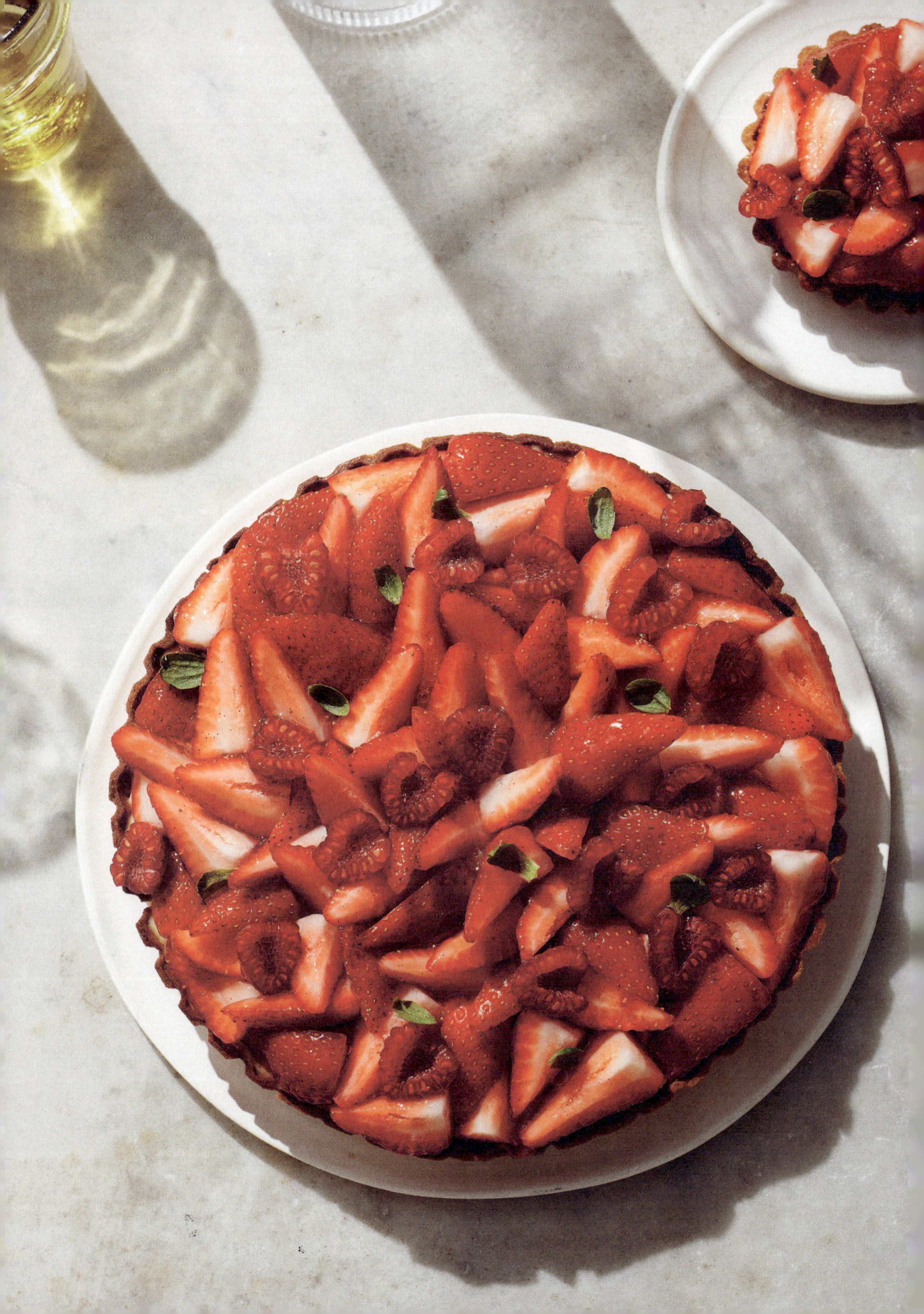

RED BERRY TART

Makes a 23 cm (9 in) tart or 8 individual tartlets

I never fully appreciated berries until I tried them in their prime as the weather warmed in the UK. They became a summer staple in my refrigerator, and this fruit tart celebrates them in a few ways. Fragrant strawberries are nestled on top of a luscious vanilla crème pâtissière, atop jammy strawberries that have been baked into almond frangipane, with a well-baked sweet vanilla tart case lathered with sweet berry jam and decorated with strawberries and raspberries.

ALMOND FRANGIPANE CREAM

1. In a food processor or high-powered blender, pulse the almonds, sugar and cornflour. Add the remaining ingredients and pulse to combine until it is a creamy texture. Set aside.

raw almonds	150 g	5.3 oz
caster (superfine) sugar	100 g	3.5 oz
cornflour (cornstarch)	20 g	0.7 oz
plant-based milk	90 g	3.2 oz
extra virgin olive oil	20 g	0.7 oz
plain (all-purpose) flour	20 g	0.7 oz
baking powder	4 g	1 tsp
vanilla bean paste	5 g	1 tsp
lemon zest		¼ lemon

BERRY JAM

2. Mix the sugar and agar-agar powder together in a small bowl, then add to a large saucepan with the remaining jam ingredients and heat over a low heat. A syrup will start to form after 2 minutes. Continue cooking and the berries will become soupy, then continue simmering for about 5 minutes until the strawberries are cooked through.

3. Pour the jam into a shallow bowl and leave to chill in the refrigerator for 30 minutes, or until set. Whisk the cooled jam to break it down into a soft spoonable texture before using.

caster (superfine) sugar	100 g	3.5 oz
agar-agar powder	2 g	½ tsp
strawberries, trimmed and quartered	200 g	7 oz
raspberries	60 g	2 oz
lemon juice	20 g	0.7 oz

TO ASSEMBLE AND BAKE

4. Make the pastry following the instructions on page 230 and use to line a 23 cm (9 in) tart case. Prebake following the instructions until golden, then remove from the oven and leave to cool.

5. Keep the oven on. Pipe the frangipane into the base of the prebaked tart case and press some of the raspberries around the frangipane. Bake for 18–20 minutes, or 8–10 minutes for small tarts, until lightly golden on top and set when pressed gently. Remove from the oven and leave to cool completely on a wire rack.

6. Pipe the crème pâtissière into the tart on top of the frangipane to fill to the top.

7. Pipe some of the berry jam into the crème pât, then use a small offset palette knife to spread the top smooth.

8. Arrange the strawberries on top, making sure to fill any gaps. Add the exotic clear glaze to a microwave-safe bowl and microwave in short bursts until melted. Alternatively, melt in a small saucepan over a low heat until it is liquid, then leave to cool for 5–6 minutes until thick and about 60°C (140°F) on a thermometer. Use a dabbing motion to generously coat the strawberries with the glaze. This helps protect the cut fruit and keeps them in place.

9. Add the remaining raspberries afterwards as they tend to be too delicate to be glazed, then decorate with baby mint. The baked tart with frangipane can be prepared and kept at room temperature for up to 4 days. The crème pâtissière and jam can be prepared in advance and kept separate. Once the tart is assembled it is best consumed on the same day.

ALSO NEEDED

Short Sweet Pastry (page 230)	400 g	14.1 oz
raspberries	125 g	4.4 oz
Crème Pâtissière (page 235)	200 g	7 oz
strawberries, hulled and halved	250 g	8.8 oz
Exotic Clear Glaze (page 239)	60 g	2 oz
baby mint leaves or sprigs from regular mint	for decorating	

VARIATION

You can also use this recipe to make 8 patisserie-sized tartlets. This recipe is also a great foundation for different seasonal fruit tarts. Swap the fruits entirely.

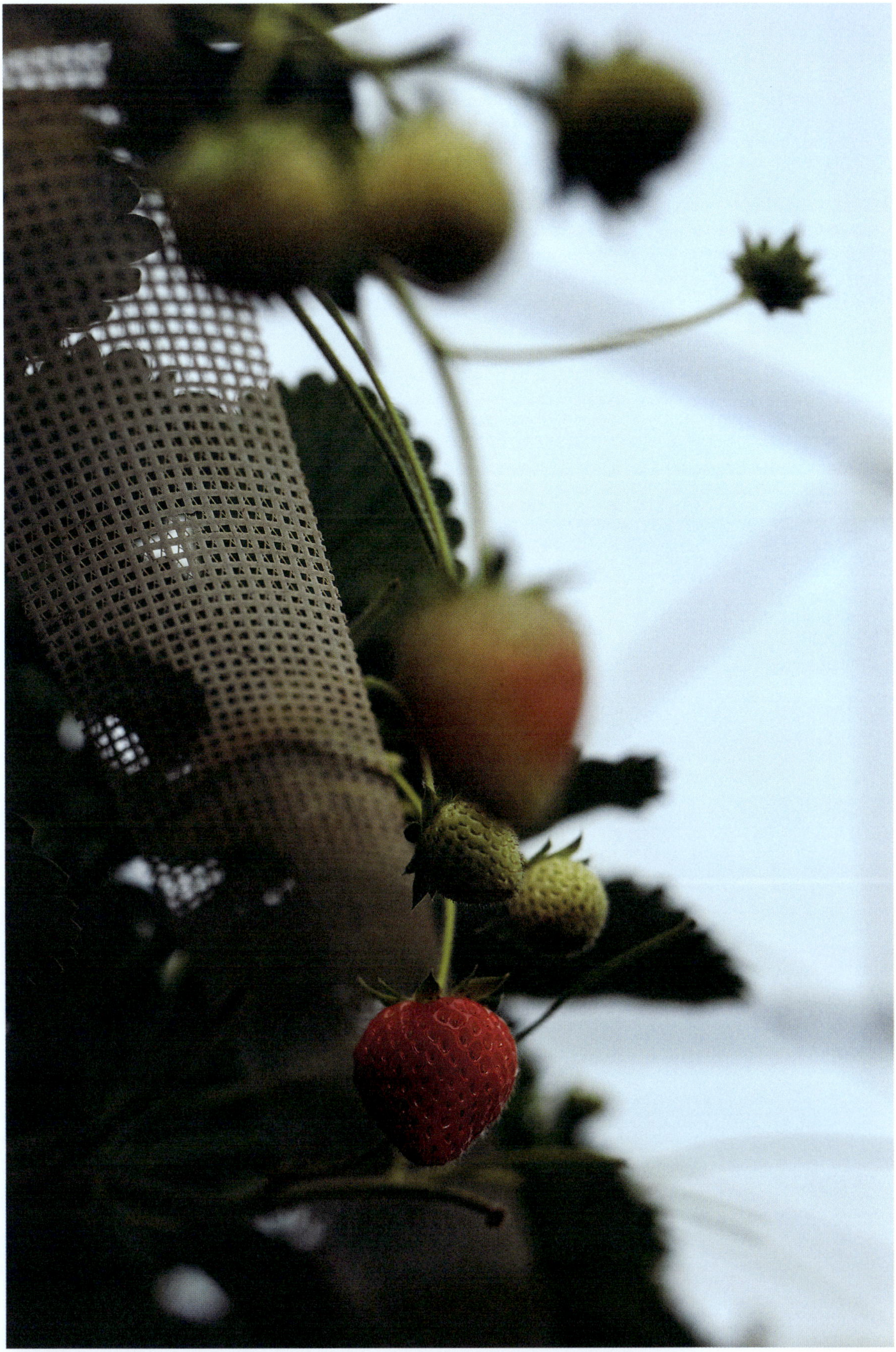

APPLE PIE

Makes a 23 cm (9 in) pie

There's something celebratory about pies. They take a bit of effort to make compared to say a modest crumble that has similar components but is assembled more haphazardly. The humble apple pie is a celebration of time well spent, honouring the people who are destined to enjoy it. More effort can be spent to make a lattice crust but avoid overdecorating with pastry. I've kept it simple. The process here is relatively straightforward and includes a small trick for keeping the apple peels in the pie – a short maceration, making the pastry, then assembling the pie ahead of baking. Using thin, raw slices of apples allows the fruit to have some bite in the middle but be jammy and soft around the edges.

APPLE PIE FILLING

1. Wash the apples well, then peel and core (compost or discard these), but keep the peels and add them to a small powerful blender and finely chop. Alternatively, finely chop by hand and reserve.

   TIP 1 kg (2 lb 4 oz) of apples contains 100 g (3½ oz) of skin. Apple skins contain significant levels of vitamins and minerals that are lower or almost non-existent in apple flesh. In fact, a raw apple with skin contains up to 312 per cent more vitamin K, 70 per cent more vitamin A, 35 per cent more calcium and potassium, and 30 per cent more vitamin C than a peeled apple.

2. Using a sharp knife, cut the apples into 2 mm (1/16 in) thick slices, or use a mandoline.

   TIP When using a mandoline, please be careful and always work slowly. As you near the end of cutting a fruit, use a guard and concentrate to avoid injury. I know all too well the perils of a mandoline but still recommend them.

3. Add the sliced apples to a large bowl with the sugar, cinnamon, vanilla, lemon juice, zest and cornflour and gently toss the apples until everything is properly combined. Leave to stand for 20 minutes to macerate – this will draw some moisture out of the apples.

apples	1 kg	2 lb 4 oz
caster (superfine) sugar	120 g	4.2 oz
ground cinnamon	5 g	2 tsp
vanilla bean paste	5 g	1 tsp
lemon juice	15 g	0.5 oz
lemon zest	3 turns	
cornflour (cornstarch)	28 g	1 oz

TO ASSEMBLE AND BAKE

4. Preheat the oven to 180°C fan (350°F/gas 4) with a baking rack in the bottom quarter of the oven.

5. Make the pastry following the instructions on page 231 and use to line a 23 cm (9 in) tart case.

6. Roll out two-thirds of the pastry between two sheets of baking parchment into a large disc, about 30 cm (12 in) in diameter and about 3–4 mm (1/8–1/6 in) thick. Roll out the remaining pastry into a 25 cm (10 in) disc and 3 mm (1/8 in) thick.

7. You can remove the top sheet of baking parchment and use the bottom sheet to help flip it over into the dish, if you like. Gently press the larger disc of pastry into a 23 cm (9 in) pie or quiche dish with a tiny overhang.

   TIP I always recommend using metal pie dishes because they conduct heat much faster (than ceramic or glass ones) to ensure the pastry is baked through and you avoid the dreaded soggy bottom.

ALSO NEEDED

Flaky Pastry (page 231)	600 g	1 lb 5 oz
Baking Glaze (page 239)	30 g	1.1 oz
Demerara sugar	for sprinkling	

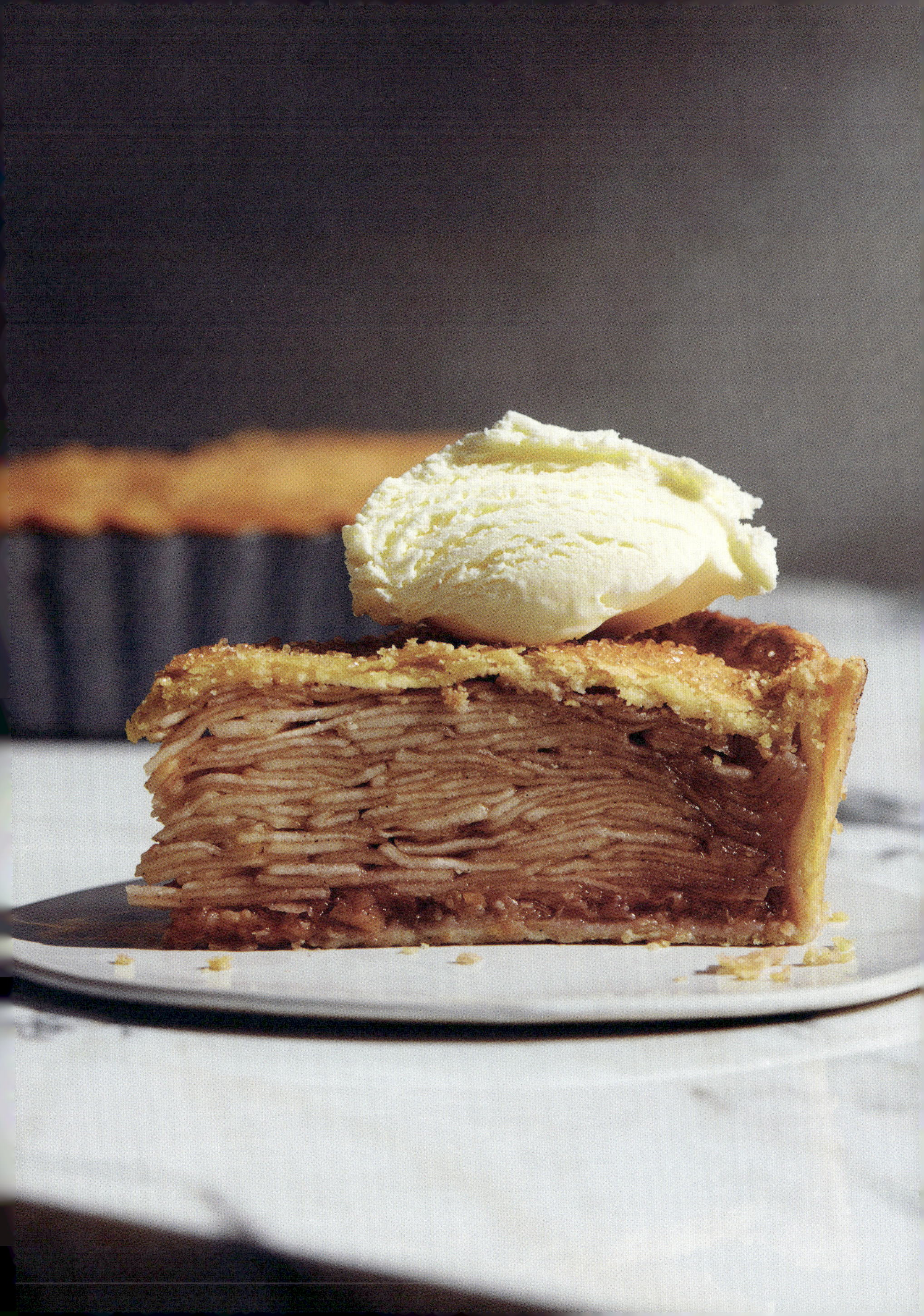

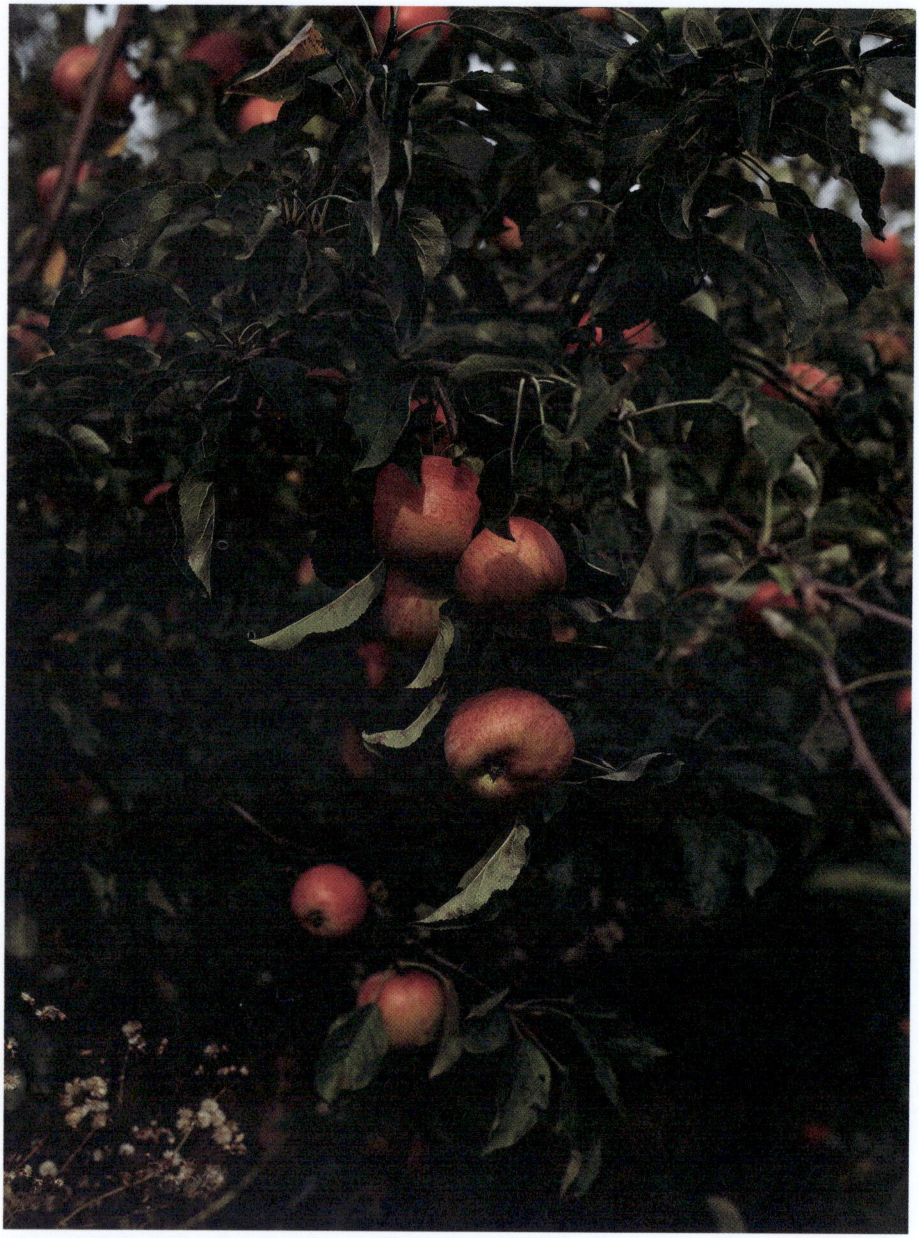

8. Arrange the finely chopped apple peels on the pastry base, then gently layer the sliced apples on top, stacking to fill all the gaps. There will be some liquid leftover from the apples, so stir to agitate any settled cornflour and drizzle it slowly over the pie. You can push the apples into a slight domed shape, if you like.

9. Brush the overhanging edge of the pie crust with water, then place the top disc of pastry over the apples and press the edges together. Trim and crimp the edges as you like.

10. Brush the baking glaze across the top of the pastry and sprinkle some Demerara sugar on top for a tantalising crunch.

11. Using a sharp knife, cut some steam holes – I like one in the centre then six in a little burst radiating from it. This reminds me of the cross-section of an apple when it's cut in half across the equator.

12. Bake for 20 minutes, then rotate and bake for another 20–25 minutes, until golden all the way across.

13. Remove from the oven and leave to stand for at least 15 minutes. Serve warm with a scoop of ice cream or pouring cream. It keeps well in a sealed container in the refrigerator for up to 4 days. I like to slice mine once cooled completely from the refrigerator to get a nice clean cut, then reheat slices in the oven or microwave.

NOTE
If you make the full quantity of the Baking Glaze, you can freeze it in an ice-cube tray, and store frozen, then defrost it in a small ramekin or bowl as needed.

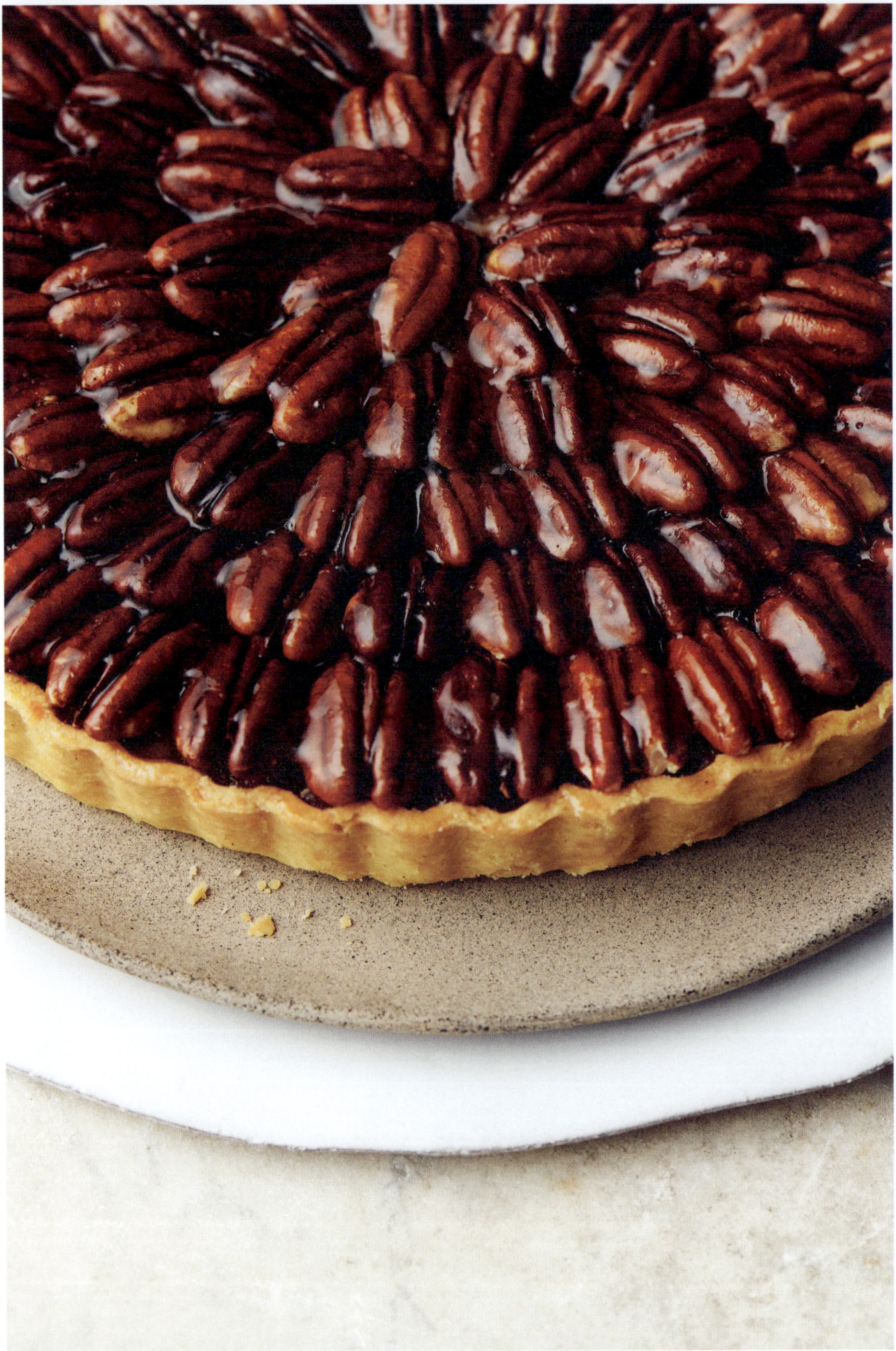

PECAN PIE

Makes a 23 cm (9 in) pie or 8 individual tartlets

This is a classic American pie. A rich and treacly filling surrounds toasted pecans for an autumnal (fall) favourite. I used unsweetened flaky pastry for this recipe as there's plenty of sugary goodness in the filling. Don't be alarmed by the sugar – the original has even more!

PIE CRUST

1. Preheat the oven to 180°C fan (350°F/gas 4) with an oven shelf in the middle of the oven. Make the pastry following the instructions on page 231 and use to line a 23 cm (9 in) tart case.
2. Roll out the pastry between two sheets of baking parchment into a large 30 cm (12 in) disc, about 3–4 mm (⅛–⅙ in) thick.
3. You can remove the top sheet of baking parchment and use the bottom sheet to help flip it over into the dish, if you like. Gently press the pastry into a 23 cm (9 in) pie or quiche dish with a tiny overhang.
4. Scrunch up one of the sheets of baking parchment and press it over the pastry, then fill with rice or baking beans to weigh down the pastry.
5. Bake in the oven for 18–20 minutes until cooked through. Remove the paper and rice and bake for another 10 minutes, or until the pastry is golden and cooked through. If the edges brown too quickly cover with kitchen foil.
6. Remove from the oven and leave to cool slightly while you prepare the filling.

TREACLE FILLING

7. Reduce the oven temperature to 160°C fan (325°F/gas 3). Spread the pecans out on a large baking sheet and roast in the oven for 10 minutes, or until they crisp up and take on some colour (and flavour!). Remove from the oven and set aside.
8. Add all the filling ingredients, except the 200 g (7 oz) of roasted pecans, to a blender or use a hand-held blender in a large bowl to pulse together until smooth. Fold in the pecans, then pour the filling into the prebaked pie crust. Bake in the oven for 30–35 minutes until the centre is just set.
9. Remove from the oven and leave to cool completely.
10. Place concentric rounds of 150 g (5.3 oz) of roasted pecans on top of the pie for decoration and extra crunch.
11. Melt the clear glaze in the microwave in short bursts or in a small saucepan over a low heat until liquid, then brush over the pecans to fix them to the top of the pie.
12. Dust icing sugar around the edges, if you like. Serve once cooled to room temperature with vanilla ice cream, or gently warm, if you like. This pie keeps well in a sealed container in the refrigerator for up to 4 days.

Flaky Pastry (page 231)	400 g	14.1 oz

pecans	200 g	7 oz
silken tofu	225 g	7.9 oz
cornflour (cornstarch)	15 g	0.5 oz
plain (all-purpose) flour	5 g	1 tsp
coconut oil (deodorised)	15 g	0.5 oz
brown or muscovado sugar	160 g	5.6 oz
maple syrup	60 g	2 oz
sea salt	1 g	¼ tsp
vanilla extract	5 g	1 tsp

ALSO NEEDED

pecans, roasted	150 g	5.3 oz
Exotic Clear Glaze (page 239)	60 g	2 oz
icing (confectioners') sugar (optional)		for dusting

TIP

Toast the pecans for the decoration in the same way as for the filling. You can roast them at the same time.

CHOCOLATE GANACHE TART

A fine simple treat. Devilishly simple and decadent.

Makes a 23 cm (9 in) pie or 8 individual tartlets

TART CASE

Short Sweet Pastry (page 230), with added cocoa variation	400 g	14.1 oz

1. Preheat the oven to 180°C fan (350°F/gas 4) with an oven shelf in the middle of the oven. Make the pastry following the instructions on page 200 and use to line a 23 cm (9 in) tart case.

2. Roll out the pastry between two sheets of baking parchment into a large 30 cm (12 in) disc, about 3–4 mm (⅛–⅙ in) thick.

3. You can remove the top sheet of baking parchment and use the bottom sheet to help flip it over into the dish, if you like. Gently press the pastry into a 23 cm (9 in) fluted tin (pan) with a removable base. For this tart, the ganache filling is quite rich so it shouldn't be too tall. Use a fork to prick the bottom of the tart so you don't get air pockets and it bakes evenly.

4. Bake in the oven for 10–12 minutes until cooked through and slightly puffed. It will be hard to tell from the colour, but if baked too long the pastry will be too crispy.

5. Remove from the oven and leave to cool completely before you prepare the filling.

CHOCOLATE FILLING

plant-based milk	450 g	15.9 oz
cornflour (cornstarch)	20 g	0.7 oz
muscovado sugar	40 g	1.4 oz
dark chocolate with at least 70% cocoa solids, coarsely chopped	350 g	12.4 oz
sea salt		pinch

6. Pour a splash (about 50 g/2 oz) of milk into a small bowl with the cornflour. Mix until all the cornflour has dissolved.

7. Heat the remaining milk with muscovado sugar and bring to a simmer. Add a splash of the hot milk to the cornflour mixture. Return everything to a low heat and stir with a silicone spatula, constantly, cooking until thick and coats the back of the spoon.

8. Add the chocolate and use a hand-blender to blend everything really well. Everything needs to be glossy and smooth. Make sure to scrape the saucepan in between.

9. Pour into the middle of the prebaked tart case. Smooth until levelled, using minimal movements.

10. Leave to chill in the refrigerator for 1 hour, until set. Remove from the refrigerator and serve at room temperature. Use a knife dipped in a tall jug (pitcher) of hot water to cut clean slices of the tart once it is set. This tart keeps well in a sealed container in the refrigerator for up to 2 days. Sprinkle with sea salt just before serving.

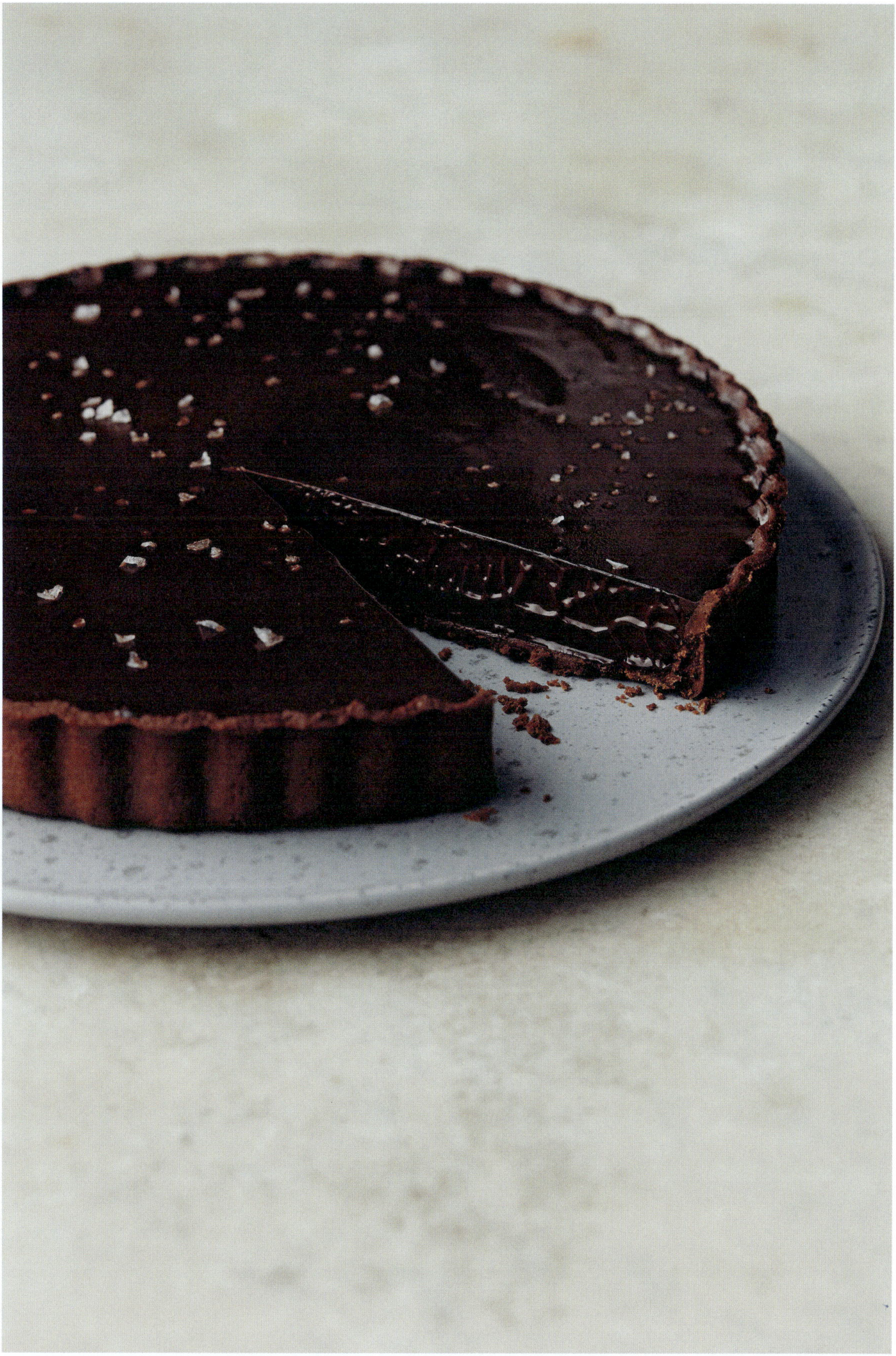

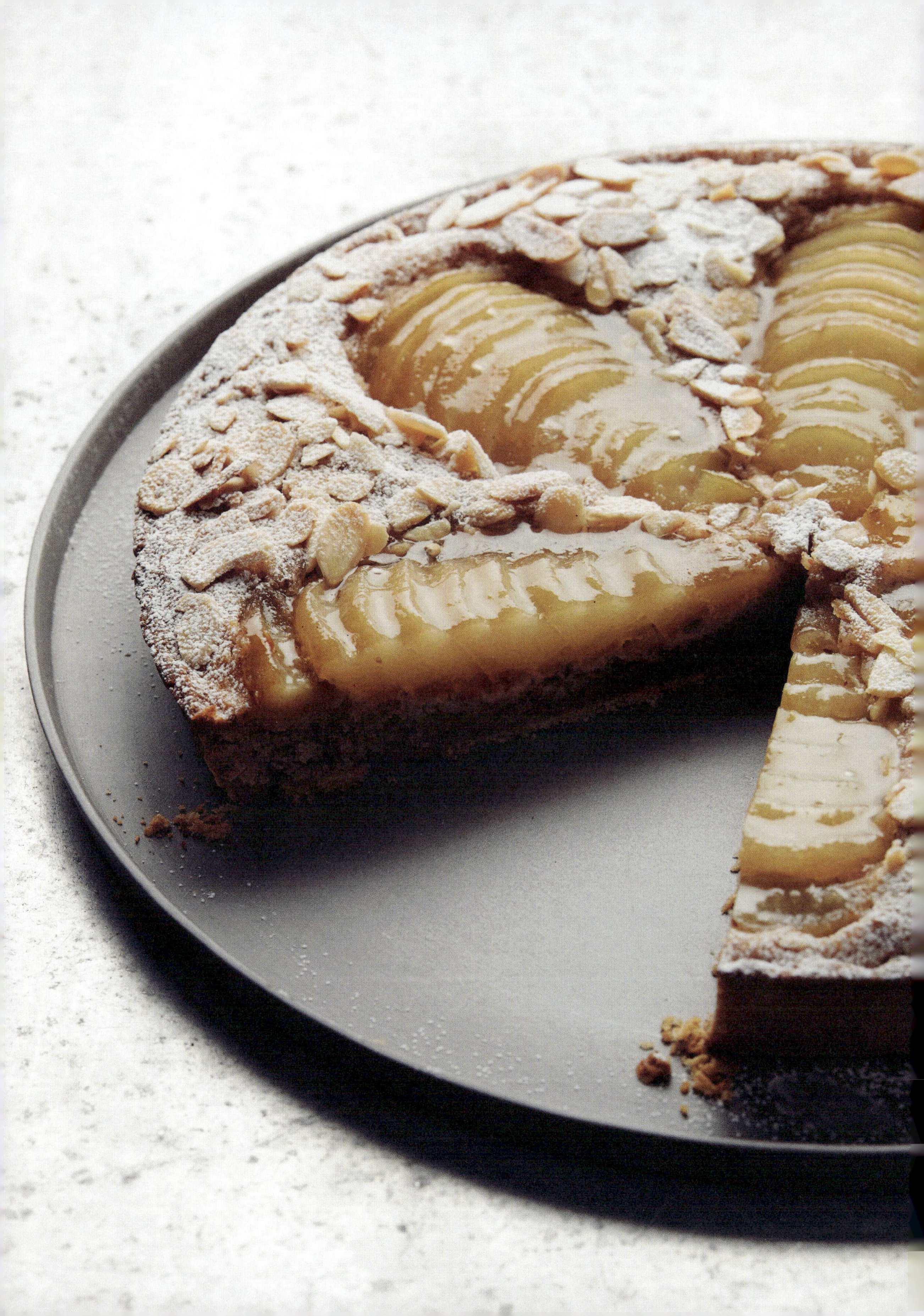

TARTE BORDALOUE

Makes a 23 cm (9 in) pie or 8 individual tartlets

Nothing says rustic French patisserie more than a pear and frangipane tart – the creamy, almond and vanilla-scented filling, flaky, well-baked pastry and cooked pears. Here I use my sweet pastry recipe and add ground almonds to the frangipane, then top with pears poached in an Earl Grey tea syrup.

EARL GREY POACHED PEARS

1. Peel the pears and cut them in half, removing the seeds.
2. Add the tea leaves to the boiling water in a heatproof bowl or jug and leave to infuse for 4 minutes, then strain into a large saucepan with the sugar and mix to dissolve. The sugar must be added after the infusion.
3. Bring to a simmer and add the pear halves. Poach for 8 minutes to start. Depending on the variety and size, it can take up to 18 minutes for very firm pears halves to cook through. They should still have some tenderness when done. Remove them from the poaching liquid with a slotted spoon and leave to drain and cool while you bake the pastry.

pears		3–4 pears
Earl Grey tea leaves	7 g	1.5 oz
water, boiling	500 g	1 lb 2 oz
caster (superfine) sugar	200 g	7 oz

FRANGIPANE CREAM

4. Pulse the almonds, sugar and cornflour in a food processor or high-powered blender. Add the remaining ingredients and pulse to combine – it will have a creamy texture. Scoop the frangipane into a piping (pastry) bag fitted with a 1 cm (½ in) plain piping tube, or cut a 1 cm (½ in) hole. Set aside.

raw almonds	150 g	5.3 oz
caster (superfine) sugar	100 g	3.5 oz
cornflour (cornstarch)	20 g	0.7 oz
plant-based milk	90 g	3.2 oz
extra virgin olive oil	20 g	0.7 oz
plain (all-purpose) flour	20 g	0.7 oz
baking powder	4 g	1 tsp
vanilla bean paste	5 g	1 tsp
lemon zest		¼ lemon

TO ASSEMBLE AND BAKE

5. To make the pastry, follow the instructions on page 230. Lightly flour a sheet of baking parchment. Press the pastry into a disc, then roll it out on the floured baking parchment until it is 3–4 mm (⅛–⅙ in) thick – the thinner the better but it will take some more skill. You want the pastry to be loose on the paper.
6. Slide the pastry over a 23 cm (9 in) tart case and gently start to press it down into the case. Work your way around the edges, pressing the pastry deeper into the corners and pricking the base with a fork.
7. Trim the top of the pastry, then chill in the freezer for 20 minutes. Preheat the oven to 170°C fan (325°F/gas 3).

ALSO NEEDED

Short Sweet Pastry (page 230)	400 g	14.1 oz
plain (all-purpose) flour		for dusting
flaked (slivered) almonds	30 g	1.1 oz
Exotic Clear Glaze (page 239) (optional)	50 g	1.8 oz
icing (confectioners') sugar		for dusting

TARTS AND PIES

8   Bake the pastry case in the oven for 10–12 minutes until puffed and only lightly golden. Remove from the oven and allow to cool. Pipe the frangipane cream into the tart case until it is halfway full.

9   Slice the pears into 3 mm (⅛ in) strips along the short length of the pear, then fan them out. Carefully lift them up with a palette knife to preserve the fanning and place them on the frangipane cream so that 5–6 halves fan out from the centre like a flower. Sprinkle some flaked almonds on the frangipane cream between the pears.

10 Bake the tart for 15–18 minutes until the frangipane is puffed and golden. Remove from the oven and leave to cool completely.

11 Brush the pears with the exotic clear glaze (if using), then dust icing sugar over the frangipane. This tart keeps well in the refrigerator for 4 days if it is well wrapped.

BANOFFEE PIE

Makes a 23 cm (9 in) pie

Use digestive biscuits (graham crackers) mixed with some dark chocolate and oil of your choice to soften it slightly to make the base, then fill with a caramel filling, followed by chunky slices of banana. Make sure your bananas are ripe and spotty – this will make sure the sweet banana aroma is present.

CHOCOLATE DIGESTIVE BASE

1. Use a food processor to pulse the biscuits to a crumb.
2. Melt the chocolate in a microwave-safe bowl in the microwave in 30-second bursts, stirring in between, or in a heatproof or stainless-steel bowl set over a pan filled with 1 cm (½ in) simmering water, stirring until melted. Mix in the oil and sea salt, followed by the digestive crumbs.
3. Pour the chocolate crumbs into a 23 cm (9 in) steel tart or pie case with removable base and press the mixture into the case with the back of a tablespoon. Leave to chill in the refrigerator to set.

digestive biscuits (graham crackers)	300 g	10.6 oz
dark chocolate with at least 70% cocoa solids, coarsely chopped	80 g	2.8 oz
peanut oil or cold-pressed sunflower oil	10 g	0.4 oz
sea salt	1 g	¼ tsp

CARAMEL CUSTARD

4. Add the sugar and water to a high-sided saucepan, making sure there is no sugar on the sides of pan, and bring to the boil over a medium-high heat.
5. Warm the soy milk (1) in another pan over a low heat until it is 60°C (140°F) on a thermometer.
6. Continue cooking the sugar syrup until it thickens and starts to colour (the time varies but it shouldn't take more than a few minutes), then reduce the heat while it caramelises. It will become a deeper golden colour quite quickly. Remove from the heat and carefully start whisking the hot milk into the caramel gradually in a stream until it is all incorporated. Be very careful as it will boil and spit.
7. Mix the remaining soy milk (2) and cornflour together in a small cup, then, while whisking, pour it into the caramel mixture. Return to the heat and cook, stirring constantly, until it thickens. Remove from the heat and add the vanilla, coconut oil and sea salt. Leave at room temperature in the pan to cool slightly, to 50°C (122°F). Whisk gently to start as the coconut oil will make the liquid slosh around. Gradually pick up speed and it will come together. Keep whisking until it is glossy and smooth and it sticks to the side of the pan.
8. Using a silicone spatula, scrape the caramel custard into the chocolate digestive-lined base. Spread gently to level. The base and caramel filling can be prepared the day before, but it should be served the same day that it is finished with the bananas and cream.

caster (superfine) sugar	225 g	7.9 oz
water	50 g	1.8 oz
soy milk (1)	375 g	13.2 oz
soy milk (2)	75 g	2.7 oz
cornflour (cornstarch)	40 g	1.4 oz
vanilla bean paste	8 g	2 tsp
coconut oil (deodorised)	50 g	1.8 oz
sea salt	2 g	½ tsp

TO ASSEMBLE

9. Slice the bananas and layer them all over the custard.

10. Whip the cream in a stand mixer fitted with whisk attachment to medium peaks, then dollop on top of the fresh banana.

11. Use a vegetable peeler to shave chocolate over the cream, then leave to chill in the refrigerator for 30 minutes to set a little further. Place the tart case on top of a small dish to help push the base upwards to remove it from the tin and place the tart on a serving dish. Serve chilled on the same day it is made.

ALSO NEEDED

bananas, ripe	4–5 bananas
Fresh Whipping Cream (page 236)	300 g 10.6 oz
dark chocolate block with at least 70% cocoa solids or cocoa powder	for serving

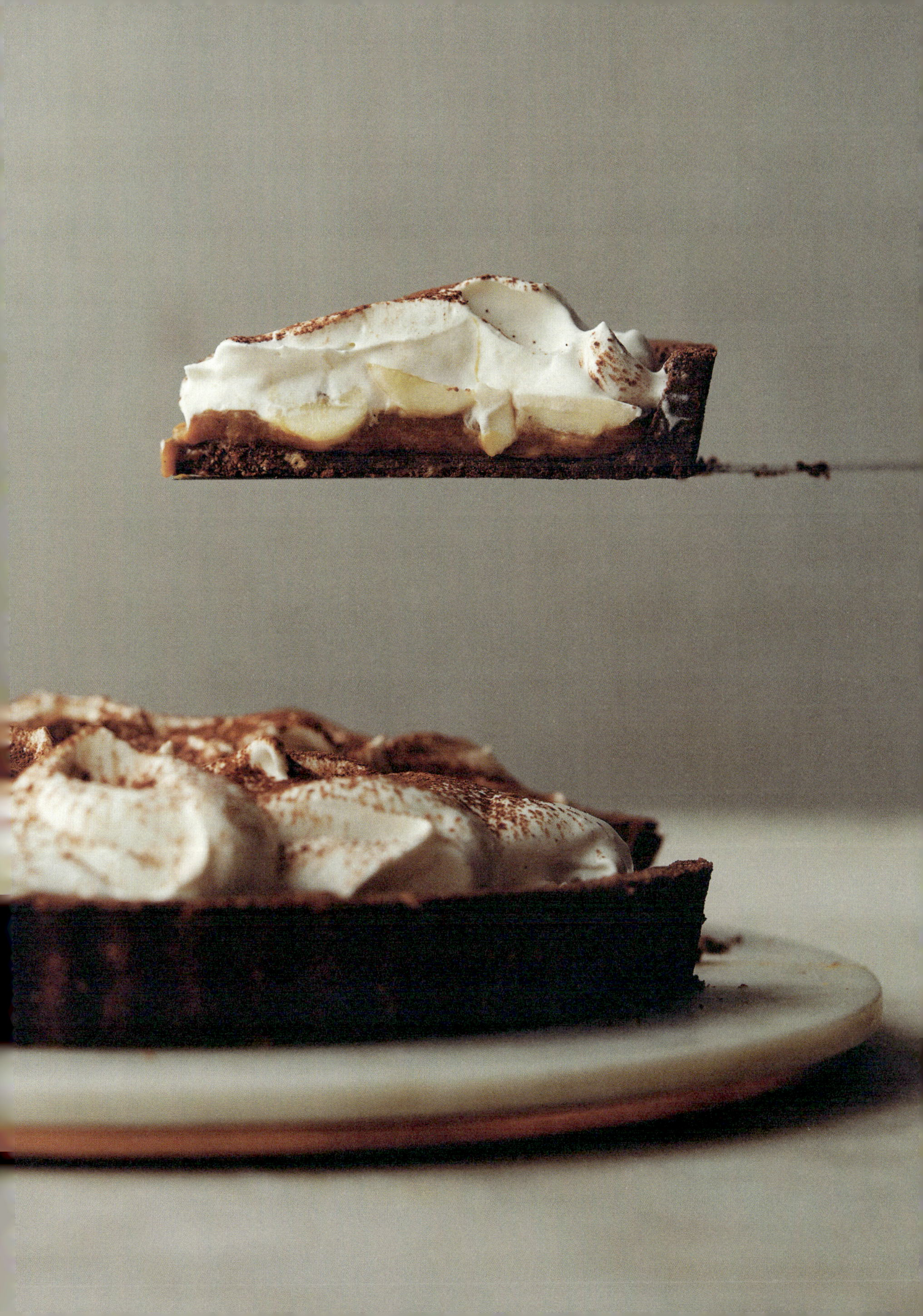

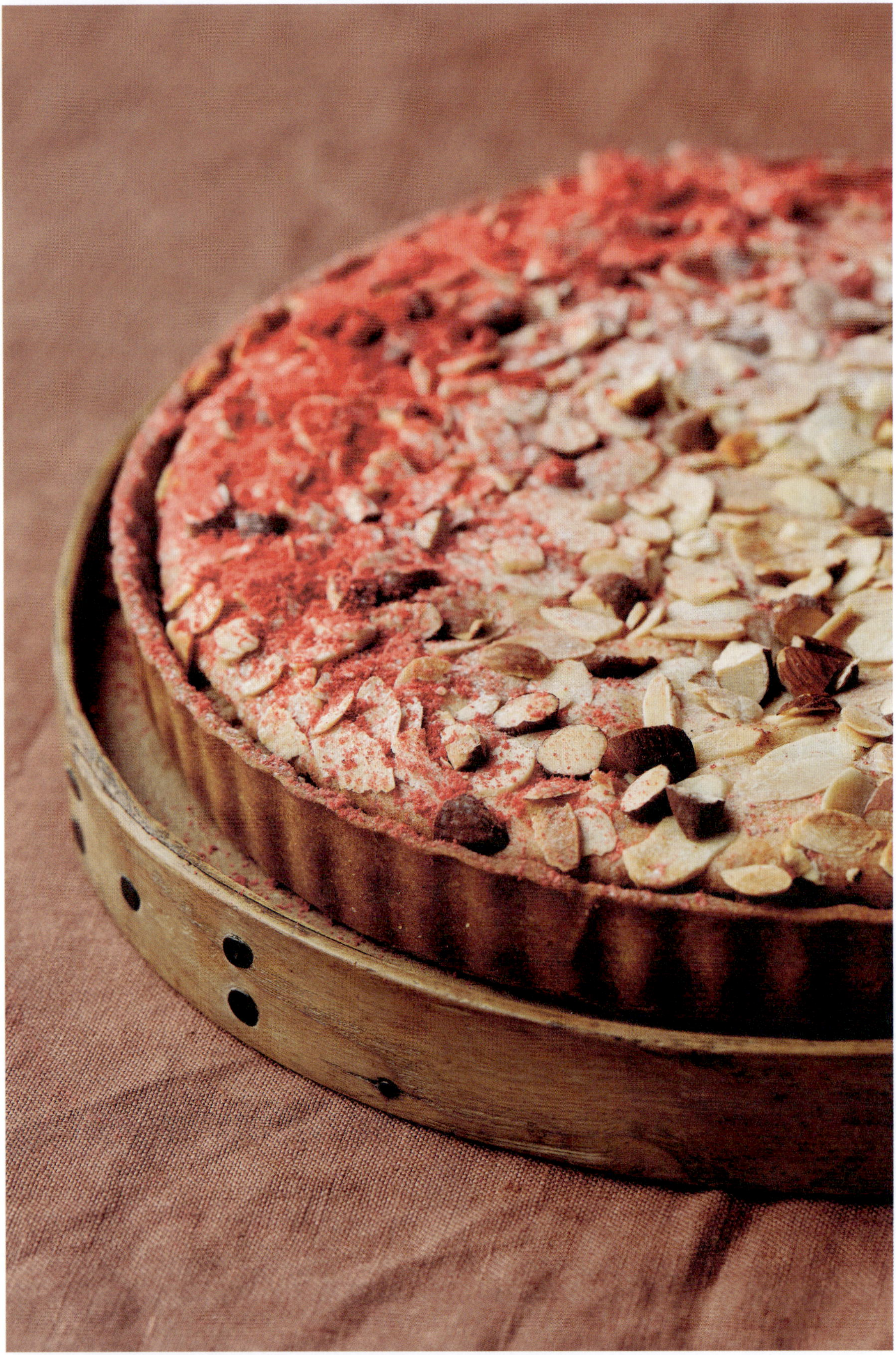

BAKEWELL TART

Makes a 23 cm (9 in) pie or 8 individual tartlets

I once visited the town of Bakewell to seek out the original tart that has become legendary, only to be very disappointed that not one shop I came across had preserved anything that resembled an authentic tart made many moons ago. So many tarts are now made with bitter almond extract and margarine, so what was authentic? This tart evokes a refined vision for the Bakewell tart with a fresh raspberry jam, very moist frangipane, topped with crunchy chopped and sliced almonds.

RASPBERRY JAM

agar-agar powder	1 g	¼ tsp
caster (superfine) sugar	50 g	1.8 oz
raspberries, fresh or frozen	100 g	3.5 oz

1. Mix the agar-agar powder with the sugar in a medium bowl and sprinkle it over the raspberries in a saucepan. Stir over the lowest heat for 3 minutes, or until the raspberries create a syrup with the sugar, then increase the heat slightly and bring to the boil. Cook for 3 minutes to allow the fruit to break down.
2. You may strain out the seeds or leave them in. I like them in.
3. Leave the jam to cool, then whisk it until it reaches a loose jam consistency that you can spread. Set aside.

   Tip Store-bought jam can be used.

FRANGIPANE CREAM

raw almonds	300 g	10.6 oz
caster (superfine) sugar	200 g	7 oz
cornflour (cornstarch)	40 g	1.4 oz
plant-based milk	180 g	6.3 oz
extra virgin olive oil	40 g	1.4 oz
plain (all-purpose) flour	40 g	1.4 oz
baking powder	8 g	2 tsp
bitter almond oil extract		4 drops

4. Pulse the almonds, sugar and cornflour in a food processor or high-powered blender. Add the remaining ingredients and pulse to combine – it will have a creamy texture. Set aside.

TO ASSEMBLE AND BAKE

ALSO NEEDED

Short Sweet Pastry (page 230)	400 g	14.1 oz
plain (all-purpose) flour		for dusting
flaked (slivered) almonds	30 g	1.1 oz
raw almonds, chopped	30 g	1.1 oz
icing (confectioners') sugar		for dusting
freeze-dried raspberries		for dusting (optional)

5. Preheat the oven to 170°C fan (325°F/gas 3).
6. To make the pastry, follow the instructions on page 230. Lightly flour a sheet of baking parchment. Press the pastry into a disc, then roll it out on the floured baking parchment until it is 3–4 mm (⅛–⅙ in) thick – the thinner the better but it will take some more skill. You want the pastry to be loose on the paper.
7. Slide the pastry over a 23 cm (9 in) tart case and gently start to press it down into the case. Work your way around the edges, pressing the pastry deeper into the corners and pricking the base with a fork.
8. Trim the top of the pastry, then bake for 10 minutes until puffed and lightly golden. Remove from the oven and leave to cool.

TARTS AND PIES

9 Preheat the oven to 180°C fan (350°F/gas 4). Pipe or spread a layer of the raspberry jam on the bottom of the cooled tart, followed by the frangipane to fill the tart about three-quarters full or leaving 5 mm (¼ in) from the top edge of the pastry.

10 Sprinkle with the flaked almonds and the chopped almonds for extra texture.

11 Bake in the oven for 12–15 minutes until the frangipane is puffed and golden. Remove from the oven and leave to cool completely.

12 Dust with icing sugar. I like to also grate some freeze-dried raspberries through a small sieve to dust the edges for some extra colour. This tart keeps well in the refrigerator for 4 days, if well wrapped. Serve at room temperature.

TIP
Remember to go very lightly with the almond oil, and seek out an extract rather than a flavouring.

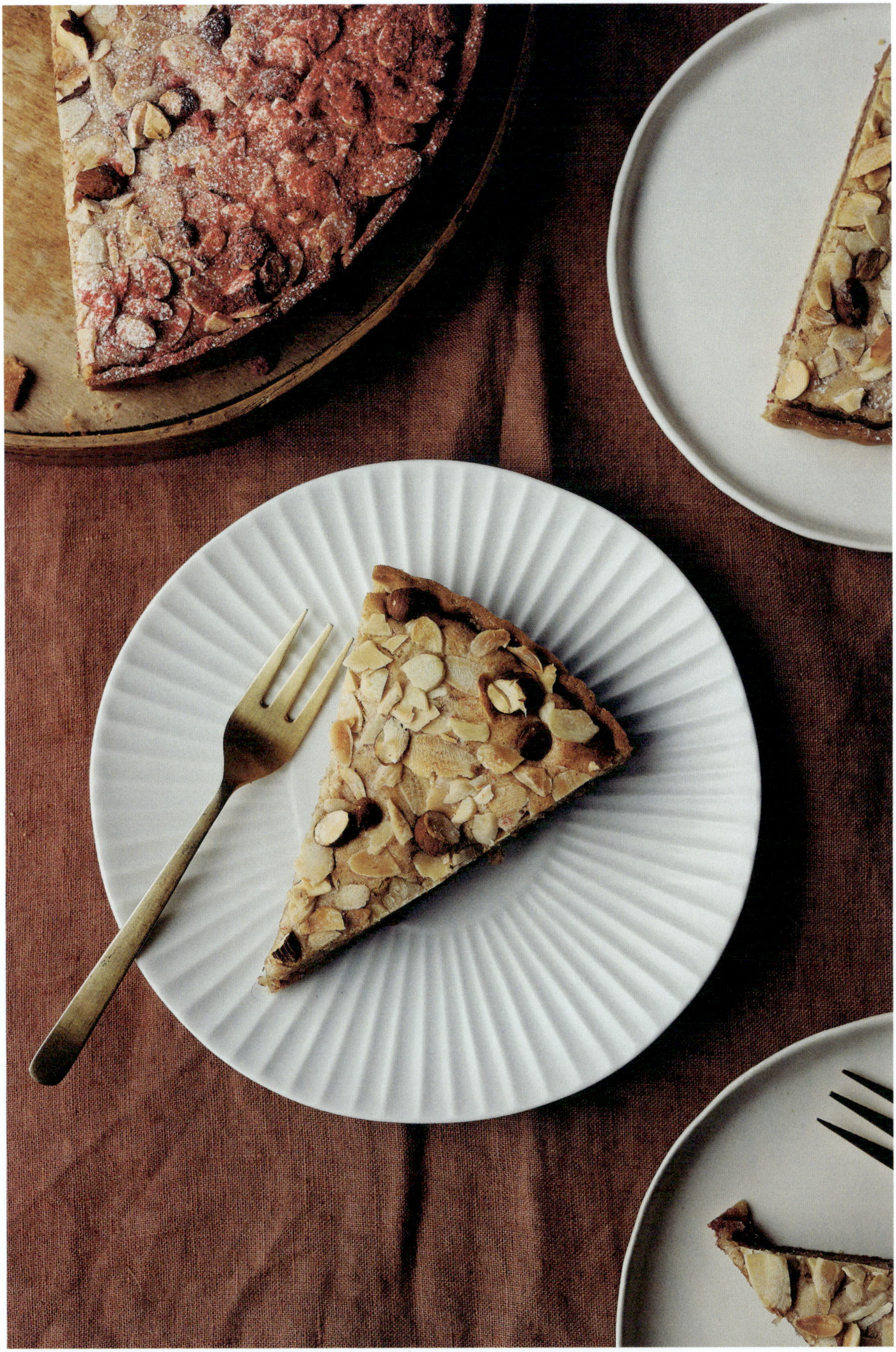

LEMON TART

Makes a 23 cm (9 in) pie or 8 individual tartlets

This lemon curd makes your lips pucker. Watch out for the blending technique of the curd – this takes the texture from flat and sad to luxurious and creamy.

TART CASE

1. Make the pastry following the instructions on page 232 and use to line a 23 cm (9 in) tart case. Prebake following the instructions until golden, then remove from the oven and leave to cool.

Sweet Flaky Pastry (page 232)	400 g	14.1 oz

LEMON CURD

2. Zest the lemon into a saucepan (zesting directly into the pan makes sure none of the aromatic oils don't go to waste), then add the lemon juice, sugar and soy milk and bring to a simmer. The acidity of the lemon juice will make the soy milk curdle but it will come back together.

3. Whisk the water and cornflour together in a medium bowl until smooth, then pour it into the pan in one go and whisk constantly. The mixture will thicken quickly.

4. Remove the curd from the heat and leave to cool to at least 25°C (77°F) – to speed this up you can pour it into a thin layer on a clean baking sheet and and leave it to chill in the refrigerator for about 20 minutes.

5. Add the coconut oil and, using a hand-held blender, blend the mixture. Something slightly magical will happen – the colour will lighten and the texture will become silky and smooth. Be careful not to over blend. Leaving out this last step will result in a set texture that's far less pleasurable to eat!

6. Pour the curd into the prebaked tart case and leave to chill in the refrigerator for 1 hour. Best served on the same day.

lemon zest	1 lemon	
lemon juice	290 g	10.2 oz
caster (superfine) sugar	220 g	7.8 oz
soy milk	190 g	6.7 oz
water	80 g	2.8 oz
cornflour (cornstarch)	60 g	2 oz
coconut oil (deodorised)	78 g	2.8 oz

TIP

To make this a lemon meringue pie, add meringue made from 80 g (2.8 oz) reduced aquafaba (page 34) and 80 g (2.8 oz) caster (superfine) sugar. Use a blowtorch to toast the meringue.

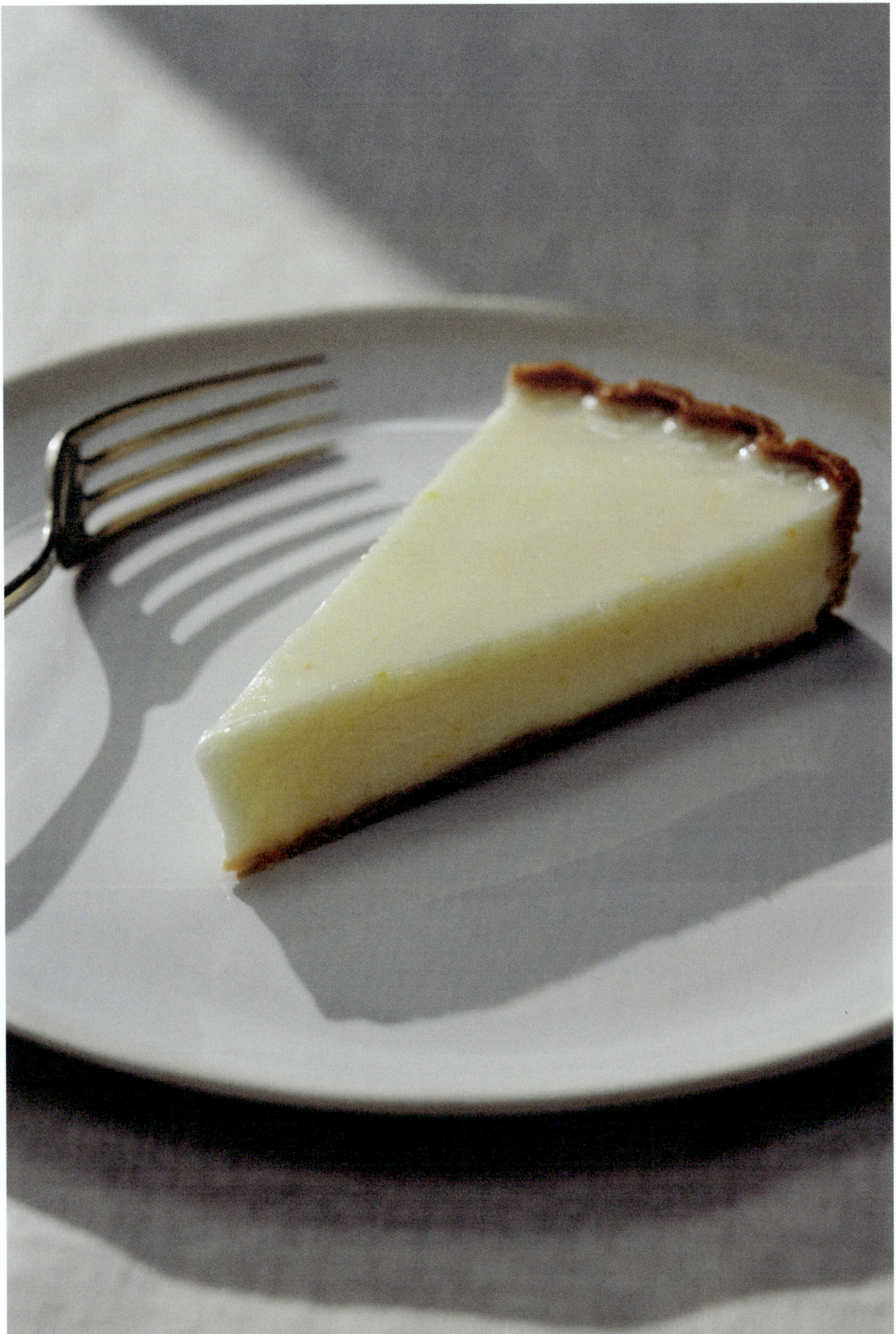

SWEET POTATO PIE

Makes a 23 cm (9 in) pie

Sweet potato pie conjures the warmth we crave in autumn (fall) and is an iconic autumnal favourite in North America, often made with pumpkin. The spiced filling is comprised of cooked sweet potato (although you can easily swap with pumpkin) that has been blended to a silky consistency with brown sugar and warming spices. Cornflour is cooked out to make a pie that slices beautifully and eats with a silky consistency.

PIE CRUST

Flaky Pastry (page 231)	400 g / 14.1 oz

1. Preheat the oven to 180°C fan (350°F/gas 4) with an oven shelf in the middle of the oven.
2. Make the pastry following the instructions on page 231. Roll out the pastry between two large sheets of baking parchment to a large 30 cm (12 in) disc, about 3–4 mm (⅛–⅙ in) thick.
3. You can remove the top sheet of baking parchment and use the bottom sheet to help flip it over into the dish, if you like. Gently press the pastry into a 23 cm (9 in) pie or quiche dish with a tiny overhang.
4. Scrunch up one of the sheets of baking parchment and press it over the pastry, then fill with rice or baking beans to weigh down the pastry.
5. Bake in the oven for 18–20 minutes until cooked through. Remove the paper and rice and bake for another 10 minutes, or until the pastry is golden and cooked through. If the edges brown too quickly cover with kitchen foil.
6. Remove from the oven and leave to cool slightly while you prepare the filling.

SWEET POTATO FILLING

sweet potato, cooked and cooled	460 g	16.2 oz
brown sugar	65 g	2.3 oz
caster (superfine) sugar	115 g	4.1 oz
plant-based milk	200 g	7 oz
cornflour (cornstarch)	53 g	1.9 oz
sea salt	2 g	½ tsp
ground nutmeg	2.5 g	½ tsp
ground cinnamon	3 g	1 tsp
ground cloves	1.5 g	½ tsp

7. Preheat the oven to 170°C fan (325°F/gas 3). Purée all the filling ingredients together in a food processor or with a hand-held blender in a large bowl for a quick finish, or purée the cooked sweet potato, then stir in all the remaining ingredients.
8. Pour the filling into the prebaked tart case all the way to the top and bake for 25–30 minutes, or until the centre is just set. Allow to cool.

TO FINISH

filo pastry		1 sheet
extra virgin olive oil		for brushing
Exotic Clear Glaze (page 239), warmed (optional)	40 g	1.4 oz

9. Preheat the oven to 170°C fan (325°F/gas 3). Gently brush some warmed exotic clear glaze, if using, onto the cooled top of the tart for an elegant shine. Brush a sheet of filo pastry with some olive oil on both sides. Use leaf cutters to cut leaves, then lay them on a baking tray and bake until golden, around 8–12 minutes. Allow to cool, then arrange on the outside of the tart.

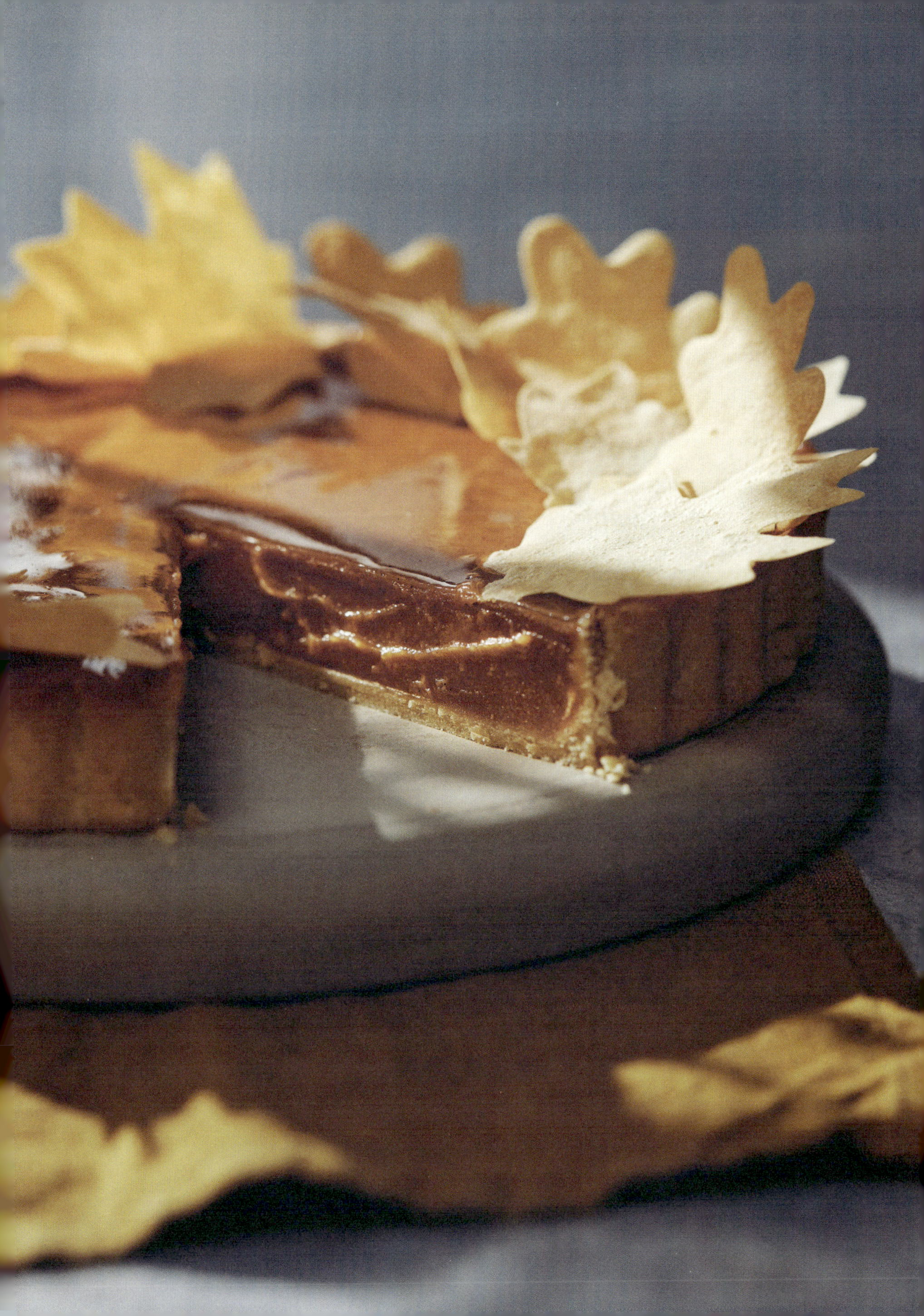

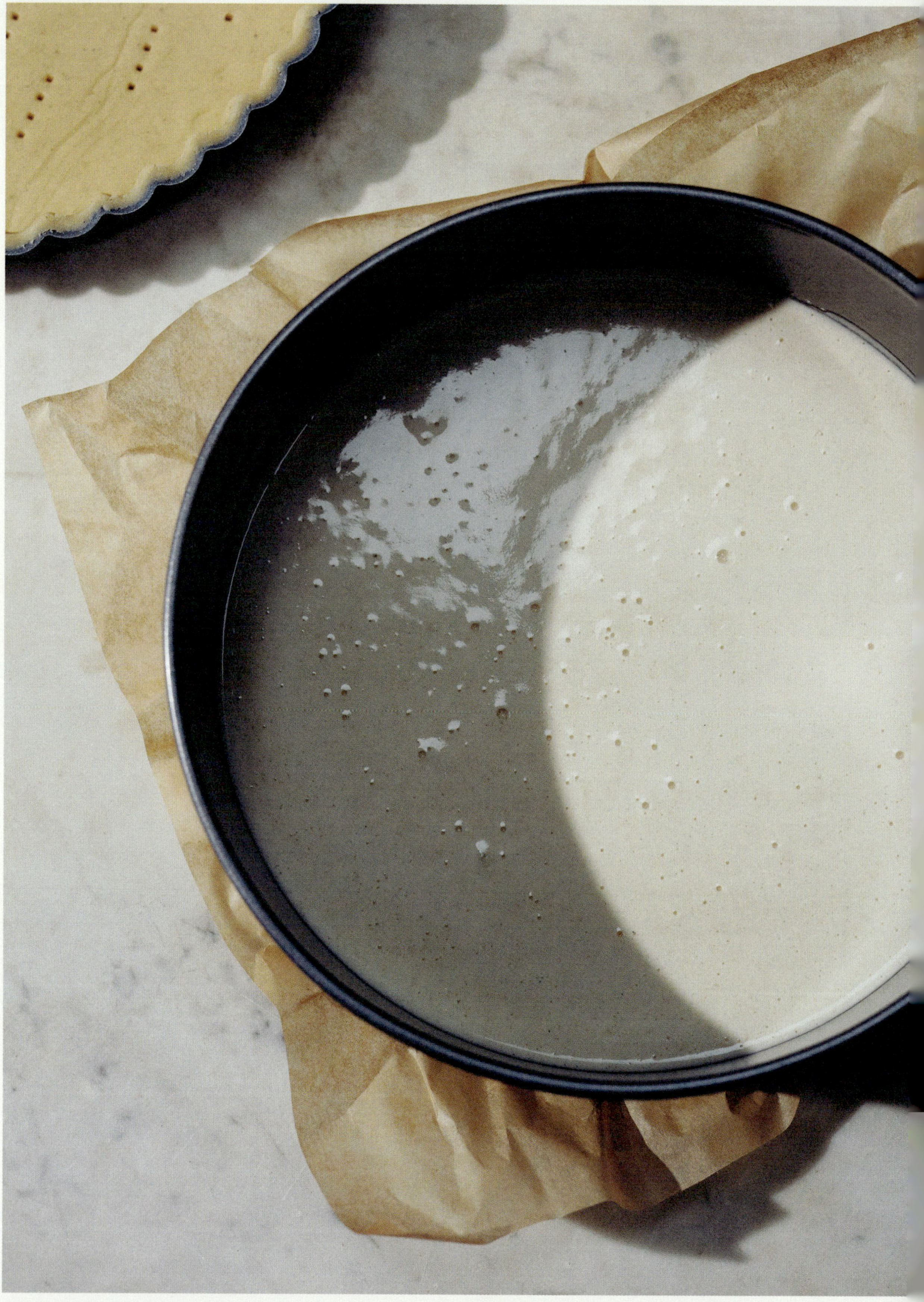

4 CAKES

The first thing I had to do when reformulating cake batters from scratch without eggs was to reduce the fat by up to 60 per cent. It turns out that in a sponge batter, the eggs and flour perform gelling functions – both gel and firm up as they bake. In the finished product, the fat in the recipe will tenderise the cake, making it soft and sumptuous. Without eggs performing their bit, there's a lot less tenderising to be done; the same amount of fat in a sponge without eggs would make the cake dense, oily and fall apart, because it has softened the gluten network of the flour too much.

The next consideration was air. Air is crucial to creating a soft and fluffy texture. In conventional cakes this is incorporated by beating butter or whipping egg whites. However, the invention of baking powders in the 19th century allowed a revolution to occur in food.

Previously, breads were the cornerstone of European and North American households. Yeast was considered a foul substance (imagine a sourdough starter but without the knowledge of hygiene and bacteria, and you get a bubbly, stinky, often mouldy mess) and baking powder emerged as a scientific breakthrough powder that produced air in the presence of water and heat.

In a time when bread making could take hours upon hours to do on a given day, almost exclusively by women, baking powders allowed flexibility and freed up time for other things. This led to a whole new category of cakes that didn't exist before, like cake-y sponges (drum-roll: Victoria sandwich), cupcakes, cake doughnuts, biscuits (cookies), scones and quick breads. Baking powder spearheaded the development of many cakes and pastries that previously relied on beating eggs or butter (without electric mixers, mind you).

Where older-fashioned cakes were versions of breads that had been enriched with honey or crude sugars, eggs and butter gave way to completely new genres of cake products.

All baking powder contains bicarbonate of soda (baking soda), an acidic powder and a starch that acts like a buffer to keep the ingredients dry and separate until they're mixed with water – a recipe to do what 19th-century cooks thought was magic!

In many recipes based on mechanical leavening where eggs or butter are beaten to incorporate air, baking powder allows for a base mixture of dry ingredients to be mixed with wet ingredients and air is produced as the result of a reaction. It is the little ingredient with a huge functional utility in the new way of baking.

Gaining an understanding of both the fat content and air within the batter opened up the gateway to cakes. The cake recipes that I have included range from simple loaf cakes to showstopping upside-down cakes and layer cakes, all of which are developed from this knowledge.

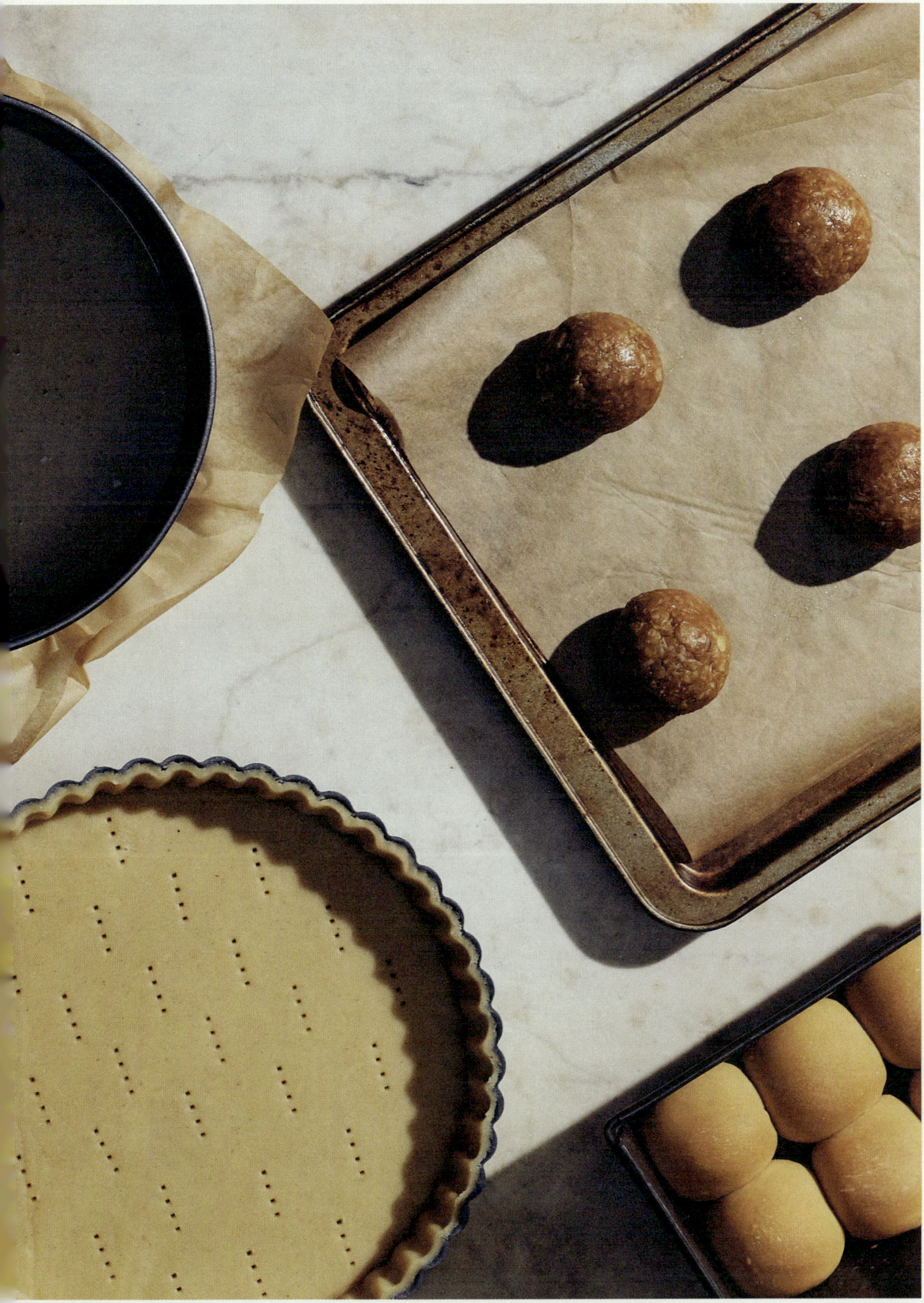

FINANCIERS

Makes 12 standard financiers (4 × 7 cm/1½ x 2¾ in)

These small cakes are memorable for their nutty flavour. I use a mix of ground hazelnut and almond to make them nutty and supremely moreish. It is traditional to bake these in a little bar mould – the name 'financier' does after all refer to the shape of gold bars. You can buy specific financier moulds made from silicone or traditional moulded steel pans. Feel free to use a muffin mould too – just fill it up halfway.

1. Blend the roasted hazelnuts, flour and sugar together in a small food processor to a fine powder.

2. Add the powdered nut mixture to a large bowl with the golden syrup, ground almonds, baking powder, olive oil and plant-based milk and mix together with a whisk until a smooth batter forms.

3. Spoon the batter into the mould, or scrape it into a piping (pastry) bag with a 7 mm (¼ in) plain piping nozzle, to fill them up halfway. You can add 2–3 raspberries, blueberries or whatever you fancy, followed by a sprinkle of flaked almonds, if you like. Rest for 15 minutes before baking.

4. Preheat the oven to 180°C fan (350°F/gas 4) with an oven shelf in the middle of the oven. Have a metal or silicone bar mould handy.

5. Bake for 12 minutes, or until nicely domed and with a deep golden colour.

6. Leave to cool in the moulds for 10 minutes on a wire rack to allow air circulation, then pop them out and leave to cool completely. Store in an airtight container at room temperature for up to 3 days.

hazelnuts, roasted	50 g	1.8 oz
plain (all-purpose) flour	100 g	3.5 oz
caster (superfine) sugar	80 g	2.8 oz
golden (or agave) syrup	20 g	0.7 oz
ground almonds	50 g	1.8 oz
baking powder	4 g	1 tsp
extra virgin olive oil	40 g	1.4 oz
plant-based milk	120 g	4.2 oz
berries, fresh or frozen (optional)	as needed	
flaked (slivered) almonds (optional)	40 g	1.4 oz

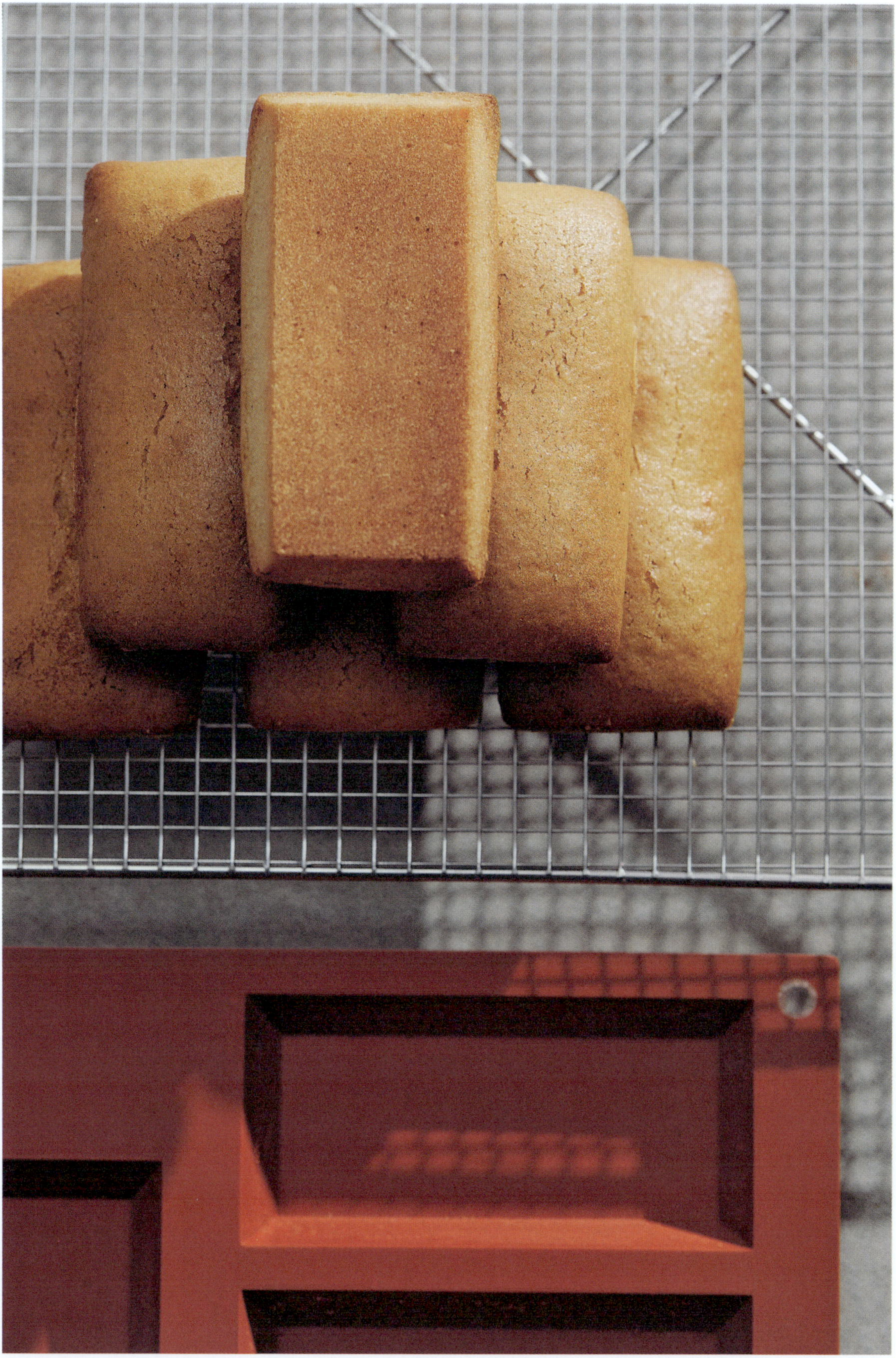

FLUFFY SCONES

Makes 12–15 scones

After working my first year in Australia's most-awarded restaurant, Quay, I sought to finish my apprenticeship somewhere I could learn the repertoire of a pastry chef. I settled on The Shangri-La Hotel in Sydney where pastry chef Anna Polyviou was bucking the trend of buying in finished products and making as much as possible in-house. I did learn a lot! Anna had worked at Claridge's in London, the famed institution, as had Alec Lowe, my very good friend and colleague (we started the job on the same day). Alec showed me the most important steps required to produce a perfectly shaped, fluffy scone (amongst many things!) and I made thousands, day in, day out over the next 2 years, every day aiming to get them closer and closer to perfection. I even used to get told off by Anna for giving each scone a nurturing little tap – something I did unconsciously without realising – maybe wishing them a perfect fluffy rise.

Scones are a tad bland on their own, so I always prefer fruit scones (which include soaked raisins) – but they are a delightful little morsel that should split perfectly in half without needing a knife, ready to be smothered with jam and cream (no matter which goes first – I'm cream first, for the record).

SCONE DOUGH

1. Using a whisk, mix the flour, baking powder and salt together gently in a large bowl to combine and 'sieve'.

2. Add the sugar, olive oil, vinegar and plant-based milk to a large measuring cup or bowl and mix together, then pour on top of the flour mixture and mix with a silicone spatula until it comes together into a dough.

3. Turn the dough onto a lightly floured work surface and gently knead, just a few times so it's a smooth dough. You also want the top of the dough ball to be smooth.

4. Wrap the dough in cling film (plastic wrap) and leave to rest for 15–20 minutes on the work surface to relax the dough so the scones cut nicely and stay round.

5. Uncover the dough, lightly dust the work surface and the top of the dough ball with some more flour, then turn the dough over so the smooth side is on the surface. Roll the dough out in both directions to 3 cm (¾–1 in) thick. If scones are rolled too thick for the size they are cut, they rise very tall and look like they have toppled.

6. Dust some more flour lightly on top of the dough – this will allow the cutter to release the round puck of dough with minimal handling – then cut decisively with a 6 cm (2½ in) round cutter. Carefully turn the scone over and place it on a large baking sheet – this gives you a nice sharp edge around the top. Repeat with the remaining dough to make 12–15 scones.

7. Leave the scones to rest for 1 hour. This will make them rise in a perfect shape, otherwise they can be tough and roughly shaped.

8. Thirty minutes before baking, preheat the oven to 180°C fan (350°F/gas 4) with the oven shelf in the middle.

plain (all-purpose) flour, plus extra for dusting	450 g	15.9 oz
baking powder	25 g	0.9 oz
fine salt	3 g	¾ tsp
caster (superfine) sugar	45 g	1.6 oz
extra virgin olive oil	75 g	2.7 oz
apple cider vinegar	4 g	1 tsp
plant-based milk	220 g	7.8 oz

9. Bake the scones for 10–11 minutes until the tops are nice and golden and the sides are still pale.

10. Remove from the oven and serve warm or leave to cool. Store the scones in an airtight container at room temperature for 3 days. Warm very briefly before serving with jam and the whipped cream.

FRUIT SCONE VARIATION

11. Add the boiled water to a cup with an Earl Grey tea bag or loose leaves and leave to infuse for 4 minutes.

12. Add the sultanas or raisins to a small bowl and strain the tea onto them, leaving them to soak for 40 minutes, or overnight in the refrigerator to make the sultanas plump and juicy. You can do this up to 4 days in advance. Store in the refrigerator.

13. Strain the soaked fruit before using and mixing into the finished dough, or halve this amount if adding to offcuts you are about to re-roll.

14. Mix into the dough before the first rest and then proceed as above.

15. Bake the scones for 10–11 minutes until the tops are nice and golden and the sides are still pale.

16. Remove from the oven and serve warm or leave to cool. Store the scones in an airtight container at room temperature for 3 days. Warm very briefly before serving with jam and the whipped cream.

ALSO NEEDED

jam		
Fresh Whipping Cream (page 236), whipped		

freshly boiled water	200 g	7 oz
Earl Grey tea bag or loose leaves	1 tea bag 4 g	bag 1 tsp
sultanas (golden raisins) or raisins	150 g	5.3 oz

NOTE

This batch is for a full batch as fruit scones. Half it if you want a mix of fruit and plain scones.

TIP

You can clump together your offcuts into a ball, leave to rest for 20 minutes, then roll and cut again. Or you can make fruit scones by adding soaked raisins at this stage and mixing until incorporated, then proceed with a 20-minute rest before rolling and cutting and the rest of the steps.

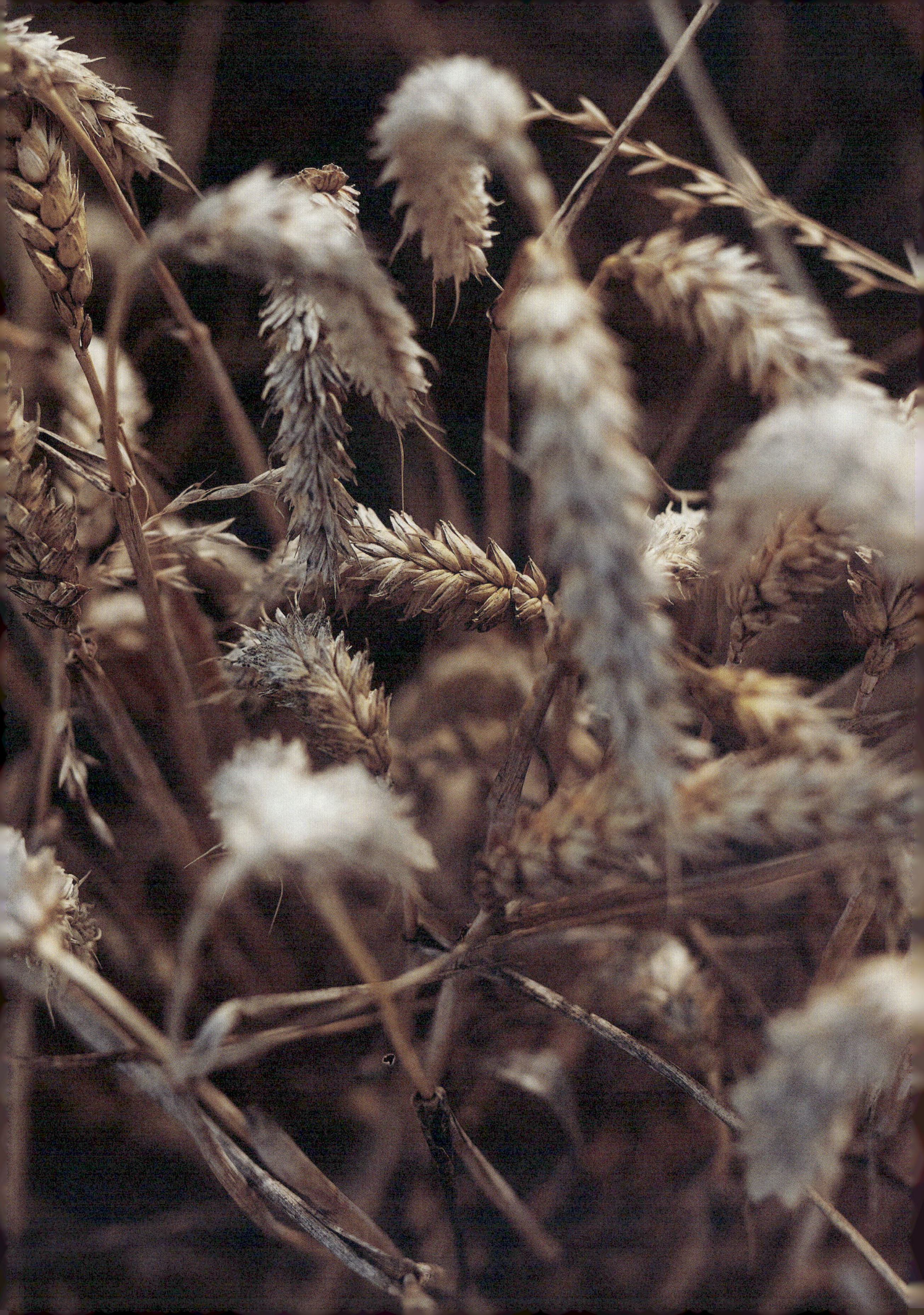

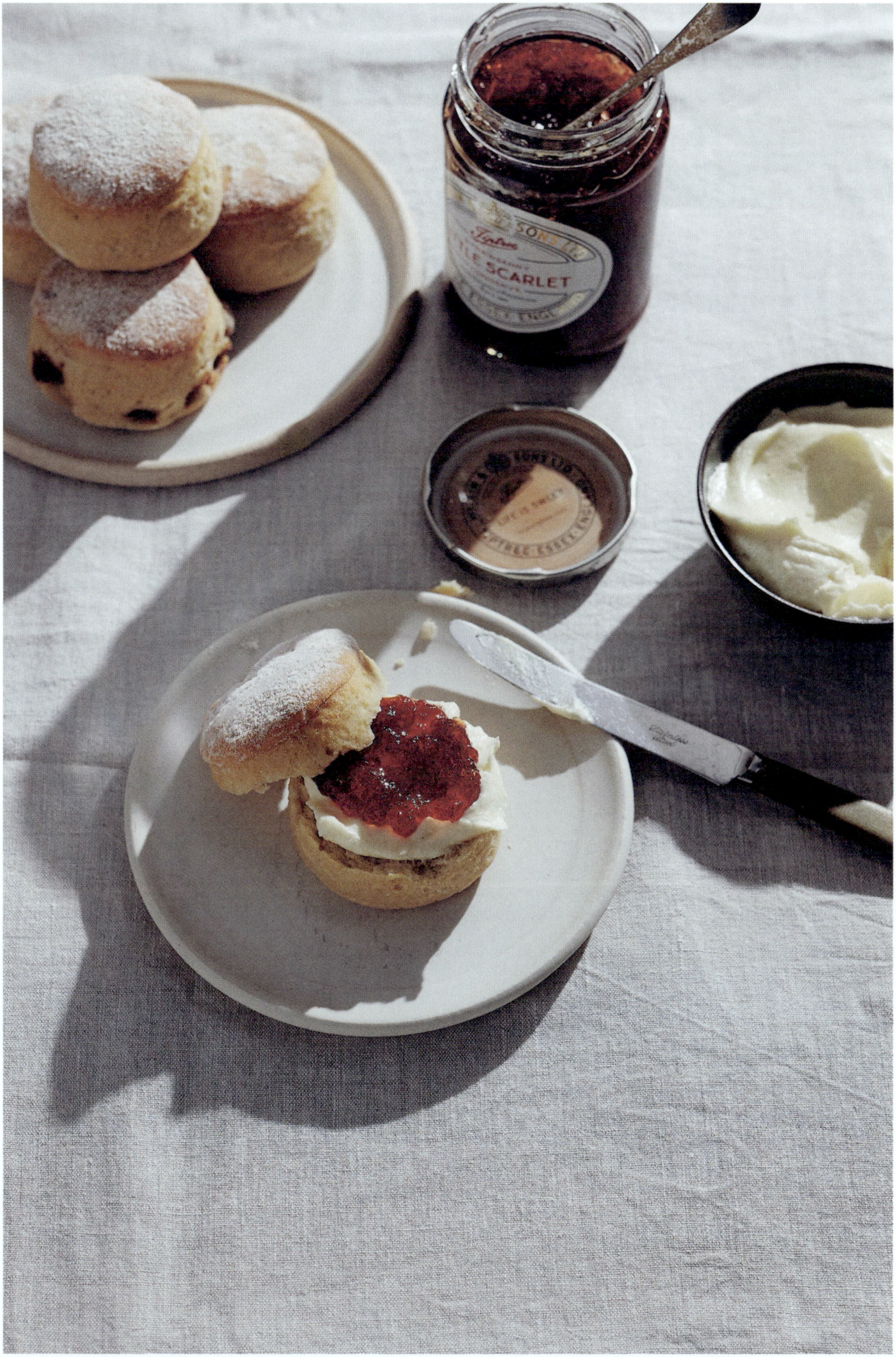
SCARLET

MADELEINES

Makes 12 madeleines

Dainty, with a noticeable bump, these iconic little cakes are baked in a shell mould. A key to getting the bump is chilling the batter for 20 minutes in the freezer before piping it into the moulds and baking. This allows the gluten to relax, the centre of the dough to remain cold and for a proud baby bump to rise at the end of a quick bake in a hot oven. You also need to reduce the temperature after 1–2 minutes.

1. Add the flour, sugar, baking powder and cinnamon to a large bowl and whisk them together just to combine.

2. Add the milk, golden syrup, vanilla paste and olive oil to the flour mixture and mix until smooth.

3. Spoon the batter into a piping (pastry) bag, cut a 1 cm (½ in) hole or use a 1 cm (½ in) plain piping tube and place it on a flat baking sheet in the freezer for 20–30 minutes to chill the dough quickly.

4. Preheat the oven (no fan) to 230°C (450°F/gas 8).

5. Pipe the batter into the madeleine mould almost all the way to the top, then bake for 1 minute (set a timer). Reduce the oven temperature to 180°C (350°F/gas 4) and bake for another 6–8 minutes until the batter in the bump is baked through and the edges are golden. The batter in the top of the bump is the last to bake, so a gentle press of the bump should spring back.

6. Leave to cool in the mould for 5 minutes on a wire rack, then push them out of the mould and allow to cool completely. Store in an airtight container at room temperature for up to 2 days.

plain (all-purpose) flour	100 g	3.5 oz
caster (superfine) sugar	70 g	2.5 oz
baking powder	2.5 g	½ tsp
ground cinnamon		pinch
plant-based milk	80 g	2.8 oz
golden (or agave) syrup	10 g	0.4 oz
vanilla bean paste	4 g	1 tsp
extra virgin olive oil	35 g	1.2 oz

TIP

For extra decadence, toss the warm madeleines in flavoured sugars. Grind a dried vanilla bean with sugar, or mix a cup of sugar with a teaspoon of cinnamon, or granulated sugar rubbed with citrus zest. You can also dip them in water icing made with water and vanilla paste, or lemon juice instead of water, and let the excess drip off on a wire rack and let the icing set for over an hour.

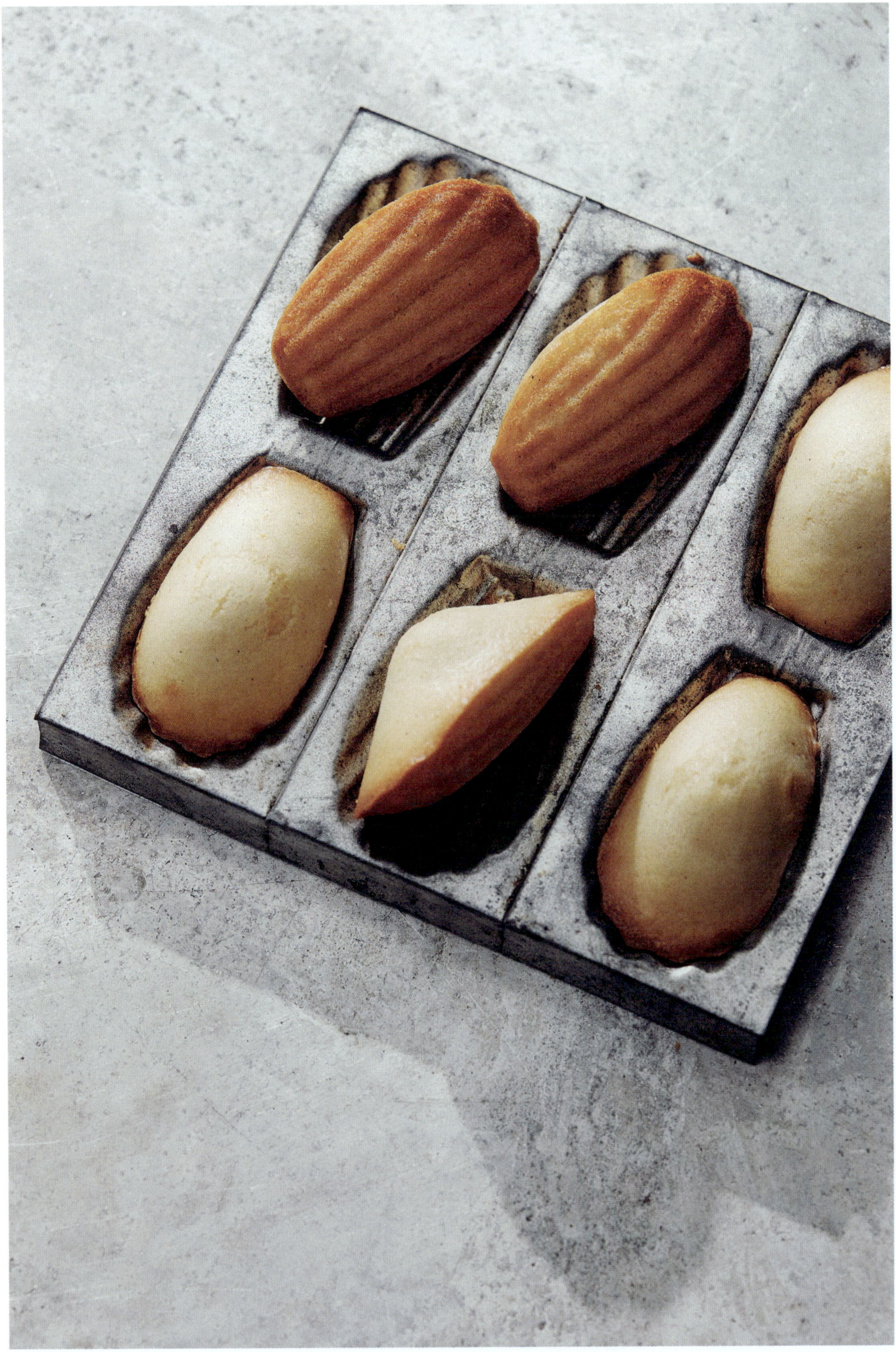

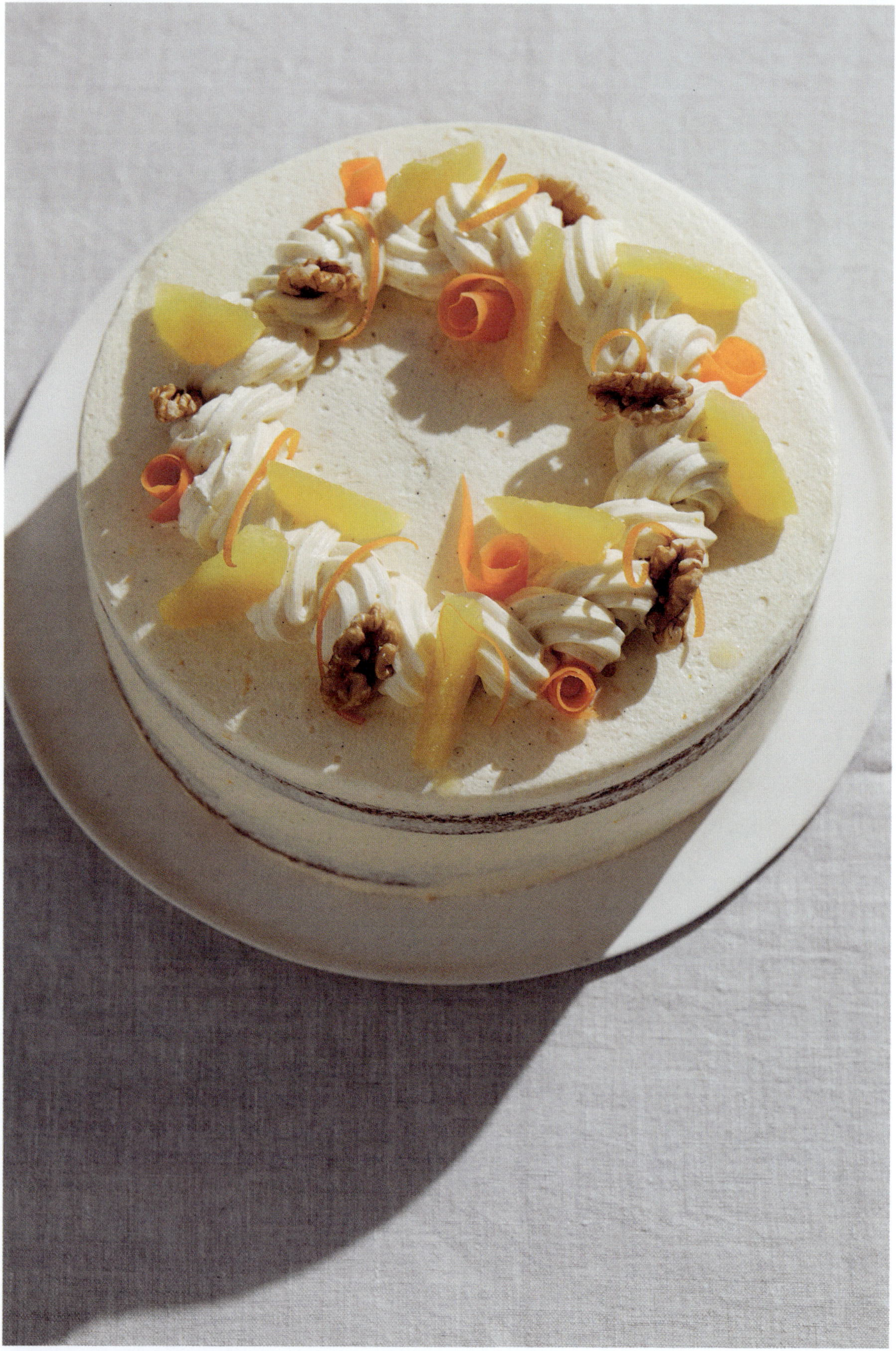

CARROT CAKE

Makes a two-layer 20 cm (8 in) cake or a single layer 23 cm (9 in)

Carrots were originally used to sweeten cakes when sugar was scarce or expensive from the Middle Ages to World War II rationing era. The modern carrot cake is spiced, usually contains walnuts and has a cream cheese frosting, which lends a luscious tang. Here, the frosting is a cooked base scented with citrus zest, which you cool and whisk with coconut oil and cocoa butter. It has the texture of a very light but not very sweet buttercream.

CAKE BATTER

1. Preheat the oven to 180°C fan (350°F/gas 4) with two oven shelves ready in the oven. Line the bases of two 23 cm (9 in) springform tins (pans) or other round baking tins with a disc of baking parchment.
2. Grate the carrots into a large bowl. Add the raisins, walnuts, both sugars, plant-based milk and olive oil and stir well with a silicone spatula to combine. In another bowl, whisk the flour, baking powder, bicarbonate of soda, spices and salt. Add the carrot mixture and mix well to combine.
3. Divide the batter into the lined tins (there should be 650 g/1 lb 7 oz in each tin) and bake for 25 minutes. Swap and rotate the tins so they bake evenly and bake for another 10 minutes, or until the top springs back or a skewer inserted into the centre comes out clean. Leave to cool in the tins on a wire rack to allow air circulation.

CITRUS FROSTING

4. Mix all the ingredients, except the shortening and sugar, in a large saucepan off the heat, then bring to the boil over a medium heat, stirring constantly with a silicone spatula so it doesn't catch. Cook for 4–5 minutes until the mixture thickens and is glossy and smooth.
5. Pour the mixture into a shallow dish, cover the surface with cling film (plastic wrap) and leave to chill in the refrigerator for 20 minutes, or until the mixture is 20°C (68°F).
6. In a stand mixer with a beater or whisk, whip the shortening and sugar until light and fluffy. Then add the room temperature base in three additions, making sure to scrape in between. Then whisk on high speed until very fluffy.

TO ASSEMBLE AND FINISH

7. Trim the curved dome of one of the cakes with a large serrated knife. Spread half the frosting on this layer, then place the other sponge on top, with the dome on top.
8. Spread the remaining frosting on top with a palette knife, or use a piping (pastry) bag fitted with a piping tube. Finish with halved walnuts, rolled-up carrot ribbons and orange segments.

TIP

If your frosting mix is cold it may look slightly curdled. If it does, it needs a bit of heat – dip the bowl into a sink of hot water for a few seconds, then remove and continue beating. Set aside.

carrots, peeled	200 g	7 oz
raisins	50 g	1.8 oz
walnuts, coarsely chopped	100 g	3.5 oz
muscovado sugar	120 g	4.2 oz
caster (superfine) sugar	150 g	5.3 oz
plant-based milk	350 g	12.4 oz
extra virgin olive oil	80 g	2.8 oz
plain (all-purpose) flour (gluten-free plain flour will also work)	300 g	10.6 oz
baking powder	8 g	2 tsp
bicarbonate of soda (baking soda)	5 g	1 tsp
ground cinnamon	2 g	1 tsp
ground nutmeg	1 g	½ tsp
salt	2 g	½ tsp
plant-based milk	300 g	10.6 oz
cornflour (cornstarch)	30 g	1.1 oz
vanilla bean paste	4 g	1 tsp
lemon juice	40 g	1.4 oz
orange zest, grated		½ orange
Shortening (page 232), chilled	165 g	5.8 oz
caster (superfine) sugar	130 g	4.6 oz

ALSO NEEDED

walnut halves	to decorate
rolled-up carrot ribbons	to decorate
orange segments	to decorate

CAKES

MAPLE CAKE

Makes a tall 20 cm (8 in) cake

Despite the simple exterior, a slice reveals an impressive multilayered cake – my nod to the infamous Medovik, an eight-layer honey cake popular in the countries of the former Soviet Union. This maple cake is on the more involved side of baking and will need two or three large baking sheets or trays (pans) to bake all the biscuits (cookies) – luckily they bake fairly quickly and you can alternate the trays. I was initially surprised that honey wasn't vegan. It turns out saving the bees isn't just about saving honey bees but the many thousands of other native bees that may not produce honey but play a critical role in pollinating so many crops and flowers. Saving the bees is about saving biodiversity. I was even more surprised that you could make an amazing layered honey cake plant-based and without honey. Who knew that the signature flavour that many have come to know and love is actually derived from the aroma of the bicarbonate of soda (baking soda) in the biscuit as it bakes and not the honey itself. Make this cake a day ahead, as something almost alchemical happens overnight as the moisture migrates from the fresh whipped cream filling to the biscuit and it melds together to make a unique confection that is both light and indulgent at the same time.

WHIPPED MAPLE CREAM

1. Add the maple and golden syrups to a large saucepan and cook over a low heat for 5 minutes until it has the consistency of thick honey and is a bit darker in colour. Pour it into a large measuring jug with the coconut oil and stir until the coconut oil has melted.

2. Add the soy milk, orange blossom water and muscovado sugar and blend with a hand-held blender for 30–60 seconds until well combined, glossy and smooth. Pour it into a shallow dish, cover the surface with cling film (plastic wrap) and chill in the refrigerator for 4–6 hours until it is 5°C (41°F).

3. Chill the bowl of your stand mixer, then use a whisk attachment to whisk the chilled mixture for 3–5 minutes until it holds a soft peak. Set aside in the refrigerator until you are ready to assemble the cake.

   TIP If your cream is not whipping after 2-3 minutes, put it in the freezer for 15 minutes and try whipping again.

maple syrup	120 g	4.2 oz
golden (or agave) syrup	60 g	2 oz
coconut oil (deodorised)	310 g	10.9 oz
soy milk, at room temperature	380 g	13.4 oz
orange blossom water	2 g	½ tsp
muscovado or dark brown sugar	50 g	1.8 oz

SOAKING SYRUP

1. Bring all the ingredients to a simmer in a large saucepan, then remove from the heat.

2. Within a couple of minutes of taking a batch of biscuits from the oven, place a disc on a wire rack set over a wide bowl or rimmed baking sheet and generously pour the hot syrup over the biscuit.

3. Tip the syrup back into the jug and continue soaking each layer as they come out of the oven.

4. Set each round of soaked biscuit on a sheet of baking parchment and leave to cool completely.

maple syrup	100 g	3.5 oz
golden (or agave) syrup	50 g	1.8 oz
caster (superfine) sugar	100 g	3.5 oz
water	250 g	8.8 oz

MAPLE DOUGH

caster (superfine) sugar	190 g	6.7 oz
water	180 g	6.4 oz
maple syrup	70 g	2.5 oz
apple cider vinegar	10 g	2.5 tsp
coconut oil (deodorised)	70 g	2.5 oz
plain (all-purpose) flour, plus extra for dusting	645 g	1 lb 7 oz
bicarbonate of soda (baking soda)	15 g	2½ tsp
fine salt	3 g	½ tsp

1. Preheat the oven to 180°C fan (350°F/gas 4) and line two large baking sheets with baking parchment.

2. Heat the caster sugar in a large saucepan over a medium heat and allow the sugar to melt and caramelise. Avoid stirring but tilt and shuffle the pan around to distribute the sugar once it starts melting. It will then caramelise.

3. Very slowly start to pour the water, maple syrup and vinegar into the caramel. Be careful: it will bubble and spit! Add the coconut oil and leave it to melt, then remove from the heat and leave to cool to below 50°C (122°F).

4. Add the flour, bicarbonate of soda and salt to a stand mixer fitted with a dough hook attachment and mix on the lowest speed to combine. Add the warm caramel liquid to the dough and mix on low speed until a dough develops that pulls cleanly away from the sides of the bowl. This dough can be mixed by hand.

5. Press your dough into four even-sized round discs to help make it easier to roll.

6. Roll one of the discs on a floured work surface until it's 1.5 mm (⅜ in) thick. Basically, this is almost as thin as most shop-bought pre-rolled pastry. Be generous with the flour and flour both sides. Roll the dough down and relax the tension by running your hand underneath, then trim to a 20 cm (8 in) disc (use a cake tin/pan as a guide). If you don't relax the dough, it will pull itself into an oval.

7. Use a fork to gently 'dock' or perforate the dough with a few holes across the surface for an even rise. Repeat with the remaining dough discs. You can re-roll all the dough offcuts until you have eight layers, by pressing them back together. Set the scraps aside.

8. Arrange a piece of dough on one of the lined baking sheets (try to fit two pieces diagonally) and bake in batches for 7–9 minutes. The 'biscuit' should be a deep golden brown and puffed up from its original height. Once it cools, it should have some slight flexibility to it but be firm enough to pick up and place on a wire rack over a roasting tray.

9. For the decoration crumbs, spread the remaining offcuts on another baking sheet lined with baking parchment and bake for 10–12 minutes until golden and dried all the way through. Blend to a fine crumb in a food processor and set aside.

TO ASSEMBLE AND FINISH

10. Place a piece of cooled soaked biscuit on the serving platter you intend to use.

11. Using a small offset spatula, spread 90 g (3.2 oz) of the whipped maple cream onto the layer of biscuit and spread evenly to the edges. The cream should be the same thickness as each piece of soaked biscuit. Repeat until you have used all the biscuit sheets and cream, then smooth the top and sides with the palette knife.

12. Sprinkle the top and sides with the dried blended biscuit crumbs.

13. Leave to chill in the refrigerator overnight to allow all the flavours to meld together. It is important to prepare this cake a day ahead so it has 10–12 hours to ensure that enough moisture from the cream has migrated to the biscuit and results in a light but indulgent texture. Store in an airtight container in the refrigerator for up to 3 days, or freeze well wrapped for a month and defrost overnight in the freezer.

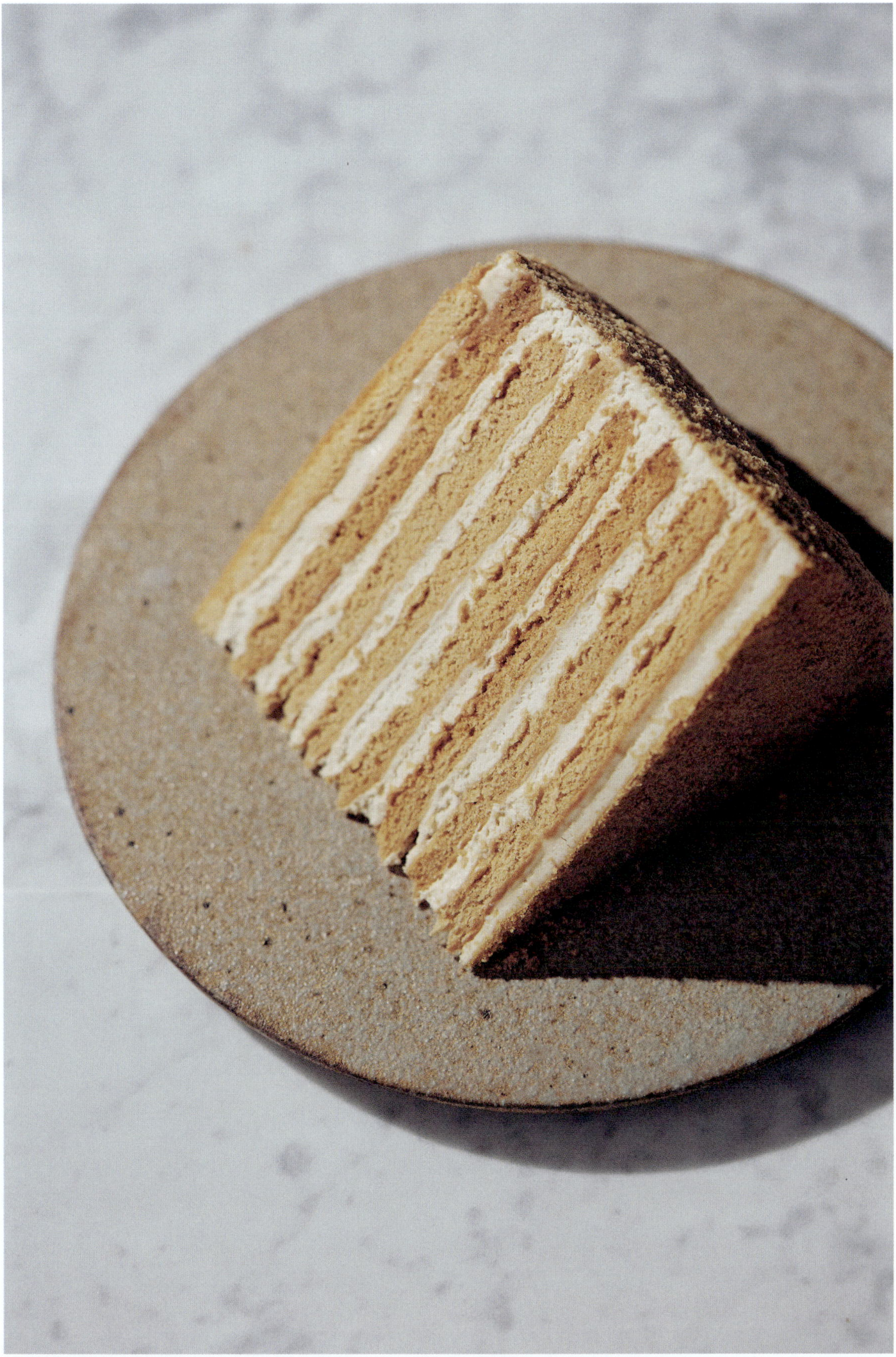

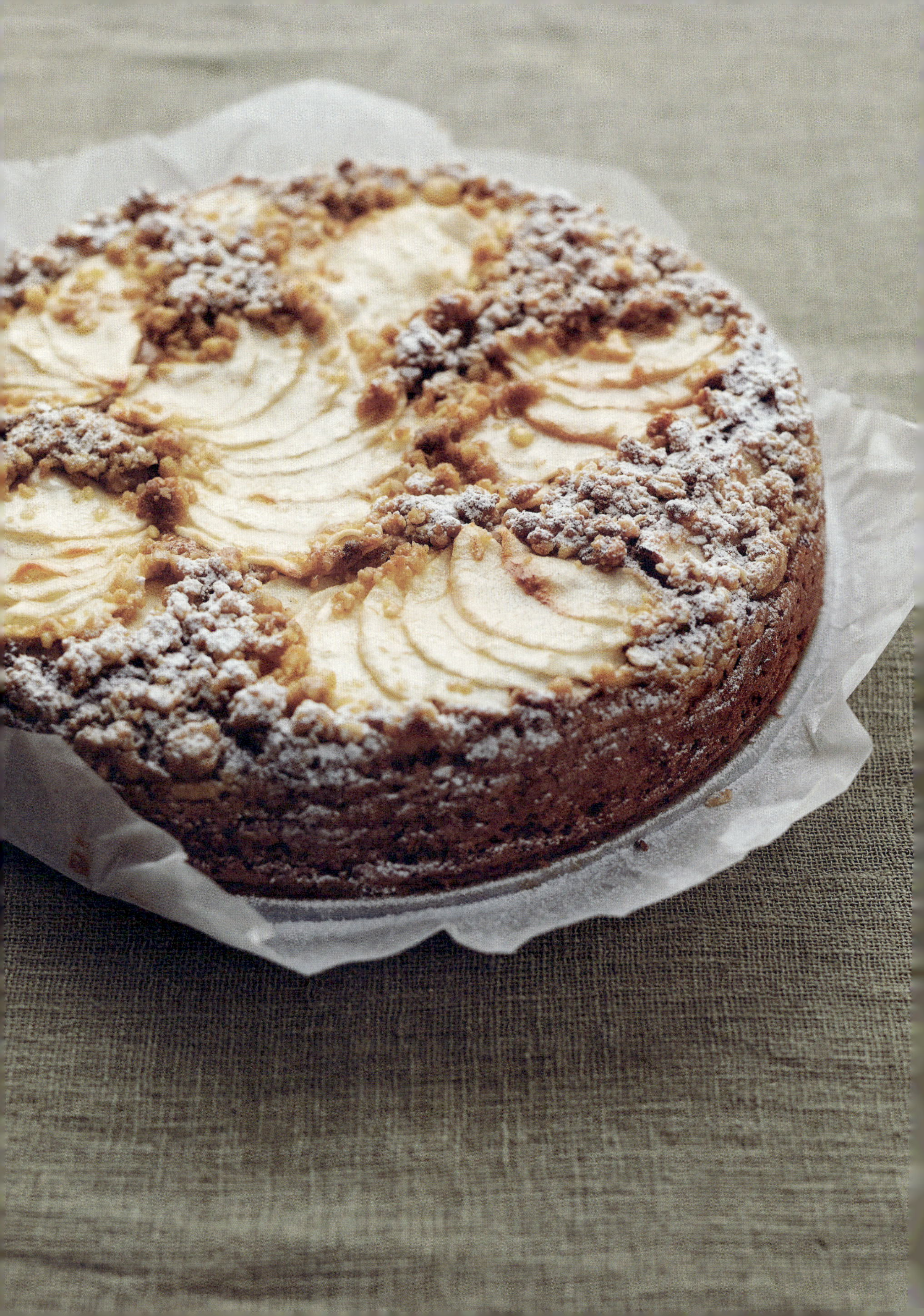

APPLE CAKE

Makes a 23 cm (9 in) cake or 12 large muffins

This cake manages to squeeze in the goodness of up to four apples. The eternally delicious combination of apple and cinnamon makes this a cake (or brilliant muffin) everyone will love. I've talked before about all the incredible nutrients you'll find in apple skins so please don't bother peeling them (easy!) and just blend the apples with the cores trimmed.

apples, cored (about 3 apples)	300 g	10.6 oz
ground cinnamon	6 g	1½ tsp
caster (superfine) sugar	180 g	6.3 oz
extra virgin olive oil	80 g	2.8 oz
plant-based milk	90 g	3.2 oz
plain (all-purpose) flour	225 g	7.9 oz
baking powder	8 g	2 tsp
bicarbonate of soda (baking soda)	4 g	1 tsp
apple, thinly sliced, for topping	1 apple	
Demerara sugar, for sprinkling	40 g	1.4 oz
Oat Crumble (page 233)	50 g	1.8 oz
icing (confectioners') sugar	for dusting	

1. Preheat the oven to 180°C fan (350°F/gas 4) with an oven shelf in the middle of the oven. Line the base of a 23 cm (9 in) cake tin (pan) with baking parchment or line a 12-cup muffin tray with paper cases.

2. Wash the apples well, quarter and cut out the seeds. There's no need to peel the apple.

3. Add the apples to a high-powered blender or food processor with the cinnamon, sugar, oil and milk and blend until smooth.

4. Add the flour, baking powder and bicarbonate of soda to a large bowl and gently whisk to 'sieve' and combine the ingredients. Add the apple purée and mix well with a whisk or silicone spatula until just combined and there are no dry streaks.

5. Pour the batter into the lined tin and top with the sliced apple, followed by the Demerara sugar and oat crumble sprinkled across the batter. Bake for 40 minutes if making the cake or 8–10 minutes for the muffins until golden and the top springs back when gently pressed with your fingertips, or a skewer inserted into the centre of the cake or muffin comes out clean.

6. Leave to cool completely on a wire rack, then remove from the tin. Serve with a dusting of icing sugar. This cake keeps very well in an airtight container at room temperature for up to 5 days.

VICTORIA SPONGE

Makes 1 cake with two 20 cm (8 in) layers

In countless tests of plant-based sponges, I was able get the perfect texture and brilliant flavour. I tinkered with (and successfully reduced) how much fat was in the sponge *but* the one thing I struggled with was getting a beautiful golden sponge – something that traditional sponges with all their yolks and butter did rather beautifully and naturally. The final piece of the puzzle came when I had worked tirelessly to develop a soft, golden fluffy vrioche. My tests started with potato and ended with sweet potato for the perfect golden hue. I've paired this cake with a beautiful, tart berry jam and vanilla whipped cream.

SPONGE

1. Preheat the oven to 180°C fan (350°F/gas 4) with an oven shelf in the middle of the oven. Line the bases of two 20 cm (8 in) round sandwich or springform tins (pans) with baking parchment.
2. Add the flour, cornflour, both sugars, baking powder, bicarbonate of soda and salt. Whisk gently to combine.
3. Add the wet ingredients and the cooled sweet potato to a blender and blend until smooth – an immersion stick blender is also great for this.
4. Add the liquid to the dry mix and mix with a whisk until smooth.
5. Pour the batter into the lined tins (450 g/15.9 oz) in each tin. Bake for 18–20 minutes, or until the top is smooth and golden and springs back when lightly pressed.
6. Leave to cool in the tins on a wire rack. Once cooled, carefully release the sponges from the tins by using a sharp paring knife and running it along the edges, carefully pushing against the tins for a clean release.

TO ASSEMBLE

7. Trim the domed top on one of the sponges. This will be your base piece of sponge.
8. Whisk the jam so it is soft and spreadable, then, using a small palette knife, spread it over the base sponge almost to the edge. You can use the ring as a guide to spread up to with a palette knife.
9. Place whole raspberries along the perimeter of the base sponge, leaving a gap in between, the same width as a raspberry.
10. Pipe alternating dots of the whipped cream between the raspberries, then pipe the cream in a spiral in the middle of the cake and out to the edge so the sponge is covered in a generous layer of cream.
11. Place the remaining piece of sponge on top and dust with icing sugar. Top with a single raspberry and serve immediately. Store in an airtight container in the refrigerator for up to 2 days.

plain (all-purpose) flour	280 g	9.9 oz
cornflour (cornstarch)	40 g	1.4 oz
caster (superfine) sugar	300 g	10.6 oz
muscovado sugar	28 g	1 oz
baking powder	8 g	2 tsp
bicarbonate of soda (baking soda)	4 g	1 tsp
salt	2 g	½ tsp
peanut (groundnut) or sunflower oil	80 g	2.8 oz
soy milk	320 g	11.3 oz
vinegar, any type	10 g	0.4 oz
vanilla extract	10 g	0.4 oz
sweet potato, cooked and cooled	55 g	1.9 oz

ALSO NEEDED

Berry Jam (page 202)	130 g	4.6 oz
Thick Whipped Vanilla Bean Cream (page 237)	200 g	7 oz
raspberries, plus 1 to decorate	125 g	4.4 oz
icing (confectioners') sugar		for dusting

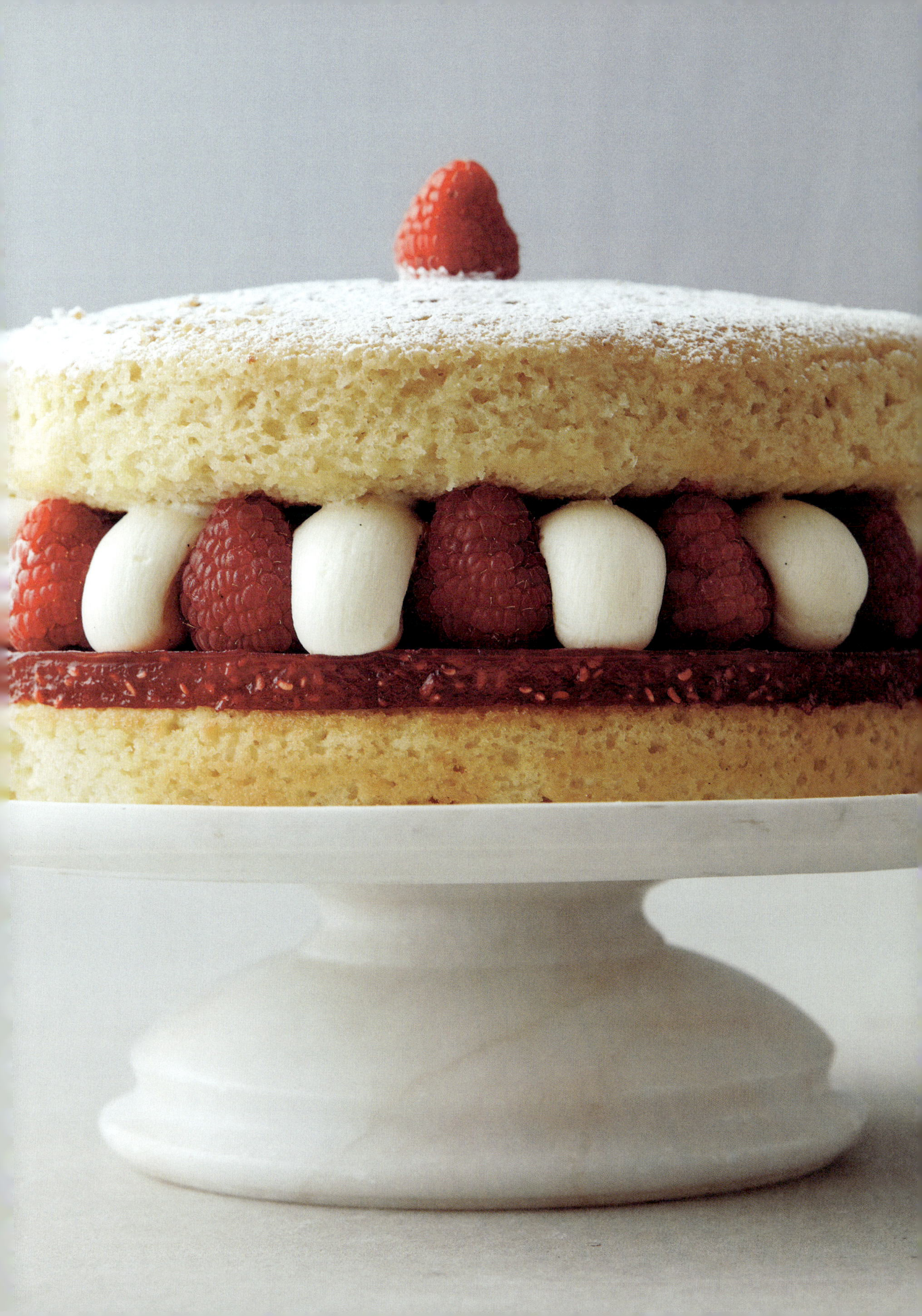

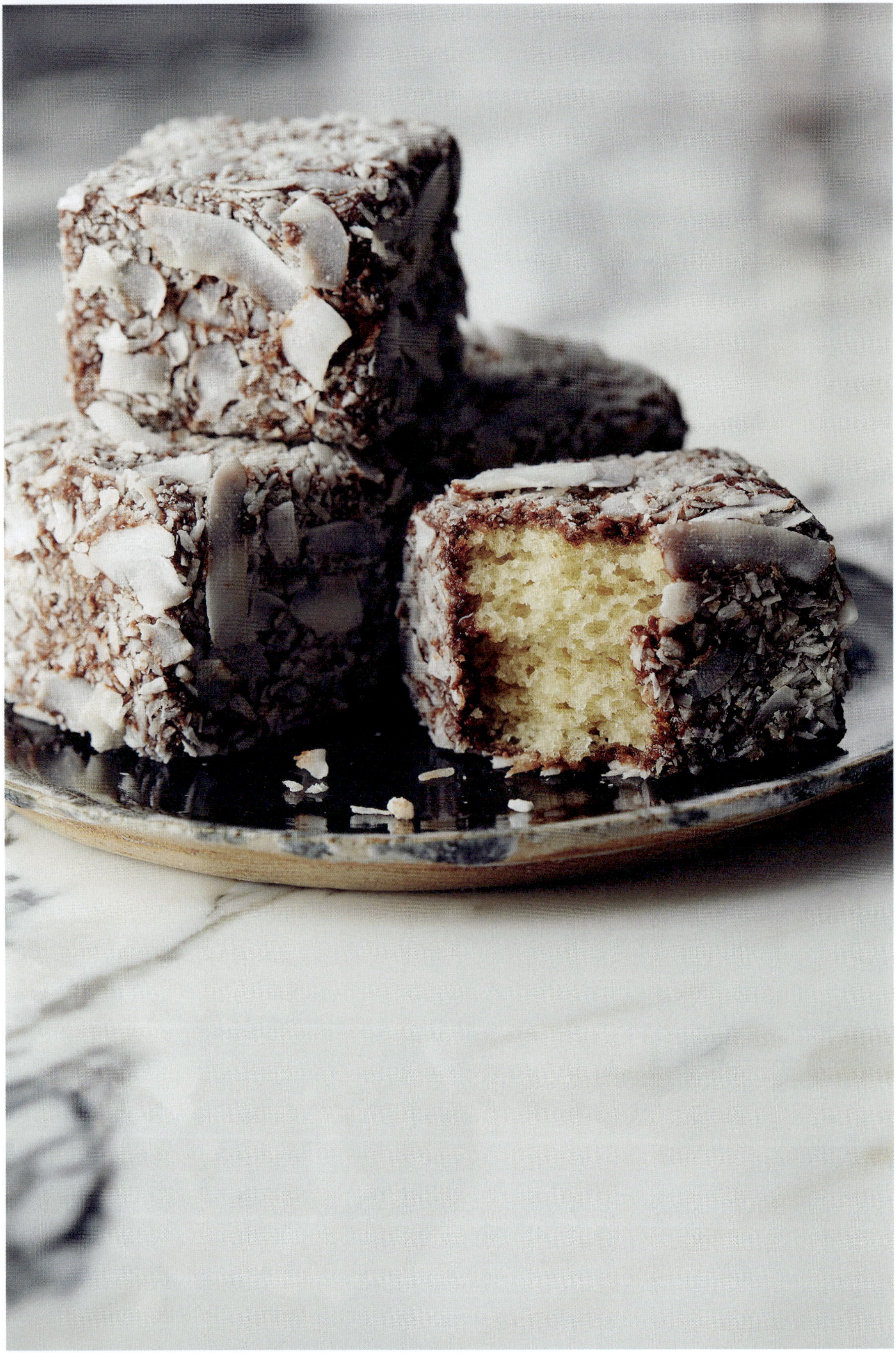

LAMINGTONS

Makes 12–15 cubes

This is a cake that stole my heart as a sweet-loving kid – or rather a treat I used to steal from my grandparents' refrigerator! One of my earliest sweet memories are the featherlight (albeit dry) shop-bought Lamingtons. This little queen of small baked goods was created in New Zealand (as determined by analysis of a 2014 study of a watercolour painting and news reports of Lord Lamington's visit!) where it was called the Wellington and 'stolen' or borrowed by Lord Lamington, the governor of Queensland. It appeared in 1902 for the first time and was credited to Lord Lamington. It is widely recognised as Australian, although a recent study of his visit to New Zealand as well as a watercolour painting revealed it had indeed originated in New Zealand. A Lamington has two main components, and there have been huge amounts of effort to elevate it (Nadine Ingham in Sydney famously dipped her sponge in a coconut panna cotta). Lamingtons are best made the day before.

LIGHT VANILLA SPONGE

1. Preheat the oven to 180°C fan (350°F/gas 4). Line a rectangular 23 × 33 × 3 cm (9 × 13 × 1 in) cake tin (pan) with baking parchment.

2. This sponge mimics the reverse creaming method pioneered by American author Rose Levy Berenbaum. Add the flour, cornflour, sugar, baking powder, bicarbonate of soda and salt to a large bowl, then add the oil and mix it in well. You can use your fingertips to help speed this up, or a stand mixer fitted with a beater attachment. Mix until the oil 'coats' the dry mix – this inhibits gluten development and creates a tight, light even crumb.

3. Mix the vanilla, coconut milk and vinegar together in another large bowl or jug, then add three-quarters of it to the dry mix and mix until you achieve a paste. I hold some of the liquid back so it is thick enough to break down any lumps of the dry mixture, then continue adding the remaining liquid and mix with a whisk until smooth.

4. Pour the batter into the lined tin and use a silicone spatula or a small palette knife to spread the mixture flat. Bake for 12–15 minutes until the top is golden and the centre springs back when gently pressed.

5. Remove from the oven and leave to cool in the tin for 2–3 minutes, then turn the sponge out onto a wire rack to cool without it sweating on the paper – if it sweats it might not pull off the sponge nicely.

plain (all-purpose) flour	280 g	9.9 oz
cornflour (cornstarch)	40 g	1.4 oz
caster (superfine) sugar	320 g	11.3 oz
baking powder	8 g	2 tsp
bicarbonate of soda (baking soda)	2 g	½ tsp
salt	1 g	¼ tsp
peanut (groundnut) oil or sunflower oil	80 g	2.8 oz
vanilla extract	10 g	0.4 oz
coconut milk	320 g	11.3 oz
vinegar, any type	16 g	0.6 oz

CHOCOLATE DIPPING SAUCE

6 Add the coconut oil to a microwave-safe bowl and microwave for 30–60 seconds until melted. Alternatively, melt in a medium saucepan over a low heat. Set aside. Pour the hot water into a heatproof container, add the coconut oil and the remaining ingredients and blend or whisk until it is a smooth, glossy sauce. Set aside.

TO ASSEMBLE

7 Once the sponge sheet has cooled down completely, using a serrated knife, cut the sheet into 12 neat cubes.

8 You need to set up two 'stations' to keep everything tidy! Working from left to right, set out the prepared sponges, a shallow bowl for the chocolate dipping sauce, followed by a flat baking sheet for the coconut.

9 For the dipping technique, use one hand (gloves are handy) to dip into the chocolate sauce, then into the coconut and roll the sponge around until coated. Press them onto a flat surface to 'tuck' the coconut in and 'flatten' the surface and sharpen the corners. When Lamingtons are judged in competitions, one of the criteria is often how square they are. Store in an airtight container at room temperature for up to 3 days.

coconut oil (deodorised)	25 g	0.9 oz
water, hot	90 g	3.2 oz
icing (confectioners') sugar	300 g	10.6 oz
cocoa (unsweetened chocolate) powder	45 g	1.6 oz

ALSO NEEDED

desiccated (dry shredded) coconut	200 g	7 oz

TIP

I like to wipe my work surface down with a moist cloth and spread a layer of cling film (plastic wrap) (is best!) on the surface, then sprinkle it with a 1 cm (½ in) layer of desiccated coconut for the coating part. You may want to split the coating in coconut into two stages to help keep the dipping sauce free of coconut and vice versa.

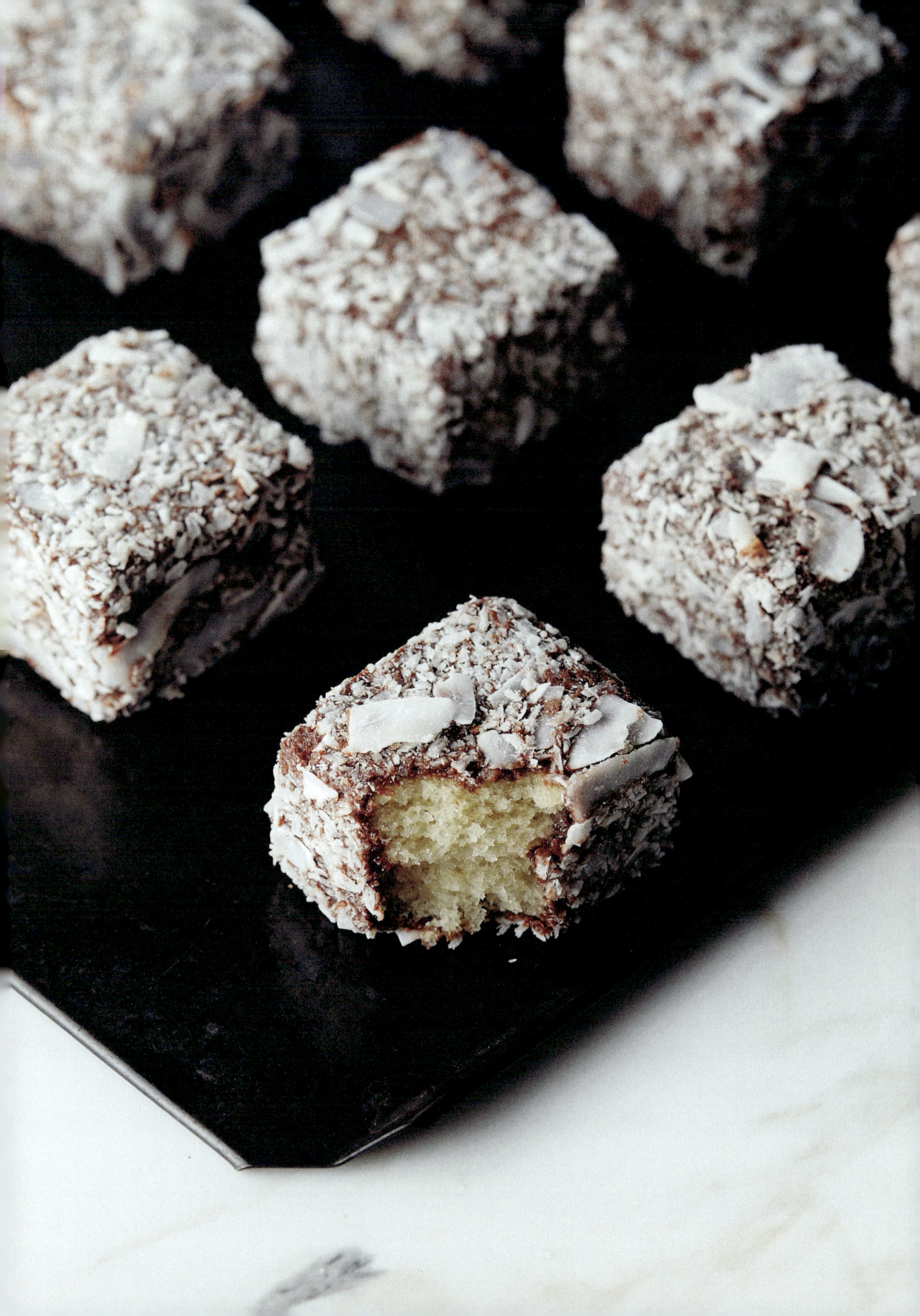

EXTRA VIRGIN OLIVE OIL CAKE

Makes a 23 cm (9 in) cake

In so many recipes of mine where I use extra virgin olive oil, it doesn't contribute a lot of flavour because not much is used, but in this recipe I wanted to celebrate its beautiful distinctive flavour. For the olive oil cream we are making an emulsion – the fancy word for blending and holding oil and water together in the silkiest cream ever known to the gods.

OLIVE OIL CAKE BATTER

1. Preheat the oven to 180°C fan (350°F/gas 4) with an oven shelf in the middle of the oven. Line the base of a 23 cm (9 in) cake tin (pan) with baking parchment.
2. Blend the chopped apple, lemon juice, mandarin segments, lemon zest, mandarin zest, soy milk, olive oil and rosemary leaves in a blender until smooth. You can also use an immersion stick blender in a large bowl.
3. Whisk the caster sugar, plain flour, baking powder, bicarbonate of soda and salt together in a large bowl.
4. Add the blended liquids to the dry ingredients and mix until mix well combined.
5. Pour the batter into the prepared tin. Sprinkle Demerara sugar over the top and bake for 30 minutes, or until golden and the top springs back when pressed with your fingertips.
6. Leave to cool completely on a wire rack, then remove from the tin.

apples, cored and chopped into 2 cm (¾ in) pieces	120 g	4.2 oz
lemon juice	28 g	1 oz
mandarin, peeled	60 g	2.1 oz
lemon zest, grated	1 lemon	
mandarin zest, grated	1 mandarin	
soy milk	240 g	8.5 oz
extra virgin olive oil	100 g	3.9 oz
rosemary	6 leaves	
caster (superfine) sugar	220 g	7.8 oz
plain (all-purpose) flour	250 g	8.8 oz
baking powder	8 g	2 tsp
bicarbonate of soda (baking soda)	4 g	¾ tsp
salt	1 g	¼ tsp
Demerara sugar	for sprinkling	

OLIVE OIL CURD

7. Pour the soy milk into a small blending jug or in a microwave bowl and microwave for 20 seconds, or until lukewarm. Alternatively, warm the milk in a small saucepan over a low heat. Add the sugar and olive oil and use a hand-held blender to blend until it is silky, thick and creamy.
8. Spread it on top of the cooled cake with a palette knife. This cake keeps very well in an airtight container at room temperature for 3–4 days.

soy milk	40 g	1.4 oz
caster (superfine) sugar	80 g	3.8 oz
extra virgin olive oil	60 g	2 oz
lemon juice	10 g	0.4 oz

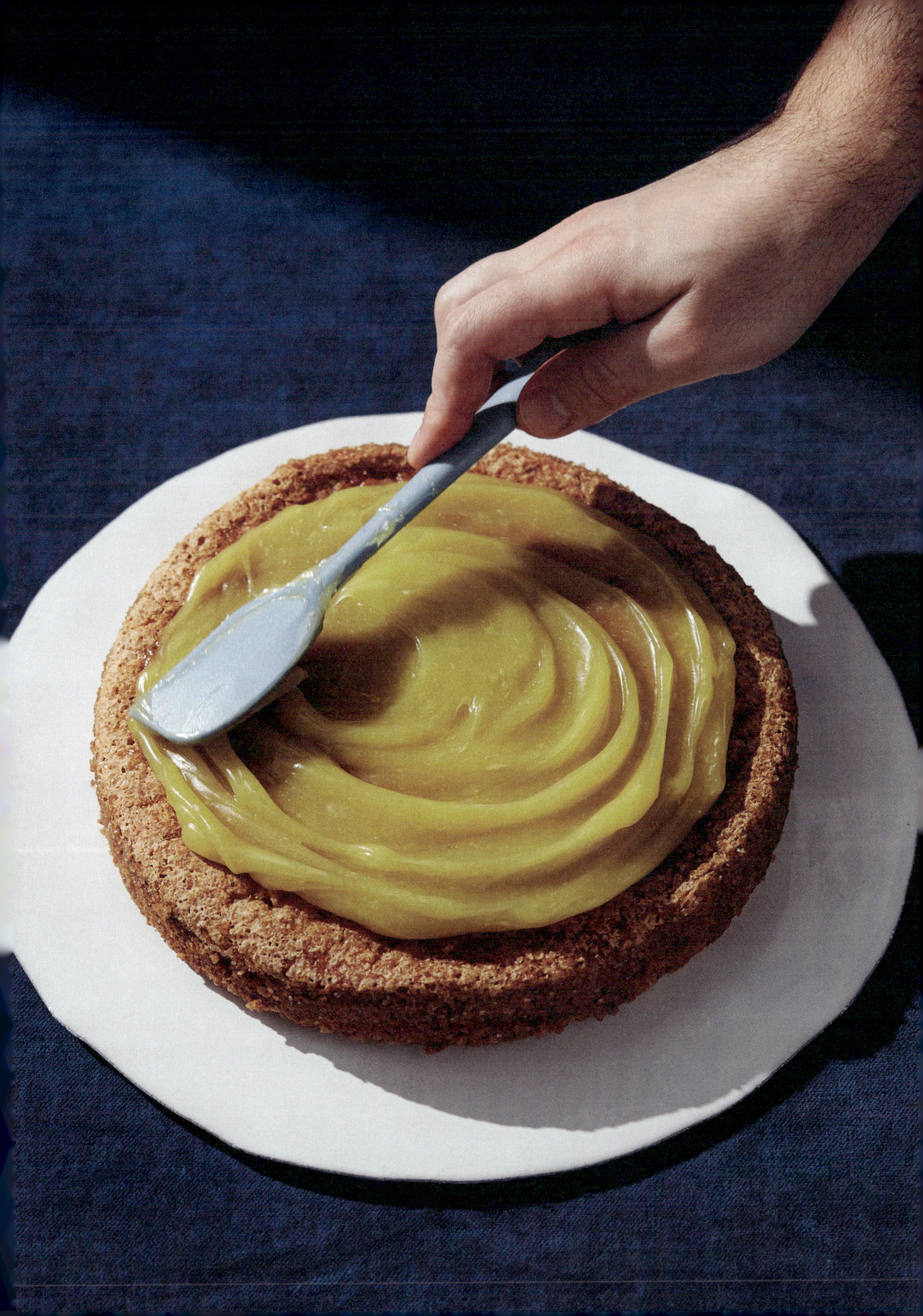

CAKES

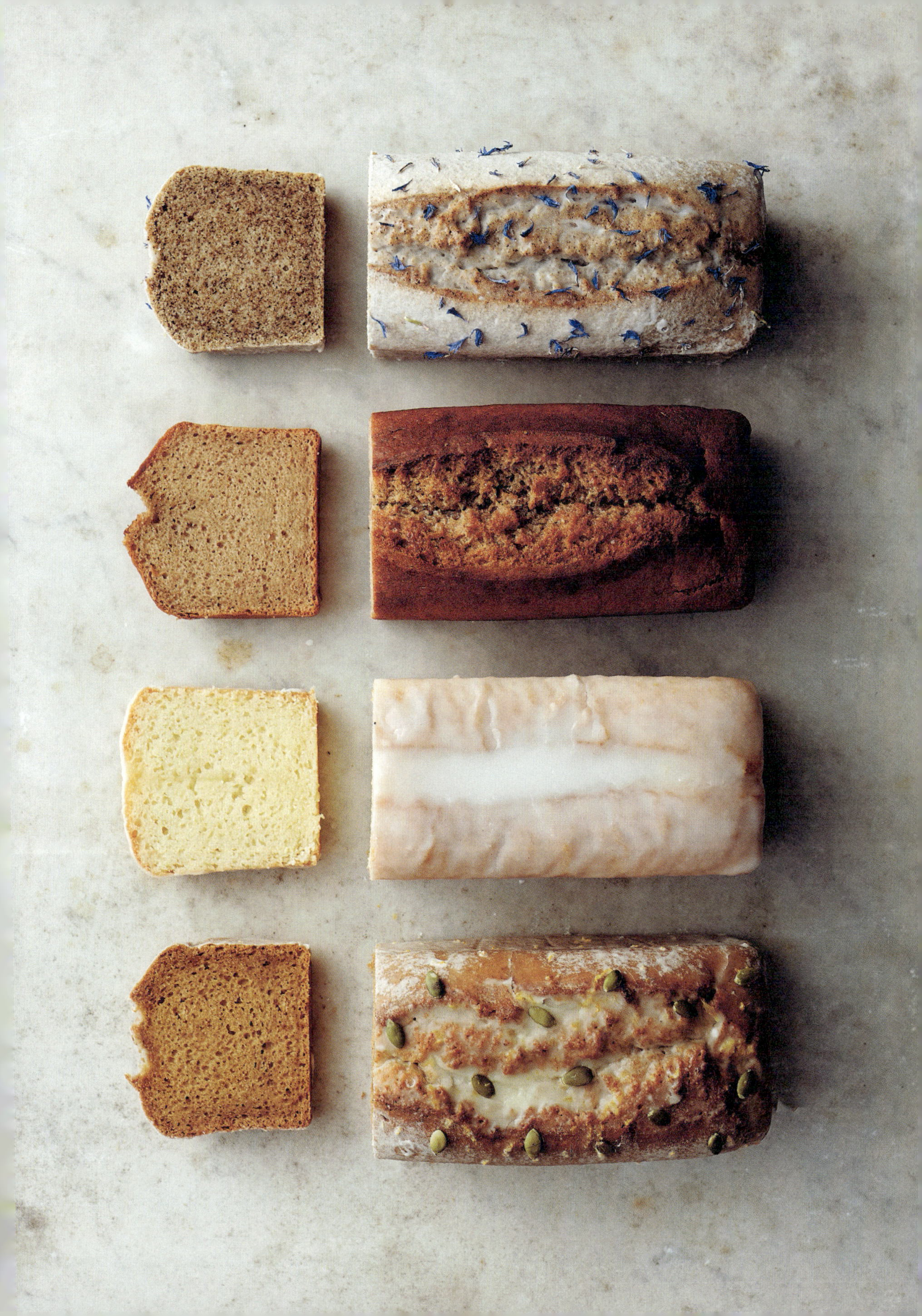

EARL GREY LOAF CAKE

Makes a 450 g (15.9 oz) loaf

Tea-flavoured tea cake has a ring to it. This little loaf celebrates the incredible perfume of bergamot (an Italian citrus fruit) essential oil which flavours Earl Grey tea – one of my first flavour loves. It awakened my taste buds and started an infatuation with Earl Grey tea.

1. Preheat the oven to 180°C fan (350°F/gas 4) with an oven shelf in the middle of the oven. Line a small 450 g (15.9 oz) loaf tin (pan) with baking parchment.

2. Add the sugar, flour and tea leaves to a high-powered blender and blitz briefly to extract the flavoursome bergamot flavour. Transfer to a large bowl and stir in the baking powder.

3. Add the olive oil and plant-based milk and use a whisk to mix all the ingredients together until fully combined.

4. Pour the batter into the lined loaf tin and bake for 30–35 minutes until golden and the top of the loaf is set and springs back when gently pressed with your fingertips, or a skewer inserted into the centre of the cake comes out clean.

5. With the help of the baking parchment, remove the loaf from the tin and leave to cool on a wire rack with a rimmed baking sheet underneath.

caster (superfine) sugar	180 g	6.3 oz
plain (all-purpose) flour (gluten-free plain flour will also work)	200 g	7 oz
Earl Grey tea leaves	8 g	2 tsp
baking powder	6 g	1½ tsp
extra virgin olive oil	60 g	2 oz
plant-based milk	200 g	7 oz

ICING AND TO FINISH

6. Slowly mix the icing sugar and water together in a small bowl or measuring jug until it is fully combined and smooth.

7. Drizzle the icing (frosting) on top of the cooled cake (still on the wire rack with the baking sheet underneath to catch the drips) and leave to set for 30 minutes–1 hour. Decorate with the blue cornflower petals. This cake keeps at room temperature, well-wrapped in cling film (plastic wrap) or in an airtight container for up to 5 days.

icing (confectioners') sugar	160 g	5.6 oz
water	45 g	1.6 oz
dried blue cornflower petals, to decorate	pinch	

LINING RECTANGULAR TINS

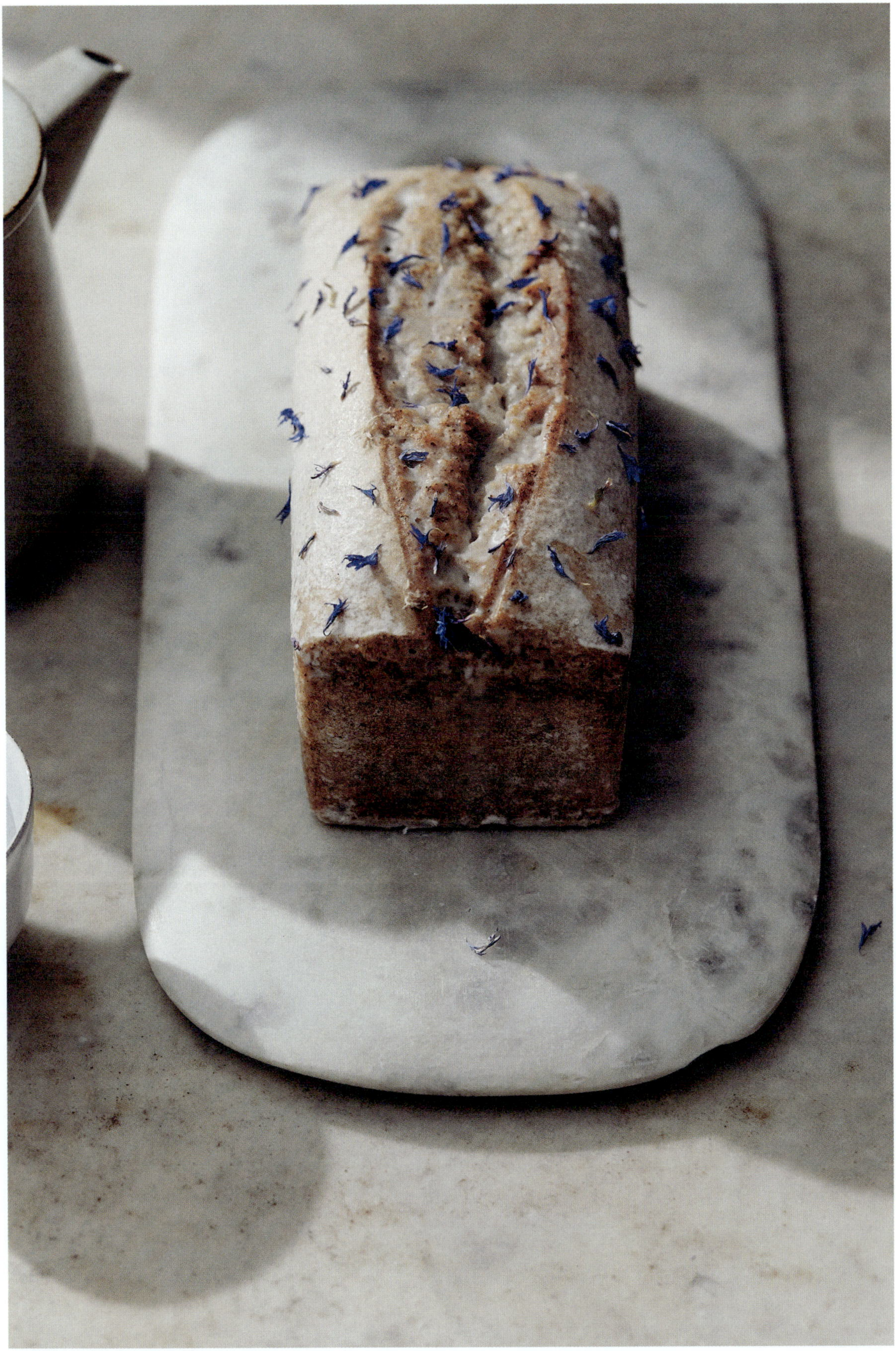

BANANA BREAD

Makes a 400 g (1 lb) loaf

Made infamous in the first Covid lockdown in 2020, banana bread may not be actual bread but this famous recipe is not far off from a quick bread (leavened by baking powder). Banana is the only ingredient in this recipe that is a non-negotiable (I lie – so is the baking powder). For the best flavour, use browning/black bananas. You can speed up their ripening by placing them in a paper bag with apples – this releases ethylene which speeds things up. I have tried many other methods and I'm sad to say they don't work – they make the bananas brown and soft but do nothing for the flavour. The recipe is very flexible – use any sugar, any oil and plain (all-purpose) flour or gluten-free flour, which all work fantasically well and you can load it up with any optional extras you like.

1. Preheat the oven to 170°C fan (325°F/gas 3) and line a 450 g (1 lb) loaf tin (pan) with baking parchment.

2. In a large bowl, mash the bananas very well with a fork. Add the sugar and mix well, followed by the oil and any optional extras.

3. In another bowl, add the flour and baking powder, then use a whisk to gently mix together until the mixture is smooth and there are no lumps of flour. Combine with the mashed or blended banana mixture.

4. Pour the batter into the lined tin and use the back of a spoon to draw an indent down the middle of the batter lengthways. Drizzle 1 tablespoon of oil down the centre – this will make a nice clean crack down the middle.

5. Bake for 35–40 minutes. The centre of the crack is the last part of the batter that will bake, so when it looks baked/dry you will know it is done. With all loaf cakes, I recommend checking it is fully cooked by using a skewer test: insert a skewer through a crack into the middle of the loaf, anda clean skewer should emerge. Use the paper to lift the bread out of the tin and leave to cool on a wire rack. Leave the paper still attached to the bread until it cools completely. Wrap well and store in the refrigerator for up to 5 days.

bananas, browning, mashed	300 g	10.6 oz
sugar (any type will work)	100 g	3.5 oz
oil, plus extra for drizzling (any type will work)	60 g	2.1 oz
plain (all-purpose) flour (gluten-free plain flour will also work)	170 g	6 oz
baking powder	8 g	2 tsp

OPTIONAL EXTRAS

walnuts, pecans or hazelnuts, chopped	50 g	1.8 oz
dark chocolate chips	50 g	1.8 oz
ground cinnamon	4 g	1 tsp

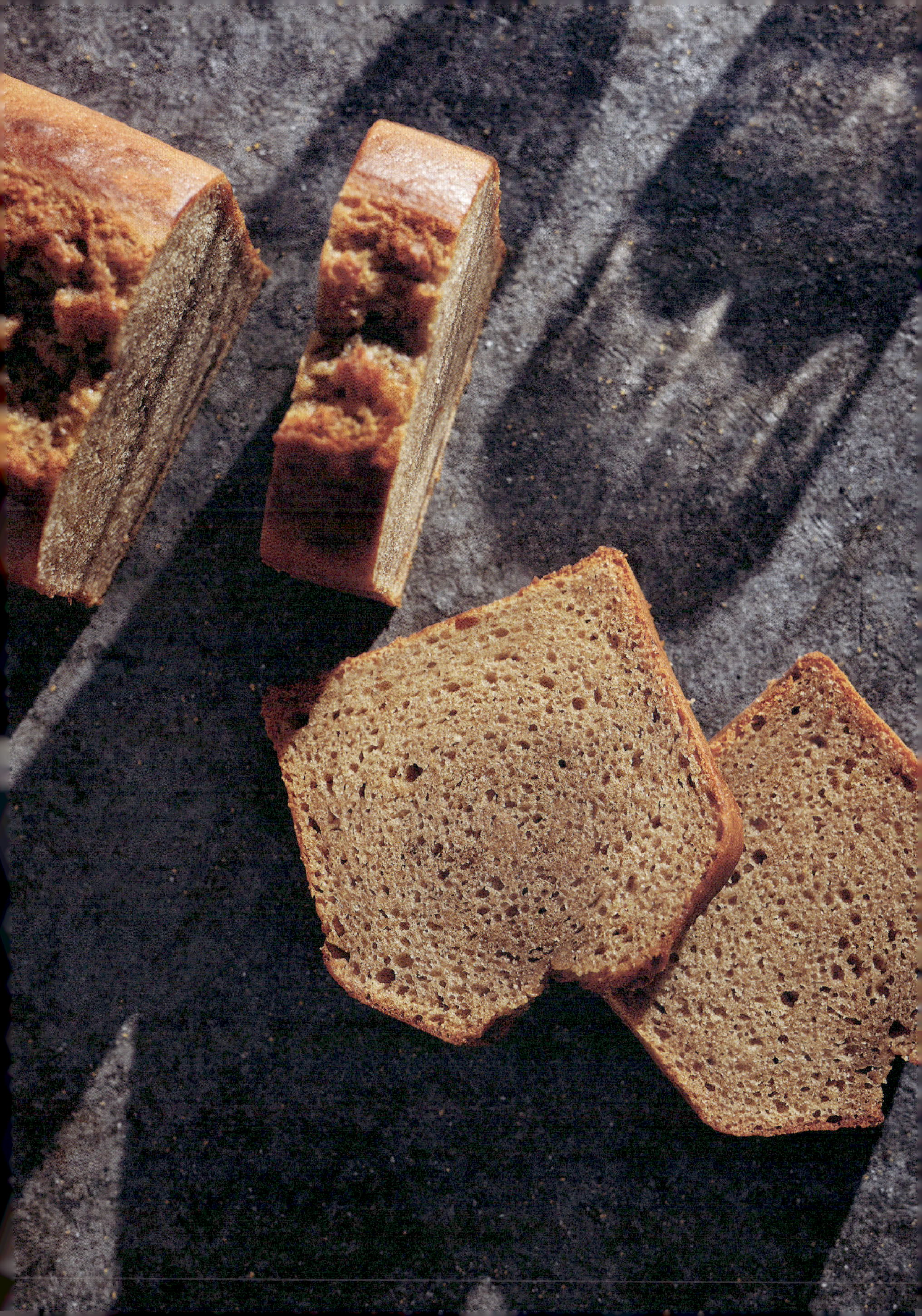

LEMON DRIZZLE LOAF

Makes a 450 g (15.9 oz) loaf

Another day, another iconic teatime treat. Most wintery days call for a lemon drizzle with it's tangy icing (frosting) that's sweet and sour enough to make you smile and pucker your lips at the same time. This cake is made with a splash of deliciously complementary extra virgin olive oil and fresh lemon. It produces a very tender crumb with less fat than is typically called for in similarly textured or 'travel cakes' – so called because they travel and keep well without refrigeration!

LEMON LOAF CAKE

1. Preheat the oven to 180°C fan (350°F/gas 4) with an oven shelf in the middle of the oven. Line a 450 g (15.9 oz) loaf tin (pan) with baking parchment.
2. Add the sugar and lemon zest to a large bowl and, using your fingertips, rub them together. This will help extract lots of juicy aromatic oils from the zest. Add the olive oil, lemon juice (1) and milk and whisk well to combine.
3. Add the flour, baking powder and bicarbonate of soda to another large bowl and use a whisk to combine the dry ingredients together. This disperses the baking powder nicely and lightens the flour.
4. Combine the wet and dry ingredients in one bowl and whisk just to combine. The batter will seem to expand slightly, but this is fine.
5. Pour the batter into the lined loaf tin and bake for 25–30 minutes until golden and the top of the loaf is set and springs back when gently pressed with your fingertips, or a skewer inserted into the centre of the cake comes out clean.
6. With the help of the baking parchment, remove the loaf from the tin and leave to cool on a wire rack with a rimmed baking sheet underneath. While hot, the lemon juice (2) onto the hot cake.

caster (superfine) sugar	180 g	6.3 oz
lemon zest	3 small lemons	
extra virgin olive oil	45 g	1.6 oz
lemon juice (1) (you can use one of the zested lemons)	20 g	0.7 oz
plant-based milk	90 g	3.2 oz
plain (all-purpose) flour	190 g	6.7 oz
baking powder	4 g	1 tsp
bicarbonate of soda (baking soda)	3 g	½ tsp
lemon juice (2) (you can use one of the zested lemons)	20 g	0.7 oz

LEMON DRIZZLE ICING AND TO FINISH

7. Slowly mix the icing sugar and lemon juice together in a small bowl or measuring jug until it is fully combined and smooth.
8. Drizzle the icing (frosting) on top of the cooled lemon cake (still on the wire rack with the baking sheet underneath to catch the drips) and leave to set for 30 minutes–1 hour. This cake keeps at room temperature, well wrapped in cling film (plastic wrap) or in an airtight container for up to 4 days.

icing (confectioners') sugar	110 g	3.9 oz
lemon juice (you can use one of the zested lemons)	20 g	0.7 oz

VARIATIONS

Lemon and poppy seed | Add 10 g (½ oz) poppy seeds to the dry ingredients and sprinkle on top of the fresh icing (frosting).

Lemon and lime | Add additional zest of 1 lime to the recipe, and use the juice and ½ teaspoon vanilla bean paste in the icing for a fragrant riff.

TIP

Add 5 g (1 tsp) more lemon juice for a thinner icing to coat the entire cake.

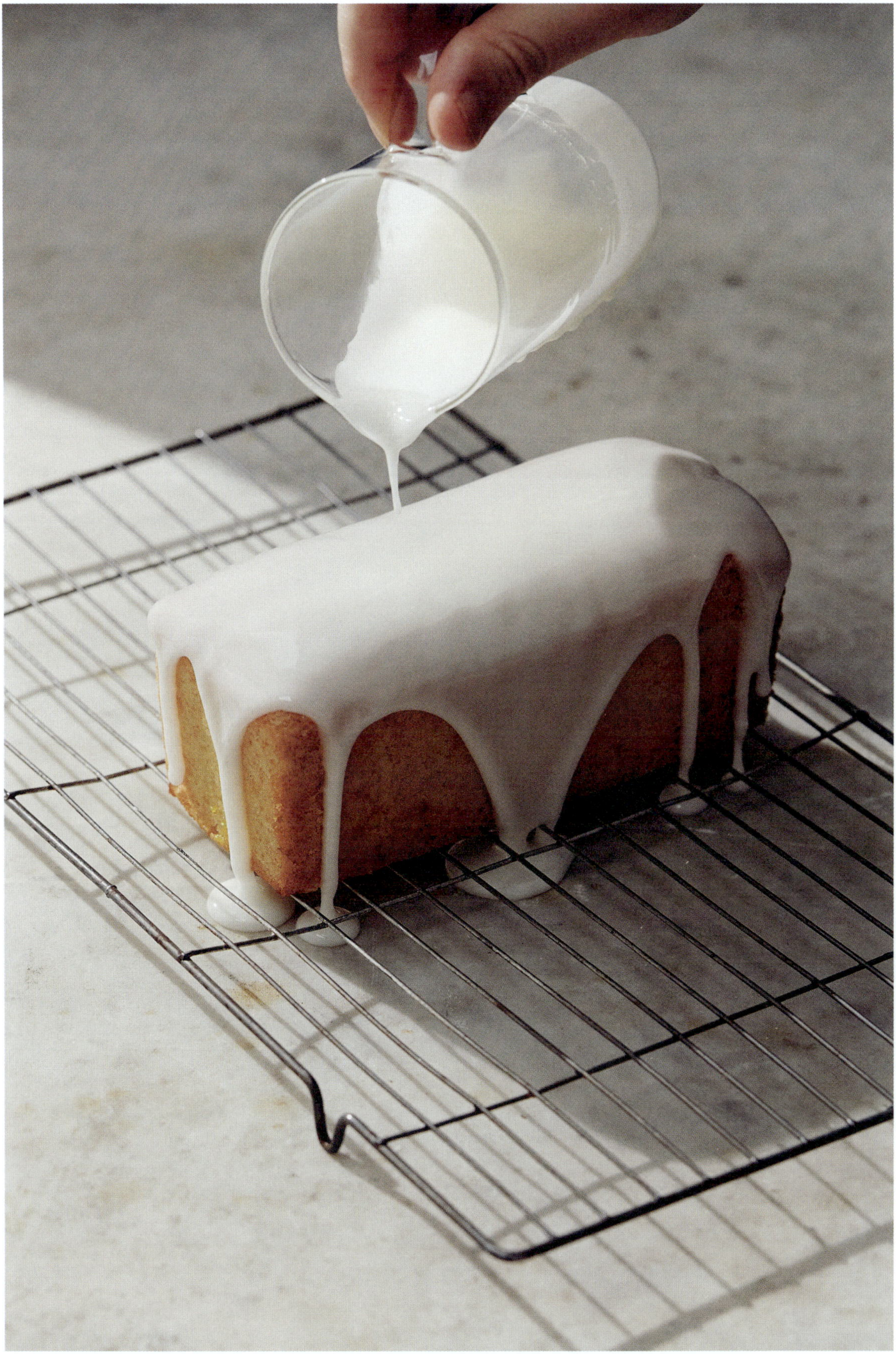

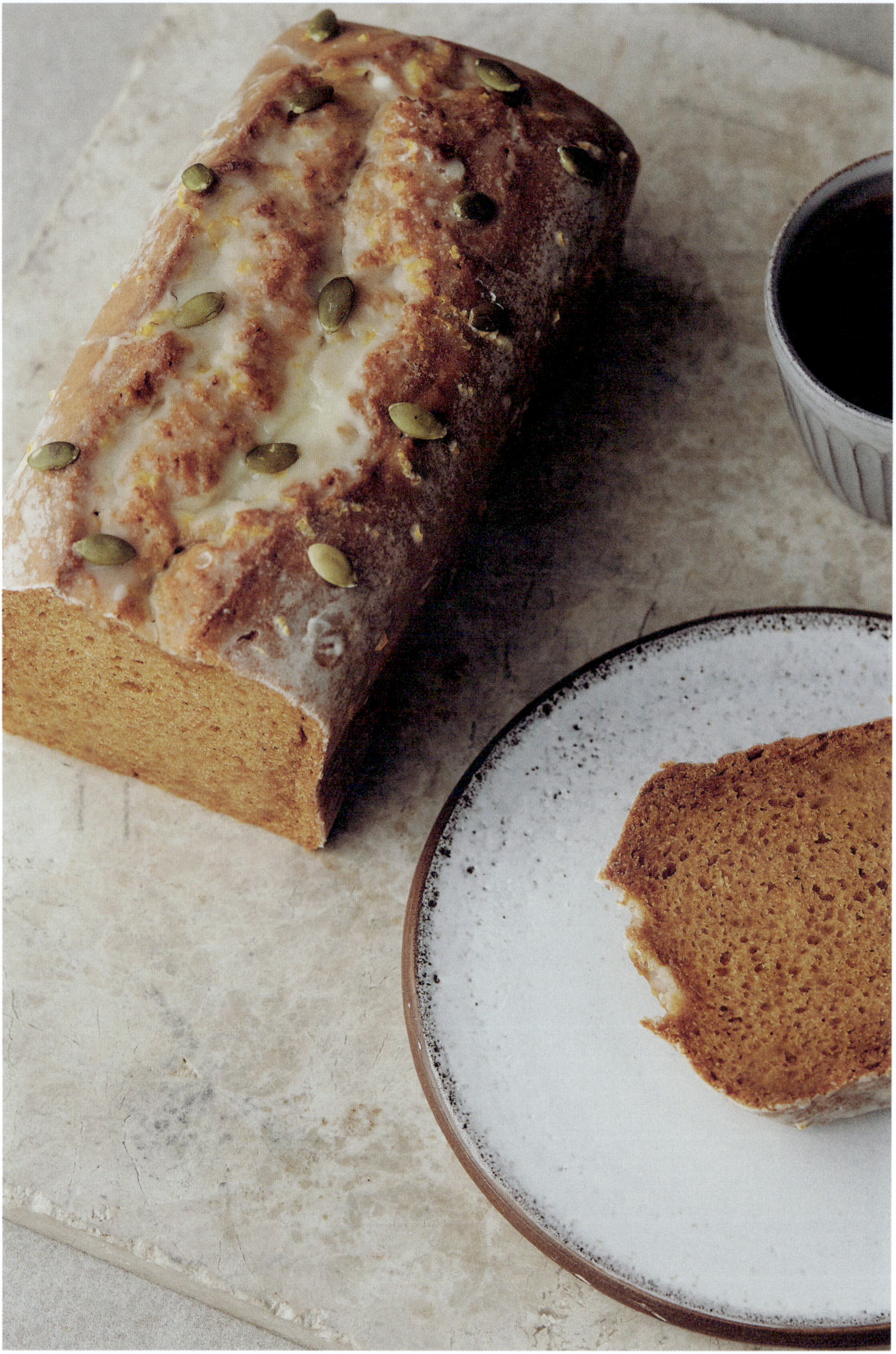

PUMPKIN SPICE LOAF CAKE

Makes a 600 g (1 lb 5 oz) loaf

#PSL takes on a new meaning with this little loaf of pumpkin spice coated in an orange-zest icing (frosting). You can also use sweet potato as a direct substitute for the pumpkin.

PUMPKIN SPICE BATTER

1. Preheat the oven to 180°C fan (350°F/gas 4) with an oven shelf in the middle of the oven. Line a small 600 g (1 lb 5 oz) loaf tin (pan) with baking parchment.

2. Cut the pumpkin into 3 cm (1¼ in) chunks, add them to a saucepan large enough to just cover them with water and simmer for 12–15 minutes until a sharp knife or skewer meets no resistance when you poke a piece of the pumpkin. Strain the pumpkin, discarding the water. Leave the pumpkin to chill in the refrigerator for 30 minutes until it is cooled to room temperature.

3. Add the cooled pumpkin, both sugars, olive oil, orange zest, milk and vinegar to a large bowl and blend with an immersion stick blender (or add to a blender) until smooth.

4. Add the flour, baking powder, bicarbonate of soda and spices to another large bowl and mix with a whisk.

5. Add the blended liquids to the dry ingredients and mix together with the whisk until combined.

6. Pour the batter into the lined loaf tin and bake for 30–35 minutes, or until golden and the top of the loaf is set and springs back when gently pressed with your fingertips, or a skewer inserted into the centre of the cake through a crack comes out clean.

7. With the help of the baking parchment, remove the loaf from the tin and leave to cool completely on a wire rack with a rimmed baking sheet underneath.

pumpkin, peeled and deseeded	150 g	5.3 oz
muscovado sugar	60 g	2 oz
caster (superfine) sugar	80 g	2.8 oz
extra virgin olive oil	40 g	1.4 oz
orange zest	5 g	1 tsp
plant-based milk, room temperature	112 g	4 oz
apple cider vinegar	5 g	1 tsp
plain (all-purpose) flour (gluten-free plain flour will also work)	150 g	5.3 oz
baking powder	4 g	1 tsp
bicarbonate of soda (baking soda)	3 g	½ tsp
ground cinnamon	1 g	¼ tsp
ground nutmeg	1 g	½ tsp
ground ginger	1 g	½ tsp
ground cloves	0.5 g	¼ tsp

ICING AND TO FINISH

8. Slowly mix all the icing (frosting) ingredients (except the pumpkin seeds) together in a small bowl or measuring jug until it is fully combined and smooth.

9. Drizzle the icing on top of the cooled loaf cake (still on the wire rack with the baking sheet underneath to catch the drips), sprinkle on the pumpkin seeds and leave to set for 30 minutes–1 hour. This cake keeps at room temperature, well-wrapped in cling film (plastic wrap) or in an airtight container for up to 5 days.

icing (confectioners') sugar	165 g	5.8 oz
orange juice	45 g	1.6 oz
orange zest		¼ orange
pumpkin seeds	8 g	2 tbsp

ORANGE AND ALMOND CAKE

Makes a 23 cm (9 in) single-layer cake

This is my version of a flourless orange cake which I love to eat. It's based on a classic Italian whole orange cake that is traditionally flourless (and gluten-free), relying on eggs to bind it, and whole oranges (pick seedless varieties) boiled in water until soft, then puréed. Polenta (cornmeal) lends a beautiful golden colour and the cake utilises a whole orange to provide a wholesome orange flavour! The skin contains a huge amount of aromatic oils that impart their beautiful citrus flavour and a hint of bitterness, and the pithy skin contains large amounts of fibre and pectins. Use a gluten-free baking powder to keep it gluten free.

1. Line the base of a 23 cm (9 in) round sandwich or springform tin (pan) with baking parchment. Rub a fingertip dipped in oil around the sides of the tin.

2. Wash the orange well, then bring to a simmer in a small saucepan of water over a low heat. Cook for 30 minutes, then remove from the water and leave to cool completely. The cooking will tenderise the skin and remove some of the bitterness from the white pith of the peel. Cut into small pieces.

3. Add the 250 g (8.8 oz) of cooled orange with milk and olive oil to a blender or food processor and purée until smooth.

4. Add all the dry ingredients to a large bowl and stir gently with a whisk to disperse all the ingredients.

5. Scrape the blended orange purée into the bowl and mix until everything is well combined. Leave the batter to rest for 1 hour to soften the texture of the polenta.

6. Preheat the oven to 180°C fan (350°F/gas 4). Pour the batter into the lined tin and bake for 35–40 minutes. You will know when this cake is ready when it has domed slightly across the top and has taken on some light browning.

7. Leave the cake to cool completely in the tin set on a wire rack, then run a sharp knife against the edge of the tin to release the sides. Decorate with fresh citrus segments. If topping with fresh fruit, this cake is best eaten on the same day but, without fruit, store the base in an airtight container in the refrigerator for up to 5 days.

extra virgin olive oil, plus extra for rubbing	40 g	1.4 oz
whole orange (approx. 1 large)	250 g	8.8 oz
oat or soy milk	160 g	5.6 oz
ground almonds	180 g	6.3 oz
baking powder	8 g	2 tsp
bicarbonate of soda (baking soda)	2 g	½ tsp
caster (superfine) sugar	180 g	6.3 oz
ground cinnamon		pinch
polenta (cornmeal)	100 g	3.9 oz
fresh citrus segments		to decorate

NOTE

One orange weighs between 200–300 g (7–11 oz). It is better to cook some more oranges in multiples of 250 g (8.8 oz), make a purée and reserve the extra purée in Ziploc bags in the freezer as the oranges should be cooked whole.

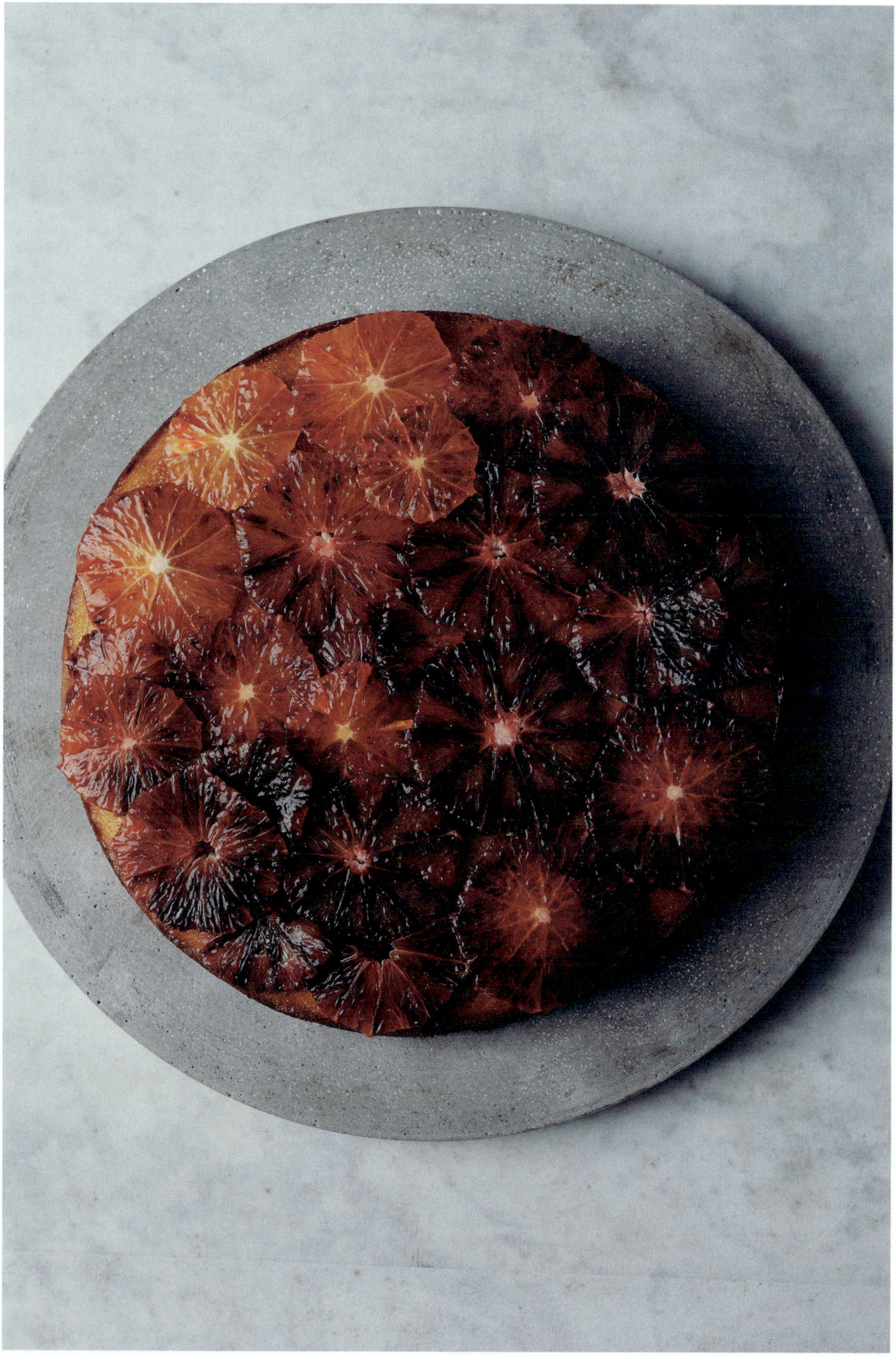

BANANA TATIN CAKE

Makes a 23 cm (9 in) cake

If you've gotten this far into the book you might have realised I love bananas. This banana cake is no exception. It's like any upside-down cake where the fruit is cooked with caramel or muscovado sugar underneath the cake, which soaks up the excess syrup from the cooking fruit. This is one of those impressive to eat but simple to make teatime cakes that can be whipped up easily. It's great as a slice of cake or warmed slightly and served as a dessert with a scoop of ice cream or pouring cream on the side.

muscovado sugar (1)	80 g	2.8 oz
bananas, whole	5 bananas	
bananas, peeled	300 g	10.6 oz
muscovado sugar (2)	100 g	3.5 oz
plant-based milk	200 g	7 oz
vanilla bean paste	10 g	0.4 oz
extra virgin olive oil	50 g	1.8 oz
plain (all-purpose) flour	240 g	8.5 oz
baking powder	10 g	0.4 oz
bicarbonate of soda (baking soda)	4 g	1 tsp
salt	1 g	¼ tsp
ice cream, cream or Fresh Whipping Cream (page 236)	to serve (optional)	

1. Preheat the oven to 180°C fan (350°F/gas 4) and line the base of a 23 cm (9 in) springform tin (pan) with baking parchment. Sprinkle the muscovado sugar (1) in an even layer onto the baking parchment in the tin.

2. Before peeling the five bananas, lay them flat on a cutting board and cut them in half. Peel off the skins, then arrange the banana halves, flat-side down, in the tin, starting on one side of the tin so the bananas line up concurrently – trim if needed.

3. Mash the 300 g (10.6 oz) of banana in a large bowl, then add the muscovado sugar (2), milk, vanilla paste and olive oil and mix to combine.

4. Add the flour, baking powder, bicarbonate of soda and salt to another large bowl and mix gently with a whisk to combine and 'sieve' the flour. Add the wet ingredients to the dry ingredients and fold in until just combined.

5. Pour the batter over the bananas in the lined tin, then cover the batter with kitchen foil and fold the sides over to capture some steam.

6. Bake for 30 minutes with the foil on, then remove the foil and bake for another 5–10 minutes so the top dries out and gets some colour.

7. Leave the cake to cool completely in the tin set on a wire rack, then run a sharp knife against the edge of the tin to release the sides.

8. Turn the cake out onto a plate so the banana is on top and serve on its own or with ice cream, cream or a dollop of whipped cream. This cake keeps well in an airtight container at room temperature for 5 days.

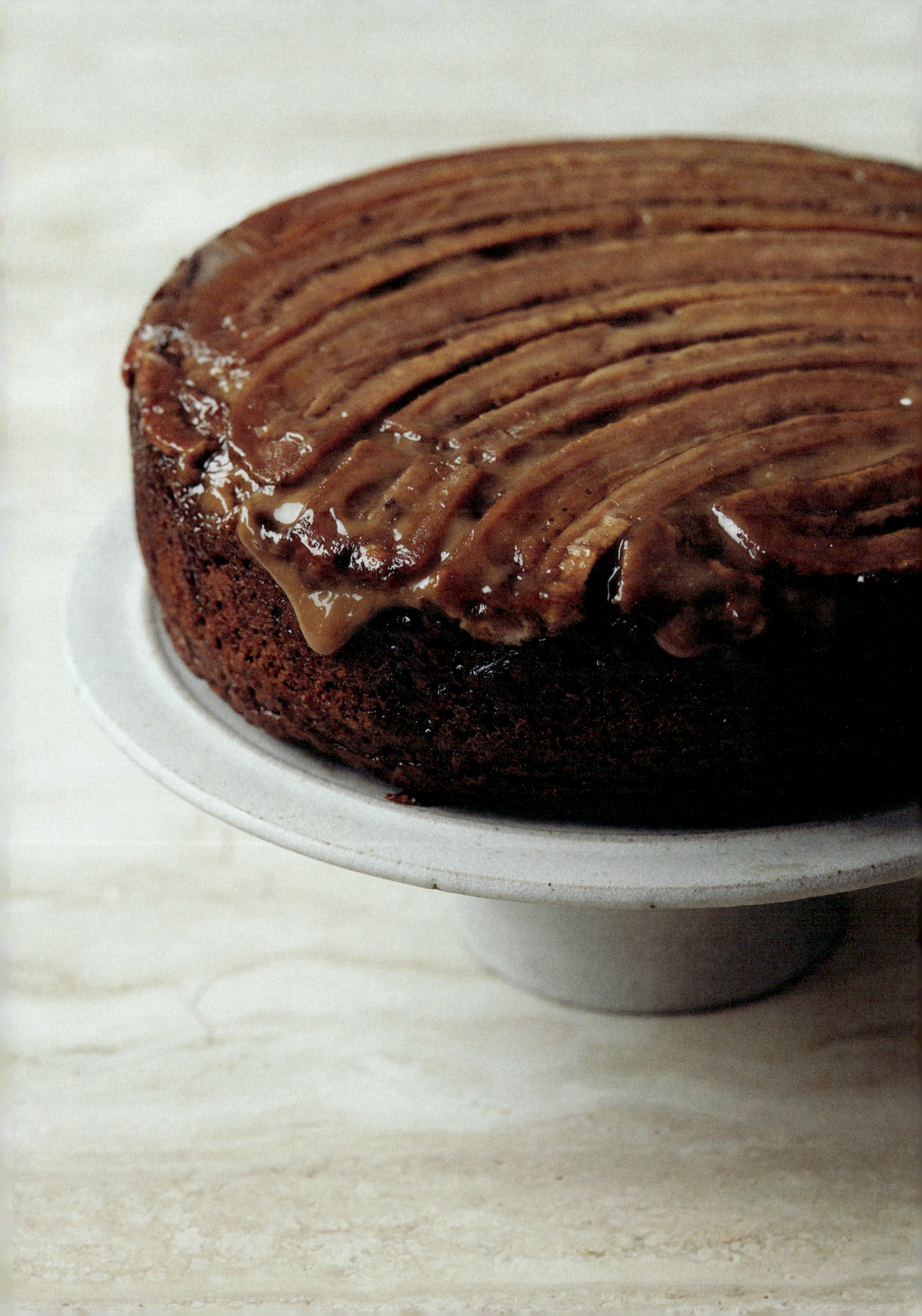

PEAR, HAZELNUT AND ALMOND GATEAU

Makes a 20 cm (8 in) cake

Sal de Riso created an iconic cake in his Amalfi coast patisserie. It was a signature cake from 1988 that came to embody the Amalfi coast and became world famous in the days of travel magazines, long before the internet and Instagram. His original cake was the sole inspiration for this one, although I have had to totally re-invent it, but I want to give credit to Sal for creating a beautiful cake to begin with.

You may notice that there are no added fat/oils; these come naturally from the nuts which are blended with the flour. This extracts a lot of oil and lends an incredible nutty flavour to the cake. Indeed, if any extra fat was added the flour wouldn't be able to do it's job of binding so well and the cake would crumble.

ALMOND CREAM

1. Blend all the ingredients in a high-powered blender. It needs to be very high powered in order to blend the almonds finely to a cream consistency. As you blend this mixture for 1 minute, it will gently heat up the mixture. The coconut oil will eventually melt and an emulsion will form. Continue blending until the almond skin (if present) looks like a tiny grain of sand. The finished mixture will be around 40–45°C (104–113°F).

2. Pass this mixture through a very fine sieve (fine-mesh strainer) – this will remove the largest almond skin particles for a silky smooth texture. This recipe will only produce 2 teaspoons of the skin which you can add to the hazelnut cake batter.

3. Pour the cream into a shallow container so it is no more than 2 cm (¾ in) thick, then cover the surface with cling film (plastic wrap) and leave it to chill in the refrigerator for at least 4 hours, or overnight.

4. When the cream is sufficiently chilled, transfer it to a stand mixer fitted with a whisk attachment and whisk on high speed to a stable peak that holds its shape. Make sure the cream is really cold (5°C/41°F), or it might not whisk. If this is the case, put the cream in the freezer for 15 minutes, before whipping again.

raw almonds	85 g	3 oz
soy milk	250 g	8.8 oz
caster (superfine) sugar	72 g	2.5 oz
xanthan gum (optional)	0.5 g	
coconut oil (deodorised)	200 g	7 oz
vanilla paste, or 2 beans, scraped	8 g	2 tsp

HAZELNUT SPONGE

5. Preheat the oven to 150°C fan (300°F/gas 2). Spread the hazelnuts out into a roasting tray and roast for 15 minutes. Remove from the oven and leave them to cool completely.

6. Increase the oven temperature to 180°C fan (350°F/gas 4) and line the base of a 20 cm (8 in) springform tin (pan) with baking parchment.

7. You may notice that this recipe contains no additional fat, and this is the magic that happens. Blend the flour, sugar and roasted nuts together in a high-powered blender or food processor until the mix starts to clump together.

8. Pour the blended mixture into a large bowl and whisk in the baking powder, bicarbonate of soda and salt.

hazelnuts	90 g	3.2 oz
plain (all-purpose) flour	140 g	4.9 oz
caster (superfine) sugar	150 g	5.3 oz
baking powder	4 g	1 tsp
bicarbonate of soda (baking soda)	2 g	½ tsp
salt	1 g	¼ tsp
soy milk, warm	200 g	7 oz
vanilla extract	4 g	1 tsp
apple cider vinegar	8 g	2 tsp

9. Make sure your soy milk is slightly warm, around 40°C (104°F) – this will just ensure that the batter isn't cold and cooks evenly. Pour it into a large jug or bowl and add the vanilla extract and vinegar.

10. Pour the liquids over the dry mixture and whisk by hand until everything is combined. Pour the batter into the lined tin and cover the top in kitchen foil. Bake for 40 minutes until risen and gently domed, then remove the foil and bake until golden and the top springs back when gently pressed with your fingertips.

11. Remove the cake from the oven and leave to cool for 10 minutes, then run a sharp knife against the edge of the tin to release the cake and turn out onto a wire rack. Leave to cool completely.

VANILLA POACHED PEARS

12. Toss the pears with the vanilla, rum, caster sugar and water in a large bowl, then transfer to a large saucepan, cover with a lid and leave to stand for 5 minutes to draw out some of the moisture and the sugar will melt into a syrup.

13. Cook the pears over a medium heat for 5 minutes, or until a skewer or sharp knife meets no resistance when poking a piece of pear.

14. Pour the pears into a sieve (fine-mesh strainer) set over a bowl and leave to chill in the refrigerator for 1 hour until chilled through.

pears, peeled, cored and cut into 1 cm (½ in) dice (2 Conference pears)	300 g	10.6 oz
vanilla bean paste	4 g	1 tsp
rum	10 g	0.4 oz
caster (superfine) sugar	100 g	3.5 oz
water	50 g	1.8 oz

ALSO NEEDED

icing (confectioners') sugar		for dusting

TO ASSEMBLE AND FINISH

15. Using a large serrated knife, cut around the edge of the hazelnut sponge (halfway up the side) and as you turn the cake around, gently cut a little deeper until the knife starts to glide through, guided by the shallow cuts, to cut the sponge in half.

16. Cut strips of baking parchment to line around the sides of the springform tin. Then, while open, replace the bottom half of the cake in the tin, and fasten it.

17. Chill the bowl of your stand mixer, then whip the almond cream with a whisk attachment until fluffy and stable (it must be very cold: 5°C/41°F). Fold in the chilled drained pear pieces and spread the mixture over the bottom piece of the sponge all the way to the edge.

18. Carefully place the remaining piece of sponge on top of the cream and chill in the refrigerator for 30 minutes.

19. Remove the ring, place the cake on a serving plate and lightly dust with icing sugar. The cake can be stored in an airtight container in the refrigerator for up to 3 days.

TIP

I find the best way to roast nuts is 'low and slow', so 150°C fan (300°F/gas 2) instead of say 180°C fan (350°F/gas 4), for about 15 minutes. This ensure that the nut is roasted all the way through, not just on the outside. For this recipe, they should only be lightly roasted.

The nuts as they get chopped release their natural oils and a lot of flavour. This oil actually coats the flour and produces a very tender cake.

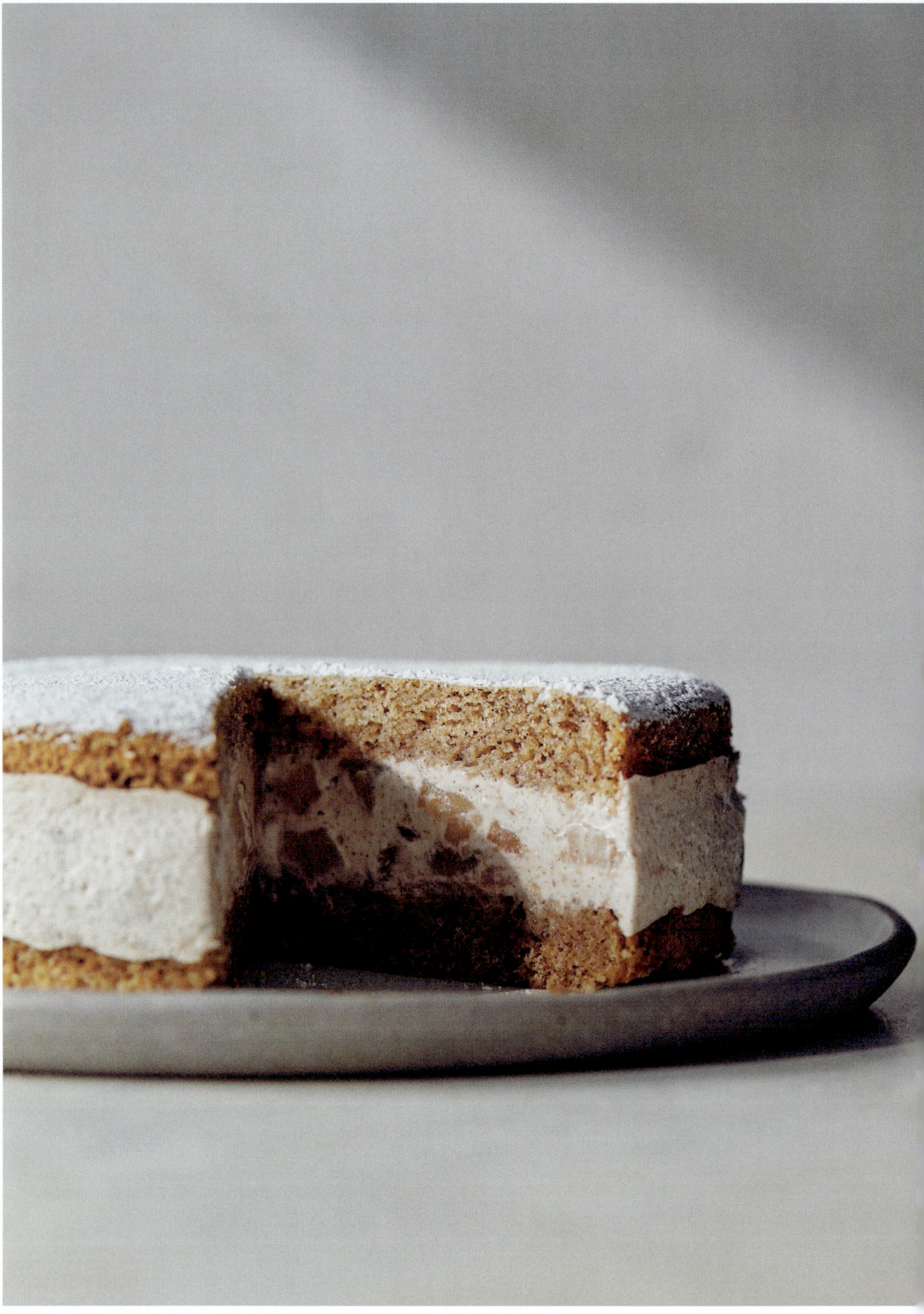

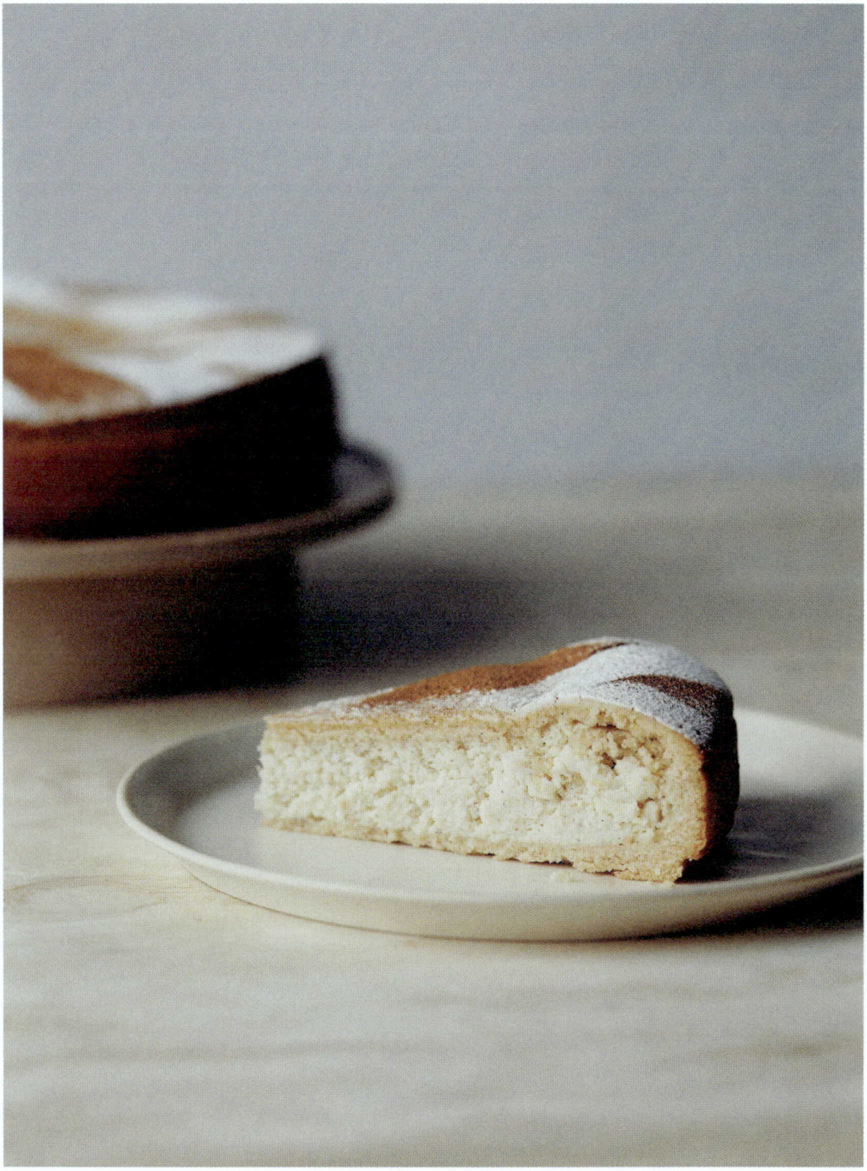

BAKED CINNAMON AND CITRUS CHEESECAKE

Makes a 20 cm (8 in) cake

This is a soft and tender crostata pastry that utilises some baking powder for a soft puff. It is somewhere in between a tender cake and shortbread and is the perfect wrap around pastry for my version of a baked cheesecake inspired by Pasticceria Papa's ricotta cheesecake from Sydney. I have added some additional candied citrus peel, but feel free to leave it out! If this is a cheesecake you want to enjoy on the same day, omit the top, but for a truly decadent eat, prepare the day before, and 'age' it in the refrigerator overnight. This will soften the pastry allowing for some moisture migration from the filling to the crust. Dust with plenty of icing (confectioners') sugar and extra cinnamon.

CINNAMON CROSTATA PASTRY

1. Add the olive oil, both sugars, the salt and water to a large bowl and whisk them together very well until the mixture is smooth, homogenous and there are no oil streaks. This is key to a dough that doesn't separate when mixed.

2. Whisk the flour, baking powder and cinnamon together in another large bowl, then add the liquid syrup. Use a silicone spatula to mix well, then turn it out onto a work surface and knead for about 5 minutes until the dough comes together into a cohesive mixture. You can also use a stand mixer with a beater attachment and mix for 1–2 minutes. The dough can look like it isn't coming together, but continue mixing on low speed until it does!

3. Wrap the dough well in cling film (plastic wrap) and leave to rest in the refrigerator for 1 hour before using.

extra virgin olive oil	60 g	2 oz
caster (superfine) sugar	80 g	2.8 oz
muscovado or brown sugar	20 g	0.7 oz
salt	2 g	½ tsp
water	60 g	2 oz
plain (all-purpose) flour	300 g	10.6 oz
baking powder	4 g	1 tsp
ground cinnamon	3 g	¾ tsp

CHEESECAKE FILLING

4. Add the silken tofu, almonds, lemon juice, grated lemon zest, caster sugar and vanilla paste into a high-powered blender and blend until smooth.

5. Add the cornflour, flour and baking powder, and pulse until combined.

6. Chill the bowl of your stand mixer, then whip the cream with a whisk attachment until it holds a soft peak. Fold into the blended silken tofu base along with candied citrus peel, if using. Set aside until ready to assemble.

silken tofu	350 g	12.4 oz
raw almonds	80 g	2.8 oz
lemon juice	25 g	0.9 oz
lemon zest, grated		½ lemon
caster (superfine) sugar	60 g	2 oz
vanilla bean paste	4 g	1 tsp
cornflour (cornstarch)	20 g	0.7 oz
plain (all-purpose) flour, plus extra for dusting	5 g	1 tsp
baking powder	4 g	1 tsp
Fresh Whipping Cream (page 236)	40 g	1.4 oz
candied citrus peel, diced (optional)	20 g	0.7 oz

TO ASSEMBLE AND BAKE

7. Preheat the oven to 170°C fan (325°F/gas 3).

8. Lightly flour your work surface, then cut the dough into three portions. Roll two pieces of dough out until they are 20 cm (8 in) in diameter (the size of your springform tin) and 3–4 mm (⅛–⅙ in) thick. Using a sharp knife and the tin, trim the dough into two neat circles.

9. Use the remaining dough to roll out a long strip that will fit around the outside of your tin, trimming to the height of your tin so it has two straight sides.

10. Place one disc of dough into the lined tin. Brush the edges with some water, and place the long strip of dough in the tin to line the sides. Allow the bottom edge to curve inward about 1 cm (½ in) so you can press the edge into the base and corners to create a seal.

11. Pour the filling into the tin leaving 1–2 cm (½–¾ in) of pastry at the top. Use a knife tip to gently fold the side pieces of pastry over the filling, then brush some water on the little ledge. Place the remaining disc of dough on top, pressing the edges down gently to seal the filling in well.

12. Bake in the oven for 45 minutes, then turn off the oven and leave to cool.

13. To demould, leave to cool completely in the tin, then pop the tin open.

14. Wrap the cake in cling film (plastic wrap) and store in the refrigerator overnight. This is where the real magic will happen and the moisture from the filling migrates to the edges and softens the crust slightly.

15. Dust with icing sugar and cinnamon before serving. This cake will keep very well wrapped in cling film or stored in an airtight container in the refrigerator for 4 days, or frozen for up to 3 months, but make sure to defrost in the refrigerator overnight.

ALSO NEEDED

icing (confectioners') sugar	for dusting
ground cinnamon	for dusting

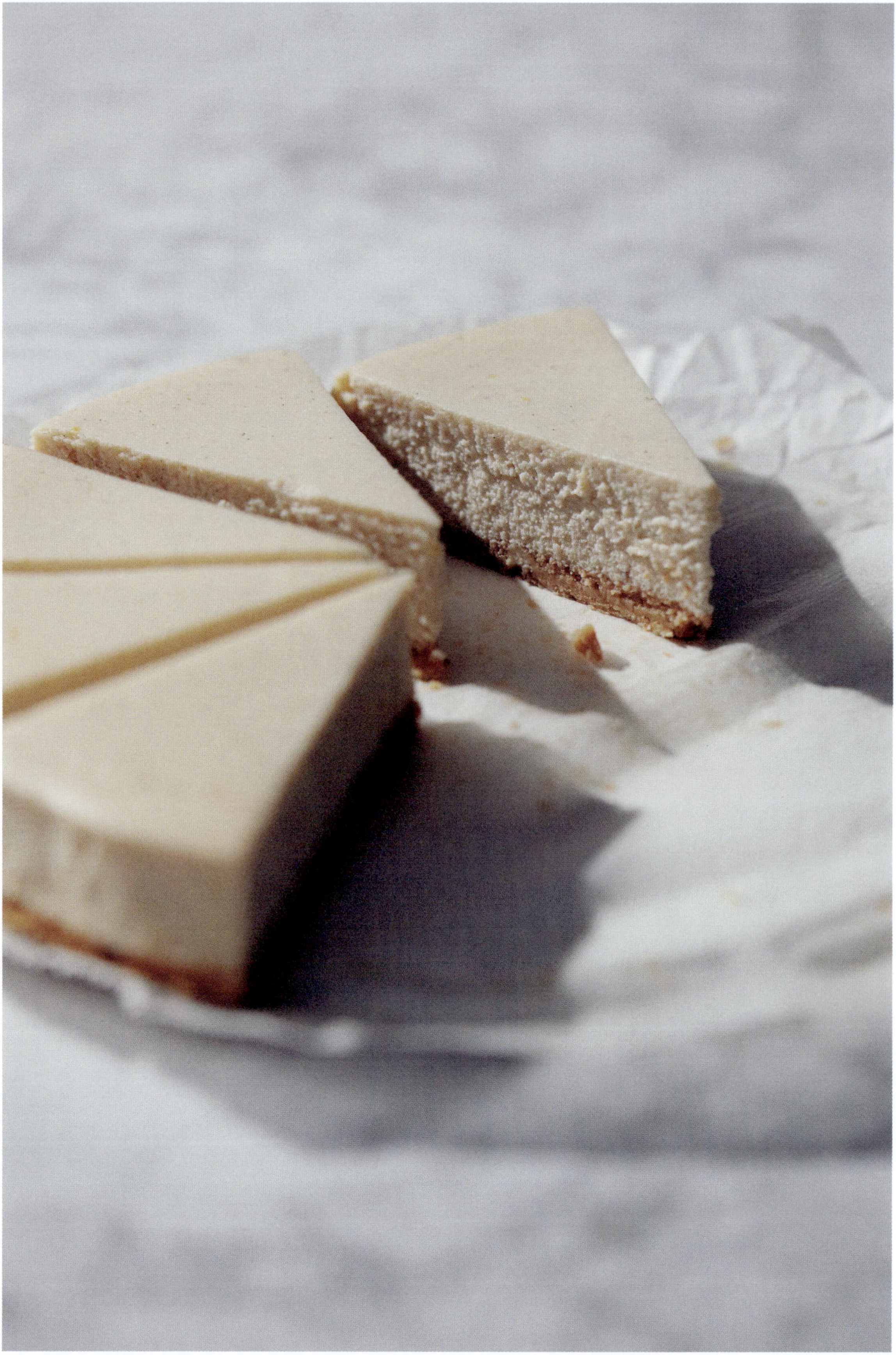

FLUFFY BAKED SILKEN TOFU CHEESECAKE

Makes a 23 cm (9 in) cake

This is more like a soufflé than a cake. Consider it a hybrid of the creamy New York cheesecake and the wobbly cotton-soft Japanese cheesecake; it is the best of both worlds. I still refer to this as a cheesecake even though the base is made from tofu, which is actually made similarly to a fresh cheese. It's super creamy and the seasoning of citrus zests and vanilla give it a classic cheesecake perfume. Go lightly on the lemon zest as a little goes a long way!

DIGESTIVE BISCUIT BASE

1. Line the base of a 23 cm (9 in) springform tin (pan) with baking parchment, then line the sides. Use two sheets of kitchen foil to create a 'sealed' barrier on the outside of the tin and place it in a roasting dish that will be filled with hot water. Set aside.

2. Use a food processor to coarsely chop the digestive biscuits to a breadcrumb consistency.

   TIP Don't overblend the digestive biscuits or it won't have a short crumbly texture.

3. Add the coconut oil to a microwave-safe bowl and microwave for 30–60 seconds until melted. Alternatively, melt in a medium saucepan over a low heat. Set aside.

4. Add the melted coconut oil, sugar, salt and cinnamon to the digestive biscuit crumbs in the food processor and pulse until the crumbs resembles moistened sand.

5. Spoon into the prepared tin and use a spoon to press the mixture into the tin to form a flat even base. Set aside.

6. Preheat the oven to 150°C fan (300°F/gas 2).

digestive biscuits (graham crackers)	200 g	7.1 oz
coconut oil (deodorised)	50 g	1.8 oz
caster (superfine) sugar	20 g	0.7 oz
salt	1 g	¼ tsp
ground cinnamon		pinch

FILLING AND BAKING

7. Use a food processor in short pulses to blend all the ingredients, except the whipping cream, together until smooth.

8. Chill the bowl of your stand mixer, then whip the cream with a whisk attachment until it holds a soft peak. Fold into the blended silken tofu base, then pour the filling into the prepared tin and pour some hot water into the roasting dish until it is a quarter to halfway up the side of the tin.

9. Bake for 35–40 minutes until the cake has a slight jiggle when the tin is gently tapped. Overbaking can make it crack.

10. Turn off the oven with the door closed and leave the cheesecake in the oven for 10 minutes before removing and leaving it to cool completely.

11. Leave to chill before serving. This cheesecake keeps well in the refrigerator, either wrapped or in an airtight container for up to 4 days. It also freezes very well in an airtight container for up to 3 months. Defrost by placing in the refrigerator overnight and serve from the refrigerator.

silken tofu	700 g	1 lb 9 oz
lemon juice	30 g	1.1 oz
yuzu or lemon zest		½ yuzu or lemon
caster (superfine) sugar	180 g	6.3 oz
vanilla bean paste	6 g	1½ tsp
cornflour (cornstarch)	50 g	1.8 oz
plain (all-purpose) flour	14 g	0.5 oz
Fresh Whipping Cream (page 236)	160 g	5.6 oz

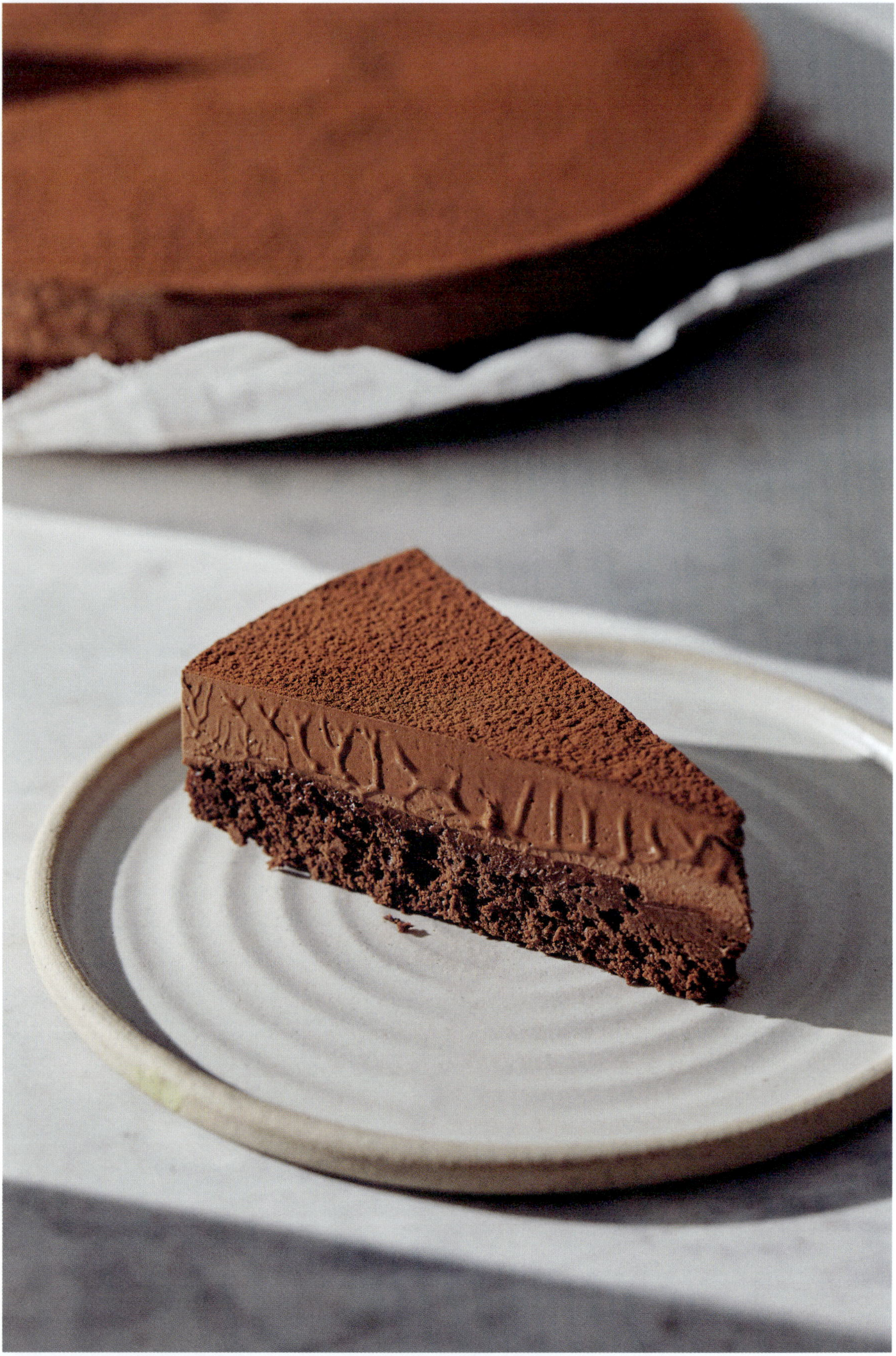

TWO-TONE CHOCOLATE CAKE

Makes a 23 cm (9 in) cake

Don't be deceived by the humble ingredients (or the three-ingredient chocolate mousse!) – a delicate touch elevates them into something sublime. Use your favourite dark chocolate because it's the show-stopping star here. The base cake also doubles as a delicious cake on its own (baked in a 20 cm/8 in tin), topped with Fresh Whipping Cream (page 236) and fresh berries. This cake is also super adaptable: it can easily be made gluten free, you can add fresh raspberries, or even swirl hazelnut praline through the mousse.

THREE-INGREDIENT CHOCOLATE MOUSSE

1. Bring the plant-based milk (1) and sugar to a simmer in a medium saucepan, then pour over the chocolate in a heatproof jug or bowl and blend with an immersion stick blender until combined.

2. Add the remaining plant-based milk (2) to the jug or bowl and blend again until the mixture is very glossy and you can see a shiny reflection of light with no oily streaks.

3. The trick here is to blend it at 30–35°C (86–95°F), then pour into a shallow dish with cling film (plastic wrap) pressed onto the surface and leave it to chill in the refrigerator for at least 3–4 hours. This will create a chocolate cream that can be whipped and piped or spread, then sets like a dreamy chocolate mousse!

4. The base will appear set but it will become liquid when agitated. Use a whisk to whisk it by hand (about 2 minutes) or use a stand mixer fitted with whisk attachment to whisk it to a stable peak. Spread on top of the cooled cake base (below) and level with a small offset spatula.

5. Leave to chill in the refrigerator for 1 hour, or until completely set.

plant-based milk (1)	250 g	8.8 oz
caster (superfine) sugar	50 g	1.8 oz
dark chocolate with at least 65% cocoa solids, callets (chips) or chopped	250 g	8.8 oz
plant-based milk, chilled (2)	200 g	7 oz

RICH CHOCOLATE CAKE

1. Preheat the oven to 160°C (325°F/gas 3). Line the base of a 20 cm (8 in) springform tin (pan) with baking parchment.

2. Heat the milk to a simmer in a medium saucepan. Pour over the chopped chocolate in a heatproof bowl.

3. Add the olive oil to the chocolate mixture and whisk well to combine (this is a type of ganache).

4. In another bowl, use a whisk to combine the flour, cocoa powder, sugar, baking powder and sea salt.

5. Add the dry ingredients to the bowl of ganache and use a silicone spatula to mix until combined.

6. Pour the batter into the lined tin and tap to level the mixture.

7. Bake for 12–14 minutes until gently domed and the top springs back slightly when pressed with your fingertips. Remove from the oven and leave to cool completely.

plant-based milk	340 g	12 oz
dark chocolate with at least 66% cocoa solids, chopped	150 g	5.3 oz
extra virgin olive oil	40 g	1.4 oz
plain (all-purpose) flour (gluten-free plain flour will also work)	75 g	2.7 oz
cocoa powder	15 g	0.5 oz
caster (superfine) sugar	100 g	3.5 oz
baking powder	1 g	¼ tsp
sea salt	2 g	½ tsp

TO FINISH

8 Remove the cake from the springform tin by releasing the clasp, then peel away the baking parchment lining the base and transfer to a serving plate.

9 For sharp clean cuts, slice with a sharp knife dipped into a jug of hot water from a tap and wiped dry between each cut. Serve with vanilla ice cream for a show-stopping chocolate dessert. Be prepared to share the recipe! This cake will keep very well wrapped in cling film (plastic wrap) or stored in an airtight container in the refrigerator for 2 days, or frozen for up to 3 months, but make sure to defrost in the refrigerator overnight.

ALSO NEEDED

cocoa (unsweetened chocolate) powder — for dusting

VARIATIONS

Add a layer of fresh raspberries onto the bottom layer of chocolate cake before adding the chocolate mousse on top.

Spread 3 tablespoons of hazelnut praline (page 181) onto the bottom layer of cake before adding the chocolate mousse on top.

TRIPLE CHOCOLATE FUDGE

Makes a two- or four-layer 20 cm (8 in) cake

A classic chocolate cake that would make Miss Trunchbull and Bruce Bogtrotter from *Matilda* both squeal with delight. A rich and pure chocolate ganache encases a fluffy, moist, richly flavoured chocolate cake.

FUDGE CAKE BATTER

1. Preheat the oven to 180°C (350°F/gas 4), no fan, and line the bases of two 20 cm (8 in) springform tins (pans) with baking parchment.
2. Add the water, vanilla extract, vinegar, olive oil and sugar to a large jug or bowl.
3. Add the cocoa powder, flour, baking powder, bicarbonate of soda and salt to another large bowl and stir gently with a whisk to combine the ingredients.
4. Add the liquids to the dry ingredients and use the whisk to stir gently until everything is combined and there are no lumps. Be careful not to overmix.
5. Pour 600 g (1 lb 5 oz) of the batter into each lined tin. If you have baking strips, soak them in water and wrap around the tin, otherwise use a length of paper towel that will fit around the cake (about 60 cm/24 in each) and fold them to fit the bottom half of the tin. Wet with water and press against the sides. Wrap the base with kitchen foil that folds up the sides – this will insulate the sides and help the cake rise evenly.
6. Bake each cake for 35 minutes, or until domed nicely and the top springs back when gently pressed with your fingertips, or a skewer inserted into the centre of the cake comes out clean.
7. Leave the cakes to cool completely in the tins, then run a sharp knife against the edge of the tin to release the sides. Place both cakes on a baking sheet or plate in the refrigerator.

water	480 g	16.9 oz
vanilla extract	10 g	0.4 oz
apple cider vinegar	10 g	0.4 oz
extra virgin olive oil	75 g	2.7 oz
muscovado sugar	420 g	14.8 oz
cocoa (unsweetened chocolate) powder	80 g	2.8 oz
plain (all-purpose) flour	336 g	11.9 oz
baking powder	8 g	2 tsp
bicarbonate of soda (baking soda)	8 g	2 tsp
fine salt	4 g	1 tsp

CHOCOLATE FUDGE GANACHE

8. Bring the plant-based milk (1) milk and sugar to a simmer in a medium saucepan, then pour over the chocolate in a heatproof jug or bowl and blend with an immersion stick blender until it is nice and silky.
9. Add the remaining chilled plant-based milk (2) to the jug or bowl and blend again until the mixture is glossy and you can see a shiny reflection of light with no oily streaks.
10. Pour the ganache into a wide shallow dish, cover the surface with cling film (plastic wrap) and leave to chill in the refrigerator for 1 hour. Remove and leave it at room temperature for another hour until set.

plant-based milk (1)	380 g	13.4 oz
muscovado sugar	150 g	5.3 oz
dark chocolate with at least 70% cocoa solids, callets (chips) or chopped	600 g	1 lb 5 oz
plant-based milk (2), chilled	380 g	13.4 oz

CAKES

TO ASSEMBLE

11 Retrieve your chocolate sponges from the refrigerator and use a long serrated knife to trim the domed top of each sponge. If you want to make it four layers, cut each layer in half.

12 Place one of the rounds on a flat serving dish and spread a third (or one-fifth if you are doing four layers) of the ganache over the top with a palette knife.

13 Place the second disc of sponge, cut-side down (so when you spread ganache on the top crumbs don't come loose), on top of the ganache, then spread another third of the ganache on the top of the sponge and the last third over the sides. Use your palette knife to smooth the ganache or leave a texture.

   TIP Be generous with the masking. It should be about 1 cm (½ in) thick as a thin ganache coating could crack due to the sponge drawing in moisture.

14 Leave the cake to set in the refrigerator for 30 minutes, then store at room temperature. If storing in the refrigerator, make sure to remove it 2 hours before so it warms to room temperature for the best eating experience. For sharp clean cuts, slice with a sharp knife dipped into a jug of hot water from a tap and wiped dry between each cut. This cake will keep very well in an airtight container in the refrigerator for 3 days, or frozen for up to 3 months, but make sure to defrost in the refrigerator overnight, and serve at room temperature.

TIP

If you increase the amount of ganache by multiplying it by a third, you will have enough to fill a piping (pastry) bag fitted with a plain or star 1 cm (½ in) piping nozzle and pipe some kisses around the edge of the cake, alternating with some small torn pieces of sponge leftover from trimming the tops of the sponges.

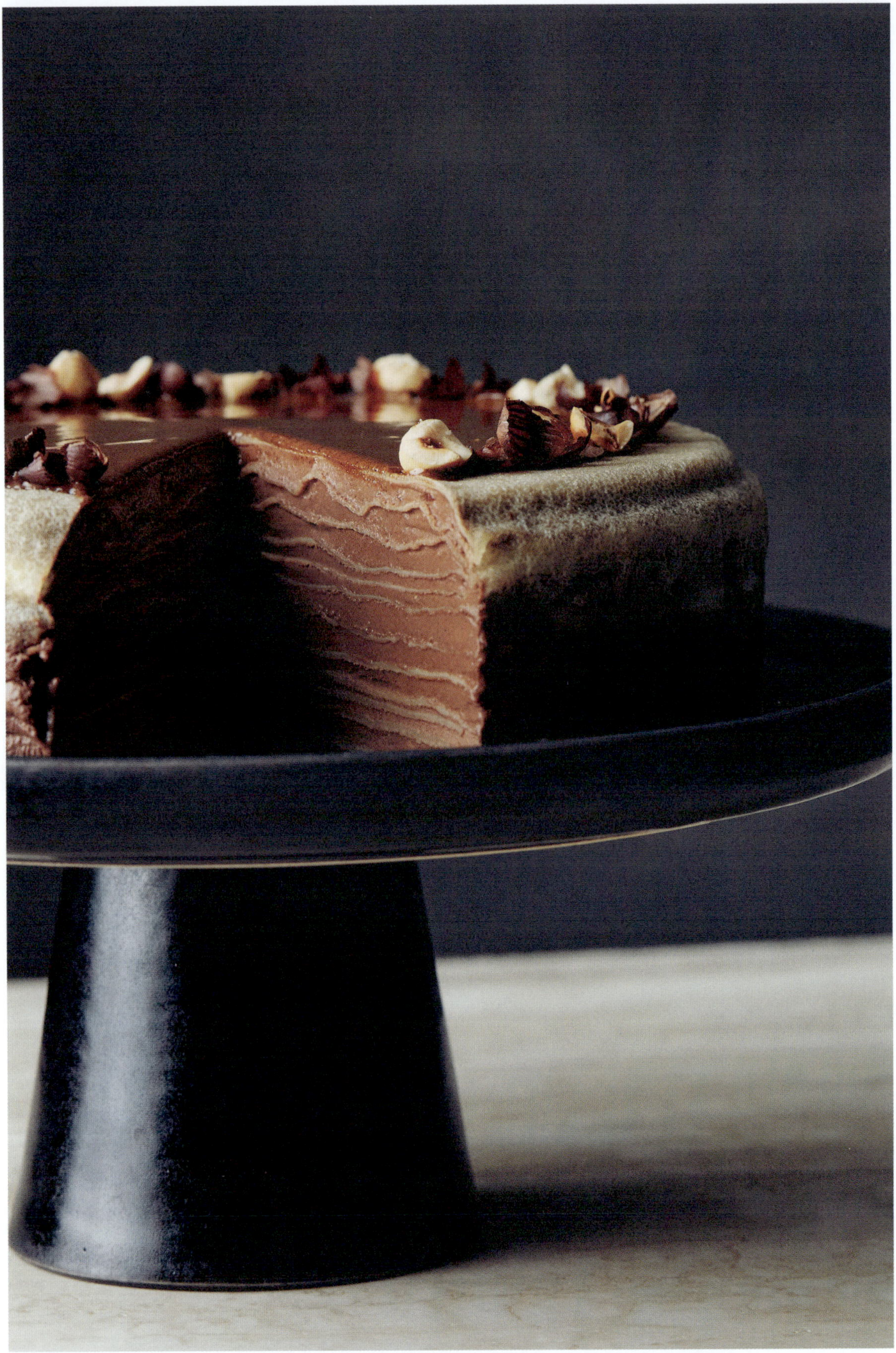

MILLE CRÊPES PRALINE

Makes a 20 cm (8 in) gateau

The name for this cake translates from French as '1,000 crêpes'. Enjoy the crêpes on their own with your toppings of choice or in this impressive and incredibly addictive gateau layered with gianduja chantilly and laced with pure hazelnut praline. Simultaneously, light and indulgent, and after you've done it the first time it's a quick one to master and whip up. Make a day ahead for the best eating texture or make it in the morning to serve for dessert at dinner. As with cutting all cakes, I recommend using a sharp knife dipped in hot water to get clean cuts that show off all the layers in this masterpiece! If you want to make this without nuts, use the Three-ingredient Chocolate Mousse (page 177) instead.

HAZELNUT PRALINE

1. Preheat the oven to 160°C fan (325°F/gas 3). Line a large baking sheet with baking parchment. Spread the hazelnuts out over another large baking sheet and roast for 16–20 minutes until they are golden, or if you carefully take one out and cut it in half, the centre should have a light golden colour. Leave to cool slightly, then transfer them to the lined baking sheet.

2. To make a 'dry caramel', heat a saucepan over a medium-high heat and add 1 teaspoon of the caster sugar. Wait until it melts, then start sprinkling in more sugar slowly while stirring or swirling the pan around. Add too much and you can get big lumps, which take longer to melt, but add the right amount more slowly and this is a quick way to melt the sugar so it starts to caramelise. Once it reaches a rich golden colour, add the vanilla pod, then carefully pour the caramel over the hazelnuts and sprinkle with the salt. Leave to cool completely at room temperature before proceeding to the next step.

3. Break up the caramel nuts and add them to a blender or food processor with the vanilla pod. Pulse to a powder. Scrape the container then keep blending. As the hazelnuts get ground finer and finer it will warm up – the oils will separate and a paste will form.

hazelnuts	200 g	7 oz
caster (superfine) sugar	100 g	3.5 oz
vanilla pod (bean) (if you have a scraped-dry one!)	1 pod	
salt	2 g	½ tsp

GIANDUJA CHANTILLY

4. Heat the plant-based milk (1) in a microwave-safe bowl or jug in the microwave for 1 minute, or in a medium saucepan on the stove until it reaches 60°C (140°F) on a digital probe thermometer.

5. Meanwhile, add the dark chocolate, hazelnut praline and coconut oil to a large heatproof bowl, then pour in the warm milk and leave to stand for 1 minute to melt the chocolate. Use a hand-held blender to blend the mixture together until it is beautiful and glossy. Add the remaining cold plant-based milk (2) and blend again. Pour it into a shallow container so it is not more than 2 cm (¾ in) deep, cover the surface with cling film (plastic wrap) and leave to chill in the refrigerator for at least 4 hours.

6. The mixture will set, but transfer it either to a large bowl if you would like to whisk it by hand or in a stand mixer

plant-based milk (1)	200 g	7 oz
dark chocolate with at least 60% cocoa solids, chopped	250 g	8.8 oz
hazelnut praline	100 g	3.5 oz
coconut oil (deodorised)	75 g	2.7 oz
plant-based milk, cold (2)	200 g	7 oz

TIP

This recipe really benefits from having a high-powered blender or food processor. If the blending chamber is big, double the amount, keep the praline in a clean glass jar and use it as a delicious spread or in other recipes. Natural oils from the hazelnut may rise to the top over time, but just stir it well. It lasts in a sealed jar for at least 2 months.

CAKES

fitted with a whisk attachment and whisk it on medium speed. The mixture will become quite liquid, so increase the speed to high and continue whisking until it reaches a stable peak. Use immediately.

CRÊPES

7   The easiest way to make this batter is to blend it together with a hand-held blender in a large bowl or in a high-powered blender. Another equally easy method is to add the dry ingredients to a large bowl, add half the liquid and mix to a paste with a whisk, then let it down with the remaining milk so you produce a lump-free batter that should be runny and coat a pan when you swirl it around.

8   Heat a flat pan at least 20–22 cm (8–8½ in) in diameter over a medium heat. Spray some oil and brush it around the pan if needed. You may need to 'sacrifice' the first one or two crêpes to find the right temperature (or prepare a 'chef's snack'!).

9   Use a small ladle and pour some batter onto the pan – it shouldn't be too hot or the batter won't spread nicely. Another reason to sacrifice the first one is so you know how much batter you should be using too. You want the crêpes to be lovely and very thin, so the batter should coat the pan in a thin layer and not overlap on itself too much as you swirl the pan around. It will cook very quickly – in less than a minute. Once swirled around, the batter will look set and start to steam. Cook for under a minute until the base of the crêpe has picked up some colour. Remove from the pan and repeat until you have used up all the batter. You can layer your crêpes with baking parchment

TO ASSEMBLE

10 Line the base and sides of a 20 cm (8 in) springform tin (pan) with baking parchment, spraying with a tiny bit of oil to help the paper stick to the sides.

11 Overlap 3–4 crêpes, then use them to line the tin so they fill the corners and hang over the top edges.

12 Use a ladle or piping (pastry) bag fitted with a 1 cm (½ in) plain tube or cut a 1 cm (½ in) hole to pipe a 4 mm (⅛ in) layer of the whipped gianduja chantilly. Use a piping bag to pipe a couple of rings of hazelnut praline or use a spoon to drizzle some praline over the cream.

13 Gently press a crêpe onto the whipped cream and repeat with another layer of cream and praline so you have at least 10–12 layers to fill your tin. Finish with a crêpe.

14 Tuck the overhanging crêpes inwards over the base, then place a heavy, flat dish on top to weigh the cake down into the tin. Chill in the refrigerator for 4 hours, or until set.

15 When ready to finish, turn the cake over onto a plate and release the clasp to remove the cake. Peel away the baking parchment, then spread a thin layer of praline over the top of the cake for a minimally decadent finish. This cake keeps well in the refrigerator for up to 4 days.

plain (all-purpose) flour	240 g	8.5 oz
caster (superfine) sugar	22 g	0.8 oz
salt	4 g	1 tsp
extra virgin olive oil	18 g	0.6 oz
plant-based milk	760 g	1 lb 11 oz
vanilla extract (remove if making savoury crêpes)	8 g	2 tsp
spray oil, for cooking		

ALSO NEEDED

hazelnut praline (see above)		
roasted hazelnuts, for decoration	40 g	1.4 oz

TIP

You can make the gianduja chantilly up to 4 days in advance and whisk it whenever you like. I like to make it the day before.

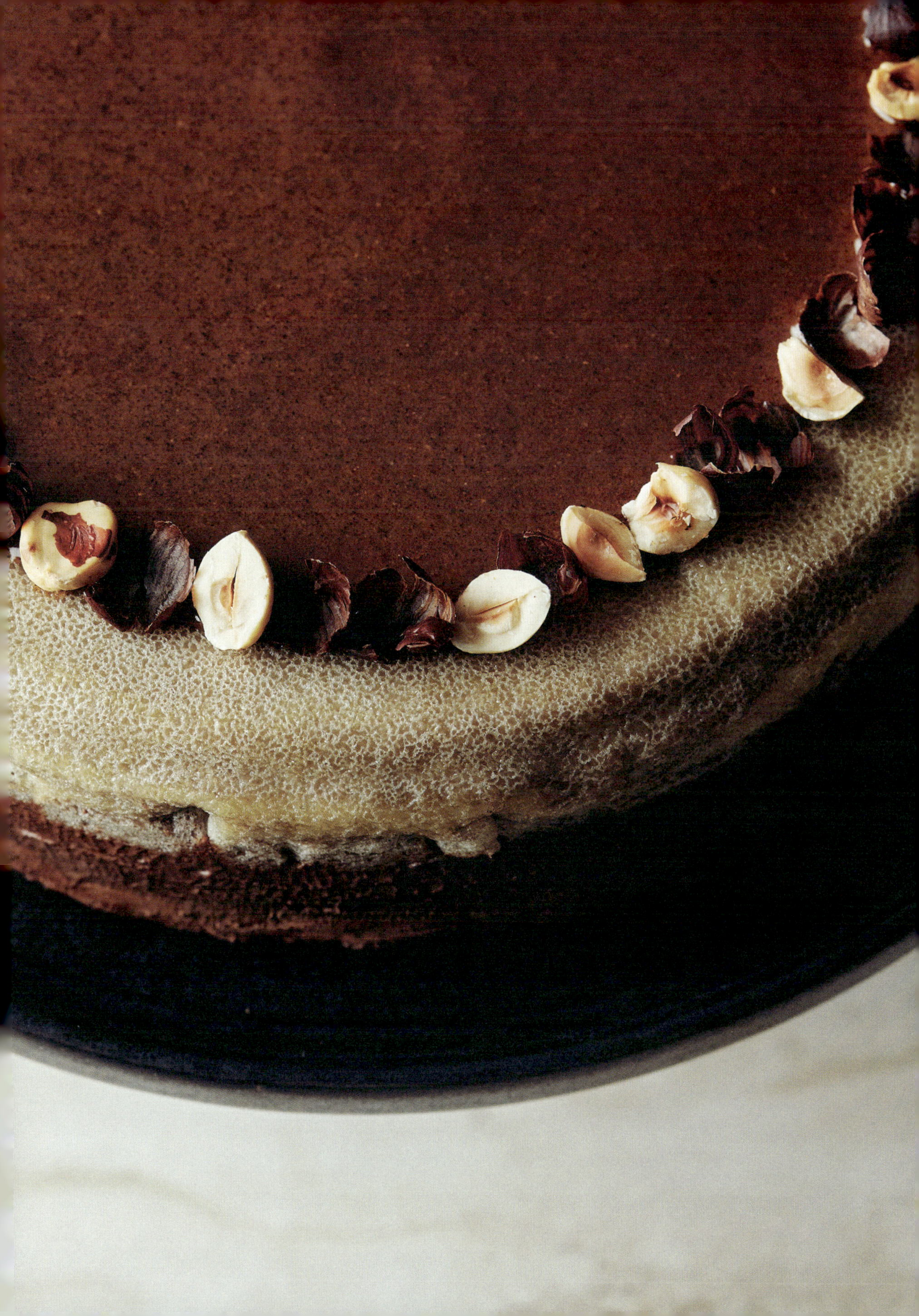

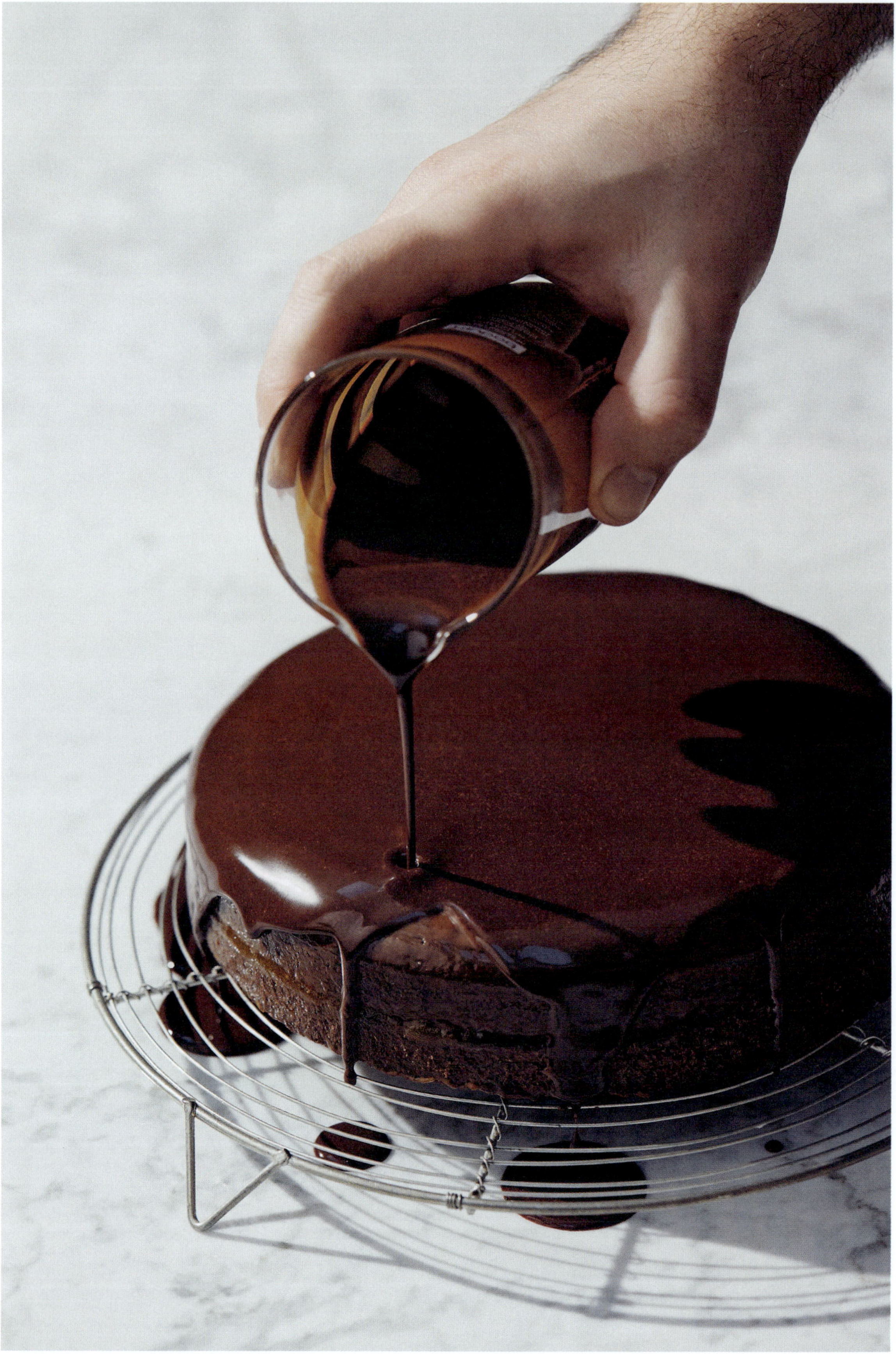

SACHER TORTE

Makes a two-layer 20 cm (8 in) cake

One of the first legendary cakes in the world, supposedly created by an apprentice at the Viennese Hotel Sacher, this cake is composed of a tender and not too chocolatey cake sandwiched with apricot jam and covered in a silky chocolate ganache. My version comes together with a not-so-secret ingredient – apricot! I have added some dried apricots to the cake batter, which are blended and rehydrated with some water. This gives the cake some extra fruitiness, and the added fibre makes for a very tender, moist cake that doesn't crumble or break apart. The sponge is based on a dark chocolate and not cocoa powder, which gives the cake its firm texture and not too chocolatey flavour.

SACHER SPONGE

1. Preheat the oven to 190°C (350°F/gas 4), no fan, and line the base of a 20 cm (8 in) springform tin (pan) with baking parchment.

2. Melt the chocolate in a microwave-safe bowl in the microwave in 30-second bursts, stirring in between, or in a heatproof or stainless-steel bowl set over a pan filled with 1 cm (½ in) simmering water, stirring until melted. Remove from the heat, add the olive oil and sugar and whisk well.

3. Blend the dried apricots and warm water together in a high-powered blender to a purée, then whisk it into the chocolate mixture until it is glossy and even.

4. In a separate bowl, whisk the flour and baking powder together. Then add to the chocolate mixture and mix to a smooth batter.

5. Pour the batter into the lined tin, smoothing until it is flat on top.

6. Cover the top and sides with a piece of kitchen foil. Bake for 35 minutes, then another 5 minutes if needed, until the top is nicely domed and will spring back when gently pressed with your fingertips.

    TIP Covering the top and sides with kitchen foil helps steam the cake and produces a smooth, uncracked dome.

7. Remove from the oven and leave to cool in the tin on a wire rack. Remove the cake from the tin once it is completely cool by running a sharp knife against the edge of the tin to release it.

8. Trim the top 1 cm (½ in) of the dome to make it slightly flat, then cut the cake in half using a cake wire slicer or a long serrated knife by gently running it around the edge of the cake as you are rotating it to make a 1 cm (½ in) deep incision, then keep rotating it around the cake so it inches slightly deeper each turn and then cuts all the way through.

dark chocolate with at least 70% cocoa solids, chopped	130 g	4.6 oz
extra virgin olive oil	20 g	0.7 oz
caster (superfine) sugar	135 g	4.7 oz
apricots, dried	50 g	1.8 oz
water, warm	250 g	8.8 oz
plain (all-purpose) flour	170 g	6 oz
baking powder	8 g	2 tsp

APRICOT JAM

9. Blend all the ingredients, in a high-powered blender until it is a smooth purée, then pour into a large saucepan.

10. Heat the filling over a medium-high heat, stirring it constantly. It is already a thick liquid so it will catch easily on the base of the pan. Cook for 5–10 minutes, or until the mixture is boiling and starts to thicken and you notice that when you scrape the bottom of the saucepan the jam doesn't immediately flow back. Leave to cool to room temperature.

   Tip I find traditional apricot jams a tad too sweet, though you are welcome to use one. I made this filling so I can control the sweetness. If fresh apricots aren't available you can make a purée by blending 80 g (2¾ oz) dried apricots with 120 g (4½ oz) water in a high-powered blender until smooth, then add the remaining ingredients, pulse to combine, and cook out on the stove as above.

   You are also welcome to use a nice pre-made apricot jam!

apricots, fresh	200 g	7 oz
caster (superfine) sugar	100 g	3.5 oz
lemon juice	10 g	0.4 oz
vanilla bean paste	5 g	1 tsp
agar-agar powder	2.5 g	1 tsp

CHOCOLATE GANACHE

11. Prepare this ganache once the cake is chilled and ready to glaze as you want to use it straight away. Bring the milk just to a simmer in a small saucepan over a low heat or in a microwave-safe bowl or jug in the microwave. Remove from the heat.

12. Add the remaining ingredients and blend with a hand-held blender until it is a smooth emulsion with no streaks.

oat milk	150 g	5.3 oz
dark chocolate with at least 66% cocoa solids	150 g	5.3 oz
glucose syrup	20 g	¾ oz

TO ASSEMBLE AND FINISH

13. Place the top of the cake with the trimmed-side down, on a flat plate. Pour most of the apricot filling into the middle and spread it to the edges. Place the remaining piece of sponge on top with the trimmed side facing the filling so the face which was the bottom of the cake is now on top, and use any excess filling to create as smooth a surface as possible. Place the sandwiched cake on a wire rack and leave to chill in the refrigerator for 1 hour.

14. Prepare the ganache above just before you use it. Set the cake on a wire rack over a rimmed baking sheet, then pour the ganache into the centre of the chilled cake, allowing the weight of the ganache to spread itself over the cake. You can tap the rack to help it along. Avoid using a spatula so you get a really nice smooth surface.

15. Leave to chill in the refrigerator for another 20 minutes. You can use some of the excess ganache in a small cornet to write 'Sacher' on top as is tradition!

16. Serve the cake at room temperature. If storing in the refrigerator, make sure to remove it 2 hours before eating so it warms to room temperature for the best eating experience. For sharp clean cuts, slice with a sharp knife dipped into a jug of hot water from a tap and wiped dry between each cut. This cake will keep very well in an airtight container in the refrigerator for 3 days, or frozen for up to 3 months, but make sure to defrost in the refrigerator overnight and serve at room temperature.

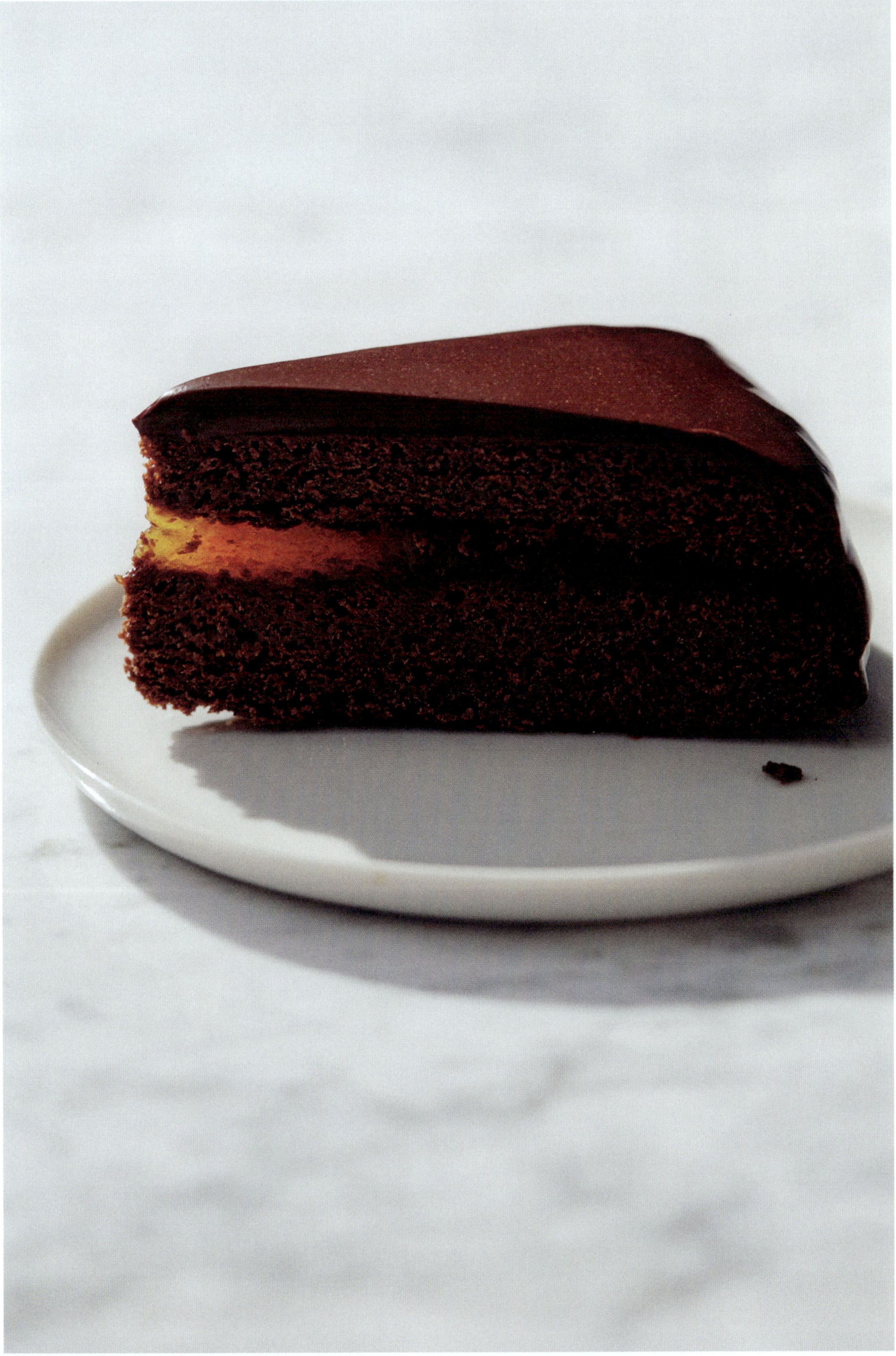

DOUBLE CHOCOLATE BROWNIES

Makes 9 × 6 cm (2½ in) square brownies

No baking book could be complete without a fudgy, double chocolate brownie – so here it is! Feel free to add in any number of mix-ins like pecans or walnuts, and maybe a pinch of cinnamon or a swirl of tahini or Biscoff spread.

1. Preheat the oven to 180°C fan (350°F/gas 4) and line a 20 cm (8 in) square tin with parchment paper.
2. Melt the chocolate in a microwave-safe bowl in the microwave or in a stainless steel bowl set over a pot with 1 cm (½ in) of simmering water.
3. Add the oil, sugars, milk and vanilla extract and use a silicone spatula to mix them to combine well. It should look silky and ganache-like.
4. Into the same bowl, add the flour, cocoa powder, baking powder, salt and chocolate chips and continue folding until all the ingredients are incorporated.
5. Scrape the mixture into the prepared tin and level.
6. Place into the oven and bake for 20–25 minutes until the brownie looks set on top and has puffed around the edges and into the middle. Remove from the oven and allow it to cool for at least 30 minutes. These will keep in a sealed container or well wrapped at room temperature for 4 days, or in the refrigerator for up to 2 weeks.

ingredient	metric	imperial
dark chocolate	80 g	2.8 oz
extra virgin olive oil	50 g	1.8 oz
caster (superfine) sugar	125 g	4.4 oz
muscovado or dark brown sugar	125 g	4.4 oz
plant-based milk	150 g	5.3 oz
vanilla extract	8 g	2 tsp
plain (all-purpose) flour (gluten-free plain flour will also work)	120 g	4.2 oz
cocoa (unsweetened chocolate) powder	60 g	2 oz
baking powder	4 g	1 tsp
fine salt	1 g	⅛ tsp
dark chocolate chips or coarsely chopped chocolate	150 g	5.3 oz

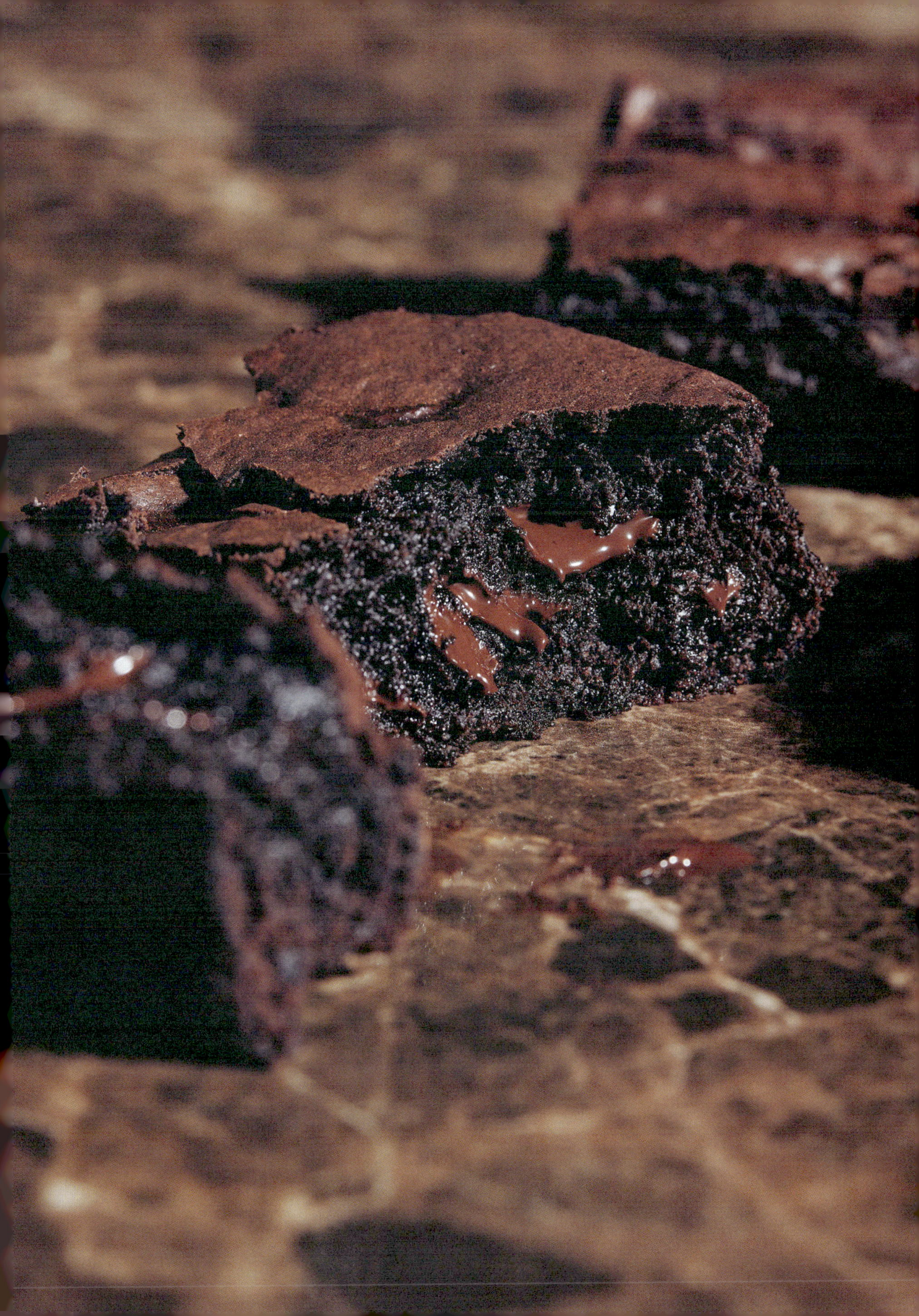

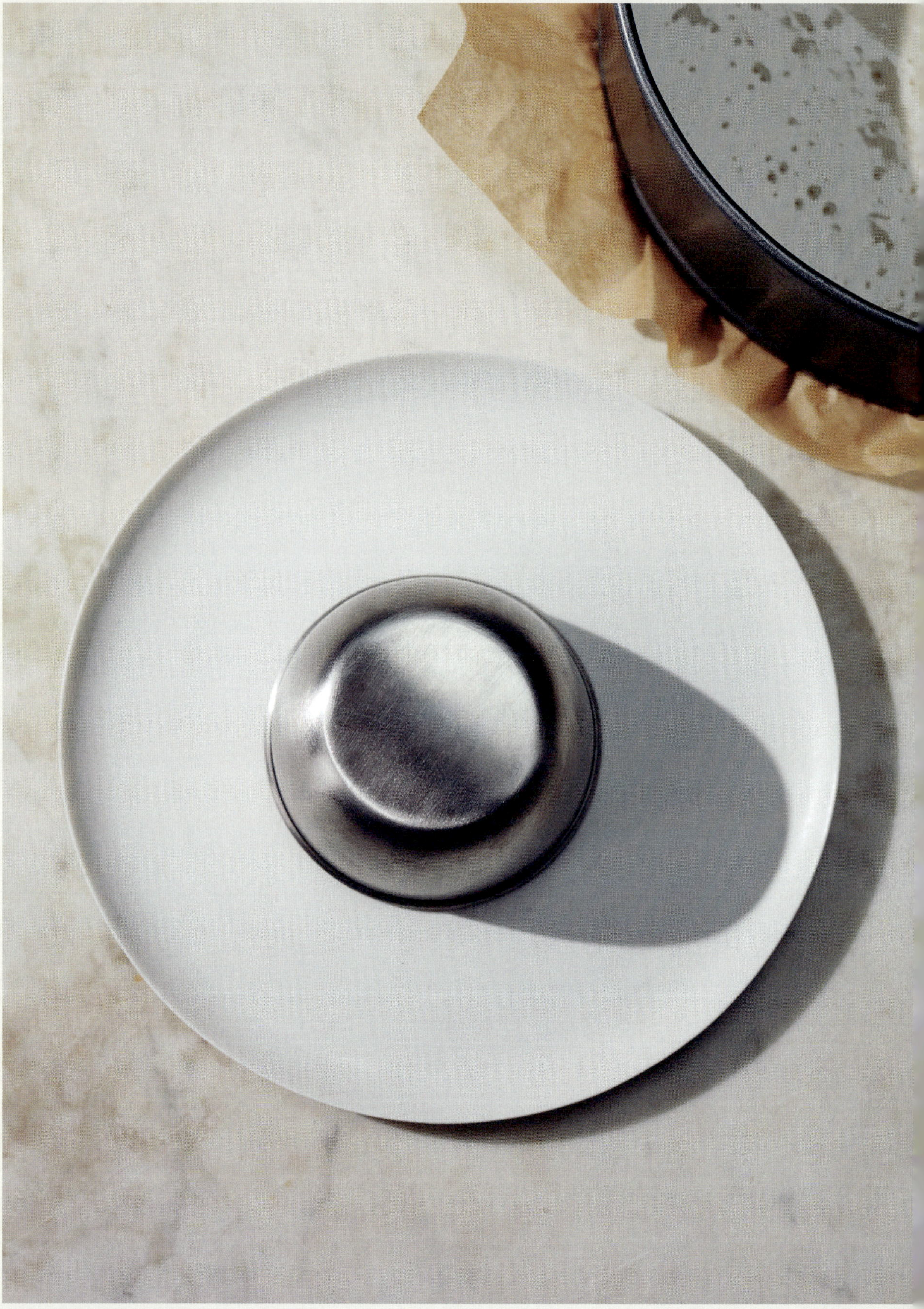

5 DESSERTS

Dessert is the last sweet course of a meal. Of course, a cake can be a dessert, but not necessarily vice versa. These are some classic desserts, reformulated, that get a chapter to themselves. I've always loved eating dessert first – and then following up with something savoury, but that's probably because I've spent my career making and developing sweet things and craved something salty afterwards. It's not a diet or lifestyle your doctor would prescribe but it's the one I chose!

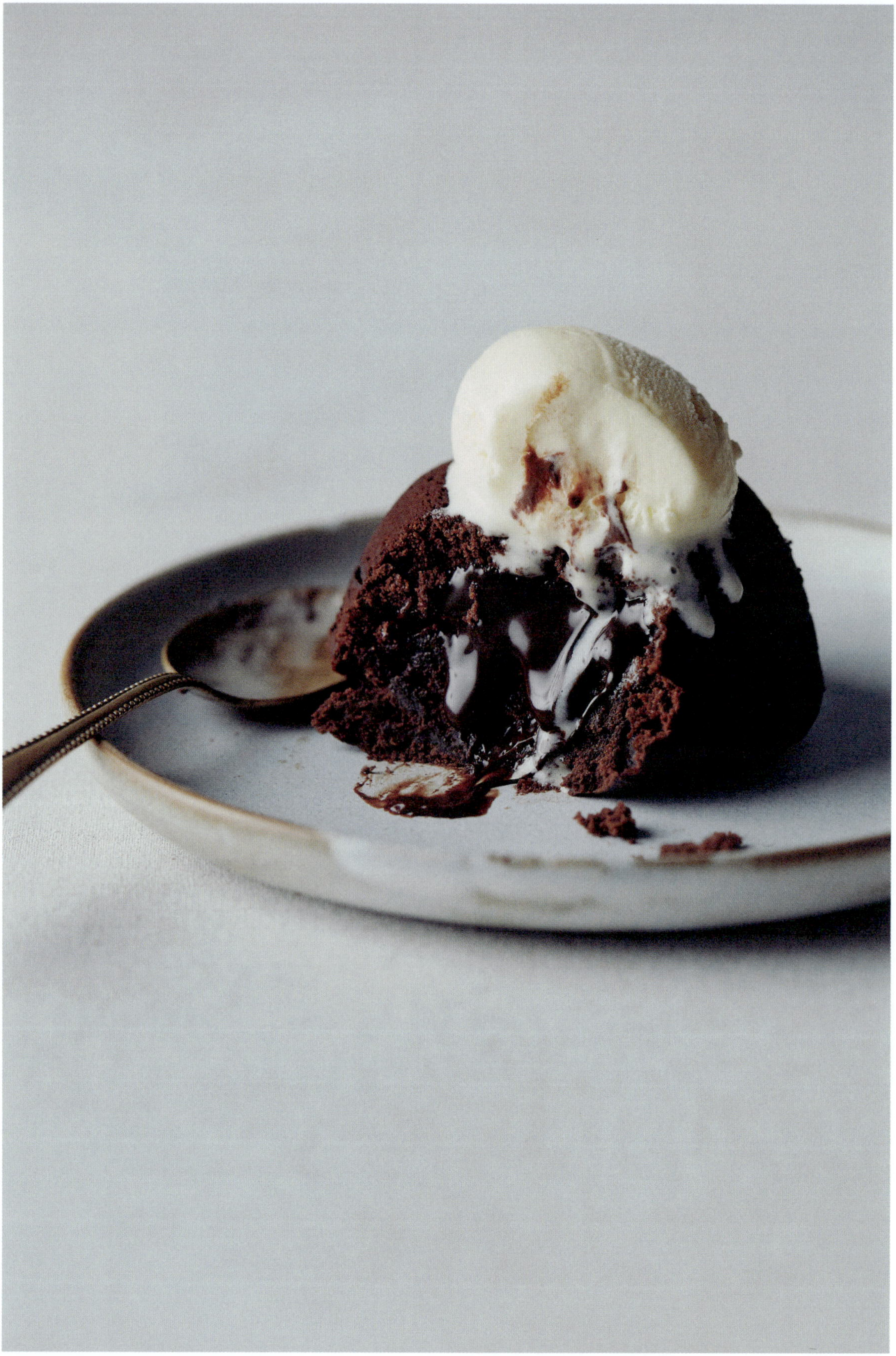

MOLTEN CENTRE CHOCOLATE CAKES

Makes 8 individual cakes

The trick to molten centre/lava cakes is a quick hot bake that cooks the outside and leaves the centre woefully warm and runny. Some professionals have evolved this by making a separate ganache which can be frozen then inserted into the batter, which keeps a distinctly separate texture. I'm sharing both recipes – the advantage of the latter option is that you can bake ahead and gently reheat for an impressive dessert, without the pressure of a time-sensitive bake! Serve with whipped cream or vanilla ice cream.

CHOCOLATE GANACHE INSERT

1. To make a core that will always stay molten, in a saucepan and using a silicone spatula, stir the oat milk and cornflour together while bringing to a simmer until thickened.

2. Pour over the chocolate in a medium heatproof bowl or measuring cup and use an immersion stick blender or silicone spatula and mix until they are completely combined. Pour into a silicone dome mould, 45 mm (1¾ in) in diameter and freeze for 4 hours, or until solid.

oat milk	150 g	5.3 oz
cornflour (cornstarch)	5 g	1 tsp
dark chocolate with at least 66% cocoa solids, callets (chips) or chopped	100 g	3.5 oz

RICH CHOCOLATE CAKE

3. Preheat the oven to 200°C (400°F/gas 6), no fan. Grease eight small chilled pudding moulds or eight holes in a large muffin tray with coconut oil and dust with cocoa powder, inverting and tapping the moulds to remove any excess cocoa.

4. Put the chocolate and sugar together in a heatproof bowl. Bring the milk to a simmer in a large saucepan, then pour over the chocolate and sugar. Whisk them together until the chocolate is melted and it is a smooth consistency.

5. Add the flour, cocoa powder and baking powder to a medium bowl and whisk gently just to combine. Add these to the chocolate sauce and mix to combine all the ingredients.

6. Use a piping (pastry) bag with a small 1 cm (½ in) trimmed opening or a spoon to fill the moulds halfway, then add a piece of frozen ganache to the centre. Press gently so the batter comes up to the sides, then add more batter to cover the frozen ganache insert.

7. Bake in the oven for 7 minutes, then remove and leave to cool for 2 minutes before turning out onto plates. Serve warm. These keep well once baked and can be stored in an airtight container in the refrigerator for up to 5 days. Reheat when ready to serve if preparing ahead for a dinner party. Preheat the oven to 170°C fan (325°F/gas 3), then place them on a baking sheet and bake for 5–7 minutes.

coconut oil (deodorised), for greasing mould	15 g	0.5 oz
cocoa (unsweetened chocolate) powder, plus extra for dusting	40 g	1.4 oz
oat or soy milk	350 g	12.4 oz
dark chocolate with at least 66% cocoa solids, callets (chips) or chopped	180 g	6.3 oz
caster (superfine) sugar	130 g	4.6 oz
plain (all-purpose) flour	200 g	7 oz
baking powder	4 g	1 tsp

TIP

You can bake and demould these desserts ahead of time. Store them in the refrigerator, then microwave on a plate for 30–40 seconds to reheat.

TIRAMISU

Serves 6

Tiramisu is so legendary you could be forgiven for thinking it has been around forever, but it is actually a relatively new concoction thought to have emerged in the 1960s in Treviso, Italy. This version maintains the simplicity the original is famous for, using simple plant-based ingredients. There is actually one big difference that I am recommending and that is to make a sumptuous and moist coffee sponge that doesn't need to be soaked in the same way as the original, which makes it a lot easier to handle and to create lovely layers.

TIRAMISU COFFEE SPONGE

1. Preheat the oven to 180°C fan (350°F/gas 4). Use spray oil to fix baking parchment to a 25 × 35 cm (10 × 14 in) baking sheet.
2. Using a whisk, combine the flour and baking powder together in a large bowl.
3. Combine the orange zest, coffee granules, milk, olive oil and caster sugar together in a jug or large bowl and whisk until the coffee has dissolved.
4. Add the wet ingredients to the dry ingredients and mix gently with a whisk until combined and completely smooth.
5. Pour the batter onto the lined baking sheet and bake for 7–9 minutes until the sponge springs back when pressed. If you overbake the sponge sheet it will have fine cracks but it will be okay. Leave to cool completely before using. If using marsala wine or coffee liqueur, brush it on top of the sponge layers.

spray oil		for oiling
plain (all-purpose) flour	200 g	7 oz
baking powder	9 g	2¼ tsp
orange zest, grated		¼ orange
instant coffee granules	6 g	3 tsp
oat or soy milk	270 g	9.5 oz
extra virgin olive oil	20 g	0.7 oz
caster (superfine) sugar	190 g	6.7 oz
marsala wine or coffee liqueur (optional)	40 g	1.4 oz

TIRAMISU CREAM DIPLOMAT

6. Whisk the whipping cream in a large bowl to a stable peak and set aside. In another bowl, whisk the crème pâtissière by hand until it's smooth.
7. Add the soft whipped cream to the crème pâtissière and fold it in until combined. Set aside until ready to assemble.

Fresh Whipping Cream (page 236)	250 g	8.8 oz
Crème Pâtissière (page 235)	250 g	8.8 oz

TO ASSEMBLE

8. Place a sheet of baking parchment on top of the cooled sponge and use another baking sheet on top to flip it over. Peel back the baking paper carefully and cut the sponge in half. Place half of a piece of sponge onto a serving or cutting board – this will be the base piece of sponge.
9. Spread half the cream on the base piece of sponge and follow with some cocoa powder, then place the next piece of sponge on top, followed by the remaining cream and spread over until it is level.
10. Leave to chill in the refrigerator for at least 2 hours, then dust with cocoa powder before cutting.
11. For sharp clean cuts, slice with a sharp knife dipped into a jug of hot water from a tap and wiped dry between each cut. This dessert keeps well in an airtight container in the refrigerator for up to 2 days.

ALSO NEEDED

cocoa (unsweetened chocolate) powder	for dusting

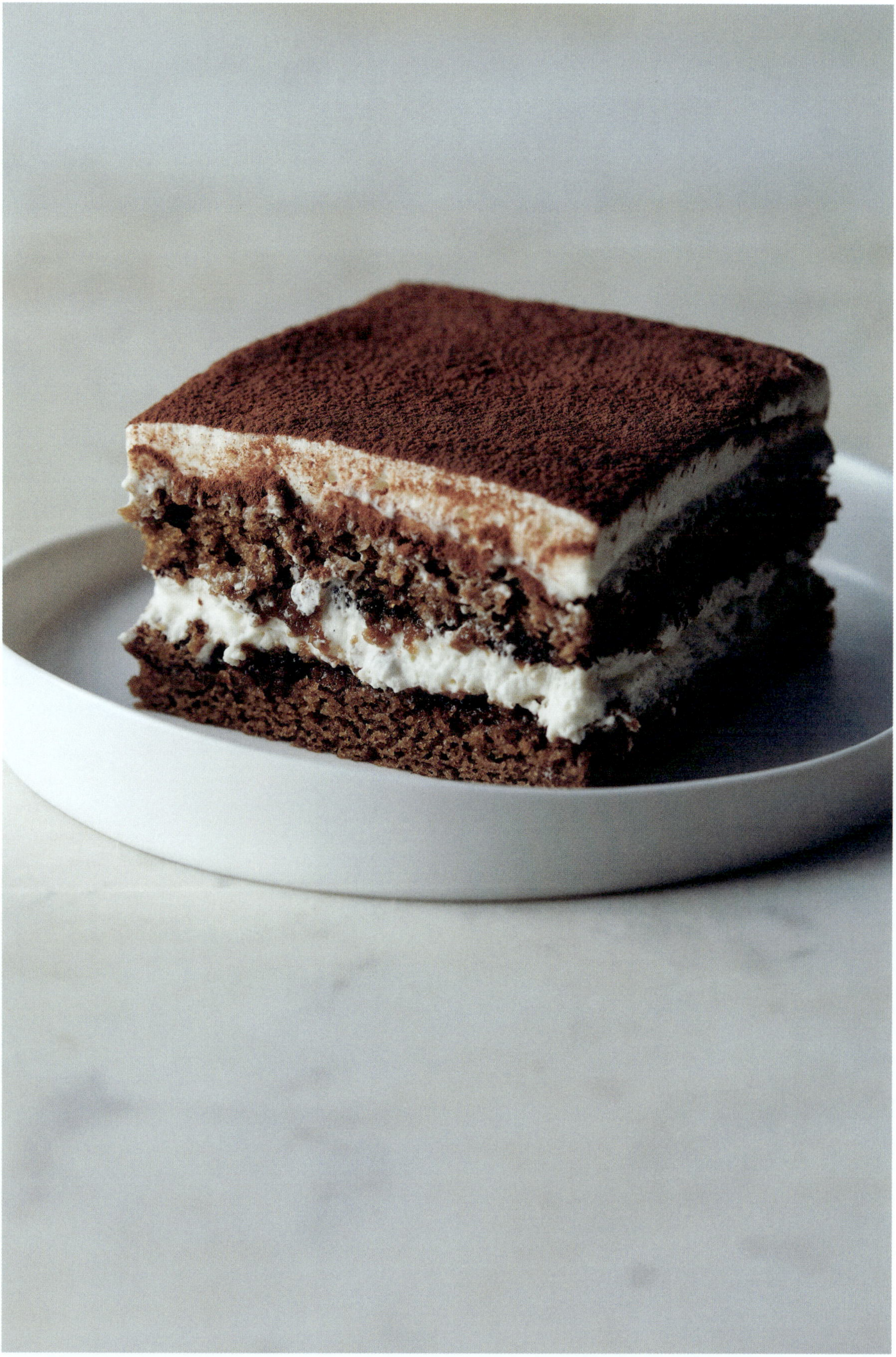

STICKY TOFFEE DATE PUDDING

Serves 8–10

This is the epitome of a winter-warming dessert. The natural fibre and sweetness in the dates binds this decadent pudding together and lends a rich moistness. I like to add a generous pinch of salt to my butterscotch sauce to temper the sweetness and give it a totally moreish (rather than sickly sweet) flavour. Serve warm with a dollop of whipped cream or vanilla ice cream.

DATE CAKE

1. Preheat the oven to 180°C fan (350°F/gas 4) and line the base of a 20 × 30 cm (8 × 12 in) rectangular baking tin (pan) or 8 individual small pudding moulds about 8 cm (3¼ in) in diameter with baking parchment.

2. Add the dates to a blender or food processor, add the boiling water and stir in the bicarbonate of soda. Leave to stand for 10 minutes. When this mixture has cooled, add the olive oil and blend it to a smooth purée.

3. Add the sugar, flour, baking powder and salt to a large bowl and whisk to combine.

4. Add the date purée to the dry ingredients and whisk until the mixture is smooth and clear with no dry lumps. Pour the batter into the lined tin and smooth the top.

5. Bake for 25 minutes, or until the cake springs back when gently pressed with your fingertips, or a skewer inserted into the centre of the cake comes out clean. Set aside in the tin.

dried dates	250 g	8.8 oz
water, boiling	350 g	12.4 oz
bicarbonate of soda (baking soda)	8 g	2 tsp
extra virgin olive oil	20 g	0.7 oz
dark brown or muscovado sugar	100 g	3.5 oz
plain (all-purpose) flour (gluten-free plain flour will also work)	200 g	7 oz
baking powder	13 g	0.5 oz
fine salt	3 g	¾ tsp

SALTED BUTTERSCOTCH SAUCE

6. Mix the milk, sea salt, cornflour and sugar together in a large high-sided, heavy-based saucepan, then bring to a rolling boil while whisking constantly.

7. Add the coconut oil and whisk until melted and well-mixed through.

TO ASSEMBLE AND SERVE

8. Pour the butterscotch sauce over the date cake still in the tin and leave to soak in a little. Slice and serve warm from the baking tin. This dish keeps well if covered in the refrigerator for up to 4 days, or wrapped and frozen for up to 3 months. Defrost in the refrigerator overnight, then preheat the oven to 150°C fan (300°F/gas 2) and reheat for 8 minutes, or until steaming. Or reheat gently in the microwave starting at 30°C (86°F).

soy or oat milk	400 g	14.1 oz
sea salt	5 g	1 tsp
cornflour (cornstarch)	20 g	0.7 oz
dark brown or muscovado sugar	100 g	3.5 oz
coconut oil (deodorised)	20 g	0.7 oz

TIP

Never blend hot liquids! It is dangerous!

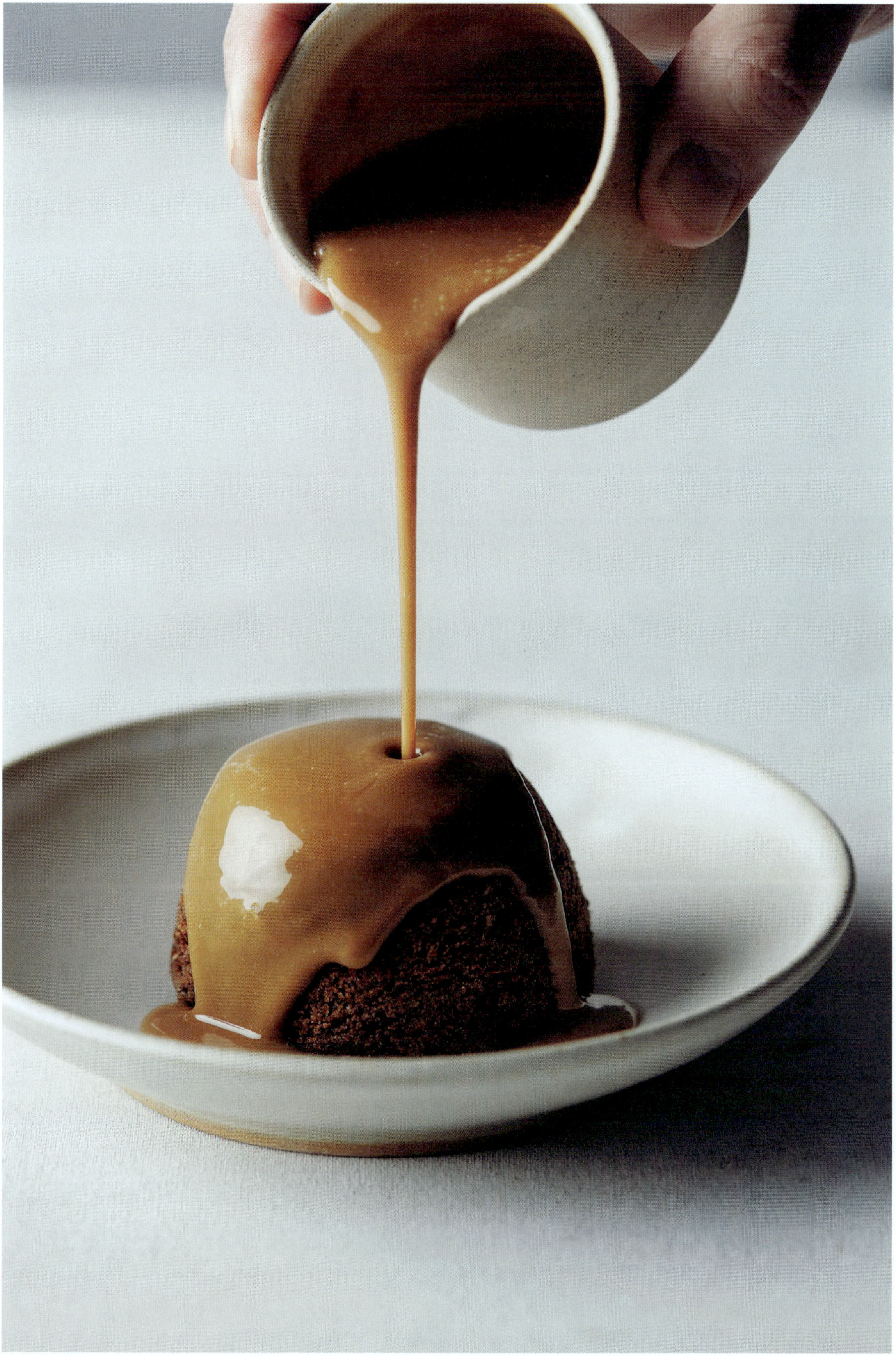

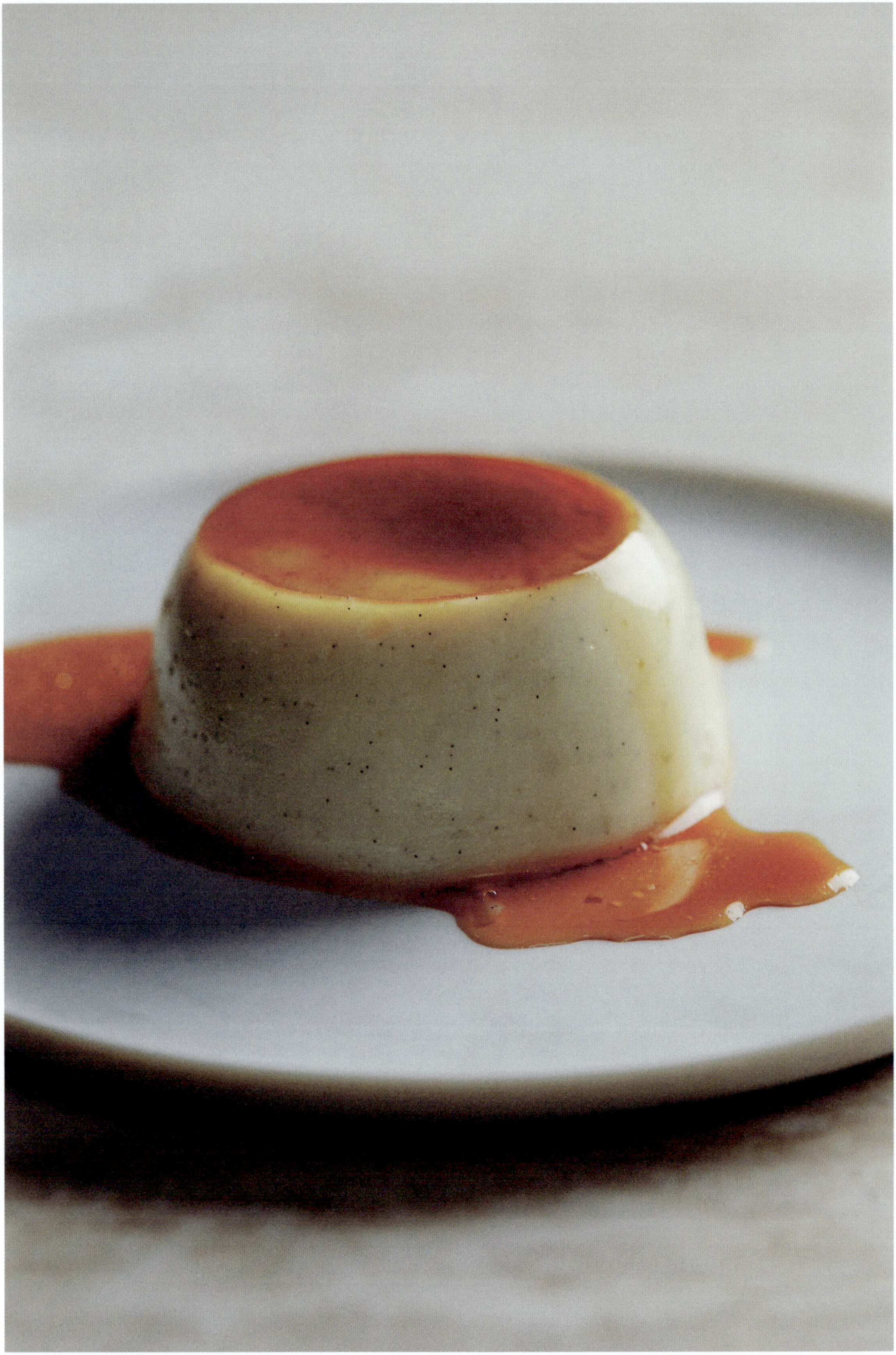

CRÈME CARAMEL

Serves 6

Hard caramel dissolves into a syrup in this self-saucing classic. The custard is simple – cooked on the stove with no chance of scrambling or tasting 'eggy'. It is also versatile (easily infused with fresh herbs, spices, tea, etc). Identical to the crème brûlée custard except that it is poured hot into the mould rather than chilled and whisked. This simple change in process gives it a perfect, just-set texture.

DRY CARAMEL

1. To prepare the 'dry' caramel that will dissolve on top of the custard, use a fingertip to wipe a drop of oil all the way round six stainless-steel, aluminium ramekins or small pudding moulds, 8 cm (3¼ in) in diameter – this will make for an easy release.

2. Use a small light-coloured saucepan so you can see the caramel colour, and heat it over a medium heat.

3. Sprinkle the sugar into the saucepan. As it dissolves, reduce the heat, pick up the pan and swirl it around so the sugar melts and caramelises to a mahogany colour. Be very careful as the sugar at this temperature is very dangerous.

4. Carefully pour in just enough caramel to cover the bottom of each ramekin or mould, about 15 g (½ oz), and leave to set at room temperature.

VANILLA CUSTARD

5. Add the milk (1) to a large saucepan with the sugar and vanilla seeds and scraped pod over a low heat until it comes to a simmer. Remove the pod.

6. Mix the milk (2), cornflour and custard powder together in a small bowl until the cornflour has completely dissolved.

7. Add the cornflour mix to the boiling milk over the lowest heat, while stirring constantly with a silicone spatula and scraping the base of the pan. The mixture will thicken on the base of the pan first so continue stirring and scraping the whole pan so it doesn't catch. Add the coconut oil and stir with a silicone spatula, gently at first, then swiftly to incorporate the coconut oil. It will look separated at first but it will come together. Keep mixing until it adheres to the saucepan sides. The mixture will be smooth, glossy, with no oily streaks.

8. Pour the custard into the prepared ramekins or moulds – about 130–150 g (4½–5 oz) per serve, and chill in the refrigerator for 4 hours. These can be prepared the day before.

9. To serve, with a fingertip, pull the edges gently to release from the sides. Put a serving dish upside down over the top of the mould and flip over, drizzle any extra syrup on top of the set custard. Serve.

oil, for greasing		
caster (superfine) sugar	120 g	4 oz

TIP

If you don't feel confident making a dry caramel, add 40 g (1.4 oz) of water to the sugar in the saucepan, making sure the sugar is wet. Then turn on medium-high heat and cook until the syrup starts to caramelise at the edge of the pan and gently swirl it around until all the syrup is caramelised evenly. Remove from the heat and allow simmering to settle.

oat or soy milk (1)	750 g	1 lb 10 oz
caster (superfine) sugar	280 g	9.9 oz
vanilla pod (bean), seeds scraped out	1 pod	
oat or soy milk (2)	80 g	2.8 oz
cornflour (cornstarch)	60 g	2.1 oz
custard powder	30 g	1.1 oz
coconut oil (deodorised)	75 g	2.7 oz

CRÈME BRÛLÉE

Serves 6

Crack through caramelised sugar into a sumptuous custard. This is a dessert that needs no introduction. For this recipe, the custard is the same as that for the crème caramel but served with blowtorched sugar in the ramekin.

VANILLA CUSTARD

1. Add the milk (1) to a large saucepan with the sugar and vanilla seeds and scraped pod over a low heat until it comes to a simmer. Remove the pod.

2. Mix the milk (2), cornflour and custard powder together in a medium bowl until the cornflour has completely dissolved.

3. Add the cornflour mix to the boiling milk over the lowest heat, while stirring constantly with a silicone spatula and scraping the base of the pan. The mixture will thicken on the base of the pan first so continue stirring and scraping the whole pan so it doesn't catch. Add the coconut oil and stir with a silicone spatula, gently at first, then swiftly to incorporate the coconut oil. It will look separated at first but it will come together. Keep mixing until it adheres to the sides of the saucepan. The mixture will be smooth, glossy, with no oily streaks.

4. Pour the custard into a shallow dish, with cling film (plastic wrap) or a silicone mat pressed to the surface to prevent a skin from forming. Chill until set, then scrape into a bowl, and whisk until smooth and there are no lumps.

5. Pour or pipe the chilled custard into the six ramekins, about 8 cm (3¼ in) in diameter and 4 cm (1.5 in) deep, until they are almost full. Leave to chill in the refrigerator. These can be stored un-brûléed in the refrigerator for up to 2 days in advance but should be served within 30 minutes of being blowtorched or the caramel will start to soften and dissolve.

6. To finish or 'brûlée' the set cream, sprinkle 1 heaped tablespoon of the sugar onto the top of the custard in a ramekin and then rotate it around to spread a thin layer of sugar over the top. Use a kitchen blowtorch to very gently melt and caramelise the sugar, slowly starting around the edges in a spiral, working your way inwards. Repeat with the remaining custards and serve.

oat or soy milk (1)	750 g	1 lb 10 oz
caster (superfine) sugar	280 g	9.9 oz
vanilla pod (bean), seeds scraped out	1 pod	
oat or soy milk (2)	80 g	2.8 oz
cornflour (cornstarch)	60 g	2.1 oz
custard powder	30 g	1.1 oz
coconut oil (deodorised)	75 g	2.7 oz

ALSO NEEDED

caster (superfine) sugar or Demerara sugar	90–100 g	3.2–3.5 oz

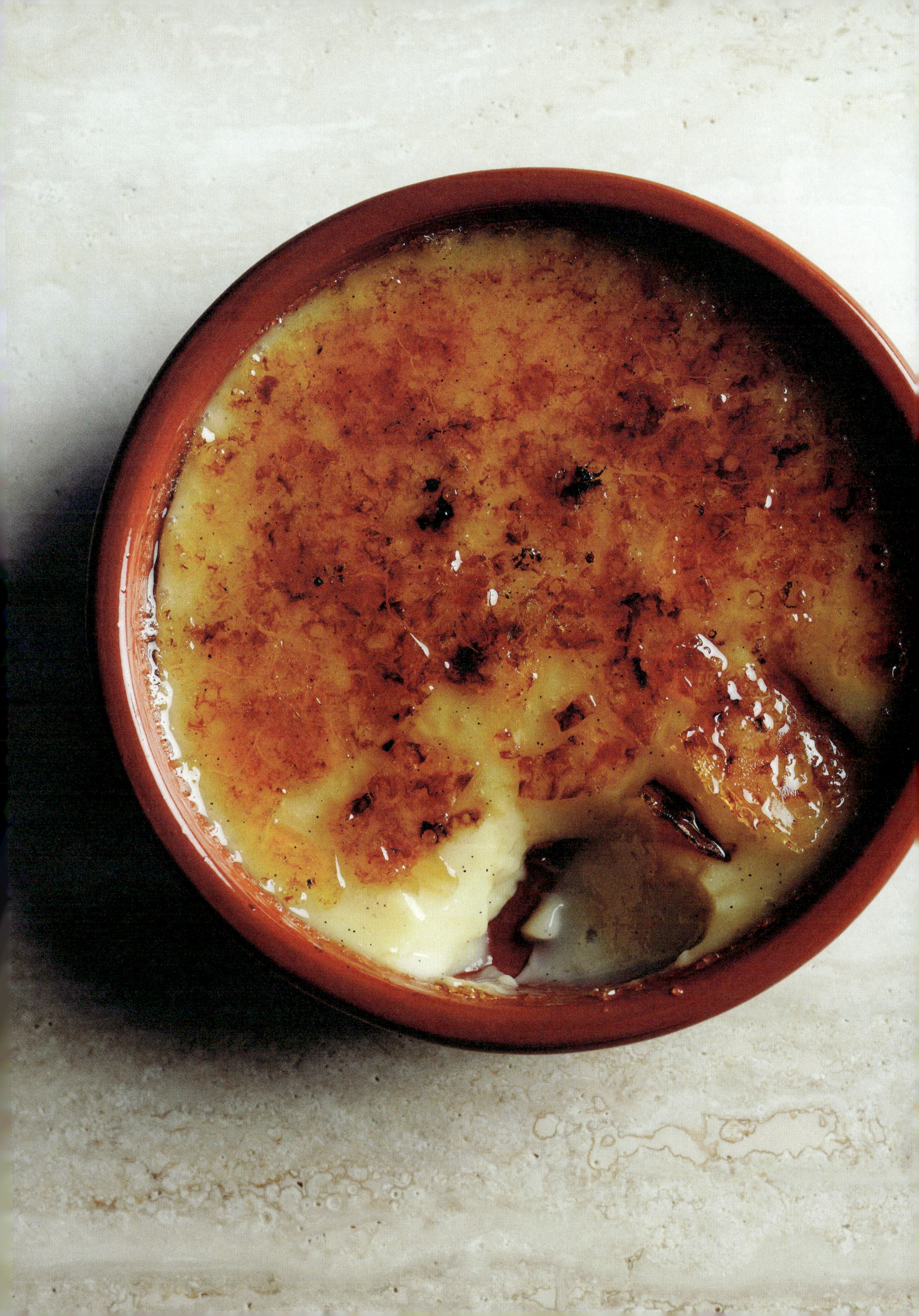

ETON MESS

Makes 6 glasses

A light but decadent dessert. I prefer Eton mess in a glass to a traditional pavlova because it is less sweet. Feel free to get creative with the fruits (I'm thinking fresh diced mango, quartered strawberries, slices of kiwi and a sexy squeeze of passion fruit for something reminiscent of a pavlova but so much better!).

MERINGUE KISSES

1. Preheat the oven to 120°C fan (200°F/gas ½) and line a baking tray with parchment paper.

2. To make the meringue, drain the chickpeas over a measuring jug. You should have around 300 ml (10 fl oz) of chickpea aquafaba liquid from the tins. Reserve the chickpeas and keep covered in the refrigerator for up to 3 days to use in other recipes – like hummus!

3. Pour the aquafaba into a saucepan, bring to the boil then reduce to a simmer. You want to reduce the volume down to 150 g (5.3 oz) which should take about 10 minutes. I set a bowl on some scales and periodically pour the reducing liquid to weigh it. If you reduce it too far, you can add some water to make up the difference.

4. Place the reduced aquafaba in the clean bowl of a stand mixer with the caster sugar and cream of tartar. Use the whisk attachment to whip for 4–5 minutes, or to a stable, fluffy meringue with firm peaks.

5. Scoop the meringue into a piping bag, fitted with a star nozzle attached and pipe small meringue kisses all over the baking paper. Bake in the oven for 30 minutes with a spoon keeping the door slightly open to allow moisture to escape, then leave to cool completely with the door slightly open.

chickpeas	2 × 400 g tins	2 × 14.1 oz tins
caster (superfine) sugar	150 g	5.3 oz
cream of tartar or vinegar	3 g	¾ tsp

BERRY JAM

6. To make the berry jam, mix the caster sugar and agar-agar together in a bowl. Add to a blender along with the berries and lemon juice and blend to a purée. Transfer to a saucepan and bring to the boil, then pour into a shallow container. Allow to cool, then place in the refrigerator to set. When ready to serve, blend or whisk the jam until smooth.

caster (superfine) sugar	30 g	1.1 oz
agar-agar	2 g	½ tsp
strawberries, trimmed	120 g	4.2 oz
raspberries	110 g	3.9 oz
lemon juice	22 g	0.8 oz

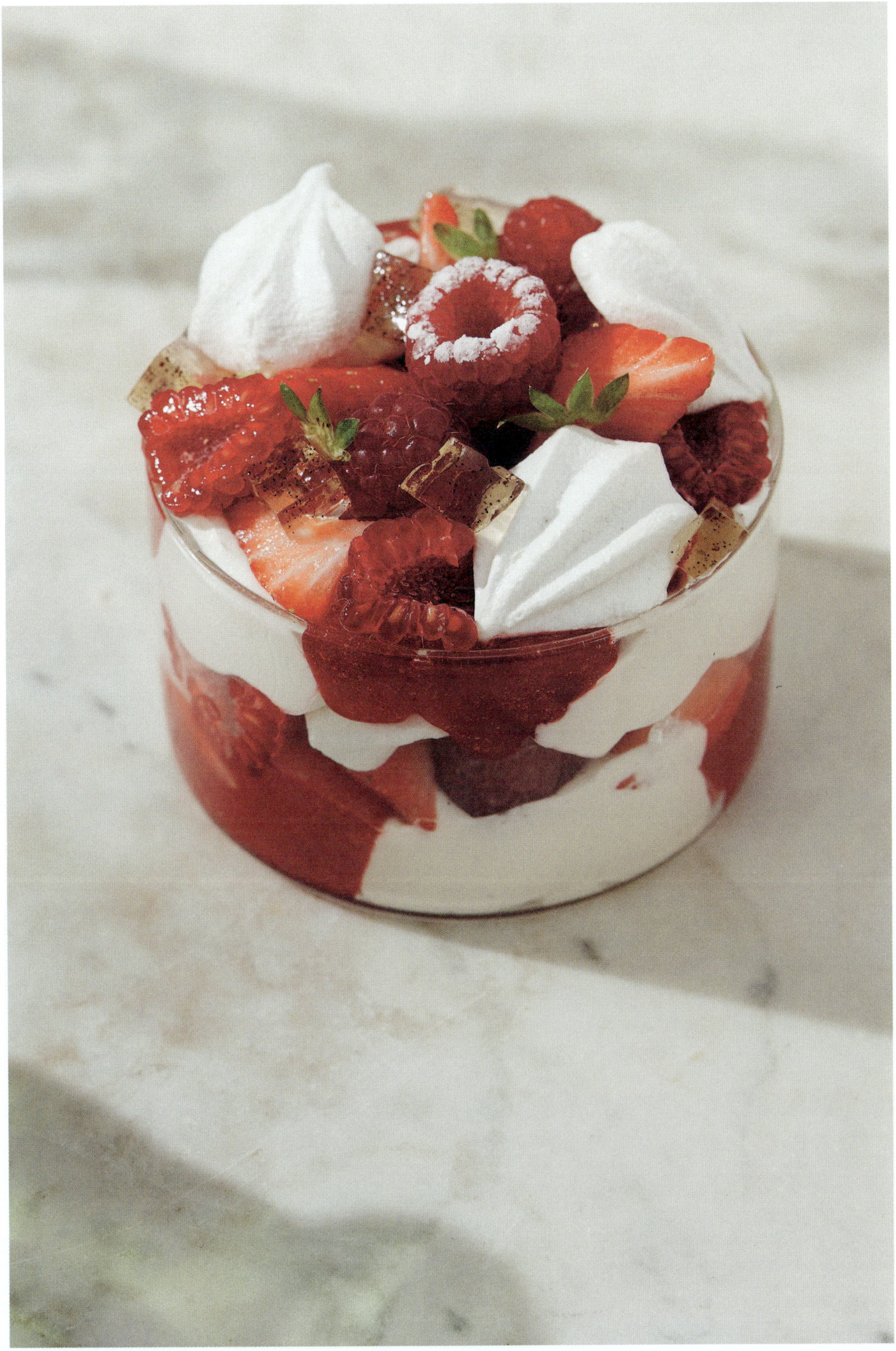

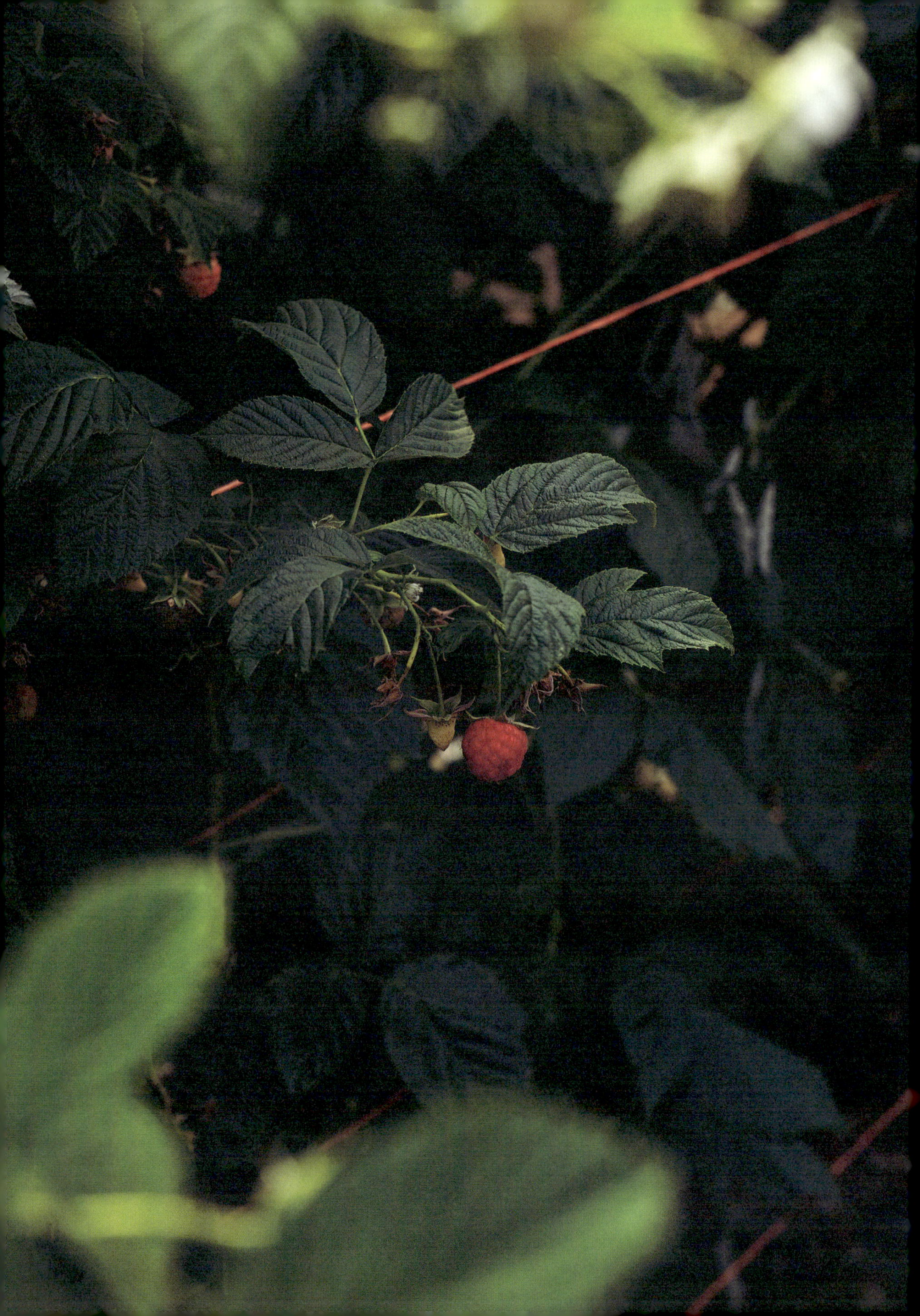

SPARKLING WINE JELLY

7. Mix the agar-agar and caster sugar together in a bowl then place in a saucepan with the sparkling wine. Bring to the boil, then pour into a container or 20 × 20 cm (8 × 8 in) square baking tin.

8. Allow to cool, then place in the refrigerator to set. When set, cut the jelly into 1–2 cm pieces.

agar-agar	2 g	½ tsp
caster (superfine) sugar	20 g	0.7 oz
English sparkling wine	150 g	5.3 oz

CHANTILLY CREAM

9. Whip the ingredients together to soft peaks.

Fresh Whipping Cream (page 236)	300 g	10.6 oz
vanilla pod, seeds scraped, or vanilla bean paste	1 tsp	1 pod
caster (superfine) sugar	30 g	1.1 oz

TO ASSEMBLE

10. Place some of the fresh berries in the bottom of each serving glass with some pieces of the jelly. Top with some meringue kisses, then pipe or spoon some of the Chantilly cream on, followed by a swirl of the berry jam. Top with more fresh berries, some meringue kisses, more jelly and finish with gold leaf, if using.

strawberries, quartered	10 strawberries
raspberries	16 raspberries
gold leaf (optional)	

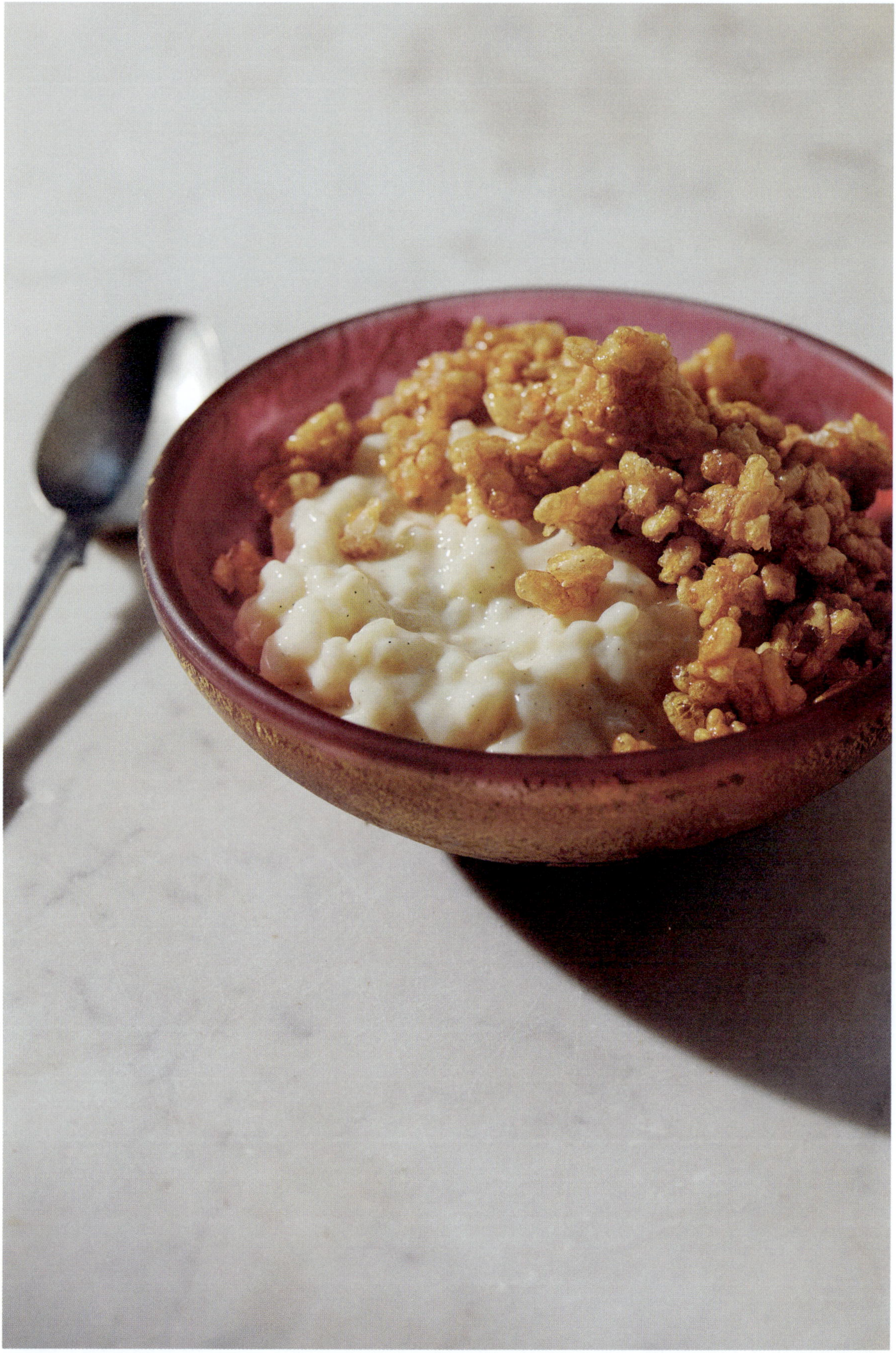

RICE PUDDING

Serves 6

Lebanese rice pudding (*Riz bi haleeb* – like my grandma used to make me as a child) is very similar to rice pudding except a tiny bit of rose or orange blossom water gives it a soft floral note. When using any floral extracts it is important to dose very carefully. A splash too much will result in something akin to pot-pourri which is not what anyone wants to eat. A famous Lebanese restaurant called Em Sherif makes the best rice pudding I have ever tasted. It is topped with puffed rice crispies that have been caramelised and served sprinkled on top of the chilled pudding. It's very smart and incredibly delicious. This recipe is my nod to it. I like using oat milk as it lends a cereal milk flavour, as well as lots and lots of vanilla 'caviar' along with the tiniest splash of rose water (which you can omit or just start with the teensiest amount) perfumes the rice and the light crunchy topping elevates it beyond the realms of a traditional rice pudding.

RICE PUDDING

1. Pour the milk (1) into a large saucepan and bring to a simmer over a medium heat. Add the rice and reduce the heat to just above the lowest heat, to maintain a gentle simmer. As it cooks, a skin will form but that's okay, just keep stirring it in. Set a timer for 35–40 minutes and cook until a tiny taste reveals no 'bite' left in the rice but it still holds its shape and some tenderness.

2. Mix the sugar and cornflour together in a large bowl, then add the milk (2) and rose water and stir to combine. Pour this mixture into the saucepan of rice and stir through over a low heat for 2 minutes, then remove from the heat.

3. Stir and serve warm, or chill in a large bowl before gently stirring to loosen up and scooping into serving dishes. It can be stored wrapped and chilled for up to 4 days.

plant-based milk (1)	700 g	1 lb 9 oz
arborio or pudding rice	100 g	3.9 oz
caster (superfine) sugar	75 g	2.7 oz
cornflour (cornstarch)	8 g	2 tsp
plant-based milk (2)	100 g	3.5 oz
rose water	2 g	½ oz
vanilla pod, seeds scraped	1 pod	
or vanilla paste	4 g	1 tsp

CARAMELISED RICE CRISPIES

4. Line a large rimmed baking sheet with baking parchment or a silicone mat.

5. Heat a stainless-steel (so you can see the colour of the sugar as it caramelises) saucepan over a medium-high heat and sprinkle 1 teaspoon of the sugar into the pan. When it melts, sprinkle in the remaining sugar and swirl the pan around to encourage it to melt, then it will start to caramelise. Once this starts to happen and you reach a golden colour, add the coconut oil and swirl the pan around to combine.

6. Remove from the heat, add the rice crispies, then use a silicone spatula to quickly stir so all the rice crispies are evenly coated with the caramel.

7. Quickly pour onto the lined baking sheet and use the spatula to spread the rice crispies in a thin layer and to break them into smaller pieces. Leave to cool before using to decorate the chilled rice puddings, just before serving. You can store the caramelised rice crispies in a small airtight container for up to 5 days.

caster (superfine) sugar	50 g	1.8 oz
coconut oil (deodorised)	10 g	0.4 oz
rice crispies	50 g	1.8 oz

TIP

Your rice should be thickened and cooked between 30–40 minutes depending on the size and variety of rice. You only need to stir it after 20 minutes to make sure nothing has caught on the base of the pan, then again 10 minutes later at the 35-minute mark (timers will work a charm here). Rice varies slightly in their time to cook, but use these times as a good guide.

NUT GELATO

Makes 1 litre (34 fl oz)

This insane ice cream has the texture and creaminess of a gelato, but are made of three to four ingredients. Pioneered in Italy, this formulation is essentially a 'nut sorbet' but with the right mix of fats, sugar and water to get a beautifully textured ice cream. Substitute any type of nut or pure nut paste you like.

nuts or smooth nut paste/butter	200 g	7 oz
water or plant-based milk	650 g	1 lb 7 oz
caster (superfine) sugar	160 g	5.6 oz
sea salt, crushed	1 g	¼ tsp

1 Depending on your ice-cream machine, there are models where you need to freeze the bowl or container and others that are self-freezing, so prepare according to the model you are using.

IF USING WHOLE NUTS

2 Preheat the oven to 150°C fan (300°F/gas 2). Spread the hazelnuts out into a roasting tray and roast for 15 minutes. Remove them from the oven and leave to cool completely.

3 Add the cooled nuts to the blender with the rest of the ingredients and leave them to stand for 30 minutes to let the nuts soften. Blend for 1 minute until any particles are very fine. Pass the mixture through a nut milk bag or muslin (cheesecloth) into a large shallow dish.

IF USING NUT PASTE OR BUTTER

4 Add the nut paste or butter with the rest of the ingredients to a high-powered blender and blend for 1 minute, then pour into a large shallow dish.

TO FINISH

5 Cover the surface of the mixture with cling film (plastic wrap) and leave to chill in the refrigerator for 3 hours.

6 Churn in an ice-cream machine according to the manufacturer's instructions and serve.

TIP

You can roast your nuts to your preference. I prefer a lower temperature to penetrate deeper into the nut for better flavour, otherwise the outside gets too toasted and the inside tastes raw.

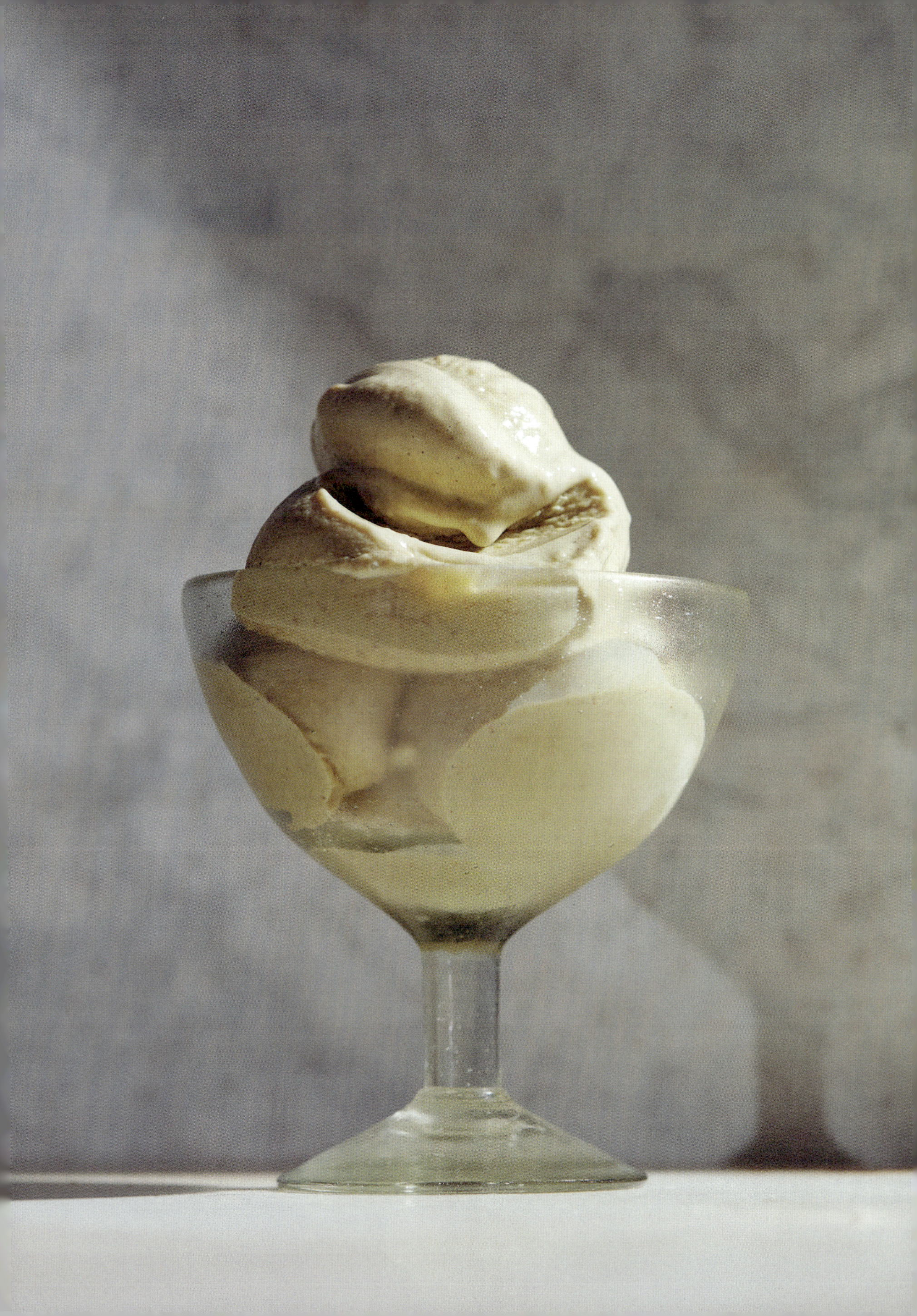

NO-CHURN ICE CREAM

Makes 900 g (2 lb)

This is an easy no-churn ice cream that you can whip up and freeze for an iced confection that is easily infused with other flavours, toppings and inclusions.

coconut oil (deodorised)	220 g	7.8 oz
oat or soy milk	290 g	10.2 oz
caster (superfine) sugar	100 g	3.5 oz
glucose (light corn) syrup	112 g	4 oz
vanilla bean paste	4 g	1 tsp
sea salt, crushed	1.5 g	⅓ tsp

1. Add the coconut oil to a microwave-safe bowl and microwave for 60 seconds, or until melted. Alternatively, melt in a medium saucepan over a low heat. Leave to cool.

2. Add the melted coconut oil to a blender with the remaining ingredients and blend very well for 1 minute. When you dip a spoon into the mixture and hold it up to the light you should see a glossy light reflection. If you can see oily streaks you need to blend more. You can also use an immersion stick blender in a large jug or bowl.

3. Pour the mixture into a large shallow dish and press cling film (plastic wrap) over the surface, then leave to chill in the refrigerator for 4 hours, or until it reaches 5°C (41°F) on a thermometer.

4. Chill the bowl of your stand mixer, then whip the chilled mixture with a whisk attachment on medium speed, starting for about 3 minutes, but up to 5–6 minutes until the mixture is fluffy and thick. Pour into a 900 g (2 lb) loaf tin (pan) or container and freeze for 6 hours, or overnight.

5. You may want to leave your container at room temperature for just a couple of minutes to soften before scooping and serving.

VARIATIONS

Fig leaf | Bring the milk to a simmer in a saucepan to infuse a washed fig leaf for 2 hours, then remove the leaf and discard, and proceed with the recipe. Ripple with fig jam at the end.

Tea | Bring the milk to a simmer in a saucepan with a tea bag for 5 minutes, then strain and proceed with the recipe.

Mango | Blend 100 g (3.5 oz) mango flesh with 50 g (1.8 oz) caster (superfine) sugar and fold through the whisked base before freezing.

Strawberry | Blend 100 g (3.5 oz) washed and hulled strawberries with 40 g (1.4 oz) caster (superfine) sugar, then strain through a sieve (fine-mesh strainer) to remove the seeds and fold through the whisked base before freezing.

Oreo | Crush 50 g (1.8 oz) Oreos and fold through the whipped base before freezing.

Nut | Fold 80 g (2.8 oz) nut butter through the whipped base before freezing.

NO-CHURN CHOCOLATE ICE CREAM

Makes 900 g (2 lb)

A no-churn ice cream recipe is super handy to have due to ice-cream machines being such a specialist and sometimes expensive piece of equipment. According to purists this would technically be an iced confection. Prepare the base cream and leave to chill in the refrigerator then whip up to soft peak and freeze! Scoop as normal.

1. Melt the chocolate and olive oil in a microwave-safe bowl in the microwave in 30 second bursts, stirring in between, or in a heatproof or stainless-steel bowl set over a pan filled with 1 cm (½ in) simmering water, stirring until melted, then remove from the heat.

2. Add the melted chocolate to a blender with the remaining ingredients and blend very well for 1 minute. When you dip a spoon into the mixture and hold it up to the light you should see a glossy light reflection. If you can see oily streaks you need to blend more. You can also use an immersion stick blender in a large jug or bowl.

3. Pour the mixture into a large shallow dish and press cling film (plastic wrap) over the surface, then leave to chill in the refrigerator for 4 hours, or until it reaches 5°C (41°F) on a thermometer.

4. Chill the bowl of your stand mixer, then whip the chilled mixture with a whisk attachment on medium speed, starting for about 3 minutes, but up to 5–6 minutes until the mixture is fluffy and thick. Pour into a 900 g (2 lb) loaf tin (pan) or container and freeze for 6 hours, or overnight.

5. You may want to leave your container at room temperature for just a couple of minutes to soften before scooping and serving.

dark chocolate, with at least 66% cocoa solids, chopped or callets (chips)	175 g	6.2 oz
extra virgin olive oil	20 g	0.7 oz
oat or soy milk, at room temperature	350 g	12.4 oz
caster (superfine) sugar	80 g	2.8 oz
glucose (light corn) syrup	100 g	3.5 oz
vanilla bean paste	4 g	1 tsp
sea salt, crushed	1.5 g	⅓ tsp

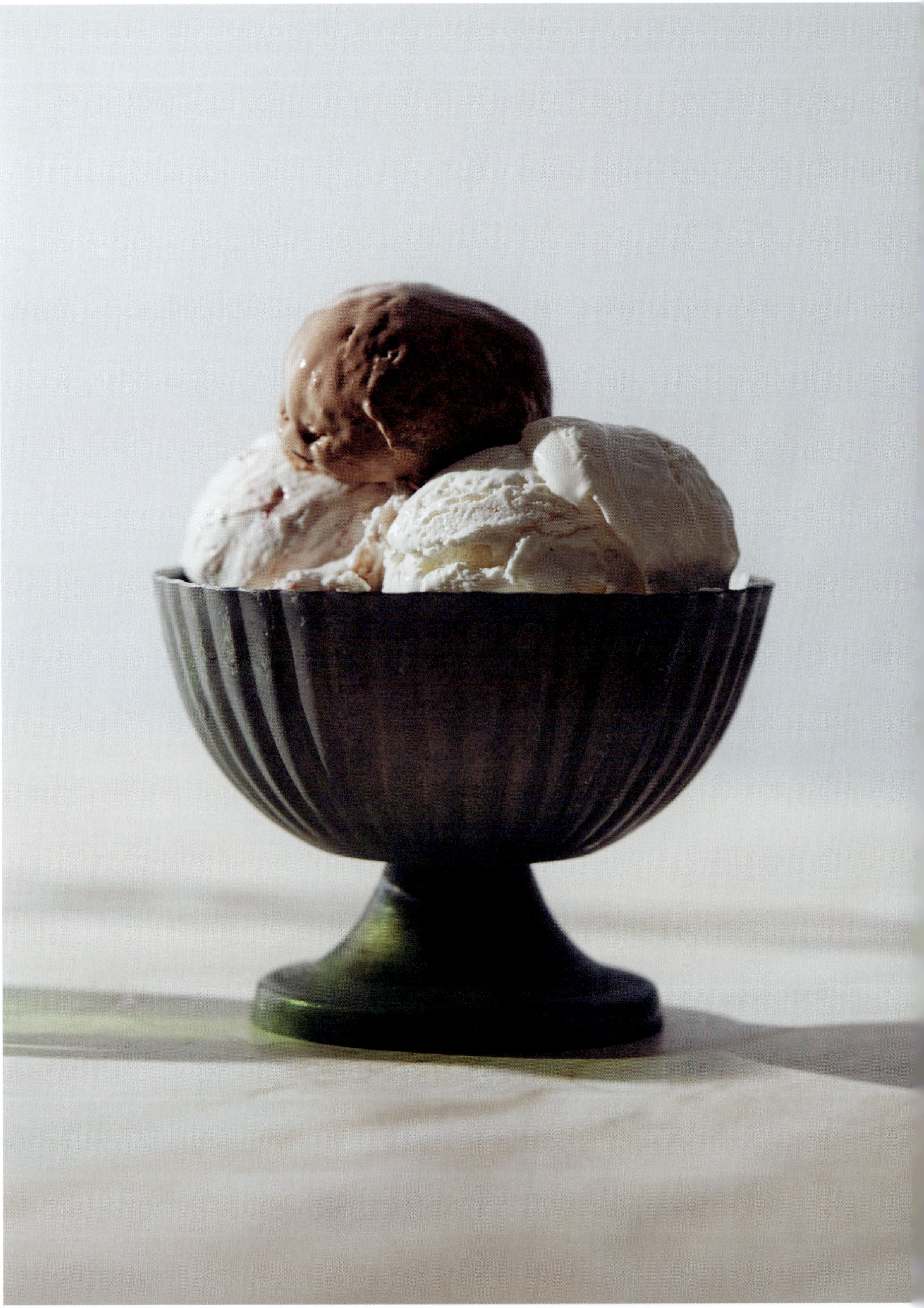

DESSERTS

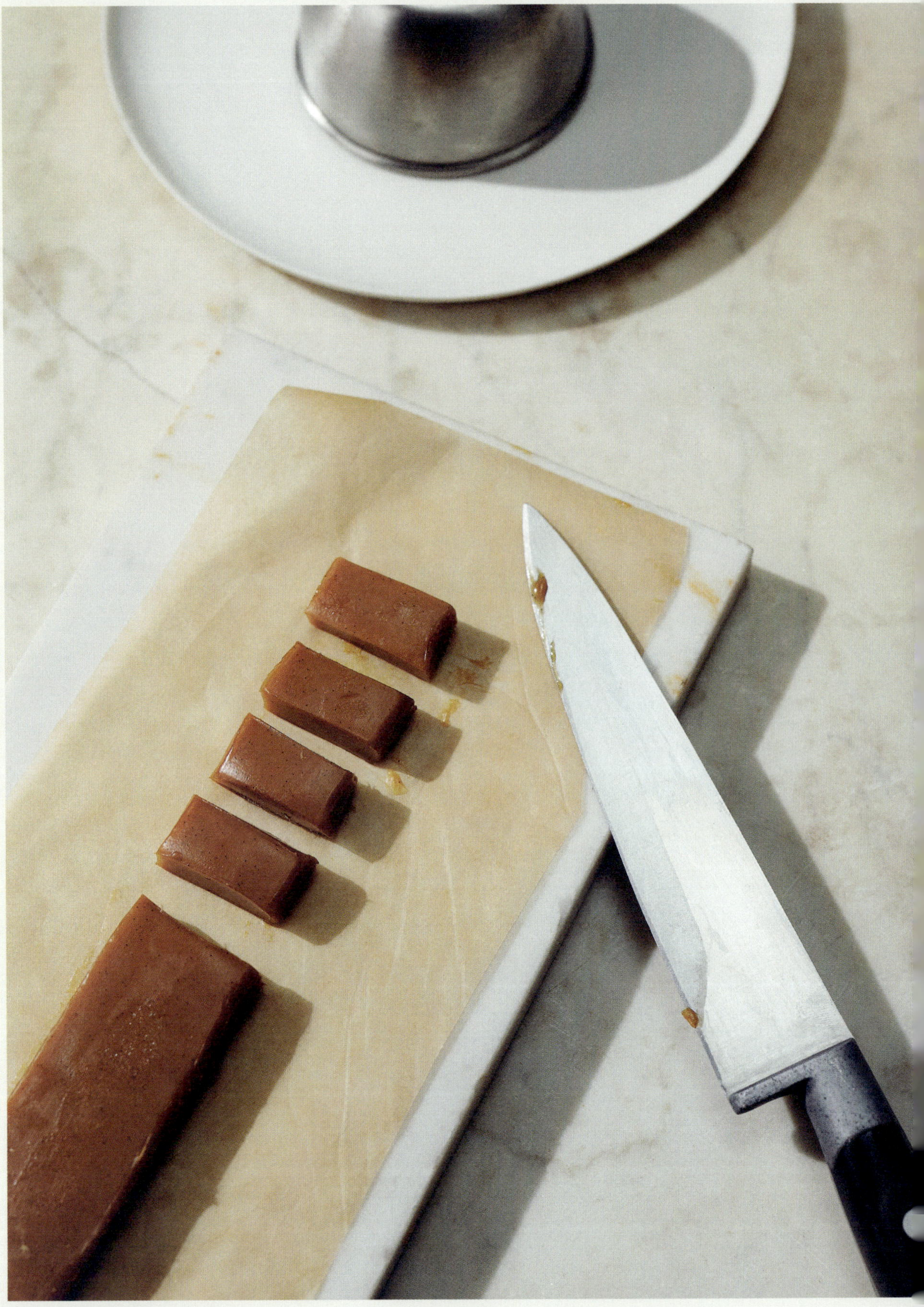

6 CONFECTIONS

Here are some little petit-fours/confections that make great gifts, or pick-me-ups at the end of a fancy dinner party. 'Petit-four' literally means 'small oven' in French. It was the term used to describe an oven that had done the bulk of its cooking and had residual heat left – in an era when ovens were fired by wood and used to bake small treats. Nowadays, a petit-four is the generic term for any small sweet bite you could enjoy at the end of a meal.

NAMA GANACHE

Makes about 36 ganache squares

This may just be the simplest recipe I have ever done. These chocolates, made by Royce', came in little sealed pouches with their own little pick to skewer your square of cocoa-dusted ganache so you didn't soil your fingers. They must be refrigerated and although they are fairly mainstream – essentially a tourist product – they need special packaging with insulated bags and ice packs to travel. They last a good 5 days in the refrigerator, and they are an awesome way to finish a meal or treat guests. The classic chocolate has alcohol added to it so feel free to add some Hennessy VSOP like Royce' does by replacing 5 per cent of the milk weight. This recipe has endless variations, but start basic and substitute some milk as you like! This recipe is another brilliant way to experience single-origin chocolates and is a great for comparing chocolate flavour profiles.

plant-based milk	200 g	7 oz
caster (superfine) sugar	20 g	0.7 oz
dark chocolate with at least 60% cocoa solids, callets (chips) or chopped	200 g	7 oz

ALSO NEEDED

cocoa (unsweetened chocolate) powder	for dusting

1. Line a 20 × 20 cm (8 × 8 in) baking tin (pan) with baking parchment.

2. Bring the milk and sugar to a simmer in a saucepan until lightly boiling, then remove from the heat.

3. Pour the milk over the chocolate in large heatproof bowl or blending jug and leave to stand until it reaches 35–40°C (95–104°F). Use an immersion stick blender or blender to blend the chocolate mixture for 30–60 seconds to get a smooth and shiny emulsion.

4. Pour the ganache into the lined tin, then tilt and tap the tin to level the ganache and remove any air bubbles.

5. Leave to chill in the refrigerator for 1–2 hours until firm. Remove the ganache from the tin by gripping the overhanging baking parchment.

6. Cut the ganache into 2.5 × 2.5 cm (1 × 1 in) squares with a sharp knife dipped into a jug of hot water from a tap and wiped dry between each cut.

7. Dust the top with cocoa powder and store in an airtight container in the refrigerator for up to 10 days. Serve with little picks so guests can keep their fingers clean!

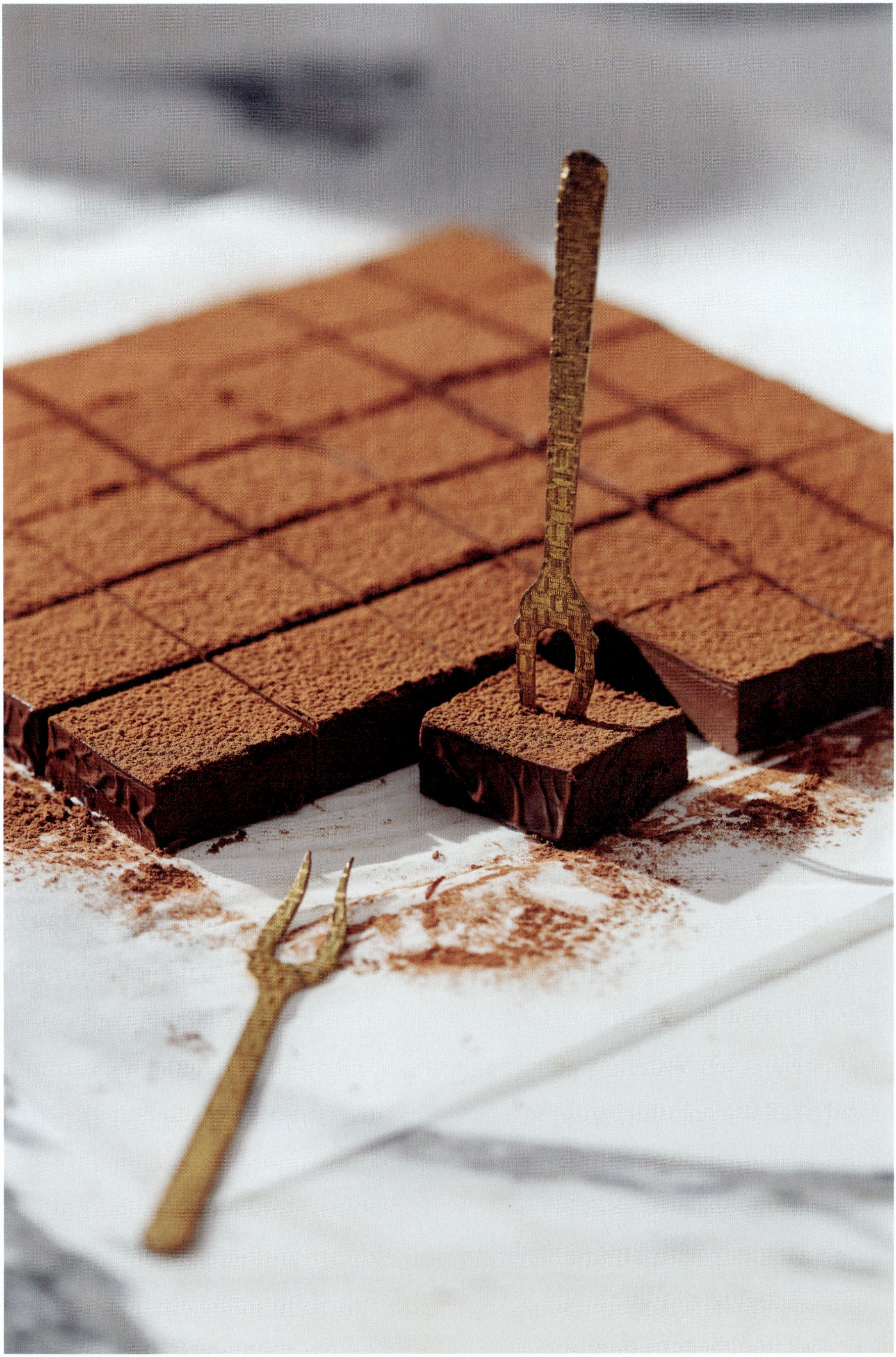

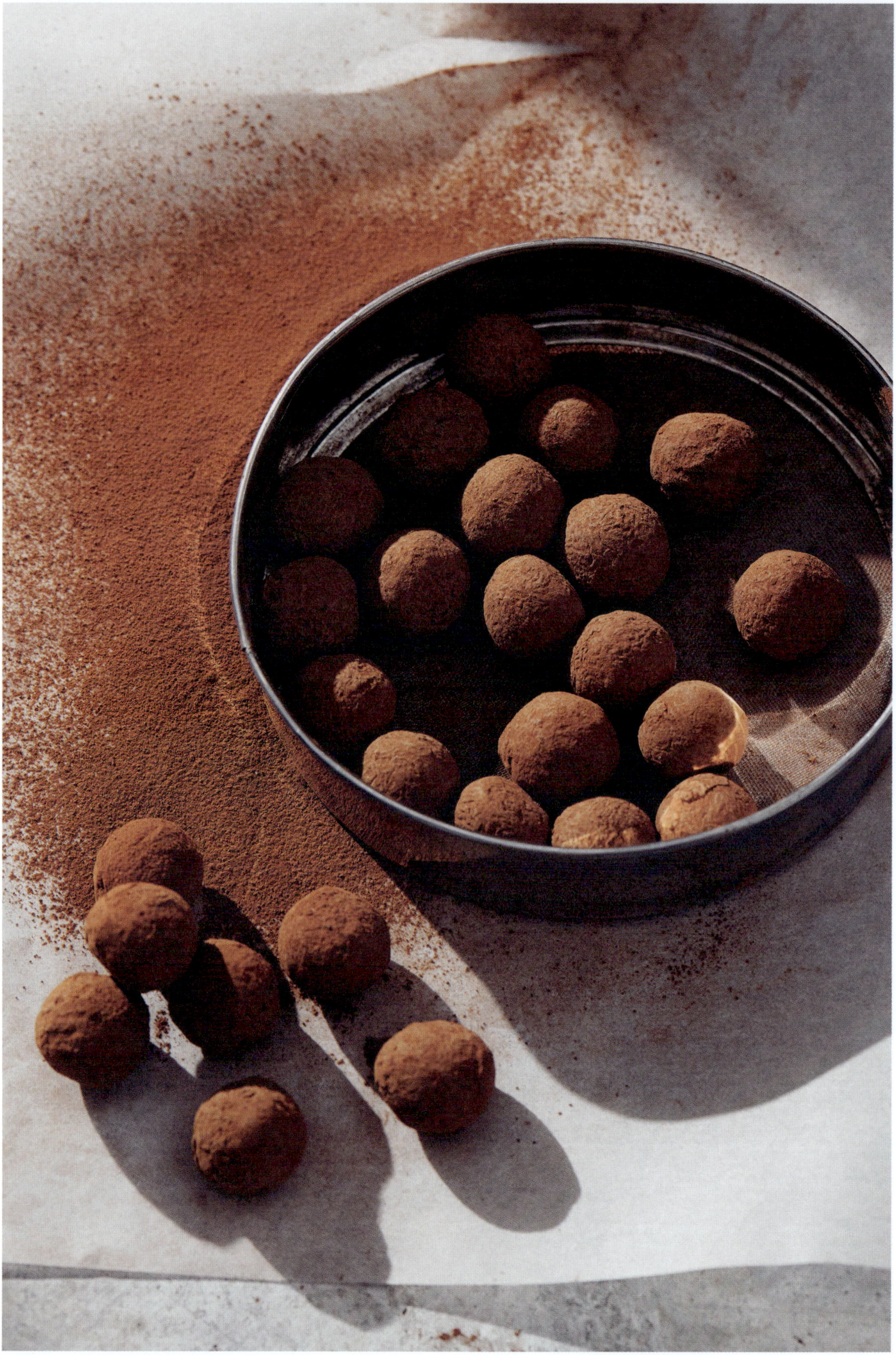

CHOCOLATE TRUFFLES

Makes 35 truffles

The concept of a water ganache blew my young pastry chef mind. How could water – the sworn enemy of chocolate – produce beautiful ganache?! The beauty of this recipe is in its simplicity and how something as pure and unadulterated as water can allow the nuances and subtleties of a fine chocolate to clearly show. Pick some interesting couvertures to try this recipe with, and feel free to replace some or all of the water with strong-flavoured juices like passion fruit or yuzu, tea infusions like Earl Grey or hōjicha or remove 5–10 per cent of the water and add alcohol at the blending stage.

water	220 g	7.8 oz
golden (or light corn) syrup	30 g	1.1 oz
dark chocolate with at least 60% cocoa solids, callets (chips) or chopped (1)	300 g	10.6 oz
cocoa (unsweetened chocolate) powder, for rolling	80 g	2.8 oz
dark chocolate with at least 60% cocoa solids, callets (chips) or chopped (2)	400 g	14.1 oz

1 Line a large baking sheet with baking parchment and set aside. Bring the water and golden syrup to a simmer in a saucepan, just until the sugar has dissolved and there are little bubbles rising to the surface.

2 Pour the liquid over the chocolate (1) in a large heatproof bowl or blending jug, then use an immersion stick blender to blend for 30–60 seconds to get a smooth and shiny emulsion. Check the temperature is 35°C (95°F) and not hotter, otherwise let it cool and blend when it reaches that temperature. This temperature is important as it needs to be hot enough to melt the chocolate, but then when you blend it needs to be closest to 30°C (86°F) so that it will set nicely and quickly and lock in the silky texture you achieved by blending (emulsifying) the ganache.

3 Pour the ganache into a piping (pastry) bag fitted with a 1 cm (½ in) round piping nozzle and lay it flat on your work surface or on a baking sheet in the refrigerator for 20 minutes.

4 Trim your piping bag and pipe long logs or rounds onto the lined baking sheet. Leave for 1–2 hours at room temperature until completely set.

5 If you piped logs, you can trim them until they are 2.5 cm (1 in) long with a knife that has been dipped into jug of hot water and dried.

6 Temper the chocolate (2).

7 Have the tempered chocolate in a bowl and the cocoa powder in another bowl on the work surface. Use one hand to pick up a truffle and the fingertips of your other hand to dab into the dark chocolate. Coat the truffles by hand rolling them, then dropping them into the cocoa powder and letting them set, tossing the bowl with every few truffles so the chocolate is coated with cocoa powder and they don't stick together.

8 Place the coated truffles in a sieve (fine-mesh strainer) and gently toss/roll them around to remove any excess cocoa. The truffles will last for a week stored in an airtight container at room temperature. You can also store them in an airtight container in the refrigerator for 2 weeks, but make sure to take out 1 hour before serving and let them come to room temperature in the closed airtight container.

TEMPERING CHOCOLATE

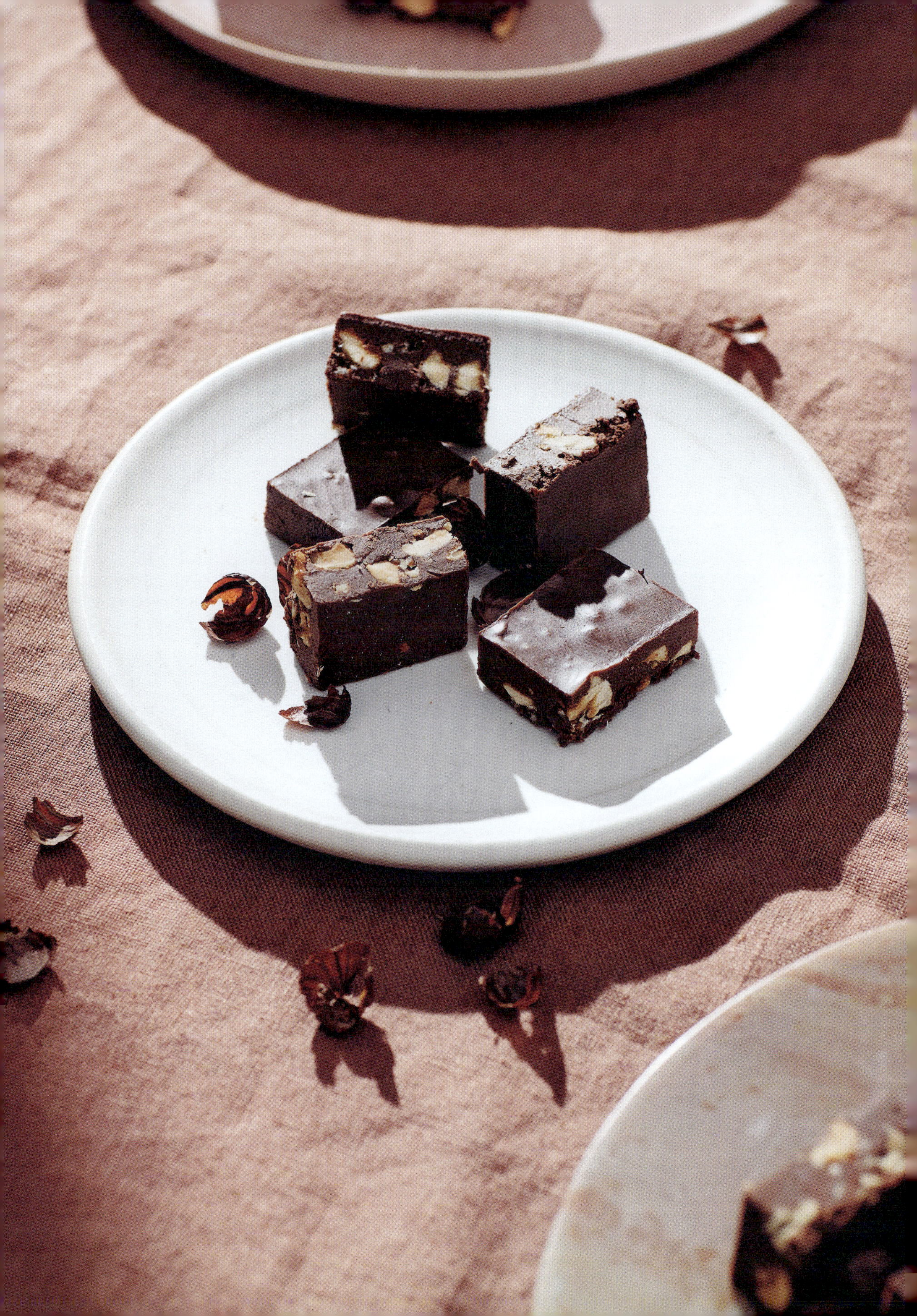

GIANDUJA

Makes 20 pieces

Gianduja is a classic treat. So simple in its formulation, and so delicious and indulgent. They take crunchy elements very well, so feel free to throw in crunchy caramelised nuts, make your own praline nut pastes, or take a shortcut withhigh-quality nut butters or praline. There are two methods for this recipe. One for using a smooth nut butter and the other for whole nuts.

raw hazelnuts or nut butter	200 g	7 oz
dark chocolate with at least 66% cocoa solids, callets (chips) or chopped	150 g	5.3 oz
caster (superfine) sugar	50 g	1.8 oz

IF USING WHOLE NUTS

1. Preheat the oven to 150°C fan (300°F/gas 2). Spread the hazelnuts out onto a baking sheet and roast for 15 minutes. Remove them from the oven and leave to cool completely.

2. Add the nuts, chocolate and sugar to a high-powered blender or food processor and start blending. The nuts will become very fine and the chocolate will melt. The mixture will become liquid and warm slightly. Continue blending until the nuts are fine, and the mixture is glossy and smooth.

3. Transfer the mixture to a bowl, scraping down the blender very well to make sure you retrieve as much of the mixture as possible. Place the bowl in the refrigerator for 3 minutes at a time and stir very well, then return to the refrigerator and repeat this step until the mixture is 22°C (70°F), then stir well again. At this stage you can add crispy inclusions like the caramelised hazelnut pieces below or leave it smooth and sumptuous.

IF USING NUT BUTTER

4. Melt the chocolate in a microwave-safe bowl in the microwave in 30-second bursts, stirring in between, or in a heatproof or stainless-steel bowl set over a pan filled with 1 cm (½ in) simmering water, stirring until melted, then remove from the heat.

5. Stir the nut butter into the bowl of chocolate and mix very well to combine.

6. Place the bowl in the refrigerator for 3 minutes at a time and stir very well, then return to the refrigerator and repeat this step until the mixture is 20°C (68°F), then stir very well again. At this stage you can add crispy inclusions like the caramelised hazelnut pieces below or leave it smooth and sumptuous.

CONFECTIONS

TO FINISH

7   If finishing here, neatly line a small rimmed baking sheet or container, about 10 × 15 cm (4 × 6 in) with baking parchment. Pour the gianduja into the lined baking sheet and leave to chill in the refrigerator for 15–20 minutes until set all the way through. You can also spoon or pipe this mixture with a piping (pastry) bag cut with 1 cm (½ in) hole into small silicone dome moulds of your choice.

8   Once set, remove the chocolates by the parchment lining and place on a cutting board. If using moulds, they should pop out easily and they're ready. Cut the chocolate into 1.5 × 3 cm (⅝ × 1¼ in) rectangles with a sharp knife dipped into a jug of hot water from a tap and wiped dry between each cut. These are ready to serve! Store in an airtight container in a cool dark palce at room temperature.

TO MAKE CARAMELISED HAZELNUT PIECES (OPTIONAL)

hazelnuts	50 g	1.8 oz
water	15 g	0.5 oz
caster (superfine) sugar	40 g	1.4 oz
coconut oil (deodorised)	4 g	1 tsp

9   Preheat the oven to 150°C fan (300°F/gas 2). Spread the hazelnuts onto a baking sheet and roast for 15 minutes. Remove them from the oven and coarsely chop them.

10 Line a large baking sheet with baking parchment.

11 Bring the water and sugar to a simmer in a heavy-based saucepan over a medium heat and allow to boil until the bubbles slow down slightly and the syrup thickens – this is called the softball stage (118°C/244°F).

12 Add the chopped nuts to the cooking syrup, remove the pan from the heat and mix very well with a wooden spoon. The sugar syrup will start to crystallise and look dry and sandy. Break up into small pieces that look like sandy white rubble.

13 Return the saucepan to a medium heat and keep stirring. Gradually the sugar will start to caramelise and melt as you stir. Continue stirring until the sugar has caramelised around the pieces. Be careful not to go too far or else they can burn. Add the coconut oil and stir well (this will help keep the nuts separate from each other).

14 Quickly pour the nuts onto the lined baking sheet, stir stir to separate in a thin layer and leave to cool. Add to the gianduja, if you like.

TIP

You can use a small bullet blender but you will need to scrape the sides down at regular intervals between pulses.

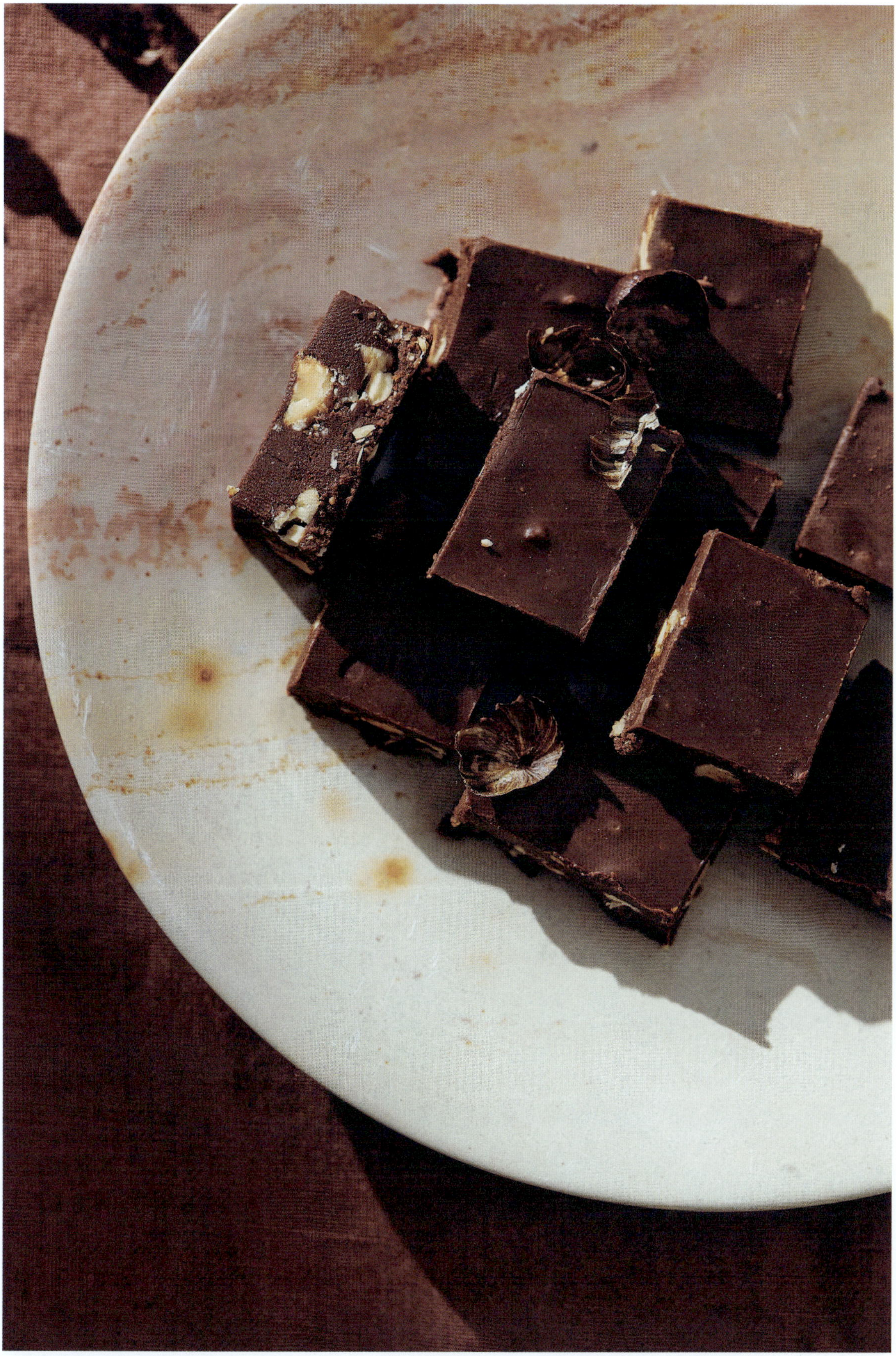

TURKISH DELIGHT / LOKUM

Makes about 30 pieces

My first taste of Turkish delight came after reading C.S. Lewis' *The Lion, the Witch and the Wardrobe*. I was dying to know what this confection tasted like. I imagined it must be incredibly delicious bordering on magical to make Edmund hurt his family to get some! I was very disappointed when I did try it as a kid, but then I grew up and one day I just found it very delicious. Like all things flavoured with floral extracts, they are easily overdosed so be careful.

coconut oil (deodorised)		for greasing
icing (confectioners') sugar	150 g	5.3 oz
cornflour (cornstarch)	150 g	5.3 oz
caster (superfine) sugar	450 g	15.9 oz
water (1)	220 g	7.8 oz
lemon juice	6 g	1½ tsp
cornflour (cornstarch)	70 g	2.5 oz
cream of tartar or lemon juice	4 g	1 tsp
water (2)	300 g	10.6 oz
rose water	30 g	1.1 oz
pistachios, shelled (optional)	100 g	3.5 oz

1. Rub a small amount of coconut oil over a 20 × 20 cm (8 × 8 in) baking tin (pan) until coated. Mix the icing sugar and cornflour together in a large bowl and set aside.

2. To make a sugar syrup, combine the caster sugar, water (1) and lemon juice in a saucepan and heat to about 110°C (230°F), whisking until it reaches a boil. Set aside.

3. Add the cornflour and cream of tartar to a wide saucepan, then while whisking pour in the water (2) and rose water and mix to combine. Turn the heat to medium and whisk until it reaches a paste consistency. This should take a few minutes.

4. Gradually, add the reserved sugar syrup, while whisking constantly, still over a medium heat.

5. Reduce the heat to low and continue cooking the mixture, while whisking constantly for 15–20 minutes. The paste will have turned a light golden colour. Keep stirring until the mixture is thick enough to see a clear line drawn through it with the spoon and it starts to leave the sides of the pan. It will be very thick and make big bubbles that burst as it cooks (be careful!). Stir in the shelled pistachios, if using.

6. While hot, pour the mixture into the oiled tin, level out the top and dust with some of the icing sugar mixture. Leave to cool completely.

7. Once fully cool, dust a cutting board with some of the remaining icing sugar mixture, then turn out the Turkish delight. Gently sprinkle and rub some more icing sugar mixture around the sides. Cut into 2.5 cm (1 in) squares with a sharp knife dipped into a jug of hot water from a tap and wiped dry between each cut. Dip the pieces into the icing sugar mixture until coated, then leave in an open container for 2–3 days to allow the outside to dry out slightly. Store in a container at cool room temperature for up to a month.

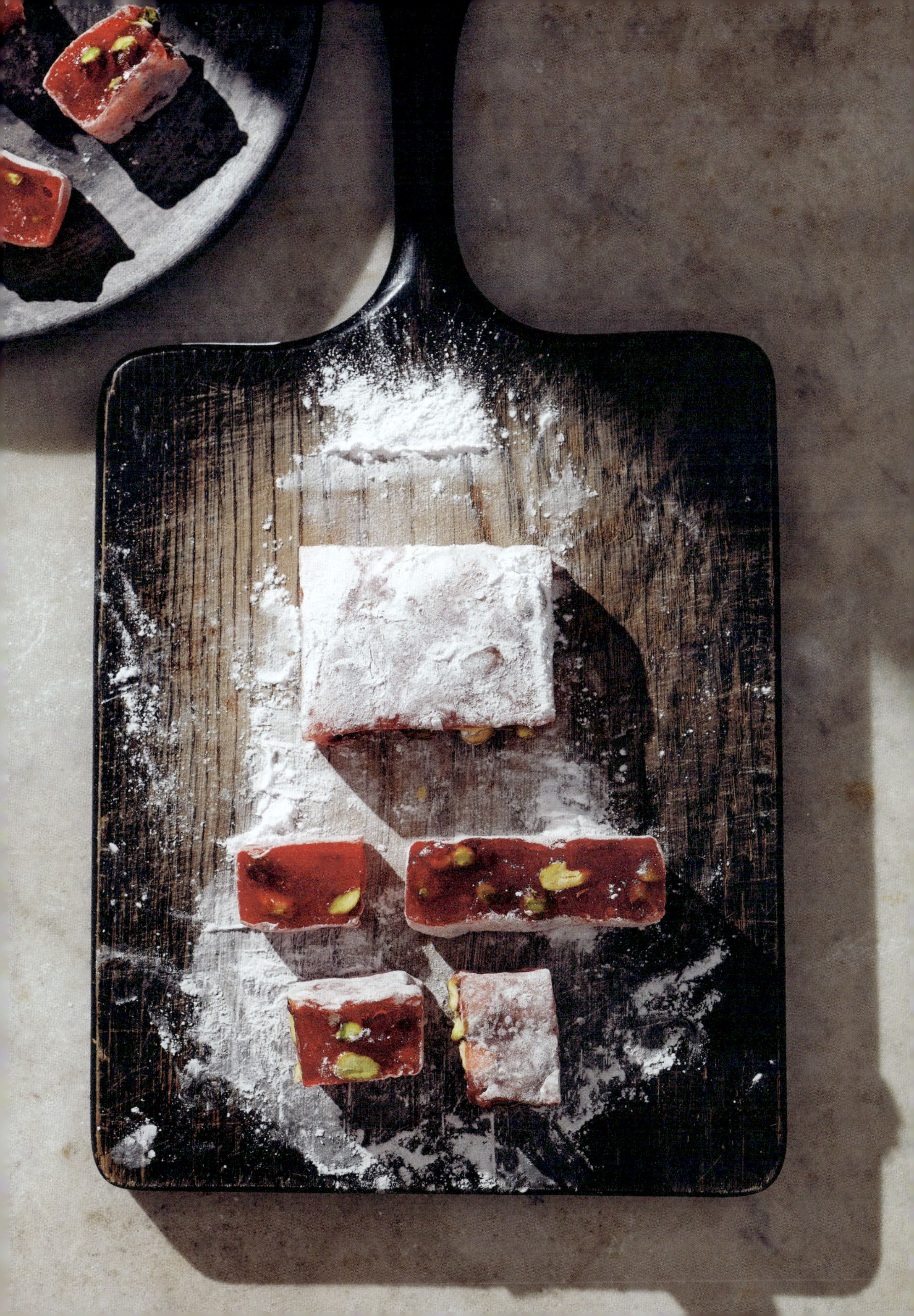

COCONUT SEA SALT CARAMELS

Makes about 40–50 caramels

I love caramel as a flavour, as a confection, in its various forms and textures, all determined (apart from a balanced recipe of course) by the temperature it has been cooked to. After initially cooking a pure caramel from sugar, deglaze with warm coconut cream and cook it again to 120°C (248°F), or firm ball stage, so be sure to check! A digital or sugar thermometer will be the quickest and easiest way to do this – not to mention the safest when working with boiling caramel!

oil		for greasing
caster (superfine) sugar	320 g	11.3 oz
water	80 g	2.8 oz
glucose (light corn) syrup	128 g	4.5 oz
coconut cream	360 g	12.7 oz
coconut oil (deodorised)	80 g	2.8 oz
sea salt	3 g	¾ tsp
vanilla bean paste	5 g	1 tsp

1. Line a 20 × 20 cm (8 × 8 in) baking tin (pan) with baking parchment, allowing at least 5 cm (2 in) of overhang on all sides. Lightly grease the baking parchment.

2. Have two saucepans ready. In the larger one (with high sides) add the sugar, water and glucose syrup.

3. In another smaller saucepan, add the coconut cream, coconut oil, sea salt and vanilla paste and bring just to a simmer while the sugar pan cooks.

4. Cook the sugar and glucose syrup over a medium heat, swirling the pan frequently, until the mixture is a nice golden colour, then remove the pan from the heat. Carefully add the coconut cream mixture in a thin stream, whisking constantly. The syrup temperature will drop when the coconut mixture is added but will climb when returned to the heat.

5. Return to a medium heat and continue cooking with a digital thermometer in the pan. Cook until it reaches 120°C (248°F), then immediately pour the mixture into prepared baking tin and leave to cool, uncovered, at room temperature, for at least 8 hours, or overnight.

6. Using the baking parchment overhang as handles, lift the caramel sheet from the baking tin, discarding the baking parchment and place on a cutting board. Using a sharp knife dipped into a jug of hot water from a tap and wiped dry between each cut, cut the caramel sheet into 15 rows, about 1 cm (½ in) wide, then cut each row into 6 pieces, about 5 cm (2 in) long, to yield 40–50 caramels.

7. Cut out 80 squares of baking parchment that will be big enough to wrap the caramels. Centre one caramel along one long edge of a baking parchment square, then roll to wrap the caramel and twist the ends to seal. Repeat with the remaining caramels. Keep these wrapped and store in an airtight container for up to 2 weeks.

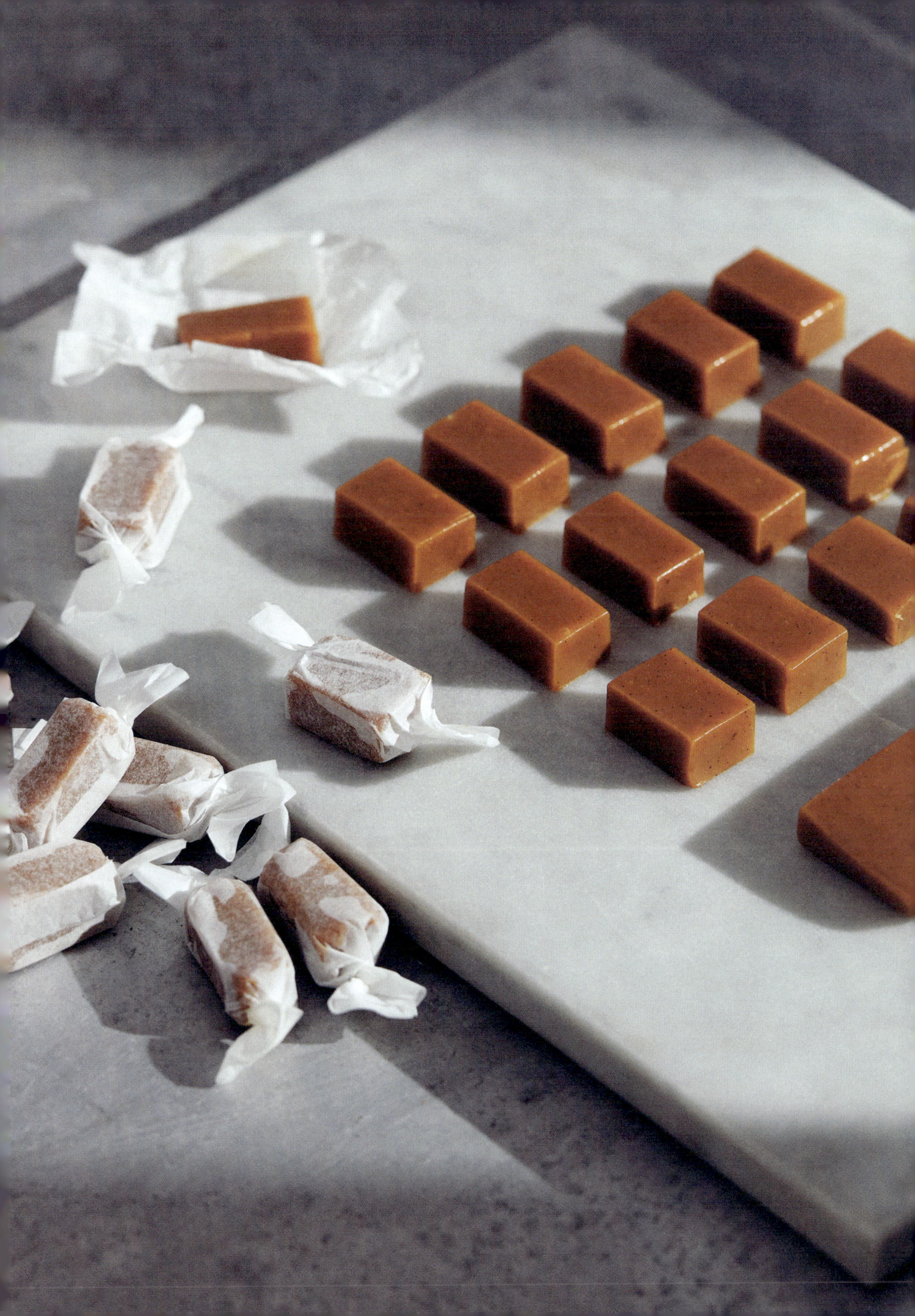

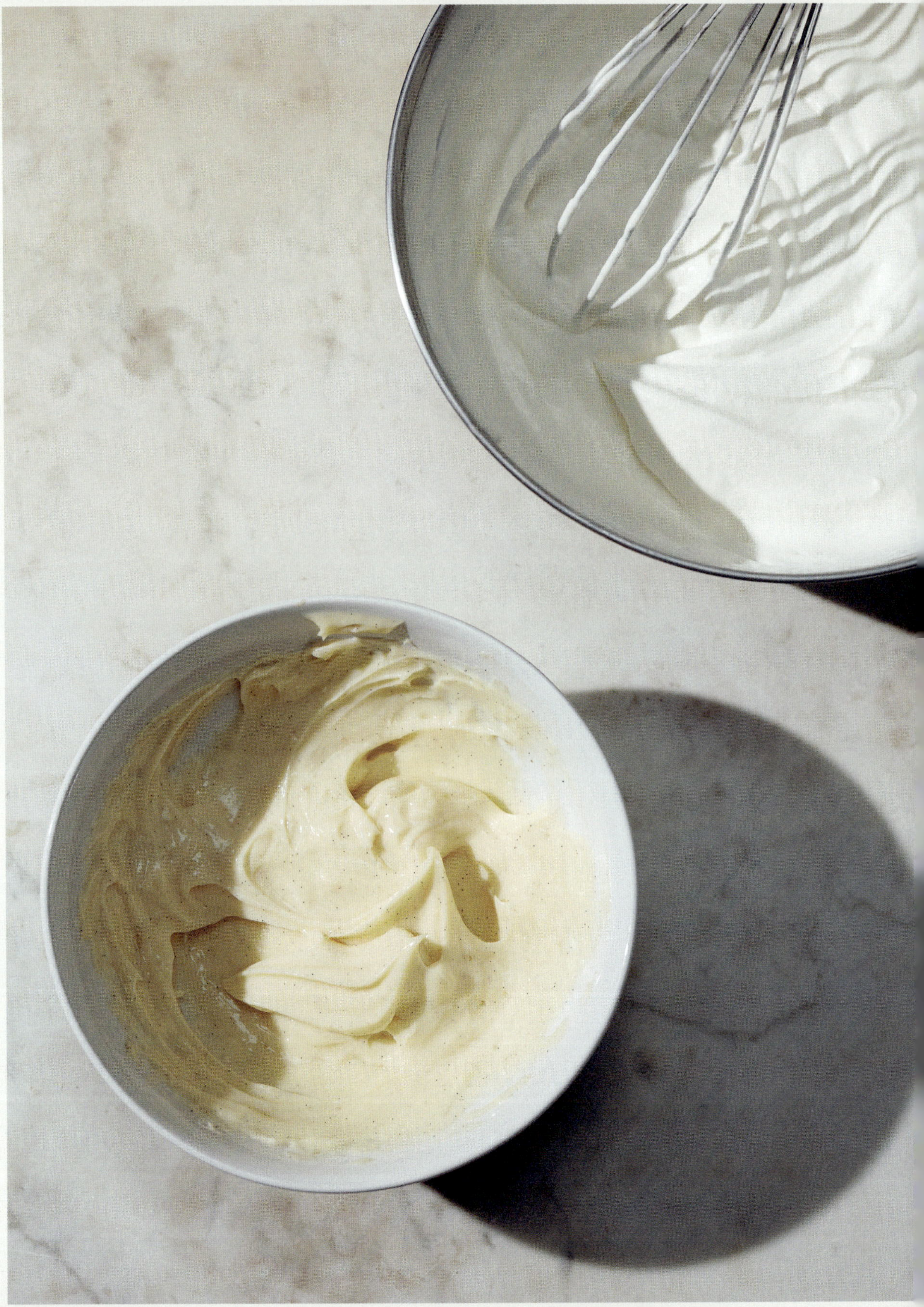

7 BASE RECIPES

These base recipes are useful to have in your repertoire. They can also be used as components in other recipes, but they aren't finished recipes in their own right! In classical baking these are some of the basic recipes that can often be adapted and multiplied very easily.

PASTRY AND CRUMBLE

These are the basic sweet, flaky and sweet flaky pastries used to make tarts, pies or crumbles. Versatile and simple, they do away with shortening and instead use virgin oils, which due to their powerful shortening effect can reduce the fat in the recipe and produce pastry that holds a wonderful array of fillings.

SHORT SWEET PASTRY

A fundamental pastry foundation that produces a crisp, short biscuit (cookie) perfect for any size tart case. This pastry doesn't shrink and can be flavoured in as many ways as you can think of.

Makes 550 g (1 lb 3 oz) / enough to line
2 × 23 cm (9 in) tart shells or 12 individual tartlets

soy milk	50 g	1.8 oz
caster (superfine) sugar	50 g	1.8 oz
muscovado sugar	50 g	1.8 oz
extra virgin olive oil or oil of your choice	100 g	3.5 oz
plain (all-purpose) flour (gluten free will also work), plus extra for dusting	300 g	10.6 oz
vanilla pod, seeds scraped		½ pod
lemon zest		¼ lemon
salt	1 g	¼ tsp

1. Make the pastry syrup in a jug by whisking the soy milk, sugars and olive oil together until the mixture is glossy and uniform in colour.

2. Add the flour, vanilla seeds, lemon zest and salt to a large bowl, then pour in the syrup and use a silicone spatula or wooden spoon to combine the mixture together until an even dough forms. Turn it out onto a work surface and press it into a 2 cm (¾ in) thick disc if rolling a round shape or square if you want to roll it into a square shape.

3. Lightly sprinkle some flour over the dough, then place it between two sheets of baking parchment and roll it out to the desired thickness: 3 mm (⅛ in) for small tarts and 4 mm (⅙ in) for large ones. You don't need to chill this dough beforehand.

4. Line the tart tin (pan) by removing the top sheet of baking parchment from the pastry and gently placing the tart tin on top of the pastry as a guide. Use a paring knife to trim the pastry around the tin, making sure there are a few extra centimetres (inches), then remove the tart tin. Use the bottom sheet of baking parchment to help flip the pastry gently into the tin, then carefully ease it into the shape of the tin with your fingertips. Use the side of your finger to press against the edges (into the flutes if the tin is fluted). Before baking, chill in the freezer for 15 minutes, then use the tip of a paring knife to 'dock' the base with a few pricks, about 2 cm (¾ in) apart, to stop the base from puffing up.

5. To blind bake, preheat the oven to 170°C fan (325°F/gas 3). Bake the chilled pastry in the oven for 9–10 minutes (no baking beans required). To fully bake, give it 3–5 extra minutes at 160°C fan (325°F/gas 3) for a golden colour all the way through.

VARIATIONS

Cocoa Remove 45 g (1.6 oz) flour and replace with 28 g (1 oz) cocoa (unsweetened chocolate) powder and add 10 g (0.4 oz) additional sugar.

Nuts Remove 20 g (0.7 oz) oil and add 30 g (1.1 oz) nut paste of your choice. The extra fat in the nut butters make it exceptionally short textured!

Matcha Remove 10 g (0.4 oz) flour and add 7 g (1½ tsp) matcha powder.

FLAKY PASTRY

This pastry dispels a number of commonly held beliefs. The results and ways of working with it made me completely rethink the way I thought that butter and other solid fats work in traditional pastry. It appears to me that the fat stops the dough from wanting to form, and the moisture does the opposite and simultaneously binds the dough through its interaction with the gluten. This paradox creates layers and a dough that doesn't want to combine, but rolling between two sheets of baking parchment makes easy work of this. This pastry can be baked on its own without weights or baking beans if the tart shape has gently sloping sides, but if it has sharp sides then do blind bake it.

Flaky pastry works great for pies with and without lids and any tart with a rich filling (I always bake mine first before the filling, even if it needs to be baked again). Oil wise, feel free to use any kind – I love using extra virgin olive oil for all my tart cases.

Makes 450 g (15.9 oz) or enough for a large 23 cm (9 in) pie base or 10 individual tartlets

plain (all-purpose) flour	250 g	8.8 oz
fine salt	3 g	½ tsp
caster (superfine) sugar	40 g	1.4 oz
cold-pressed oil	100 g	3.5 oz
sweet potato, cooked and cooled	20 g	0.7 oz
water, cold	40 g	1.4 oz

Makes 750 g (1 lb 10 oz) or enough for a large 23 cm (9 in) pie and lid

plain (all-purpose) flour	450 g	15.9 oz
fine salt	5 g	1 tsp
caster (superfine) sugar	70 g	2.5 oz
cold-pressed oil	180 g	6.3 oz
sweet potato, cooked and cooled	30 g	1 oz
water, cold	75 g	2.7 oz

1. Prepare the pastry by mixing the flour, salt and sugar together in a large bowl. Add the oil and use a silicone spatula or your hands to mix it into the flour. The oil should coat all the flour.

2. Add the sweet potato. I always cook my sweet potato in advance and keep it in a sealed container in the freezer for up to 3 months.

3. Add the cold water and mix until the dough just comes together. Don't overmix because the dough will start to separate and become more difficult to handle.

4. Place the dough between two sheets of baking parchment to roll out until it is 3–4 mm (⅛ in) thick.

5. Line the tart tin (pan) by removing the top sheet of baking parchment from the pastry and gently placing the tart tin on top of the pastry as a guide. Use a paring knife to trim the pastry around the tin, making sure there are a few extra centimetres (inches), then remove the tart tin. Use the bottom sheet of baking parchment to help flip the pastry gently into the tin, then carefully ease into the shape of the tin with your fingertips.

6. Leave to chill in the refrigerator for 15 minutes, then use the tip of a paring knife to 'dock' the base with a few pricks, about 2 cm (¾ in) apart, to stop the base from puffing up.

7. This pastry can be blind-baked. Preheat the oven to 170°C fan (325°F/gas 3). Scrunch up some baking parchment, then unfurl it, press it into the pastry-lined tart case and fill it with rice or baking beans. Preheat the oven to 180 °C fan (350F/gas 4) .Bake for 12 minutes at for individual or small tart shells, adding 2 minutes at a time (up to 18 minutes total) for larger tarts until nicely golden. I always fully bake my bases because once they are filled they don't take on a whole lot of colour. If the edge is browning early, cover with a piece of kitchen foil.

TIP

I always prefer to blind bake my tart cases (except for the Apple Pie, page 102) to prevent a soggy bottom, and they seem to last longer and develop more flavour.

FLAKY PASTRY

LINING PASTRY CASES

BASE RECIPES

SWEET FLAKY PASTRY

This pastry follows the same principles as the flaky pastry (page 231), but with more sugar and without sweet potato.

Makes 450 g (15.9 oz) or enough for a large 23 cm (9 in) pie base or 10 individual tartlets

plain (all-purpose) flour	250 g	8.8 oz
caster (superfine) sugar	50 g	1.8 oz
salt	2 g	½ tsp
cold-pressed oil	100 g	3.5 oz
water, cold	40 g	1.4 oz

Makes 750 g (1 lb 10 oz) or enough for a large 23 cm (9 in) pie and lid

plain (all-purpose) flour	450 g	15.9 oz
caster (superfine) sugar	90 g	3.2 oz
salt	3 g	¾ tsp
cold-pressed oil	180 g	6.3 oz
water, cold	75 g	2.7 oz

1. Mix the flour, sugar and salt together in a large bowl. Add the oil and use a silicone spatula or your hands to mix it into the flour mixture. The oil should coat all the flour and clump together when pressed.

2. Add the cold water and mix until the dough just comes together. You won't want to overmix because the dough will start to separate and become more difficult to handle. Press it into a disc if your final shape is a large pie or rectangle if you are lining small tarts.

3. Place the dough between two sheets of baking parchment and roll out until it is 3 mm (⅛ in) thick.

4. Line the tart tin (pan) by removing the top sheet of baking parchment from the pastry and gently placing the tart tin on top of the pastry as a guide. Use a paring knife to trim the pastry around the tin, making sure there's a few extra centimetres (inches), then remove the tart tin. Use the bottom sheet of baking parchment to help flip the pastry gently into the tin, then carefully ease it into the shape of the tin with your fingertips.

5. Leave to chill in the refrigerator for 15 minutes, then use the tip of a paring knife to 'dock' the base with a few pricks, about 2 cm (¾ in) apart, to stop the base from puffing up.

6. This pastry can be blind-baked. Preheat the oven to 180°C fan (350°F/gas 4). Scrunch up some baking parchment, then unfurl it, press it into the pastry-lined tart case and fill it with rice or baking beans. Bake for 12 minutes for individual or small tart shells, adding 2 minutes at a time (up to 18 minutes total) for larger tarts until nicely golden. Carefully remove the baking parchment and beans and bake for another 5–10 minutes until golden. I always fully bake my bases because once they are filled they don't take on a whole lot of colour. If the edge is browning early, cover with a piece of kitchen foil.

SHORTENING

This is a recipe for a vegetable shortening if you need one, although most recipes include the fat required. I often make this recipe and leave it in a sealed container or jar in a cool dark place. Using deodorised oils means it won't go rancid for a couple of months, and it is ready to use whenever required.

Makes 500 g (1 lb 2 oz)

coconut oil (deodorised)	200 g	7 oz
cocoa butter (deodorised)	180 g	6.3 oz
sunflower oil	120 g	4.2 oz

1. Add the coconut oil and cocoa butter to a saucepan and melt over a low heat. Direct heat is the fastest way to melt solid fats. Pour into a container along with the sunflower oil and chill in the refrigerator for 2–3 hours until firm. Once it's firm, remove from the refrigerator and leave at room temperature until the centre reaches room temperature (this is about 19°C/66°F) to use.

2. Store in a container at room temperature for up to 2 months.

NUT BUTTER

Nuts contain a high percentage of fats. In order to get the most flavour, a raw dried nut should be roasted at a lower (and slower) temperature of around 150°C fan (300°F/gas 2) for about 15 minutes depending on the size of the nut. This ensures an even roast all the way through and lowers the chance of burning. You need a food processor or a high-powered blender to make a nut butter and I insist on a pinch of salt to enhance the flavour.

Depending on the size of your blender, you may need to use a lot of nuts for the grinding mechanism to catch and grind your nuts efficiently (in which case it might be sensible to buy ready-made nut butters). I like to use a small Nutribullet-style high-powered blender for nut butters as then I don't have to make too much. To do this, fill the jug with roasted nuts (at least 250 g/8.8 oz and a pinch of salt) so it generates enough friction and you don't burn out the motor. Pulse a few times, making sure to open the jug and scrape it down in between pulses. It will start to look like wet sand, so scrape again and blend until it is wet and smooth. The mixture will heat up a bit but this is normal.

OAT CRUMBLE

This moreish muscovado and oat crumble tops any roasted fruit compote perfectly (plums and apples are my favourite). Top with pouring custard for an easy, seasonal, crowd-pleasing dessert.

Makes 400 g (14 oz)

cold-pressed sunflower oil	80 g	2.8 oz
plant-based milk	60 g	2 oz
muscovado sugar	50 g	1.8 oz
plain (all-purpose) flour	230 g	8.1 oz
baking powder	4 g	1 tsp
fine salt	1 g	¼ tsp
rolled oats	60 g	1.8 oz

1. In a measuring cup or jug, add the oil, milk and sugar, then blend with a hand-held blender until smooth and emulsified. Alternatively, use a whisk and whisk until smooth and homogenous. This is the syrup.

2. Add the flour, baking powder, salt and rolled oats to a large bowl and use a whisk to gently combine them together.

3. Pour in the syrup and mix with a silicone spatula until everything is just combined. You don't need to mix it until a dough forms as it should be crumbly.

4. Spread the mixture out on a baking sheet and bake according to the recipe.

BASE RECIPES

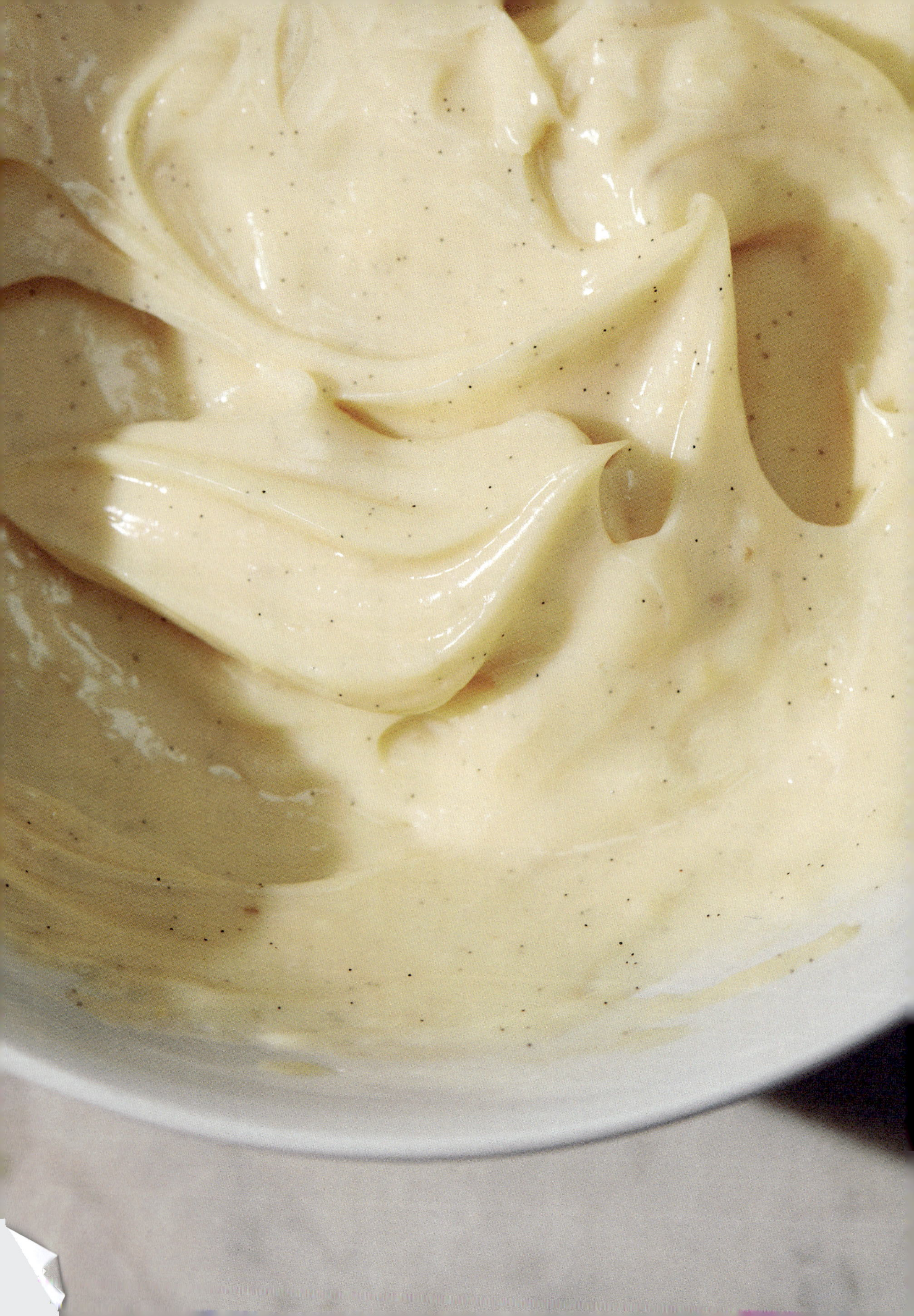

CREAMS

Recipes from light whipping, to thick, rich and sturdy, these are base recipes that can easily be infused with extra flavour.

CHOCOLATE CRÈME PÂTISSIÈRE

A rich chocolate crème pât.

Makes 500 g (1 lb 2 oz)

plant-based milk (1)	230 g	7 oz
caster (superfine) sugar	90 g	3.2 oz
cocoa (unsweetened chocolate) powder	13 g	0.5 oz
plant-based milk (2)	30 g	2.1 oz
dark chocolate with at least 70% cocoa solids	130 g	4.6 oz
cornflour (cornstarch)	13 g	0.5 oz

1. In a high-sided saucepan, add the milk (1), caster sugar and cocoa powder and stir with a whisk to combine. Bring to a simmer over medium heat.

2. Place the cornflour and milk (2) in a small bowl, and mix them to dissolve the cornflour and ensure there are no lumps. When the milk in the saucepan comes to a simmer, turn the heat to low then pour in the cornflour mixture and continue stirring. The mixture will immediately thicken. Continue stirring until it comes to a boil and the mixture starts to bubble, then remove from heat.

3. Add the chocolate and mix it in to melt. Continue mixing with a silicone spatula until it is fully incorporated, glossy smooth and clings to the sides of the saucepan.

4. Pour the mixture into a shallow dish with a layer of cling film (plastic wrap) pressed to the surface to prevent a skin from forming. Refrigerate until firm and set. Store in the refrigerator for unto 4 days.

5. Before using, take what you need in a small bowl and whisk it until smooth and there are no lumps.

CRÈME PÂTISSIÈRE

Crème pât for short! This thick and rich custardy cream is super versatile. It's used in many recipes, from social slice, to Pain aux Raisins (page 53), or folded with whipped cream in a Tiramisu (page 194).

Makes 500 g (1 lb 2 oz)

plant-based milk (1)	290 g	10.2 oz
caster (superfine) sugar	90 g	3.2 oz
vanilla bean paste	5 g	1 tsp
or vanilla pod, seeds removed	1 pod	
cornflour (cornstarch)	28 g	1 oz
custard powder	15 g	0.5 oz
plant-based milk (2)	40 g	1.4 oz
coconut oil (deodorised)	30 g	1.1 oz

1. In a high-sided saucepan, add the milk (1), caster sugar, custard powder and vanilla paste (or the scraped seeds of a vanilla pod) and stir with a whisk to combine. Bring to a simmer over medium heat.

2. Place the cornflour and milk (2) in a small bowl and mix them to dissolve the cornflour and ensure there are no lumps. When the milk in the saucepan comes to a simmer, turn the heat to low then pour in the cornflour mixture and continue stirring and the mixture will immediately thicken. Continue stirring until it comes to a boil and the mixture starts to bubble, then remove from heat.

3. Add the coconut oil and mix it in to melt. Whisk in gently as it may start to look separated, then continue mixing until it is fully incorporated, glossy smooth and clings to the sides of the saucepan.

4. Pour the hot mixture into a shallow dish with a layer of cling film (plastic wrap) pressed to the surface to prevent a skin from forming. Refrigerate until firm and set. Store in the refrigerator for unto 4 days.

5. Before using, take what you need in a small bowl and whisk it until smooth and there are no lumps.

FRESH WHIPPING CREAM

Fresh whipping cream or chantilly is a versatile staple in the vegan repertoire. This recipe is simple but with a tiny trick. It is best made as a base, stored in the refrigerator and whipped whenever required. It is used to lighten mousses and other creams and can be used in any recipe that calls for a double (heavy) or whipping cream of 35 per cent fat. I have sucessfully used oat milk to make whipping cream, but I much prefer soy milk. Please use deodorised coconut oil and the resulting cream will have a beautiful neutral flavour. Using virgin coconut oil will leave a strong taste and make it prone to spoiling and having an off-taste.

Makes 500 g (1 lb 2 oz)

coconut oil (deodorised)	200 g	7 oz
caster (superfine) sugar	40 g	1.4 oz
soy milk	275 g	9.7 oz

1. Add the coconut oil to a microwave-safe bowl and microwave for 30–60 seconds until melted. Alternatively, melt in a medium saucepan over a low heat. Set aside.

2. Add the sugar mixture to the soy milk in a large bowl and use an immersion stick blender or high-powered blender to blend them together.

3. Add the melted coconut oil to the mixture, then, using a thermometer, test the temperature. It should be 35°C (95°F), so warm or cool the mixture as required. Use the immersion stick blender for 30–60 seconds until the mixture has emulsified.

4. Pour the mixture into a shallow dish and press cling film (plastic wrap) onto the surface. Leave in the refrigerator for at least 4 hours to chill and 'crystallise' fully – this is where the solid fat particles cool to the temperature they turn solid and completely solidify. The fat particles should be dispersed throughout the cream in a homogenous, creamy mixture that won't go grainy.

5. Pour the mixture into the chilled bowl of a stand mixer fitted with a whisk attachment, or whisk by hand or with electric beaters making sure to chill your bowl first, until soft peaks are formed that hold their shape. Use immediately or reserve the whipped cream in the refrigerator until needed.

    TIP If the cream is not whipping, place the mixture in freezer for 15 minutes, before whipping again. Make sure to chill the mixing bowl before whipping.

6. To store, transfer to a container, cover with cling film (plastic wrap) on the surface of the cream and use the same day. The unwhipped cream can be stored in the refrigerator in a sealed container or jar for up to 4 days.

TIP

Temperature is crucial so before emulsifying the mixture, it should be closest to the temperature that the fats start to crystallise or set, to ensure it whisks beautifully.

THICK WHIPPED CREAM

A thick, more stable whipped cream akin to light butter cream on the slightly richer side compared to the fresh whipped cream (page 236). This one is useful as a layer in a Victoria sponge or sandwiched inside a lamington.

Makes 500 g (1 lb 2 oz)

caster (superfine) sugar (1)	70 g	2.5 oz
cornflour (cornstarch) or custard powder	40 g	1.4 oz
plant-based milk	300 g	10.6 oz
vanilla bean paste	6 g	1⅓ tsp
Shortening (page 232)	120 g	4.2 oz
caster (superfine) sugar (2)	50 g	1.8 oz

1. Mix the sugar (1) and cornflour in a small saucepan, then add the plant-based milk and vanilla paste. Mix well to combine. Bring to a simmer over a medium heat, while stirring constantly with a silicone spatula until thickened.

2. Remove from the heat and leave to cool completely. Pour the mixture into a shallow dish, cover the surface with cling film (plastic wrap) and leave to cool at room temperature. It should be 15–20°C (59–68°F) when you use it.

3. Add the shortening and sugar (2) to a stand mixer fitted with a whisk attachment or use electric beaters in a large bowl. Whisk until very pale and fluffy. While whisking, add the cooled custard mixture, a little at a time until it is all incorporated. It will become fluffier and fluffier. Use immediately.

NOTE

Plant-based stick butter can be used in place of the shortening. It is different to spreadable version. It is usually wrapped in a wrapper rather than in a tub. It has a higher proportion of fat that are solid at room temperature than the spreadable variaties, which have more oil and are much softer. Spreadable will not work in this application.

TIP

The shortening and custard base need to be at the same (room) temperature. If your mixture starts to look curdled, it could be too cold. Dip into a sink of hot water for a few seconds to gently add some heat, then continue beating. Repeat if needed.

JAMS, GELS AND GLAZES

I love to make my own jams (jellies) and glazes because I like controlling the sweetness and letting the fruit flavour shine through. Shop-bought jam can often be too sweet. These jams work brilliantly in cakes as a fresh component to add a fruit flavour in a bright way that can support a cake. There are a few different recipes based on whether you need to freeze the cake, or would like to serve it from the refrigerator, or are keeping it at room temperature on the work surface.

FRUIT JAM WITH PECTIN NH

In the professional kitchen we have access to many specialist ingredients that can help us create different gels of varying texture. I often use pectin NH extracted from fruits to make my gels and jams, so I have supplied a base recipe.

Makes 490 g (17.3 oz)

caster (superfine) sugar	60 g	2 oz
pectin NH	8 g	2 tsp
fruit juice, purée or soft fruit pieces, peeled and cut into small pieces	400 g	14.1 oz
lemon juice	30 g	1.1 oz

1. Mix the sugar and pectin NH together in a small bowl. Add the fruit juice or purée to a large saucepan, then add the sugar mixture and whisk well to combine. Bring to a simmer over a medium heat while stirring constantly. Add the lemon juice, then pour the mixture into a container or directly into a mould or lined cake tin (pan) to set. The gel will set at room temperature or in the refrigerator and also freezes and defrosts very well.

TIP

If you use the gel directly it will have a set jelly-like texture but, if you blend it, it will be a thick creamy texture.

NOTE

Pectin NH is different from general pectin, which is what professionals call yellow pectin or pectin jaune which needs high sugar and high acidity to create a gel.

FRUIT JAM WITH AGAR-AGAR

I have made a recipe from agar-agar powder because of it's wide availability and because it's easy to use! Agar-agar sets at room temperature and melts at 40°C (104°F) so it won't melt in the mouth. It is important to use very accurate microscales when using agar-agar so you have control over the texture – 2 g will produce a softer gel, while 8 g (2 tsp) will produce a firm and brittle gel, which can be whisked smooth. Use this recipe where freezing the finished cake is not a priority; if frozen, the water in the recipe can be released once it thaws and will affect the texture.

Makes 280 g (9.9 oz)

agar-agar powder	2–6 g	½– tsp
caster (superfine) sugar	50–100 g	1.8–3.5 oz
fruit juice, purée or soft fruit piece, peeled and cut into small pieces	200 g	7 oz

1. Mix the agar-agar powder with the sugar in a medium bowl. Add the fruit juice to a large saucepan, then add the sugar mixture and bring to the boil. Reduce the heat to low and simmer for 1 minute to fully activate the agar.

2. Pour the gel into a mould or container and it will set as it cools, around room temperature. Once set, cut into cubes, or whisk to make a smooth jam or compote. Store in the refrigerator for up to 4 days. Do not freeze.

EXOTIC CLEAR GLAZE

This is a brilliant glaze to help protect cut fruits from the elements and give a tasty and attractive shine to finished bakes. Inspired by the glaze that Pierre Hermé makes with citrus peels and vanilla, which I used to joke with my colleague who introduced to me to it as the 'eau de pâtissière, this glaze can be microwaved to melt as its high water content will heat up quickly. If it needs to be reheated on the hob, you will need to break it with a whisk and add a splash of water before reboiling it.

Makes 450 g (15.9 oz)

water	350 g	12.4 oz
agar-agar powder	4 g	1⅛ tsp
caster (superfine) sugar	100 g	3.5 oz
lemon peel		1 strip
orange peel		1 strip
vanilla pod (upcycle a scraped-out pod)		½ pod
mint		1 sprig

1. Pour the water into a large saucepan. Weigh the agar-agar accurately in a small bowl, add the sugar and mix to combine, then add to the saucepan of water.

2. Peel a couple of strips of lemon and orange and add them to the water together with the vanilla and mint.

3. Bring the mixture to a simmer for 2 minutes, then remove from the heat and leave to infuse for 30 minutes, before straining the mixture through a sieve (fine-mesh strainer).

4. The mixture should be used as it cools – you will notice it starting to thicken. If it cools or clumps, reheat it in the microwave in short bursts or in a saucepan over a low heat. The glaze sets firmly.

5. Set the glaze aside in the refrigerator for up to 2 weeks. When needed, cut a small piece off and heat it in the microwave in short bursts to melt it, or in a saucepan.

BAKING GLAZE

Makes 300 g (10.6 oz)

soy milk	200 g	7 oz
golden (or agave) syrup	40 g	1.4 oz
sweet potato, cooked and cooled	50 g	1.8 oz
xanthan gum (optional)	0.2 g	
caster (superfine) sugar (optional)	10 g	0.4 oz

1. Blend all the ingredients together with an immersion stick blender or other high-powered blender. Pour into a shallow saucepan and bring to the boil for 2 minutes. Strain the mixture through a very fine sieve (fine-mesh strainer) and leave to cool.

2. Pour into an ice-cube tray and put in the freezer. Once frozen, store in a freezer bag. Defrost and use a cube at a time by heating in a small dish in the microwave or leave at room temperature to melt.

TIP The xanthan gum is optional but gives the glaze some body, which helps it stay on the baked goods.

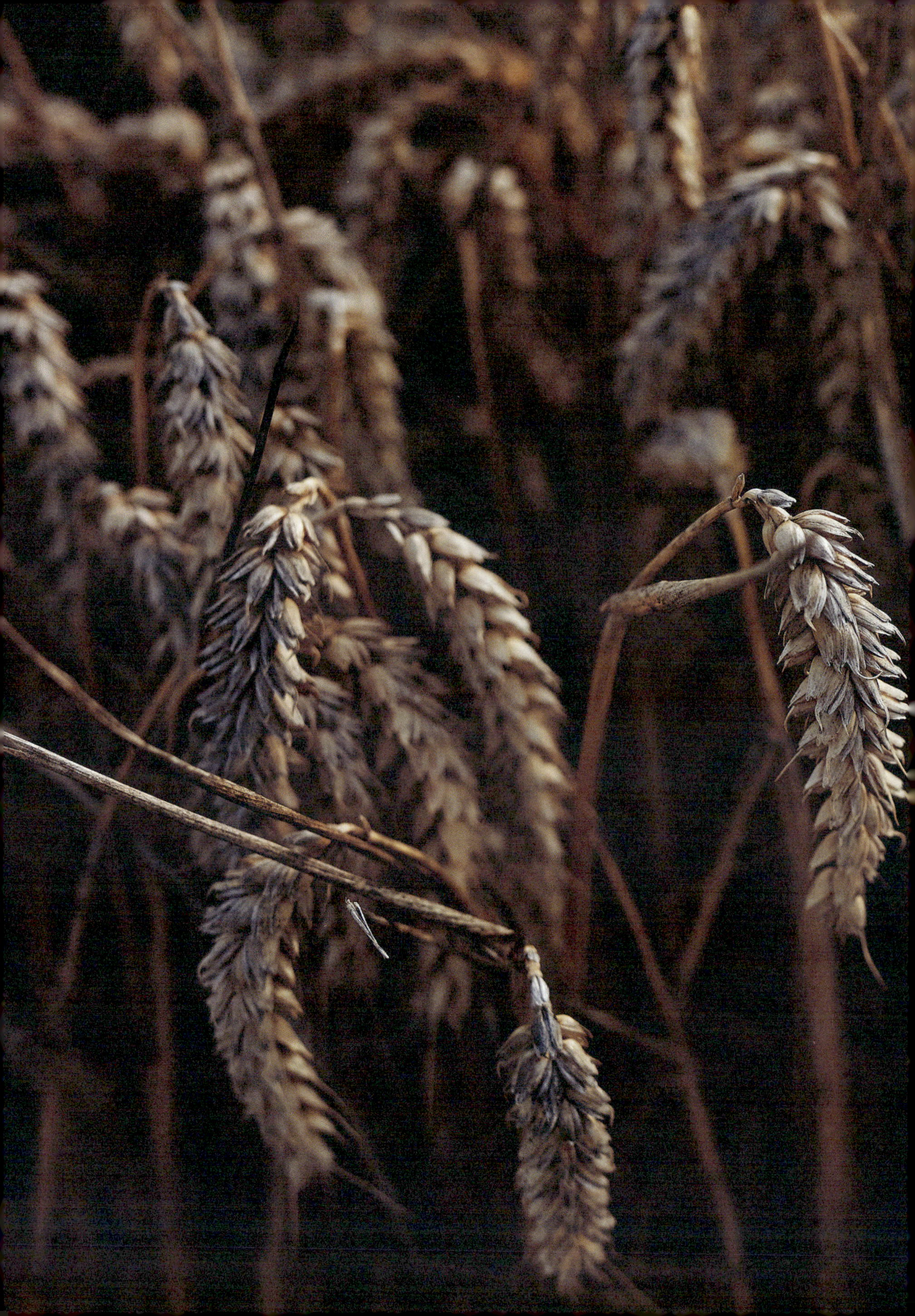

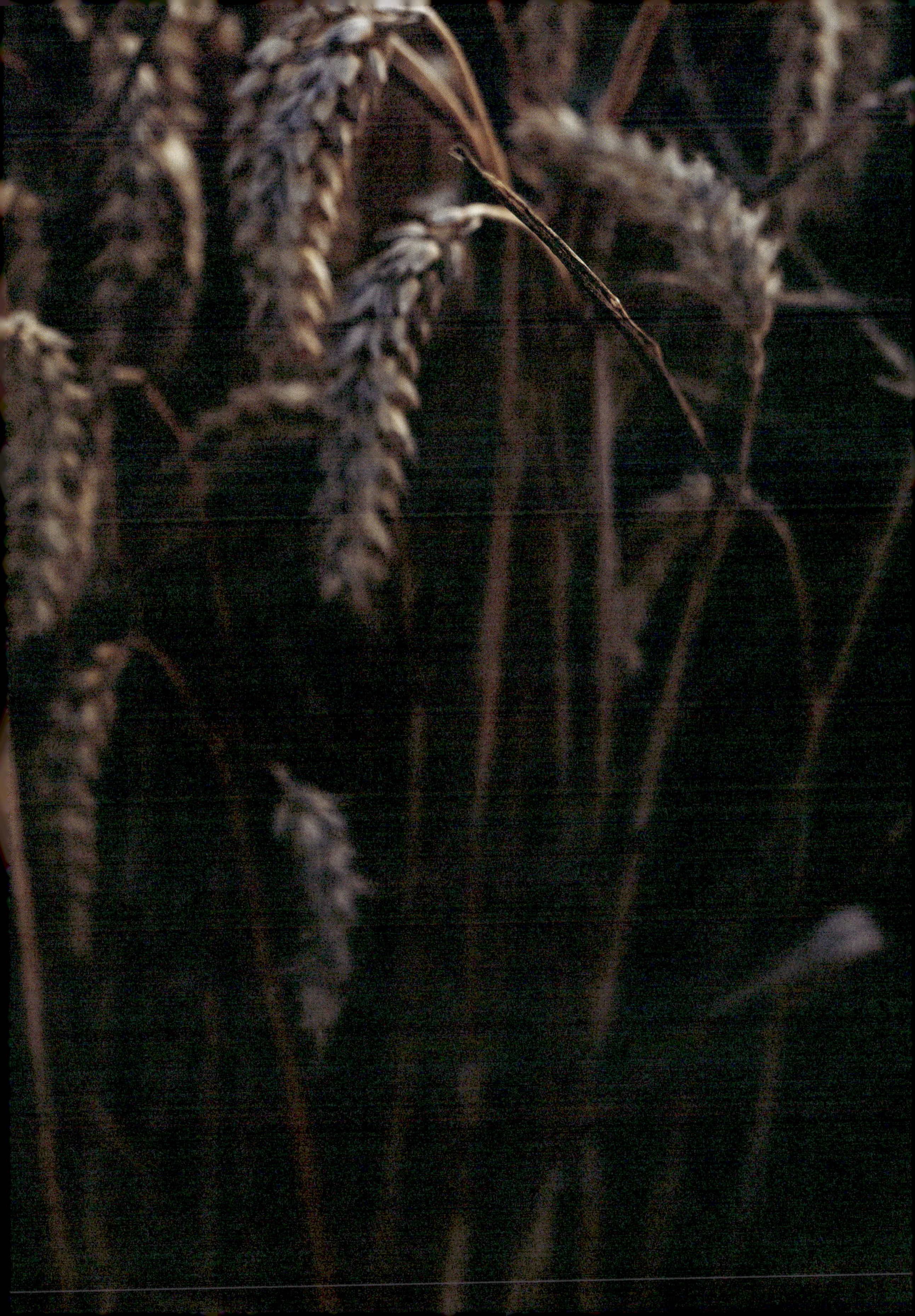

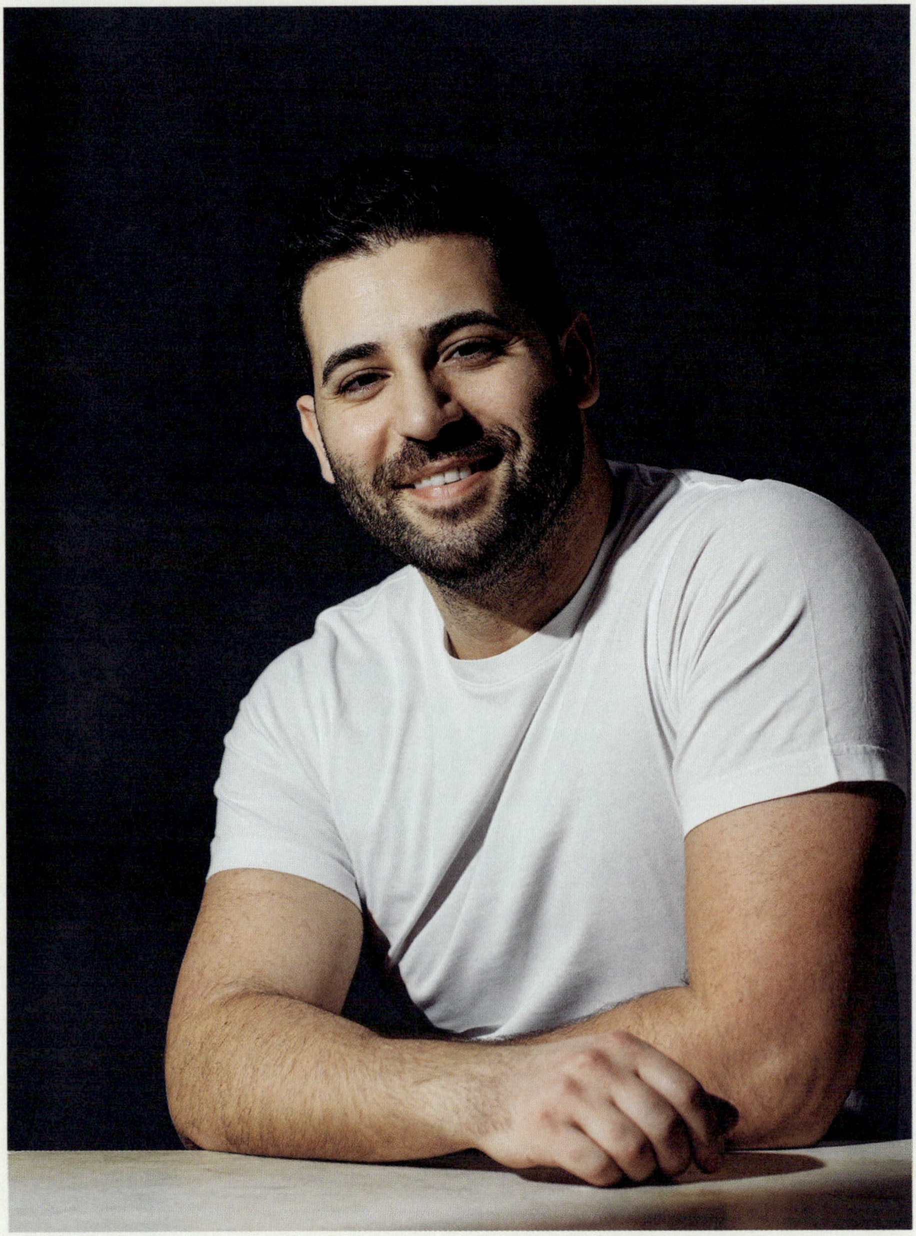

ABOUT THE AUTHOR

Philip Khoury is an award-winning Australian pastry chef, of Lebanese descent, known for his innovative and delicious creations made from plants. Originally from Australia, he started his career at Quay, one of the country's most highly acclaimed restaurants, before becoming Adriano Zumbo's right-hand and launching hundreds of patisserie lines in his native country. Over time, he began to realise the wider food industry's unsustainable reliance on animal exploitation and decided to focus on creating plant-based desserts that were not only delicious but also environmentally friendly.

Philip is currently the resident plant-based expert and head pastry chef at Harrods in London, where he has introduced plant-based and allergen-friendly patisserie in addition to the iconic made-in-house ranges. His dedication to sustainability and creating desserts that are both ethical and indulgent has earned him a reputation as one of the most innovative and forward-thinking pastry chefs in the industry.

Philip shares his expertise and insights into creating innovative and delicious cakes, bakes and desserts from plants, providing guidance and inspiration for anyone looking to explore the world of plant-based desserts.

THANKS GO TO

My mum who taught me to have an open mind and heart. My dad, a visionary, who always pushed me to think outside of what I know and to imagine worlds with new realities, as well as always encouraging me to work backwards to build them. It would seem only natural that with these two influences I would embark on this book. When the task I'd set myself seemed overwhelming, they reminded me to break it down and just start with a piece of cake. Perfect solutions don't exist and when you accept that you can make the little steps forward. Thanks also go to my huge family – in Australia, Lebanon and beyond – for the culture and love we've shared.

Mike – my rock through sometimes harrowing times – from my delusional era when I thought that making this book and then insisting on recording 90+ videos would be 'easy' or at worst 'manageable' to the nights I'd be curled up on the couch in foetal position paralysed by the seemingly enormous task at hand, on top of having a demanding full-time job. Mike was MVP through this whole process. Also, my best friend Eleni – love you.

My agent, Emily Sweet (I know – what a name), saw my and my book's potential. In the business of publishing books, new, untested ideas (especially from a new author!) proved too much for most. Emily helped me strike a balance in the contents of the book which has, over the course of 2 years, reshaped my approach to plant-based pastry. Huge thanks also to Eve Marleau who 'got it' immediately. I remember taking some bakes to a meeting to try and sell the book to Eve, but I think Eve was already sold. Eve and, later, Eila Purvis have been steadfast in the crafting of this book. Thanks, Eila, for being so endlessly patient and kind, keeping me on time and to task, and for taking in my endless amendments and updates down to the final days before print. I think I would be lost without you – you're a bespectacled angel! Thanks to Paul Nichols from p2d! Thanks also to Laura Eldridge, Alice Hill, Iman Khabl and Kajal Mistry and the wider team at Hardie Grant for your belief in this undertaking! Matt Russell, for jumping in his car and coming out to a farm in Essex in September 2022, for imbuing this book's photographs with a stunning natural beauty and for representing my work so beautifully!!! I insisted on a picture for every recipe and you made it happen!!! Thank you for your persistence, talent and friendship. And to Alexander Breeze – a powerhouse of creative energy and style – stunnin'! Thanks to Jess Geddes, for helping keep stress levels down on shoot and to Evi O and team for taking every part of the brief and giving back a beautiful book design that really felt simple and clean, natural and beautiful. I hope readers take joy in the clarity of the layout – it was designed with intention. Evi and team are wondrous!

The biggest influence on my work as a pastry chef has been Adriano Zumbo. He plucked out of his production kitchen when I showed some promise and let me eventually lead research and development for his business. He helped me believe in myself and instilled in me the mantra of 'if you can dream it, you can make it'. I am indebted to him for his trust, and for passing on his knowledge and skills so generously. Kirsten Tibballs is my pastry fairy godmother, who has always seen my potential. Her Savour School in Melbourne, Australia, is a centre of excellence for specialist training. It is where long-time exec chef, Paul Kennedy, taught me fundamental chocolate skills!

All the professionals who I have encountered through my career: Peter Gilmore and the team at Australia's Quay Restaurant where are I started as an apprentice all the way to Anna Polyviou and Giovana Falanga; Alec Lowe; Jessica Timpano at the Shangri-La in Sydney; Alejandro Luna; Marky McDonald; Rosalba; Amelia; Nelly, Karen, Mat, Matteo, Aurelio; and the huge team from Zumbo days.

And most recently, Markus Bohr, and the wonderful and very big, talented pastry team at Harrods, especially Alistair Birt, in whom I found a friend, confidante and honest taste tester, as well as being my line manager and an immensely talented pastry chef. Thanks for your trust! Thanks to our amazing pastry team that come in and make magic everyday from underneath Harrods' famed Food Halls. Thanks Bastien, Theresa, Kevin, Charles and all past and present team members!

Harrods is the most luxurious department store in the world – what is made two floors underneath the famed Food Halls is pure magic – it is deserving of its own book(s). It takes a special business environment to allow all this to happen. Thanks to a business that has nurtured my experimental nature and supported me; showing that anything is possible, constraint is creativity and that everything must happen for a reason – whether it's the right thing to do, or just to express pure, unbridled creativity. Thanks Amy Broomfield for the introduction to Eve! Ashley Saxton, Andre Lewis, Ciaran, Fenja, Emilie, Abi, Andy, Garrett, Olga, Vicky, Tayla, the Lucys, Jen, Jess, Hope and Stella to name but a few of the many supporters I am so lucky to have at Harrods. Special thank you to Julie Ishmael whose critically keen eyes were much appreciated at final proof stages and who tested some of my recipes and mentally prepared the rest of them to check everything was in line!

The whole fabulous London/UK food scene – how beautiful and vibrant you are! I have been lucky to find a community of beautiful, open, creative and passionate individuals, food writers, chefs and suppliers. Gurd Loyal, with whom I shared a book development timeline, always a step ahead and so open with his knowledge, experience and encouragement. He also introduced me to Ravneet Gill – a huge supporter of so many and someone who found the industry in a state and imagined a world where it could be better and did something about it and has been a supporter of mine. Thank you, Gemma Bell! Thanks to everyone who shared such kind words too: Helen, Yotam, Adriano, Rachel! Matt Adlard thanks for your support and friendship this past 5 years! Thanks Min Chai, Dave Katague and Gabriel Virata from Sydney!

Pastry chefs around the world that inspire and propel us all forward. We have an immensely expressive and beautiful craft. Thanks for sharing your passion and skill. Thanks to all the vegan pioneers, the environmentalists, animal rights activists and plant pushers who've nurtured an important cause from the marginalised fringes, long before it was popular. Slowly but surely, more people will realise how everything is connected and progress only comes through compassion.

THANKS GO TO

INDEX

A

agar-agar 35
    Bakewell tart 117–18
    Eton mess 202–5
    exotic clear glaze 239
    fruit jam with agar-agar 238
    red berry tart 99–100
almond amaretti 94
baked cinnamon and citrus cheesecake 170–1
almond milk 33
almonds
    almond amaretti 94
    baked cinnamon and citrus cheesecake 170–1
    Bakewell tart 117–18
    financiers 128
    orange and almond cake 162
    pear, hazelnut and almond
        gateau 166–7
    red berry tart 99–100
    tarte bordaloue 111–12
    vostocks 61
Anzac biscuits 77
apple cake 143
apple pie 102–5
apples
    apple cake 143
    apple pie 102–5
    extra virgin olive oil cake 150
apricots
    Sacher torte 185–6
aquafaba 30
    Eton mess 202–5
    sugar cookies 91

B

Bakewell tart 117–18
baking glaze 239
baking powder 20, 126
banana bread 156
banana chip cookies 82
banana tatin cake 164
bananas
    banana bread 156
    banana chip cookies 82
    banana tatin cake 164
    banoffee pie 113–14
banoffee pie 113–14
bicarbonate of soda 20
biscuits & cookies 75
    almond amaretti 94
    Anzac biscuits 77
    banana chip cookies 82
    chocolate chip cookies 84
    chocolate tahini cookies 88
    glazed gingerbread 81
    maamoul 93
    nut shortbreads 78
    sugar cookies 91
bread
    chocolate hazelnut babka 67–8
brownies
    double chocolate brownies 188
buns & rolls 49
    hot x buns 71–3
    pistachio (and rose) vostocks 62
    sticky date and cardamom buns 54
    vostocks 61
    vrioche 49–51

C

cacao 32
cakes 125–6
    apple cake 143
    baked cinnamon and citrus cheesecake 170–1
    banana bread 156
    banana tatin cake 164
    carrot cake 137
    double chocolate brownies 188
    Earl Grey loaf cake 154
    extra virgin olive oil cake 150
    financiers 128
    fluffy baked siken tofu cheesecake 173
    fluffy scones 130–1
    Lamingtons 147–8
    lemon drizzle loaf 158
    madeleines 134
    maple cake 138–40
    mille crêpes praline 181–2
    molten centre chocolate cakes 193
    orange and almond cake 162
    pear, hazelnut and almond vanilla cream gateau 166–7
    pumpkin spice loaf cake 161
    Sacher torte 185–6
    triple chocolate fudge 177–8
    two-tone chocolate cake 175–6
    Victoria sponge 144
caramel
    coconut sea salt caramels 226
    crème brûlée 200
    crème caramel 199
cardamom
    sticky date and cardamom buns 54
carrot cake 137
caster sugar
    crème pâtissière 235
    exotic clear glaze 239
    fresh whipping cream 236
    fruit jam with agar-agar 238
    fruit jam with pectin NH 238
    short sweet pastry 230
    sweet flaky pastry 232
    thick whipped cream 237
    Turkish delight / lokum 224

cheesecakes
    baked cinnamon and citrus cheesecake 170–1
    fluffy baked siken tofu cheesecake 173
cherries
    almond amaretti 94
chocolate 32
    banana bread 156
    banana chip cookies 82
    banoffee pie 113–14
    chocolate chip cookies 84
    chocolate crème pâtissière 235
    chocolate ganache tart 108
    chocolate hazelnut babka 67–8
    chocolate tahini cookies 88
    chocolate truffles 219
    double chocolate brownies 188
    gianduja 221–2
    mille crêpes praline 181–2
    molten centre chocolate cakes 193
    nama ganache 216
    no-churn chocolate ice cream 211
    Sacher torte 185–6
    triple chocolate fudge 177–8
    two-tone chocolate cake 175–6
chocolate chip cookies 84
chocolate crème pâtissière 235
chocolate ganache tart 108
chocolate hazelnut babka 67–8
chocolate tahini cookies 88
chocolate truffles 219
cinnamon slice 56
cocoa butter 32
    shortening 232
cocoa powder 32
    chocolate truffles 219
    Lamingtons 147–8
coconut, dessicated
    Anzac biscuits 77
    Lamingtons 147–8
coconut cream
    coconut sea salt caramels 226

coconut oil 25
    coconut sea salt caramels 226
    fresh whipping cream 236
    maamoul 93
    maple cake 138–40
    no-churn ice cream 210
    shortening 232
coconut sea salt caramels 226
coffee
    tiramisu 194
cold-pressed oil
    flaky pastry 231
    sweet flaky pastry 232
confections 215
    chocolate truffles 219
    coconut sea salt caramels 226
    gianduja 221–2
    nama ganache 216
    Turkish delight / lokum 224
cookies. see biscuits & cookies
cornflour/cornstarch 35
    thick whipped cream 237
    Turkish delight / lokum 224
cream
    banoffee pie 113–14
    Eton mess 202–5
    fresh whipping cream 236
    thick whipped cream 237
    tiramisu 194
cream, vanilla bean
    fluffy baked siken tofu cheesecake 173
    thick whipped cream 237
    Victoria sponge 144
crème brûlée 200
crème caramel 199
crème pâtissière 194
    chocolate crème pâtissière 235
    cinnamon slice 56
    pain aux raisins 53
    red berry tart 99–100

D

dates
    maamoul 93
    sticky date and cardamom buns 54
    sticky toffee date pudding 196
desserts 191
    crème brûlée 200
    crème caramel 199
    Eton mess 202–5
    molten centre chocolate cakes 193
    no-churn chocolate ice cream 211
    no-churn ice cream 210
    nut gelato 208
    rice pudding 207
    sticky toffee date pudding 196
    tiramisu 194
double chocolate brownies 188

E

Earl Grey loaf cake 154
Earl Grey tea
    Earl Grey loaf cake 154
    fluffy scones 130–1
    tarte bordaloue 111–12
Eton mess 202–5
exotic clear glaze 239
extra virgin olive oil cake 150

F

financiers 128
flaky pastry 231
flour
    gluten free 30
    wheat 19
fluffy baked silken tofu cheesecake 173
fluffy scones 130–1
frangipane
    pistachio (and rose) vostocks 62
    red berry tart 99–100
    tarte bordaloue 111–12
    vostocks 61

fruit
    fruit jam with agar-agar 238
    fruit jam with pectin NH 238

G

gianduja 221–2
gingerbread
    glazed gingerbread 81
glazed gingerbread 81
glazes
    baking glaze 239
    exotic clear glaze 239
glucose (corn syrup) 29
    chocolate truffles 219
    coconut sea salt caramels 226
    no-churn chocolate ice cream 211
    no-churn ice cream 210
gluten free flour 30
golden syrup 29
    baking glaze 239
groundnut oil 24

H

hazelnuts
    chocolate hazelnut babka 67–8
    financiers 128
    gianduja 221–2
    mille crêpes praline 181–2
    pear, hazelnut and almond gateau 166–7
    hot x buns 71–3

I

ice cream
    no-churn chocolate ice cream 211
    no-churn ice cream 210
    nut gelato 208

J

jam
    fruit jam with pectin NH 238

L

Lamingtons 147–8
lemon drizzle loaf 158
lemon tart 120
lemons
    baked cinnamon and citrus cheesecake 170–1
    carrot cake 137
    exotic clear glaze 239
    extra virgin olive oil cake 150
    fluffy baked siken tofu cheesecake 173
    lemon drizzle loaf 158
    lemon tart 120
lokum 224

M

maamoul 93
madeleines 134
mandarins
    extra virgin olive oil cake 150
maple cake 138–40
maple syrup
    maple cake 138–40
marzipan
    stollen 65–6
milk, plant based 33
mille crêpes praline 181–2
mixed peel
    stollen 65–6
molten centre chocolate cakes 193

N

nama ganache 216
no-churn chocolate ice cream 211
no-churn ice cream 210
nut butter 233
nut gelato 208
nut shortbreads 78
nuts 36
    banana bread 156
    nut butter 233
    nut gelato 208
    nut shortbreads 78

O

oat milk 33
    crème brûlée 200
    crème caramel 199
    molten centre chocolate cakes 193
    no-churn chocolate ice cream 211
    no-churn ice cream 210
    orange and almond cake 162
    sticky date and cardamom buns 54
    tiramisu 194
oats
    almond amaretti 94
    Anzac biscuits 77
    oat crumble 233
oils 23–5
olive oil 23–4
    extra virgin olive oil cake 150
    short sweet pastry 230
orange and almond cake 162
orange blossom water
    maamoul 93
oranges
    baked cinnamon and citrus cheesecake 170–1
    carrot cake 137
    exotic clear glaze 239
    orange and almond cake 162
    pumpkin spice loaf cake 161
    tiramisu 194

P

pain aux raisins 53
pastries
    cinnamon slice 56
    pain aux raisins 53
pastry
    flaky pastry 231
    short sweet pastry 230
    sweet flaky pastry 232
peanut oil 24
pear, hazelnut and almond gateau 166–7

pears
    pear, hazelnut and almond gateau 166–7
    tarte bordaloue 111–12
pecan pie 107
pecans
    pecan pie 107
pectins 35
    fruit jam with pectin NH 238
pistachio (and rose) vostocks 62
pistachios
    maamoul 93
    pistachio (and rose) vostocks 62
    vostocks 61
plant-based milk 33
    apple cake 143
    Bakewell tart 117–18
    banana tatin cake 164
    banoffee pie 113–15
    carrot cake 137
    chocolate ganache tart 108
    Earl Grey loaf cake 154
    financiers 128
    lemon drizzle loaf 158
    mille crêpes praline 181–2
    nama ganache 216
    oat crumble 233
    pumpkin spice loaf cake 161
    red berry tart 99–100
    rice pudding 207
    sweet potato pie 122
    tarte bordaloue 111–12
    thick whipped cream 237
    two-tone chocolate cake 175–6
polenta
    orange and almond cake 162
pumpkin spice loaf cake 161

R

raising agents 20–1
raisins
    carrot cake 137
    stollen 65–6

raspberries
    Bakewell tart 117–18
    Eton mess 202–5
    red berry tart 99–100
    Victoria sponge 144
red berry tart 99–100
rice pudding 207
rolls. see buns & rolls
rose water
    pistachio (and rose) vostocks 62
    Turkish delight / lokum 224

S

Sacher torte 185–6
scones
    fluffy scones 130–1
semolina
    maamoul 93
short sweet pastry 230
shortbread
    nut shortbreads 78
shortening 232
    thick whipped cream 237
soy milk 33
    baking glaze 239
    chocolate crème pâtissière 235
    crème pâtissière 235
    extra virgin olive oil cake 150
    fresh whipping cream 236
    Lamingtons 147–8
    lemon tart 120
    maple cake 138–40
    pain aux raisins 53
    pear, hazelnut and almond
        gateau 166–7
    short sweet pastry 230
    sticky toffee date pudding 196
    Victoria sponge 144
    vrioche 49–51
sticky date and cardamom buns 54
sticky toffee date pudding 196
stollen 65–6

strawberries
    Eton mess 202–5
    red berry tart 99–100
sugar 27–9
sugar cookies 91
sultanas
    fluffy scones 130–1
    hot x buns 71–3
sunflower oil 24
    oat crumble 233
    shortening 232
sweet flaky pastry 232
sweet potato 30, 47
    baking glaze 239
    cinnamon slice 56
    flaky pastry 231
    pain aux raisins 53
    stollen 65–6
    sweet potato pie 122
    Victoria sponge 144
    vrioche 49–51
sweet potato pie 122

T

tahini
    chocolate tahini cookies 88
tangzhong 47
    chocolate hazelnut babka 67–8
    cinnamon slice 56
    hot x buns 71–3
    pain aux raisins 53
    pistachio (and rose) vostocks 62
    sticky date and cardamom buns 54
    vostocks 61
    vrioche 49–51
tarte bordaloue 111–12
two-tone chocolate cake 175

tarts & pies 97
  apple pie 102–5
  Bakewell tart 117–18
  banoffee pie 113–14
  chocolate ganache tart 108
  flaky pastry 231
  lemon tart 120
  pecan pie 107
  red berry tart 99–100
  short sweet pastry 230
  sweet flaky pastry 232
  sweet potato pie 122
  tarte bordaloue 111–12
tin sizes 43
tiramisu 194
toffee
  sticky toffee date pudding 196
tofu, silken
  baked cinnamon and citrus cheesecake 170–1
  fluffy baked siken tofu cheesecake 173
  pecan pie 107
tools 41–2
triple chocolate fudge 177–8

truffles
  chocolate truffles 219
Turkish delight 224

V

vanilla bean paste
  crème pâtissière 194
  thick whipped cream 237
Victoria sponge 144
vostocks 61
  pistachio (and rose) vostocks 62
vrioche 49–51

W

walnuts
  carrot cake 137
  stollen 65–6
wheat flour 19
wine, sparkling
  Eton mess 202–5

Y

yeast 21

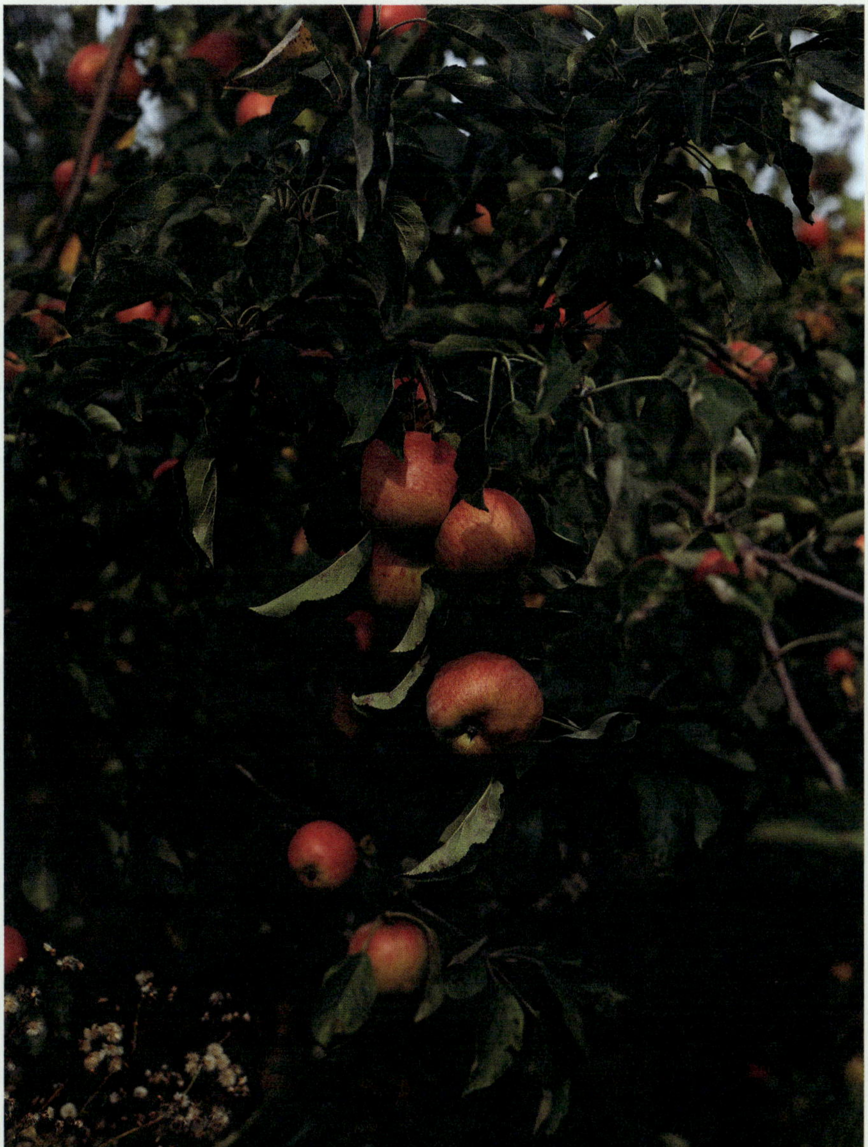

Published in 2023 by Hardie Grant Books,
an imprint of Hardie Grant Publishing

Hardie Grant Books (London)
5th & 6th Floors
52–54 Southwark Street
London SE1 1UN

Hardie Grant Books (Melbourne)
Building 1, 658 Church Street
Richmond, Victoria 3121

hardiegrantbooks.com

All rights reserved. No part of this publication may be reproduced, stored in a retrieval system or transmitted in any form by any means, electronic, mechanical, photocopying, recording or otherwise, without the prior written permission of the publishers and copyright holders.

The moral rights of the author have been asserted.

Copyright text © Philip Khoury
Copyright photography © Matt Russell
Copyright illustrations © Evi-O Studio

British Library Cataloguing-in-Publication Data.
A catalogue record for this book is available from the British Library.

A New Way to Bake
ISBN: 978-1-78488-592-2
10 9 8 7 6 5 4

Publishing Director: Kajal Mistry
Acting Publishing Director: Emma Hopkin
Commissioning Editor: Eve Marleau
Senior Editor: Eila Purvis
Art Direction: Evi-O.Studio | Evi O.
Design: Evi-O.Studio | Evi O. & Katherine Zhang
Photographer: Matt Russell
Photography Assistant: Matt Hague
Food Stylist: Philip Khoury
Food Stylist Assistant: Jessica Geddes
Prop Stylist: Alexander Breeze
Copy-editor: Kathy Steer
Proofreader: Suzanne Juby
Indexer: Cathy Heath
Production Controller: Sabeena Atchia

Colour reproduction by p2d

Printed and bound in China by Leo Paper Products Ltd.

MIX
Paper | Supporting responsible forestry
FSC™ C020056